Gerald D. Nash sees World War II as one of the major turning points in the history of the American West. Like the coming of Europeans to the New World and the land and mining booms of the nineteenth century, the changes wrought by the Second World War left an indelible imprint on the American West.

This volume traces the social and cultural impact of World War II within the context of rapid economic growth in the American West. Subjects discussed include the expansion of cities and the consequent changes in the lives of black Americans, Spanish-speaking Americans, and American Indians. The book also charts the extraordinary influence of the war on science in the West, and on the burst of cultural activities spearheaded by a talented group of European émigrés in southern California.

Nash demonstrates how the war transformed the West from a sparsely populated, underdeveloped region bearing many of the characteristics of a colonial society into a dynamic growth area that has paced the nation in the four postwar decades.

GERALD D. NASH is editor of *The Historian* and author of *The American West in the Twentieth Century* and numerous other books.

The
American West
Transformed

GERALD D. NASH

The American West Transformed:

The Impact of the Second World War

89-680

INDIANA UNIVERSITY PRESS
BLOOMINGTON

Photo Credits

Franklin D. Roosevelt Library: illus. 1–5 Oregon Historical Society: illus. 6–10 Oregon State University Archives: illus. 11, 23 Denver Public Library: illus. 12, 14, 22, 24–26 U.S. National Archives: illus. 13, 15–17 U.S. Air Force: illus. 18–21 Los Alamos Scientific Laboratories: illus. 27–30 National Atomic Museum, Albuquerque, N.M.: illus. 31–33 Marta Feuchtwanger: illus. 34

Library of Congress Cataloging in Publication Data

Nash, Gerald D.
  The American West transformed.

  Bibliography: p.
  Includes index.
  1. World War, 1939–1945—Economic aspects—West (U.S.)
2. World War, 1939–1945—Social aspects—West (U.S.)
I. Title.
HC107.A17N37 1985   330.978′032   83-49524
ISBN 0-253-30649-3
1 2 3 4 5 89 88 87 86 85

Contents

Preface

This book has a simple theme: that the Second World War transformed the American West. No other single influence on the region—
not the Mexican War, not the Civil War, not World War I, nor even the
Great Depression—brought such great and cataclysmic changes to the
West. It transformed a colonial economy based on the exploitation of
raw materials into a diversified economy that included industrial and
technological components. It spawned another significant population
boom and brought unprecedented expansion to most western cities.
It greatly diversified the ethnic and racial composition of the West,
particularly by encouraging the influx of large numbers of black
Americans and of Spanish-speaking people. It opened up new opportunities for Native Americans at the same time that it created new
problems for them. In addition, it unveiled new directions for science
in the West and served to quicken and deepen the cultural life of the
region. In four short years the war brought a maturation to the West
that in peacetime might have taken generations to accomplish. It
transformed an area with a self-image that emphasized colonialism
into one boasting self-sufficiency and innovation.

Such a transformation should be viewed not as an isolated event
but as one of the crucial turning points in the broad sweep of western
history. In the development of the region during the last four hundred years only a few major events have had such an extraordinary
impact. One such turning point was the arrival of the first European
explorers and settlers to the region beginning in the sixteenth century. Another was the California Gold Rush of 1849 and related land
and mining rushes in the trans-Mississippi West in the ensuing two
decades. These promoted a major population movement into the
area, followed by intensive settlement and development. The lure of

gold drew the Spaniards and other Europeans to the West as explorers who introduced European culture and institutions. The search for minerals and land induced Americans to become developers who undertook the first large-scale settlement of the region. In World War II Americans transformed the West to a more mature stage, one in which it began to shed its colonial status. It constituted another major watershed in the region's history.

In evaluating the impact of the Second World War on the West I have attempted to place the subject within the broader context of the major influences that have shaped the lives of westerners in the twentieth century. Since 1890 several generations of historians obsessed with the theories of Frederick Jackson Turner have emphasized the dominant influence of the frontier and of free land as a determining force in the development of the West. Whatever merit such theories may have had to explain growth patterns during the nineteenth century, consideration of the environmental factor alone cannot be conducive to an understanding of twentieth-century developments. By this time, influences such as technological changes, demographic movements, federal government policies, the changing values of Americans, and also wars and depressions and a growing concern for national security were becoming far more significant than they had been a hundred years earlier in determining the parameters of western history. The total impact of these major influences on the West in the twentieth century still awaits scholarly studies in the future. The present work seeks to make an initial contribution to this broader problem by demonstrating how wartime experiences changed the nature of western life.

A brief note on the organization of this book is in order. Its main focus is on the social and cultural impact of the war, since I expect to analyze economic influences in greater depth in a separate volume. In the present work I include a brief sketch of economic changes only as these provide a context for social and cultural developments. When the war transformed the western economy, it set another population boom into motion. The opening up of new job opportunities drew millions of Americans westward, most of them settling in urban areas. Ethnic and racial diversity was characteristic of the wartime migration, and succeeding chapters deal with the particular experiences of minorities. The rapid peopling of the West in wartime also stimulated cultural development. As one haven for refugees who constituted the cream of European intelligentsia, the region profited from their presence as they contributed significantly to a flowering of cultural life and institutions. And the war also hastened the unprecedented expansion of scientific research which made the region one of the science centers of the nation. Cumulatively, the war wrought a social and cultural transformation.

But it should be emphasized that this work is designed to be suggestive rather than exhaustive. Many aspects of life in the West during the Second World War remain to be explored and are barely touched upon in this study. This is true of the experiences of women in the West during this period, a major subject not yet treated with the depth it deserves. Nor have I delved deeply into particular subregions in the West, or into the history of Texas, subjects that in themselves require major books. My hope is that the present work will stimulate the completion of detailed studies about these and other topics.

The West discussed in this work mainly encompasses eleven states: California, Washington, Oregon, Nevada, Idaho, Utah, Montana, Colorado, Wyoming, Arizona, and New Mexico. Other states in the trans-Mississippi West, such as Kansas, North Dakota, and South Dakota on the Plains, Texas and Oklahoma in the Southwest, and Alaska and Hawaii share many characteristics with the other eleven, but they receive less emphasis because of the vastness of the subject. My own purpose is to provide a suggestive overview with appropriate illustrations to chart the broad dimensions of the impact of the Second World War on the West.

In the preparation of this book I have incurred many debts and obligations. A grant from the University of New Mexico Research Allocations Committee enabled me to inaugurate the project. A Fellowship from the Henry E. Huntington Library in San Marino, California, made it possible for me to exploit the riches of that great institution. In 1981 I was fortunate to receive a Senior Fellowship from the National Endowment for the Humanities. Without this generous support it would not have been possible for me to visit libraries and archives in fourteen western states to gather materials for this study. Special thanks are due to archivists and librarians who made materials available at the Colorado Historical Society, Special Collections at Arizona State University, the Oregon State Historical Society, the Bancroft Library at the University of California, the Federal Records Center in South San Francisco, the Nevada State Archives, Special Collections at the University of California, Los Angeles, the Federal Records Center at Laguna Beach, the Library of the Psychoanalytic Institute in Los Angeles, Special Collections at the University of Montana, the University of New Mexico and the Eugene C. Barker Library at the University of Texas. No adequate appreciation can express the debt I owe to the efficient staff at the National Archives in Washington, D.C., especially Richard Crawford and Jerry Hess, and the Manuscript Division of the Library of Con-

gress. Essential materials were also provided by the staff of the Franklin D. Roosevelt Library in Hyde Park, New York, and the Harry S.
Truman Library in Independence, Missouri. Without the cooperation
of the professionals in the archives the work of historians of twentieth
century America would be more difficult. I also owe a debt of gratitude to my wife and family for their patience and indulgence during
the course of my preoccupation with this project. I alone am responsible for the final product.

Albuquerque, N.M.

The
American West
Transformed

Part I
Before the Transformation,
1939–1941

CHAPTER ONE

The West on the
Eve of War,
1939–1941

In an impassioned plea, the well-known historian and publicist
Walter P. Webb sought in 1937 to arouse the consciousness of his
fellow westerners to their colonial status in relation to the East (or the
North, as he termed it). "I believe," wrote Webb, "that there have
developed in this country three fairly distinct cultures . . . each with its
own mores, ways of life, and culture complexes." Extending his argu-
ment further, he continued: "Back of the North's present [1937]
might and behind its increasing control of . . . the West is its undisputed command of the mighty forces of the industrial revolution in
America. . . . At the present time the North owns 80 or 90 per cent of
the wealth of the United States. . . . The economic imperial control by
the North over the . . . West . . . grew stronger as the political imperial-
ism grew weaker."[1] Webb was only stating what many westerners felt
in their hearts, namely that as America's youngest region the West still
occupied a subordinate or colonial status in relation to the older states
of the American commonwealth. That status implied a significant
economic dependence on the industrial East, a minority position in
the American political arena, and on the importation of almost every
aspect of culture from the East.[2] As a colony the West was also closely
tied to federal largesse emanating from the nation's capital. On the
eve of World War II, therefore, when the national mood was still
largely shaped by the Great Depression, the West too, like a barometer, reflected the cautious and hesitant outlook about the future that
swept America as a result of the economic crisis.

This cautious mood pervaded most aspects of life in the West
during this period. The 1930s had been truly an era of limited expectations. That was reflected in the western economy, in the decline of
population growth, and in its cultural life. The nation's leading

3

economists—particularly those of the stagnation school—belabored the myth that the disappearance of the western frontier had greatly restricted further economic growth in the United States. "It is not possible, I think," wrote Professor Alvin H. Hansen of Harvard University, a leading economist of the period, "to make even an approximate estimate of the proportion of the new capital created in the nineteenth century which was a direct consequence of the opening of new territory. . . . What proportion of new capital formation in the United States went each year into the Western frontier we do not know, but it must have been very considerable. . . . The opening of new territory and the growth of population were together responsible for a very large fraction—possibly somewhere near one-half—of new capital formation in the nineteenth century." And then he added, reflecting the pessimism of his day: "These outlets for new investments are rapidly being closed. . . . This movement ended in the Great Depression."[3] The same assumption, merely stated in a different context, had been articulated by Webb in his indictment of western colonialism: "If the frontier was a dominant force until 1890, the *absence* of the frontier has just been as dominant *since* 1890. . . . The frontier was a powerful stimulant injected into the veins of democracy to raise its spirit and speed its growth. Now that the effects are dying out, democracy cannot escape a hangover. . . . The closing of the frontier brought fundamental changes and compelled the government . . . to substitute another form."[4] Thus, while an economist like Hansen rationalized federal deficit spending policies and Keynesianism on the basis of restricted economic growth due to the alleged closing of the frontier, a historian like Webb arrived at similar conclusions through historical analysis. Both were perpetuating the myth of the closing of the frontier in 1890 to bolster their analysis of contemporary depression problems.

Within four years this analysis was to be shattered by wartime experiences which transformed the erstwhile mood of pessimism into an undaunted optimism. Writing in 1946, Wendell Berge, a prominent corporation lawyer who was then Assistant Solicitor in the Department of Justice in charge of anti-trust problems, noted that "before 1941 it was assumed that the passing of a geographic frontier also meant the disappearance of economic opportunities. The realities of war compelled a reorientation of our economic potentials and our attitudes. The economy was not mature or senile, but asleep, unaware of its own powers in technological progress and in terms of new fields waiting to be explored."[5] But who could foresee such portentous changes in 1941?

For on the eve of World War II the West still occupied a colonial status. In the classical mold of the relation between a colony and the mother country the region was shipping its raw materials out to be processed in the East—which also retained a major portion of the profits derived from their fabrication. Agricultural and mining industries still provided the major income for the West. Manufactures were extremely restricted, accounting for less than 5 percent of the region's income in 1940. That was in part due to decisions made by Wall Street bankers and the Interstate Commerce Commission in Washington who imposed discriminatory freight rates and the basing point system on the West.[6] Just how restrictive such policies were in retarding western economic growth was reflected in the award of federal war contracts in the incipient stages of mobilization during 1940 and early 1941. Of the major defense contracts awarded by the Army and Navy Departments from June 1, 1940, to February 28, 1941, the thirteen states receiving the smallest amounts were all located in the West. On the other hand, of the thirteen states receiving the largest amounts of war orders California and Washington were the only western states to be included—and that was largely related to their aircraft production.[7] The situation was similar in the award of defense installations financed by the federal government. Of the twelve states which received no such funds during this period only two were east of the Mississippi River. As Chester C. Davis, a prominent member of the National Defense Advisory Commission, said in an address to the Southern Governors' Conference in New Orleans on March 15, 1941:

> I was somewhat shocked a few days ago to see a tabulation of the distribution of defense orders to date. . . . Included in the tabulation were $ eleven and a half billions of prime contracts awarded between June 15 of last year and February 15 of this year. . . . Of this vast total . . . 80 per cent has gone to 62 companies (mostly in the East). There is rich food for thought in these figures. I believe they are closely related to the mediocre success we have had in apportioning . . . this new defense industry to the states.[8]

In short, the West in 1941 was mainly a raw materials producer, with few manufactures of its own—with a prime dependence on the East.

It is true, of course, that throughout the 1930s dependence on the East was being lessened as the federal government assumed an increasingly important role in the western economy and poured increasing amounts of capital into the region. New Deal programs had a pervasive impact on the West. Between 1933 and 1939 the federal investment there totaled more than $7,582,434,000, according to one careful estimate.[9] In a sense, public funds were replacing private capital in fostering development of the trans-Mississippi area. That shifted some attention of westerners from Wall Street to Washington, D.C., although it did little to change the colonial mentality.

The mood of restricted expectations in 1939 and 1940 was intensified by continued hard times for western farmers. On the Great Plains, farmers had just lived through one of the most trying times within memory. In North Dakota in 1933 per capita income dropped to $145 (compared to the U.S. average of $375). One-third of that state's farmers had faced the agony of living through the foreclosure of their farms and homes. The number of farms declined, farm population dropped by 17 percent, and more than 120,000 people were forced to leave the state to look for a livelihood elsewhere. One-half of the population was on relief. Neighboring states such as South Dakota and Montana found themselves in a similar position—although they were to reach unprecedented production records just a few years later.[10] In the Rocky Mountain area the impact of the agricultural depression was not quite so severe, but in states like Wyoming, Nevada, Colorado, and New Mexico farm income in 1939 was considerably below levels a decade earlier. West Coast farmers had recovered from some of the most severe effects of the depression but had hardly made a full recovery on the eve of war.[11] Fortunately, by 1939 some of the terrible weather conditions of the past decade which had plagued farmers on the Plains were becoming memories. In that year a significant improvement in weather conditions began which was to extend for more than another decade.[12]

Like farmers, western cattlemen had just lived through a difficult decade. In fact, between 1936 and 1939 per capita meat consumption in the United States continued to decline as Americans faced continuing unemployment and depression, from 68.9 pounds of beef and veal annually in 1936 to 62.3 pounds by the end of 1939. Although prices for beef improved slightly between 1936 and 1939 this was not sufficient to lift most cattle growers out of the depression. Their net incomes continued to remain low. In 1938, one survey revealed, two-thirds of the cattlemen on the Great Plains earned less than $1,000 annually, an amount which contemporary economists considered to be a bare subsistence income.[13] Meanwhile, in 1938 and in 1939 hordes of grasshoppers destroyed significant stretches of rangelands, further adding to the woes of western cattlemen. Small operators were the most vulnerable victims of economic crisis and were forced out in increasing numbers. That was also reflected in the increasing size of family-owned ranches on the Plains.[14] The mood of the cattlemen and women on the Plains in the years just before Pearl Harbor was therefore somber and cautious.

Similarly, western miners saw few bright spots on the horizon in the late 1930s. Revenues from mining operations steadily declined during the decade and made only a limited recovery. Arizona's copper industry—providing fully one-half of the nation's needs—

reflected the sluggishness of the national economy. Between 1930 and 1940 its production steadily declined.[15] In 1939 the immediate outlook was still bleak. A hopeful sign in that year was Congressional enactment of the Strategic Minerals Act—a measure which westerners had advocated with great enthusiasm. The act authorized the U.S. Bureau of Mines and the U.S. Geological Survey to engage in accelerated prospecting for new minerals sources and to provide scientific information for prospectors, particularly small operators. Led by Senator Pat McCarran of Nevada, Congressional delegations from western states rallied to support this early phase of the national mobilization program.[16]

Western oil producers were also still chafing under the hardships of the depression. Between 1936 and 1939 the production of motor fuels and fuel oil barely increased. Sales continued to be dull; the retail price of gasoline actually declined during that three year period. Meanwhile, the consumption of gasoline by passenger cars remained on a plateau in the decade after 1929. At the same time, exports of American petroleum products declined. In 1939 crude oil exports from the United States were lower than in the preceding year. And this was true of total petroleum exports from the United States as well.[17] On the eve of war the western oil industry had been mired in stagnation and depression for a decade, hampered by shrinking market demands both at home and abroad. No wonder that the mood of the industry, as reflected in its trade journals, was gloomy.

Just before World War II, manufacturing in the West was extremely limited, contributing no more than 8 percent to the value added by manufactures in the United States, as Table 1 indicates (see Appendix). California was the most important manufacturing state in the West. Its production of petroleum products, leisure clothes, automobile assembly, and small machinery made it eighth in national ranking of manufacturing states. But elsewhere in the West manufacturing activities were insignificant. South Dakota's contribution to the nation's manufacturing income in 1939 was but a mere $19.9 million, and that outpaced New Mexico's contribution of $8.7 million.[18] Nor did westerners profit from expansion inspired by slow mobilization during 1939 and 1940. Almost all of the new defense contracts awarded by Washington went to large business enterprises. But in the West almost all manufacturing was performed by small scale operations. Thus, the West seemed to be losing out again as new economic opportunities beckoned.

Some cities—such as Los Angeles—became so alarmed over this development that in the spring of 1940 the Los Angeles Chamber of Commerce established a special office in Washington, D.C. with the specific purpose of soliciting government business for its clients. As

James Ingrebretsen, manager of this office, explained, 4,000 firms in the Los Angeles area employed fewer than 25,000 employees, and 850 other businesses fewer than 50 people each.[19] Just as small businesses during the depression suffered more than large firms, so they experienced greater difficulties in securing their share of federal contracts. Delegations of chamber of commerce representatives from Montana and North Dakota who journeyed to the nation's capital in search of federal contracts dejectedly returned empty-handed.[20] In the rush toward mobilization these small western businesses seemed to pale in the competition with bidders from larger corporations.

Many westerners felt that, apart from the Great Depression, institutional barriers erected by easterners were a major stumbling block to economic expansion. In particular, discriminatory freight rates charged by railroads and the basing point system commonly used by some eastern industries were real impediments to western economic growth. This had been true since the early 1880s when railroads controlled by eastern financiers first established a system of freight rates that discriminated against western manufactures. Over the years the Interstate Commerce Commission enshrined these schedules in administrative regulations. At the same time many major industries—steel and cement provided notable examples—adopted the basing point system.[21] Under this scheme they calculated delivery costs from base cities in the East, whether or not in fact their products were shipped from these base points. The net effect of this system—created in the late nineteenth century when most of the trans-Mississippi West was still a sparsely populated region—was to discourage local manufactures in the West since manufacturers there could reap no competitive advantage over their eastern competitors by being close to the local markets.

This increasingly anomalous situation prompted a chorus of western (and southern) protests which grew louder during the Great Depression. Governors of various southern states met formally in 1934, 1935, and 1937 to press their case with the Interstate Commerce Commission. In 1938 they also secured the open support of President Franklin D. Roosevelt.[22] In the following year Representative Robert Ramspeck (Georgia) announced that he planned to organize a western-southern bloc in Congress to assure remedial legislation. Appropriate committees dealing with interstate commerce in both the House and in the Senate held hearings in February and March, 1939 during which a broad spectrum of westerners and southerners presented their complaints.[23]

Although Congress did not enact desired legislation in that year, the anger of those who had testified and the determination of Congressmen and Senators from the South and West had a decided im-

pact on the members of the Interstate Commerce Commission. They
not only stepped up their activities concerning regional freight rate
discrimination but disposed of pending cases in favor of western and
southern interests.[24] Before the year was out Congress enacted a resolution directing the ICC also to begin an inquiry into regional freight
rate differentials. Meanwhile, on July 29, 1939, the ICC inaugurated
the most far-reaching investigation in its history—an inquiry into all
class rates east of the Rocky Mountains.[25] At the same time Senator
Harry S. Truman—together with his colleague, Burton Wheeler of
Montana—introduced a bill in the Senate on March 30, 1939, which
amended the Interstate Commerce Act of 1887 by prohibiting discrimination by railroads against regions, districts, or territories.
Known as the Transportation Act of 1940, the measure received
President Roosevelt's signature on September 18, 1940.[26] These were
the first hopeful signs in over half a century for westerners hoping to
throw off the bonds of eastern corporate and financial domination.

The sluggishness of the western colonial economy during the
1930s was clearly reflected in a notable slowing of the population
influx into the region during that decade. In 1940 California could
look back on ten years that saw the slowest rate of population increase
since the Gold Rush, no more than about 21 percent.[27] Elsewhere in
the West, the population growth was proportionately small, with
significant losses due to outmigration experienced by states on the
Great Plains. North and South Dakota each lost about 15 percent of
their citizens during the period, while a similar outflow of people
occurred in Montana and Nebraska. Rocky Mountain states like Wyoming lost one-third of their inhabitants during the decade.[28] To a
considerable extent these losses were due to the movement of individuals from such distressed areas further west. The Dust Bowl states
of the Southwest contributed to this stream of emigrants on their way
to the Pacific Coast. This was clearly a distress migration, prompted
not so much by economic opportunities on the West Coast as by the
severity of the depression and a rather futile search for jobs. Since the
majority of newcomers arrived by automobile, their geographical
background was more varied than in previous years. Most came from
towns and cities, not from rural areas. The fictional account of the
Joad family from Oklahoma described by John Steinbeck in *The
Grapes of Wrath* notwithstanding, a majority of the migrants were not
farmers but small shopkeepers, tradesmen, and people employed in
service industries.[29] That was to be significant once the national war
mobilization program increased its momentum after Pearl Harbor
because the resident population of the West was well geared not only
to urban living but to jobs and occupations familiar in an urban set-
ting.

The slowing of the westward population movement was reflected in conditions that prevailed in many western towns and cities. Just before the outbreak of World War II municipal officals looked back on a decade during which they were preoccupied with economic crisis and unemployment rather than with growth and expansion. Colorado's cities, for example, had grown little. Population in such cities as Denver and Colorado Springs remained constant and the outlook of their businessmen for the future was gloomy. Young people were leaving the state in search of better opportunities elsewhere. By 1940 the Chamber of Commerce of Colorado Springs was particularly desperate as the flow of tourist traffic registered a sharp decline. In Arizona, Phoenix had profited from slow growth of the past three decades, but its population of 65,000 in 1940 hardly made it a major population center. It was a lethargic retirement community as was Tucson, its southern neighbor, which had 37,000 inhabitants.[30] Las Vegas, Nevada, was a sleepy little town of 8,422 souls just before Pearl Harbor. Its chamber of commerce was hoping at the time that the recent completion of Lake Mead near Boulder Dam would bring in a modest influx of families and tourists. Reno's population of 21,000 remained stable during the 1930s as that city enjoyed the distinction of being the largest urban area in the state.[31] If coastal cities had larger populations, they were hardly bustling. San Diego counted 190,000 people, and Los Angeles and San Francisco had increased little since the Great Crash.[32] Portland, Oregon, and Seattle, Washington, remained remarkably stable during that period, reflecting the condition of many smaller towns in the Pacific Northwest's interior. On a national scale, few urban communities in the West ranked as major cities. In fact, in the census of 1940 the only western cities to rank among the largest twenty-five urban areas in the United States were San Francisco, Los Angeles, and Denver. Although the West contained one-half of the area of the United States, it had as yet only 14 percent of its population.[33]

Western towns and cities had a diverse population in terms of racial and ethnic backgrounds, yet minority groups tended to be acquiescent and often almost invisible. Most lived in self-contained neighborhoods and rarely ventured into the mainstream of American life. They were generally not accepted in the dominant business elites of their community, were largely excluded from the social life around them, and lived in a cultural milieu of their own. This was true of the very small black population in western urban enclaves, of the more numerous Spanish-speaking peoples in the barrios, and of the isolated Chinese- and Japanese-Americans living their lives in tightly knit islands amidst their more numerous American neighbors. Even more isolated was the American Indian population of the West, concentrated on remote reservations usually far removed from large towns and cities.

In 1940 few black Americans lived in the West. According to the census of that year they comprised less than 5 percent of the population. The Watts area of Los Angeles was typical of black communities in the West. The inhabitants lived quietly and unobtrusively, eager not to call special attention to themselves. Except for those who worked as sleeping car porters on the Santa Fe or Southern Pacific Railroads they were largely restricted to menial or unskilled jobs. Irrespective of their training, discrimination kept blacks out of white collar jobs or those requiring special training and skilled trades. Social integration of blacks with whites was extremely rare, and schools were segregated in fact if not in law. Segregation was a common pattern. As a minuscule minority in the community, they exercised little political influence. Despite variations, similar conditions prevailed in other western cities such as Portland, Denver, and Tucson.[34]

Spanish-speaking people were the most numerous minority in the Southwest. California, like Texas, had a large Spanish-speaking population, numbering nearly 1 million, only a small number of whom were descendants of the original Spanish or Mexican settlers of California. The majority were either descendants of Mexican immigrants or immigrants themselves. By 1940 more than 600,000 lived in the barrio of East Los Angeles, with substantial concentrations also in Denver, Tucson, El Paso, San Antonio, and smaller towns along the Texas-Mexican border. In New Mexico they lived clustered in small, rural communities, many in the northern part of the state. Most were poor, engaged as they were in marginal farming. The minority who lived in towns and cities were largely unskilled or semi-skilled workers. If the median income for the state of New Mexico in 1940 was less than that for the United States as a whole, it was largely due to the 40 percent of its population that was of Hispanic origins.[35]

During the 1930s smaller Spanish-speaking communities also sprang up in towns throughout Arizona, Colorado, Utah, and Montana, as migratory field workers drifted there during off-peak seasons. Most Spanish-speaking Americans worked at unskilled or semi-skilled jobs, providing labor for the sugar beet growers of the West, railroad track maintenance on the Santa Fe, Southern Pacific, and other railroads, or in service occupations. Mexican-Americans occupied the bottom rungs on the economic ladder of income scales in the West. Suspended between their native Mexican cultural tradition and dominant American cultural values, they lived within their own unique ethnic enclaves in the barrios. Most experienced discrimination in employment—and in the use of public facilities such as housing, swimming pools, restaurants, and movie theaters, and places of entertainment. Although Mexican-Americans as individuals may have chafed under such restrictions, nevertheless they had little political consciousness or influence as a group. Anxious not to displease, they bore their burdens in silence.[36]

Within the Spanish-speaking communities social cohesion was tight. Language, cultural values, and an emphasis on family provided Hispanic-Americans in the Southwest with a life style that differed from that of their Anglo neighbors. That close-knit society was just beginning to foster a sense of political solidarity. It was reflected in the growth of LULAC (League of United Latin-American Citizens) to represent their interests. This organization gave strong support to U.S. Senator Dennis Chavez (N.M.), the only member of the U.S. Senate who was of Hispanic-American background. Elected in 1936 as an ardent New Dealer, he was by 1940 in the process of making himself a national spokesman for Spanish-speaking westerners.[37] Nevertheless, a strong political consciousness was still in the future. Just before the war Hispanic-Americans were still an economically disadvantaged minority with their own distinct cultural traditions.

Western Indians were similarly outside the mainstream of American life. Isolated on their reservations, they were mired in poverty more grinding than that experienced by most other Americans at the time. Even those who were fortunate enough to own herds of sheep or cattle were fearful in 1939 and 1940 because the Office of Indian Affairs under Commissioner John S. Collier was then engaged in a forceful reduction of their herds to prevent overgrazing of the western ranges. With different language and cultural backgrounds than most Americans, Indians frequently failed to understand the purpose of many federal policies to which they often were vehemently opposed. But as they were painfully aware, their political power was minimal, for most even lacked the right to vote. The gulf between their life styles and that of the majority of Americans was so wide that assimilation seemed farfetched. Before the war, the American Indian was America's outsider, its most isolated minority with its own distinct cultural traditions.[38]

The more than 120,000 Japanese who lived in western cities tended to be concentrated in isolated racial enclaves that were dominated by leaders emphasizing traditional values and customs. Although most had been born in the United States, they remained largely unassimilated in American society and lived outside the mainstream of American life. That was true of the large Japanese-American colony in Los Angeles, which numbered 80,000, representing a majority of the Japanese in the United States.[39] It was also true of the Japanese-American community in San Francisco and of the smaller Japanese settlements in Sacramento, Portland, Oregon, and

Seattle. Their economic pursuits were largely limited to agriculture and landscaping, and to trade within the Japanese ethnic neighborhoods. Other occupations in the mainstream of American life were largely closed to them. Their social life centered around their own ethnic and cultural institutions within their mostly segregated communities. And as a political force in local or state governments their influence was minimal.[40] Maintaining a low profile, fearful of antagonizing their white neighbors, the Japanese lived quietly and unobtrusively, dependent on the sufferance of the majority.

The cultural life of the American West on the eve of World War II was still largely colonial, despite the invigorating effect of many of the New Deal's cultural programs during the Great Depression. Since the beginning of the twentieth century and the appearance of writers like Charles Lummis, westerners had been seeking to forge a distinct cultural life that would not only be independent of the East but would also reflect the unique elements of the western environment and the values which it engendered among the people. That effort took the form of regionalism during the 1920's which saw notable accomplishments in literature, folklore, art, architecture, music, and other cultural endeavors. These forms of cultural expression were strengthened by the various programs of the Works Progress Administration. Its writers program produced the famous guidebooks for individual states and encouraged the collection and publication of local and native folklore. The WPA theatre program provided an outlet for local dramatists and stimulated the production of plays with local motifs. The music program not only stimulated local musicians, but encouraged the collection of hitherto unpublished native folksongs in the Southwest. The arts program resulted in innumerable murals in public buildings executed around local or regional themes. These varied federal programs during the 1930s did much to improve the quality as well as the quantity of western cultural activities.[41] It should be noted, however, that with few exceptions these were of a regional nature, and as yet received little national or international acclaim.

And Hollywood, the West's most visible dispenser of popular culture, was ending the decade with an emphasis on mass entertainment. Between 1935 and 1940 the films produced by Hollywood studios emphasized light, frothy entertainment and escapism. Driven by perceptions of what the American public would reward at the box office, Hollywood producers created a dream world in a variety of vehicles, including musicals, gangster films, and flimsy romances.[42] Perhaps a generation wracked by the depression needed escape from stark reality. The late 1930s were not a great age of filmmaking in Hollywood. Contemporary intellectuals were wont to sneer not only at the films

Hollywood produced, but also at what the film colony represented symbolically as an expression of culture—in the United States as a whole as well as the West.

On the eve of war, therefore, the American West was still very much an underdeveloped region, a colony dependent on the older East for much of its economic well being, for its population growth, and for its cultural sustenance. An economy based primarily on the exploitation of raw materials made the West dependent on eastern manufactures. The further development of sparsely populated areas of the West as well as the expansion of its towns and cities waited upon the return of prosperity to the industrial East. And the growth of cultural activities was largely dependent on the importation of eastern talent and ideas. It was hardly surprising that the mood of many westerners about the future in 1939 was somber and cautious, a mood of limited expectations.

But within four short years the West underwent a metamorphosis. Under the impact of war the horizons of westerners were transformed as they came to embrace an unbounded optimism about their future based on the expectation of unlimited possibilities for the region. The war transformed the erstwhile colonial economy. It prompted a vast new surge of population and triggered the dynamic growth of western cities. And it made Hollywood the propaganda capital of the free world and an increasingly distinguished cultural center. By 1945 the war had transformed the West and made it the pace-setting region of the nation. Just how this transformation was accomplished and how it changed so many aspects of western life is a story that will be detailed in the pages to follow.

Part II
The Transformation,
1941–1945

CHAPTER TWO

The New West: War and Economic Transformation

Between Pearl Harbor and V-J Day the economy of many portions of the West underwent a profound transformation. The colonial economy of the region, heavily dependent on raw materials production before 1941, now became increasingly diversified and self-sufficient. Changes that would have taken more than a generation in peacetime were accelerated by war mobilization in a four-year period. Mobilization speeded up the activities of the extractive industries such as mining, accelerated industrial development, and ushered in what Daniel Bell has described as the post-industrial era.[1] As a region rich in natural resources the West profited from the nationwide demand for its raw materials as it had not for more than a decade during the depression. At the same time military demands stimulated the establishment and expansion of manufacturing and industrial assembly plants. Somewhat unexpectedly, the war crisis greatly spurred new aerospace and electronics industries in the West and, in their wake, a host of profitable new service industries so characteristic of the post-industrial society.[2] In short, as no other single event in the history of the West, the war stimulated economic growth. The erstwhile colony emerged from the war as an economic pace-setter for the nation.

How was this transformation accomplished? A major influence was the dynamism of the federal government, which invested at least $40 billion in the West during wartime. More than ever, the West became a federal province. Federal monies poured in through the establishment of new factories and award of vast contracts for war materiel. At the same time the large-scale expansion of military installations—air and naval bases, supply depots and training camps—provided an extraordinary stimulus to the regional economy. It would be inaccurate to say that the federal government was solely responsi-

17

ble for the spurt in the area's economic growth. But the federal presence provided the spark that set a pattern of other economic activities into motion. The influx of federal monies created hundreds of thousands of new jobs; these openings attracted men and women from all over the nation (not unlike the Gold Rush of 1849) and set off a population boom, increased population, particularly in towns and cities, proved a boon to service industries of all kinds, and created demands for new social and cultural services.

Of course, the ingredients for the realization of this vast economic potential had long been present. As Walter P. Webb bemoaned in 1937, eastern industrial interests had been consciously seeking to inhibit western economic growth. Webb pointed to the discriminatory freight rate system then sanctioned by the Interstate Commerce Commission as one important reason for western subservience to the East. The concentration of investment capital in eastern financial centers was undoubtedly another contributory factor. As one admirer of Webb, John Crowe Ransom, himself a distinguished spokesman, said:

> We all know about the inequalities of the economic structure. . . . Within the Northern states you have your masters of capital on the one hand, and against them your farmers and employees. . . . But . . . [in] the West you have almost your whole population in this latter status. . . . The North owns and operates the national economy; the South and West work under its direction. . . . The West bears a colonial relation to the North because the North actually colonized the West.[3]

Webb's arguments had a ring of truth, of course, although they oversimplified a somewhat more complex situation. As a relatively young and underdeveloped section, the West reflected many of the characteristics of third-world underdeveloped nations in the twentieth century. Before the Second World War its population in many areas was still too sparse to sustain local manufactures; its internal transportation arteries were not as well developed as those in eastern states; it lacked well-developed financial institutions that could provide the capital necessary for further growth; and in a national and international economy wracked by depression, as in the 1930s, westerners could hardly expect to find markets for their goods.

But in 1941 the potential seemed limitless. The West still had open spaces to harbor a vast new population; changing transportation patterns, particularly the growth of the motor truck industry and the emergence of expanding air traffic, lessened the importance of rail transport and freed the region from the shackles of the basing point system; remoteness became a positive virtue with the development of new scientific and technological processes which required vast open spaces for testing and development; and the balmy climates of many portions of the West became a positive attraction with the growth of more affluent life styles. The development of air conditioning and climatic control further enhanced the economic potential of the desert areas which in previous years had been considered by many easterners to be uninhabitable.[4]

In a sense, then, the boom triggered by World War II was not entirely unexpected. Wartime mobilization stimulated an expansion in which the West cast off some of the constraints which had hampered its growth in the preceding decade and at the same time acquired vast sums of new capital investments which made expansion possible. How this process took form constitutes a fascinating chapter in the annals of western history.

The exigencies of war prompted a massive influx of federal monies into the West. Certainly such an investment was not a totally new departure for the federal government. To bolster the first American settlements in the trans-Mississippi West during the early nineteenth century Congress had poured large sums into the region—through military installations, transportation development, and river and harbor appropriations. During the 1930s New Deal programs accelerated the flow of public expenditures into the West. But beginning in 1941 the scale of federal investment reached unprecedented levels. Congress authorized the expenditure of approximately $70 billion in the West from 1941 to 1945, with almost half of that sum earmarked for California. In fact, that state secured one-tenth of all federal monies expended during World War II.[5]

This federal largesse flowed westward through various channels. Some was expended by existing agencies such as the U.S. Army Corps of Engineers and the Bureau of Reclamation; in addition, Congress created new agencies to purvey capital to the West. One major source was the Reconstruction Finance Corporation which established various subsidiaries to carry out plant expansion in the West. The challenge of creating "instant industries" in the region was met by the Defense Plant Corporation (DPC), the Rubber Reserve Corporation, and the Metals Reserve Corporation, to name three of the subsidiaries which were especially significant in the West. The experience of new manufactures had usually been accomplished by private enterprise—at times perhaps with federal aid. Even in the First World War, 90 percent of new war-induced investments ($6 billion) came from private sources. But in the Second World War the situation was very different. The Defense Plant Corporation supplied the capital for 96 percent of new rubber plants, 58 percent of new aluminum plants, 90 percent of new magnesium plants, and 71 percent of the aircraft factories. With the exception of synthetic rubber, almost all of these enterprises were west of the Mississippi River. Of the fifteen largest aircraft plants built in World War II fourteen were financed by the Defense Plant Corporation.[6] If before 1941 the federal government had been a junior partner with private business in financing new enterprises in the West, during World War II it became a dominant influence in western industrial expansion.

Established by Congress on August 22, 1940, to expedite the lagging mobilization program, the DPC came to be the largest investor in the history of the region. During the next five years it built 344 plants in the West at a cost of $1,853,634,000. These included a wide range of manufacturing facilities. Outstanding were the vast new steel mills established in Provo, Utah, and Fontana, California, the only such complete steel fabricating facilities west of the Mississippi River. The DPC also erected the largest magnesium plant in the world near Boulder Dam, just outside the sleepy little railroad town of Las Vegas. And it constructed a whole new complex of aluminum fabricating plants in the Pacific Northwest. As noted, virtually all of the aircraft manufacturing plants on the Pacific Coast were built with DPC funds.[7]

Although most of the DPC's projects were designed to increase production, the Corporation also engaged in research and development. Such was the case with the plan hatched by Howard Hughes and Henry J. Kaiser for the "Spruce Goose," a giant cargo plane. With their vivid imaginations, Hughes and Kaiser in 1942 envisaged an eight-engine, 200-ton aircraft capable of carrying an entire company of soldiers with all of their equipment. At a time when German submarines were seriously impeding the flow of American supplies to England such a proposal seemed attractive to the administration and the President himself gave a green light for the program. The DPC spent $18 million for a proposal to build three of these planes, one prototype and two for use in testing. As metals were scarce in 1942, the DPC directed that they be made of wood.[8]

Hughes undertook construction of one of the planes in his California plant, indulging his ever-increasing penchant for secrecy. No outsiders were permitted to watch progress in the building of this, the world's largest aircraft, not even Henry Kaiser, it was rumored. But even after the DPC had expended more than $13 million, the prototype was still far from completion. Thus, in 1943 Donald Nelson, chairman of the War Production Board, decided to cancel the contract. Hughes hurried to Washington to plead his case. His persuasiveness led President Roosevelt to order Donald Nelson to reinstate the contract. Although the DPC agreed to pay the remaining $5 million of the loan to Hughes, it also required him to pay additional needed costs out of his own pocket. At that point Kaiser dropped out of the project while Hughes invested at least $10 million more, according to the estimate of Jesse Jones, chairman of the Reconstruction Finance Corporation. Not until November 2, 1947, with Hughes himself at the controls of the prototype, did the Spruce Goose lift off for a two-minute flight near his plant in California. As public confidence in the venture waned, that of Hughes increased. His faith in the project remained unshaken, but he placed the plane in storage in a huge hangar in Long Beach, California, where it languished until 1980 when the Hughes estate sold it to promoters who made it a public tourist attraction in Long Beach.[9]

The West was also affected by the activities of the Metals Reserve Corporation. Another major subsidiary of the Reconstruction Finance Corporation, it became the federal government's principal agent for the purchase of more than $2,750,000,000 of metals in the western states, not to speak of another $1 billion of purchases overseas. As the major metals procurement agent for the armed services it scoured the West for copper, tin, tungsten, zinc, chrome, bauxite, and more exotic metals. It also constructed the world's largest tin smelter in Texas City, Texas, despite efforts by executives of Phelps-Dodge and American Metals Company to retain the facility in the East, near their operations in Baltimore. Through the subsidies it paid to western miners the Metals Reserve Corporation greatly stimulated metals production in California, Idaho, Nevada, Colorado, and Utah, and in most other western states. Even metals that had been imported into the United States before 1940, such as chrome, were produced domestically during wartime as miners—spurred by the Corporation's subsidies—combed unexplored reserves throughout the region. In Montana, for example, they discovered rare chrome deposits in the Custer National Forest. These finds supplemented limited quantities imported from South Africa and Rhodesia. And the western aluminum industry could not have flourished during wartime had it not been for the Metals Reserve extensive program to exploit Arkansas deposits.[10]

Synthetic rubber was another of the new industries fostered by the federal government in the West. Twenty-three new synthetic rubber plants built by the Rubber Reserve Corporation were erected either on the Pacific Coast or in the Texas Gulf region. Almost overnight, the Rubber Reserve Corporation created an important new industry for the West.[11]

At the same time, the Rubber Reserve Corporation undertook extensive experiments to grow natural rubber in California, Arizona, and other portions of the West. Supervision of these operations was largely by the U.S. Department of Agriculture and the Forest Service. Discerning the possibility of developing this new industry in the West, Senator Sheridan Downey of California early in 1942 urged his col-

leagues in the Senate to consider the possibilities of large-scale production of the guayule shrub. Although native to northern Mexico,
guayule was well adapted to arid areas in California, Arizona, New
Mexico, and Texas. Senator Downey estimated that four-year-old
shrubs would yield about 1,250 pounds of raw rubber to the acre.[12]
On March 15, 1942, a subcommittee of the Truman Committee, the
Senate Special Committee to Investigate the Defense Program, accompanied Senator Downey to Salinas, California, to hold hearings
on the feasibility of growing guayule in that area. Meanwhile, on
March 5, 1942, Congress approved the law sponsored by Senator
Downey to empower the Department of Agriculture to buy up all
rights and properties of the Intercontinental Rubber Company, the
only private firm in the United States to cultivate and process guayule.
At the same time, the Department of Agriculture also started ninety
test plantings throughout the West, although plantings in California
promised the most immediate success.[13] The Forest Service collaborated in the program by planting seedlings for 45,000 acres in the
Salinas area. The main problem with guayule was that it would take
four to seven years to produce rubber at prevailing world prices. Even
with the crash program, Forest Service specialists estimated that it
would take at least twelve months to grow the seedlings. But the
executives of the International Rubber Company estimated that the
nation's total rubber needs could be met by planting 1,460,000 acres
on four-year cycles. By 1942 four extraction plants in Mexico were
already producing about 7,000 tons annually. Although the program
bore great promise, it was suspended late in 1942 as synthetic rubber
production promised to supply defense requirements in a much
shorter time span than guayule.[14]

Businessmen and state officials in western states that were primarily agricultural saw the war mobilization program as an unusual opportunity to secure long-desired manufacturing facilities. In North
Dakota, for example, the Governor and other state officials were eager in the fall of 1941 to secure federal contracts. They encouraged a
group of local businessmen to form the North Dakota War Resources
Committee to develop specific proposals. Another group of businessmen organized the Greater North Dakota Association, which
hired a paid lobbyist to solicit federal funds in the nation's capital. In
1942, this individual, Frederick Frederickson, introduced the state's
political leaders and members of the Association's War Resources
Committee (of which he was chairman) to key federal officials. They
made the rounds of the War Production Board, the Reconstruction
Finance Corporation, and the War Department, but unfortunately
met with no success. A somewhat similar experience befell a group of
businessmen and political leaders from Wyoming.[15]

On the other hand, when a western state had a powerful politician as a spokesman, it fared better. Nevada was a case in point. With Senator Key Pittman's death in 1940 the state lost an influential voice in the United States Senate. But within a short time Senator Pat McCarran took up his mantle. A shrewd political manipulator, he was instrumental in 1941 in securing more than $200 million from the Reconstruction Finance Corporation for the construction of the world's largest basic magnesium plant at Henderson, near Las Vegas. The site—between Las Vegas and Boulder City—was not far from the recently completed Boulder Dam, which promised to provide an ample supply of cheap power. Nearby Nye County also contained extensive magnesium deposits. McCarran intervened at the highest level and secured President Roosevelt's direct, personal support. "I am glad to be able to advise you," Roosevelt wrote him in 1941, "that a project for producing 23,000,000 pounds of magnesium annually has already been approved by the Materiel Division, U.S. Army Air Corps. . . . The new plants will be located at Gables, Mead, and Las Vegas, all in the state of Nevada." With evident pride McCarran reported his accomplishment to Joe Cook, editor of the *Nevada State Journal,* noting that he had first written to the Chief Executive on this matter on June 14 after holding several conferences in Washington, D.C., with "appropriate authorities." As McCarran wrote, he had done "all to securing for Nevada a share in this defense program," for he was sure that the plant was a "promise of increased industrial development activity for our state."[16]

By September 1941 the RFC had rushed the completion of the plant, which operated until November 1944, at times with more than 15,000 employees. When federal stockpiles of magnesium grew large toward the end of the war, the Defense Plant Corporation closed the facility. During the period of operation, however, Basic Magnesium not only created the new boom town of Henderson, but invigorated the economy of the entire southern portion of the state.[17]

Although disappointed about much hoped-for federal funds to speed industrialization, those western states that failed to receive substantial war orders nevertheless still prospered from the wartime boom, which spurred mining and agriculture and new military installations. Almost as a consolation prize western states were the beneficiaries of government largesse in the form of new military installations. Remoteness and isolation now came to be virtues that provided a magnet for vast new facilities in every western state. A recapitulation of their history would entail many volumes. It is true, of course, that since 1850 the West had received a substantial portion of its income from army posts and supply depots.[18] But the scope of this expansion in World War II was unprecedented, and more than ever made the West increasingly dependent on federal largesse.

The defense installations of Utah provide a striking example of the growing pervasiveness of the federal presence in the West. In Utah, by 1942 the federal government established ten major military bases. Three were training facilities, one a research and testing installation, while the others were huge supply depots and repair and maintenance bases. They included the Ogden Arsenal, Hill Air Force Base, Ogden Defense Depot, Deseret Chemical Depot, Tooele Army Depot, Naval Supply Depot at Clearfield, Camp W. G. Williams and Fort Douglas, Wendover Air Force Base, Kearns Air Force Base and Dugway Proving Ground. In addition to more than 60,000 military personnel stationed in Utah in wartime, the bases employed another 60,000 persons.[19]

In fact, a sizable portion of federal investment throughout the West during wartime came through the establishment of new military installations. Training camps, air bases, testing facilities and storage depots came to dot the West, making the region—in contrast to World War I—a major site for the nation's expanding military-industrial complex. Its open spaces, remoteness, and mild climates made the West particularly desirable for such installations, given the state of technology at the time. Moreover, in 1941 the United States was also engaged in a Pacific war and the proximity of the West to that area made it more important than ever as a major arsenal.[20]

Although the federal government provided about 90 percent of the new investment capital that flowed into the West during wartime mobilization, it also did much to stimulate private banking in the West. Capital funds of banks west of the Mississippi River increased by about 20 percent between 1940 and 1945. The Bank of America was certainly not a typical western financial institution, but its wartime growth did mirror the expansion of other banks throughout the West. During World War II it supplied increasing amounts of capital to local industries and significantly freed many western businessmen from their reliance on eastern financiers. Between 1941 and 1945, for the first time in its history, the bank entered upon large-scale investment programs in cooperation with eastern syndicates. To stimulate corporate expansion on the Pacific Coast, it floated large debt issues for corporations like Bendix, Chrysler, RCA, and Westinghouse. It also supplied most of the private funds needed for the expansion of private shipyards on the Pacific Coast, in collaboration with the major banks in the Pacific Northwest. Although the influence of the western banks in Washington was still less than that of Wall Street lobbyists, war mobilization significantly increased their importance and their influence. The Smaller War Plants Corporation and the Federal Reserve Board's Regulation V were among the concrete manifestations of that influence. At the same time the war-induced boom on the Pacific Coast greatly boosted the bank's business. Although in 1942 the Comptroller of the Currency was loath to issue the Bank of America more permits to open new branches, he really had no choice. The extraordinary demand for new banking facilities in new housing developments, army camps and naval installations, and war-related factories forced his hand. Thus, the war accelerated the trend toward branch banking, particularly for the Bank of America. But its experience was closely watched—and soon widely imitated—in many other western states.[21]

The large influx of federal investment funds—supplemented by expansion of private financial institutions—sparked an enormous economic boom throughout the West. It spawned new factories and new service industries, stimulated many spheres of Western mining, and created a vast network of military installations and new science centers. That boom, of course, did not affect all parts of the West in an even-handed fashion. It was most pronounced on the Pacific Coast, quite noticeable in the Southwest, muted in the Rocky Mountain area, and perhaps least significant on the Great Plains. On the other hand, wartime-induced demands for agricultural goods brought a revival of prosperity to the Plains and ended more than a decade of hardship inaugurated by the Great Depression.

Industry on the Pacific Coast experienced the most striking wartime boom. California alone secured 12 percent of all war orders in the United States with heavy concentration in shipbuilding, aircraft manufactures, food processing, and clothing and light manufactures. In 1939, California was in a good position to attract war orders. Its large metropolitan areas contained a vast array of small machine shops, auto assembly and food processing plants, and clothing manufacturers who could convert to wartime production on short notice. And shipyards and aircraft manufacturers who had developed during the First World War had managed to survive the hazards of the Great Depression. Blessed with a mild climate and strategically located near the Pacific theater of war, California appeared particularly appealing to the Washington chiefs of staff who favored some decentralization of the nation's industrial capacity in the interests of national security.[22]

The influx of more than $70 billion in federal funds into California between 1941 and 1945 set a chain of events into motion that ultimately created the nation's largest urban military-industrial complex in the state. In that complex the aircraft industry was preeminent, stretching from San Diego northward to Long Beach, Santa Monica, Burbank, Inglewood, and other communities in the Los Angeles area. During the peak of production in 1943 the aircraft plants of southern California employed 243,000 workers drawn from all parts of the nation. Their function was not unlike that of the mines in the Gold Rush of 1849. By June of 1945 aircraft plants in Los Angeles had secured $7,093,837 in federal orders while those in San Diego received $2,136,119.[23] The names of once obscure airplane manufacturers now came to be household words in America. Who in World War II had not heard of Douglas Aviation's Flying Fortresses (B-17s) or Liberator Bombers, or of Lockheed's famed P-38 fighter? Not only aviation enthusiasts but the general public now followed the latest production records of Hughes Aircraft or Northrop, Consolidated-Vultee or North American Aviation as popular magazines and newspapers filled their pages with the exploits of the nation's newest corporate heroes in the West.

Much of California's boom town atmosphere during wartime was due to its vast shipbuilding activities. As southern California became the hub of the West's aircraft industry, so the northern part of the state became a significant shipbuilding center. By 1943, the shipyards in the San Francisco area and those in Los Angeles employed 280,000 workers. Three-fourths of the $4.7 billion which the federal government spent for shipbuilding on the Pacific Coast was awarded to yards in the Bay region, and Richmond, Vallejo, Sausalito, Alameda, and South San Francisco became boom towns over night, complete with trailer camps, ramshackle streets, and bawdy entertainment houses.[24]

Of the Big Three manufacturing industries that sprang up in the West during World War II steel was another newcomer. President Roosevelt himself decided early in the rearmament program, in the spring of 1941, that steel manufacturing in the West needed to be greatly expanded. Consequently, in 1942 the Reconstruction Finance Corporation provided subsidies and loans for the construction of a vast new steel manufacturing complex in Fontana, California. The proximity of Fontana to the major shipyards of the Pacific Coast was a major factor in the decision to build this, the only major steel manufacturing facility west of the Mississippi River with the exception of the Geneva Steel Works in Provo, Utah.[25]

The Big Three industries in California generated a vast network of subcontractors, resulting in the extraordinary expansion of thousands of small businesses. Airplane parts, electrical equipment, plastics, machinery, and pumps of infinite variety were made and processed. The value of California's manufactures jumped from $2,798,000 in 1939 to $10,141,000 just five years later. And the number of production workers in California employed in manufacturing grew as dramatically, from 271,290 in 1939 to 530,283 eight years later.[26]

In many ways the "can do" spirit of western industry was personified by the West's (and the nation's) outstanding industrialist,

Henry J. Kaiser. He was born in Canajoharie in upstate New York of a poor family. Forced to leave school at the age of eleven, he went to work for a local photographer as an errand boy. Before he was out of his teens, he had bought out his boss and operated the photography business, spending summers in Lake Placid and winters in Florida to tap the tourist trade. When he fell in love with one of his photographic subjects, Bessie Hannah Fosburgh, and asked for her hand, her father insisted that he ply a more "regular" trade. So in 1907 Kaiser went to Spokane, Washington, where he secured a job with J. B. Hill and Co., a paving contractor who was then building Spokane's expanding street network. Within six years Kaiser founded his own paving firm specializing in highway construction as increasing use of automobiles created a boom in that field by the 1920s. In 1921, his first large project was building the road between Redding and Red Bluff, in California. With wife and children in the back of his car he was always on the move during these years, supervising his various construction projects while building a modest home in Oakland and earning a reputation for efficiency. Kaiser's was one of the Six Companies that built Boulder Dam, completed in 1935, and also built the piers for the Oakland–San Francisco Bay Bridge. From these vast ventures he moved to even greater challenges with the building of Bonneville and Grand Coulee Dams just on the eve of World War II. Meanwhile, in 1939 he had also entered into the cement manufacturing business with the establishment of the Permanente Company.

Kaiser came to shipbuilding somewhat accidentally. While he was having two old cement carrier ships repaired in the Todd Shipyards in Seattle, he talked with the president, John Reilly, in January 1941. He decided on a partnership—Todd–California Shipbuilding Company—to garner lucrative government contracts. They separated just two months later, but by then Kaiser was well on his way. Using the good offices of his friend and sometime financier, A. P. Giannini of the Bank of America, he made initial contacts with the White House. Within a year Kaiser had secured contracts for fully one-third of all the merchant ships then under construction.[27]

Once engaged in large-scale shipbuilding, Kaiser became concerned about securing a steady supply of prefabricated steel for his yards, and so became involved with the expansion of the western steel industry at Fontana. Eastern industrialists still had a virtual monopoly on the manufacture of finished steel products and did not look favorably on losing control of their western markets. But President Roosevelt himself felt strongly that the decentralization of industry—particularly the steel industry—was highly desirable. Such decentralization was needed not only for greater national security but also in the event of possible enemy air attacks. Dispersion would also limit the monopolistic practices of industries such as steel which had just recently been laid bare by the investigations of the Temporary National Economic Committee and the Anti-Trust Division of the Department of Justice under Thurman Arnold. Thus, Kaiser's plans found receptive ears in the Roosevelt administration. In 1942, Jesse Jones, chairman of the Reconstruction Finance Corporation, authorized a $150-million loan to Kaiser to enable him to build a brand-new steel manufacturing facility at Fontana, California, largely at government expense.[28]

The restless vision of this remarkable entrepreneur also led him to assume leadership in the development of a new aluminum industry in the West. Kaiser keenly perceived that light metals would have burgeoning markets in the immediate future, not only for the building of aircraft, ships, and autos, but for thousands of other civilian uses. Thus, he applied to the Reconstruction Finance Corporation for federal loans to build and operate five new aluminum plants in the Pacific Northwest. Since the power to be used by these factories was to be supplied by Bonneville and Grand Coulee Dams which he had just completed, Kaiser was in a particularly favorable position to win approval for his plans, once again financed largely by federal funds.[29]

Kaiser's career paced the West Coast's economic growth. He was representative of the region's outlook and its desire to utilize its undeveloped capacity and its still untried potential. The war forever demolished the myth that the frontier had closed and ended the West's capacity for growth and expansion. The war stimulated the West's traditional optimism which had been blunted—if not virtually extinguished—during the Great Depression. The war unlocked a sense of purpose and determination that westerners quickly translated into striking accomplishments in industrial expansion. With a growing population, a highly skilled labor force, vast areas of unpopulated lands, abundant natural resources, and an increasing array of scientific and technological skills the West was in an excellent position to embark on another surge of economic growth. The ingredients that had been missing in the 1930s—namely a supply of new investment capital and also a sense of optimism—were now provided.

If the pace of war-induced industrialization was slightly less hectic in the Pacific Northwest than in California, the transformation there was no less complete. Between 1941 and 1945 manufactures increased 265 percent in the region. Seattle alone secured war contracts totaling $5.6 billion. A significant portion of this total flowed to the Boeing Company in Seattle which hired 40,000 new workers. Although headquartered in Seattle, Boeing's activities reached into many parts of the region in view of extensive subcontracting and the establishment of branch plants in Renton, Bellingham, Aberdeen,

Chehallis, and Everett, Washington.[30] Seattle and Portland hummed also with extensive shipbuilding activities as the vast new Kaiser shipyards in Portland and the Puget Sound area helped to pace large-scale construction of Liberty ships and baby aircraft carriers. The shipyards of the Pacific Northwest were also involved in large-scale repair activities. Much of the Navy's fleet salvaged from the disaster at Pearl Harbor, for example, was refitted in the Portland shipyards. In addition, many smaller plants were engaged in significant war production, such as the Pacific Car and Foundry Company which converted to producing Sherman tanks.[31]

The Pacific Northwest also benefited from wartime demands for aluminum. The recent completion of the Bonneville Dam in 1942—and the availability of cheap power from that source—was a key factor that led the Roosevelt administration, particularly Donald Nelson and Jesse Jones, to locate nine major new aluminum plants on the Pacific Coast, built primarily with funds advanced by the Defense Plant Corporation, and operated by the Aluminum Corporation of America (Alcoa), Reynolds Aluminum, and Henry Kaiser. Federal intervention in the industry effectively broke the monopoly which Alcoa had cherished until 1941.[32] Moreover, it brought a major new industry to the Pacific Northwest and established mutually advantageous relationships with the booming aircraft industry.

In the Rocky Mountain area the war also stimulated industrial development, if on a smaller scale than on the Pacific Coast. Denver, Colorado, secured a significant share of wartime contracts. The Rocky Mountain Arsenal there, operated by Remington-Rand, employed more than 20,000 people at the peak of wartime production, fabricating munitions and poisonous gases. Denver became something of a shipbuilding center as well, specializing in the fabrication of submarine chasers. The yard produced more than sixty such vessels, which were shipped to the Mare Island Naval Yard in the San Francisco Bay Area by railroad. It was an eerie sight indeed to see ships moving over mountains. Once they arrived at Mare Island, workers there undertook assembly and gave them a second launching.[33]

War industries moved into selected areas of the Southwest, most notably Arizona, where the Goodyear Company opened a vast new plant in Phoenix that attracted a number of smaller companies. Tucson profited from war orders also, primarily with the growth of small establishments that worked as subcontractors for the large corporations on the Pacific Coast.[34]

If the war greatly stimulated the economy of Utah, it was due not only to the large number of federal military installations and supply depots there but also to the establishment of the Geneva Steel Works at Provo, operated by the United States Steel Corporation. A small steel making facility had been operating there before 1941, but at that time, in an effort to decentralize steel manufacturers, and to have an available supply for shipyards on the Pacific Coast, President Roosevelt himself decided on the construction of a vast new facility in Provo. At the President's behest the Defense Plant Corporation expended more than $200 million in establishing the operation, which became the largest steel manufacturing plant west of the Mississippi River.[35]

Industrialization as a result of war was more limited in the Rocky Mountain states, yet mobilization did much to stimulate mining activities in that area. The Rocky Mountain West, as it had been for a century, was still the nation's storehouse for precious metals. The U.S. Geological Survey and the Bureau of Mines embarked on extensive prospecting in the region in a crash effort to make the United States self-sufficient, and by and large they succeeded. When Japanese occupation of the Dutch East Indies cut off a major source of tin, for example, the Survey was able to locate new supplies in western states. When in 1942 German submarines in the Atlantic made the shipment of tungsten from Spain highly erratic, the Survey's scientists found vast new deposits in Idaho, and lesser ones in California, Washington, Nevada, Colorado, Arizona, and Utah. They also found hitherto unexploited veins of copper and chrome that made the nation virtually self-sufficient in these metals during wartime. Their intensive search for minerals even extended to Indian reservations, where they found substantial deposits of needed lead, zinc, and coal.[36]

In many ways the access to important minerals in the Rocky Mountain region facilitated the expansion of manufacturing activities on the Pacific Coast. Without the U.S. Geological Survey's discovery of impressive new iron deposits in California, Oregon, Arizona, New Mexico, and Utah, it is doubtful whether the administration's plans for expanding steel production in the West would have succeeded. Similarly, had not the Survey found hitherto unknown deposits of bauxite in the West, most likely the Defense Plant Corporation would have been more hesitant to build what was virtually a new aluminum industry in the Pacific Northwest. Arkansas came to be the major source of bauxite during wartime, but Washington, California, and Idaho also yielded significant amounts of this vital raw material.[37]

The contribution of many of the Plains states to the war effort was largely in supplying needed agricultural products. An exception was Wichita, Kansas, where the Boeing Company established a large satellite operation, supplementing a growing number of aircraft manufacturers who were already located there.[38]

Although the new plants spawned by federal largesse did much to boost the industrial capacity of the West, they stimulated the expansion of large rather than small business enterprises. On a national scale, federal agencies awarded two-thirds of wartime contracts to the 500 largest corporations in the nation. Thus, westerners understandably were particularly concerned about the fate of small business, so characteristic in the region.

Their views were clearly articulated by Secretary of the Interior Harold Ickes. He was among the most vocal national leaders who hoped that wartime mobilization would also benefit the long-range industrial development of the West. Early in 1942, Ickes submitted an extensive report to Congress on his views concerning the future development of the West's enormous resources. Addressing his remarks to Senator Joseph C. O'Mahoney (Wyoming), chairman of the Temporary National Economic Committee, on February 6, 1942, Ickes noted:

> I have little to add at this time to my earlier statement to the Committee that, for the wider development of the West, there should be more fabrication of raw materials into finished products and more diversification of industries. . . . I have been urging upon the war agencies that they give consideration to locating . . . plants . . . in the West. . . . Unless adequate consideration is given to these matters, the result will be that at the end of the war the people of the West will be . . . at the mercy of . . . the larger companies of the country.[39]

From O'Mahoney's final report, written in 1941, it was clear the Senator shared Ickes's concern:

> The concentration of economic power has caused the development of our productive and distributive mechanism frequently without primary concern for efficiency and economy in the production and distribution of goods. Attempts of various localities to lure factories from other cities and efforts by some industrialists to escape the more enlightened practices of advanced communities have fostered unsocial movements of industries. Ghost towns have appeared frequently without justification.
>
> Moreover, in the present emergency the National Government is confronted for the first time with the practical problem of the proper location of important industries, a problem which will have widespread influence on the economic practices of the country.
>
> The Temporary National Economic Committee urges upon the President, the Congress, the States, and local governments, and private enterprise, that serious attention be given to the manifold economic and social problems involved in the proper location of our strategic industries. . . . We therefore submit . . . the desirability of decentralizing industry.[40]

O'Mahoney's fears were shared by other westerners, notably by Senator James E. Murray of Montana. Born in Canada and educated at New York University, Murray settled in Butte, Montana, where he opposed corporate interests and became known as a progressive Democrat. Succeeding to the U.S. Senate seat of Thomas J. Walsh in 1934, he became known as a strong New Dealer. By 1940, Murray had already become greatly concerned about acceleration of economic concentration of industry in the United States, particularly in light of the reports of the Temporary National Economic Committee which had been publishing forty-four of its studies on particular industries in the years between 1937 and 1941.[41] Consequently, in October 1940 Murray prevailed upon his colleagues in the Senate to authorize establishment of a Special Committee to investigate small business. The Committee was authorized to study "all the problems of American small business enterprise which would aid the Congress in enacting remedial legislation."[42] Throughout the years from 1940 to 1946 the Committee made dozens of exhaustive investigations about the impact of the war on small businesses, particularly in the West.

The Committee did more than play a symbolic role, however. Its influence led directly to strong advocacy of the domestic mining industry before the War Production Board, to the award of war contracts to small businesses by a wide range of federal agencies, and to the creation of the Smaller War Plants Corporation. Philosophical as well as practical interests dictated Murray's course as he relentlessly pursued his goals. Bemoaning the dangers of further economic concentration in the heat of the mobilization program, he declared in 1941 that "Small business for many years has been waging a losing fight against its big competitors. The growing concentration of economic control and the extension of monopolistic practices has become appalling. . . . A continuing concentration of economic power will be certain to result in an undermining of the very foundations upon which our system of free enterprise was built." President Roosevelt, who endorsed Murray's position, wrote him in August 1942 that "I am glad that you have called my attention to the hardships that may be suffered by many small businesses as a result of the war effort. The problem is one that has concerned me for some time, and I wish very much that a solution might be found."[43]

The fear of increased corporate concentration was also shared by Senator Harry S. Truman who in 1941 had just been selected as chairman of the new Senate Committee to Investigate National Defense Expenditures. Truman was particularly concerned about the predominance of big business executives from the East in most federal war emergency agencies. Popularly known as "Dollar a Year" men, they brought the outlook of corporate America to Washington at the same time that they undoubtedly followed patriotic motives to serve their country. "It is only natural," said Truman, "that such men should believe that only companies of the size and type with which they were associated have the ability to perform defense contracts; that small and intermediate companies ought not to be given prime contracts; that the urgencies of the defense program are such that they have no time to consider smaller companies."[44] His statement was particularly applicable to the West, of course.

In California small businessmen sought to overcome the problem by organizing pools and then bidding for federal contracts. The idea originated in San Jose, California, where seventy machine shops pooled their financial resources and their manufacturing facilities. Henceforth it became known as the "San Jose Plan," and was copied by small businesses in central California. Despite some success in securing federal contracts in 1942, after one year of operation small businessmen felt that the program had only limited potential. As Donald Nelson, head of the War Production Board, noted in April 1942: "The experience with pools is not as good as I should have liked to have seen."[45]

Among those who watched the bidding pool experiment with great interest was A. P. Giannini, founder and chairman of the Bank of America. That institution's rise to financial eminence between 1920 and 1940 had been based largely on its liberal lending policy toward small business and the establishment of branches in dozens of localities throughout California. As the pace of mobilization quickened in the fall of 1941 Giannini and the officers of the bank became increasingly concerned over the plight of many of their small business clients who had problems in securing scarce raw materials at the same time that they failed to secure lucrative defense contracts. The attitude of bank officers was that it would be desirable for the economy of California if federal contracts were distributed to include thousands of small subcontractors. That would avoid what they feared might otherwise become a boom and bust economy. "It means," said Giannini, "the continued functioning of local industry, maintenance of payrolls, stabilization of the skilled worker in established surroundings . . . and a big step towards the cushioning of the readjustments which must follow the ultimate curtailment of the defense program." Giannini persuaded Governor Olson of California in 1941 to call a conference on the problem. Meanwhile, the Bank of America's branches organized local meetings with businessmen throughout the state on the theme, "Convert Your Plant to National Defense."[46]

In November 1941 the Bank extended its activities to Washington. There it opened an Office of Defense Information at the Mayflower Hotel to advise its clients (and others) who might be seeking war contracts within the maze of the federal bureaucracy. Under the di-

rection of Theodore Granick, a Washington lawyer, the office provided contacts for small businessmen from California with federal
procurement agencies. Just during the first three months of its operation it secured 1,900 contracts worth $42,500,000. A friendly Con-
gress also enacted a most helpful law allowing banks to accept assign-
ment of government contracts as a collateral for loans.

But the Gianninis hoped for a more broadly gauged effort and
urged creation of a federal agency which would extend the Bank of
America Plan on a national scale. Obviously, with many of its loans
tied to small rather than large businesses, the Bank of America stood
to profit from such an agency. When the Senate Committee on Banking and Currency held hearings on the plight of small business in
1942, Mario Giannini sent one of his best lobbyists, E. A. Mattison, to
represent the Bank's interests. After listening to Donald Nelson's
testimony endorsing creation of an agency to aid small business Mattison jubilantly wired his boss: "Your entire program endorsed by Mr.
Nelson."[47]

But Murray believed that the administration needed to do still
more, and throughout March and April of 1942 urged Donald Nelson to establish a new division within the War Production Board
which would extend federal loans and contracts to small business. As
he plied Nelson with successive drafts of proposed legislation, he
secured his somewhat reluctant assent. Nelson was aware that the War
Production Board, largely staffed by representatives from large corporations, and seeking shortcuts to meet maximum production
quotas, was not particularly oriented toward granting contracts to
small or untried enterprises.[48] Meanwhile, Murray laid the groundwork for his plan to authorize creation of a new agency. He secured
unanimous support for the bill in the House and Senate which on
June 11, 1942, authorized creation of a Smaller War Plants Corporation (SWPC). As the Reconstruction Finance Corporation had provided federal funds for big business so the framers of the SWPC
hoped the new agency could stimulate small business and impede
further economic concentration in wartime. The SWPC was designed
to extend loans to enterprises employing fewer than 500 employees,
ensuring them of at least a share of war contracts.[49]

Much of the success of the Smaller War Plants Corporation depended on its administration. During its first year the agency was
plagued with two chairmen who seemed unable to nudge it to become
an active and effective instrument for fulfilling its purposes. At the
insistence of Senator Harry S. Truman, Donald Nelson appointed
Lou Holland as first chairman. Holland, a small businessman from
Kansas City, met strong opposition from armed services procurement
officers, however, who were skeptical about the ability of small busi-

ness to supply their needs.[50] His successor was Colonel Robert W. Johnson, head of Johnson and Johnson, a well-known pharmaceutical manufacturer. A good friend of President Roosevelt, Johnson could not cope with the Corporation's problem any better than his predecessor.[51] In an effort to revitalize the SWPC, Roosevelt agreed to appoint Maury Maverick as chairman in January 1944. That fiery Texan, a former Congressman and mayor of San Antonio, breathed new life into the agency. A strong believer in small business, he aggressively expanded the volume of federal loans and contracts to small businesses, particularly in the West, a region for which he held a special affinity.[52]

In ensuing months he aggressively expanded the volume of federal loans and contracts to small business. "The Government is an umpire," Maverick said in 1944, "but let's get this umpire business straight. It shouldn't let a team of supermen that has a patent pool on its side, plus cartel agreements, take on a team of sand lot boys. . . . The Government should step in where such inequalities exist, and give the small businessman a chance to compete. Then, if he can't hit the ball, let him be called out." Maverick was part of a small group of western anti-trust advocates during World War II that included Senator James Murray, Thurman Arnold, Joseph C. O'Mahoney, Wendell Berge, and others who were staunch upholders of the anti-trust tradition.

Western states benefited almost immediately from the activated SWPC under Maverick. One of his first actions as chairman was to expand regional offices, and set up new ones in Los Angeles, San Francisco, and Seattle. The number of projects in the West also increased significantly, especially after Maverick's extended tour of the western regional offices late in 1944. Each region had its own regional director, and a board of governors composed of between ten and twenty local businessmen, representing the various enterprises in the particular area.

The war thus had a profound influence in transforming the western economy. Mobilization wrought major changes in the economic life of the region and brought long-sought-for diversification. In addition to the basic resource industries, the massive influx of new capital provided by the federal government now resulted in the establishment of major new manufacturing facilities—mainly in aircraft, shipbuilding, aluminum, and steel—with related industries. But the West did more than gain a new manufacturing base in World War II. Its economic growth was further stimulated by the founding of new technologically oriented industries characteristic of a post-industrial society, namely aerospace and electronics. These had as yet barely developed in the older and more stratified economy of the industrial

Northeast. In a sense, the underdeveloped economy of the West in 1941 proved to be an advantage, because it offered unlimited opportunities for experimentation with new industries such as nuclear energy, aerospace, and electronics. Along with extensive military installations, these industries did much to promote the service trades which were already becoming increasingly significant in the national economy. In 1941 the Western economy had been backward, characterized by a raw-materials, nonindustrial base. By 1945 the region had not only developed the bases for a manufacturing complex; it had moved into the next stage of economic development with the growth of a technological and service economy. In four short years, the erstwhile backward section had become a pace-setter for the nation.

CHAPTER THREE

Westward Migrations:
Expanding the Labor Force

The economic expansion prompted by the war triggered a spectacular population boom in the West. Of course, the region was no stranger to population booms. Throughout much of its history, western settlement had been characterized by spurts rather than by a pattern of gradual and steady population growth, beginning with the gold and silver rushes of the 1850s and 1860s. The decade after the First World War witnessed another major surge of people pouring into the West, particularly into urban areas. But the depression of the 1930s brought this expansion to a halt. Some of the more sparsely settled parts of the region such as the Dakotas and Montana actually lost population as migrants sought work in more heavily industrialized areas. As by 1941 mobilization created new job opportunities, these served as a magnet for Americans in every part of the United States and created yet another wave of migration.[1]

If the expansion of industries, such as shipbuilding, aircraft manufactures, and small-scale manufacturing, was most striking on the Pacific Coast, it also affected interior cities like Denver, Phoenix, Tucson, El Paso, and Salt Lake City. Equally dramatic was the establishment of new aluminum plants in Portland, Tacoma, and Seattle, new magnesium facilities near Las Vegas, and burgeoning steel plants at Provo, Utah, and Fontana, California. The flow of people into these areas provided an enormous impetus to the expansion of their service industries—banks, food establishments, health care services, and schools. Although strained to the limit by the influx of newcomers, western communities welcomed the vast reservoir of new job opportunities. At the same time the unprecedented expansion of federal installations in the West also created thousands of new civilian openings.[2] As land had served as a magnet for western migrants in the later nineteenth century, so wartime mobilization set into motion another major population expansion movement in the trans-Mississippi West. Indeed, it could be said that the entire American West became a giant boom town in the World War II era.

Within the region, however, population gains were uneven. Urban areas experienced the most dynamic expansion, sometimes with spectacular growth reminiscent of nineteenth-century western boom towns. The pace of growth was not as hectic in rural localities. If the wartime appearance of some neighborhoods in western cities tended to be somewhat ramshackle, haphazard, or nondescript, it was in part due to development characterized by fits and starts rather than by a gradual process. In many ways the cities of the West, with a century of experience with the boom town syndrome, were better able to cope with frantic wartime conditions than cities in other parts of the nation.[3]

Of the more than 8 million people who moved into the trans-Mississippi West in the decade after 1940 almost one-half went to the Pacific Coast. California gained three and a half million individuals, leading to a population surge from 6,907,000 in 1940 to 10,586,000 in 1950. The state's growth rate continued to be significantly higher than in the nineteenth century. And 72.2 percent of that growth was due to in-migration. Elsewhere, the population increase was not as spectacular. In the Rockies population increased by 15 percent, in the Southwest by 40 percent, while the Great Plains lost 3 percent. The precise number of those who went West to work in western war industries and then returned East is difficult to determine, but it seems to have been fewer than one million.[4]

This wave of western migrants shared certain common characteristics. In contrast to the nineteenth century, when many migrants hailed from east of the Mississippi River, this migration had a substantial proportion of men and women born and raised in western states. As a group they tended to be youthful (under 30) and not highly skilled, and the vast majority came from urban rather than rural or farm backgrounds. Culturally, they were geared to city life. Significant also was the influx of racial and ethnic minorities, particularly blacks, Mexican-Americans, and Indians (from reservations to the cities).[5]

The urban origins of this migration helps to explain why the newcomers gravitated to metropolitan areas. In his *Grapes of Wrath* John Steinbeck etched a vivid portrait of western migrants during the Great Depression. Who can forget the Joads, farmers ruthlessly torn from their native Oklahoma soil, arduously making their way to California? Vivid as it was, that portrait was hardly accurate, for even for the 1930s the census statistics reveal that many of the Okies and

Arkies had not been tillers of the soil, but rather small shopkeepers, gasoline station owners, or tradespeople in towns which were heavily dependent on farmers displaced by the depression. The waves of the 1940s did not differ significantly in their urban origins and orientation. They too came by automobile (three out of four) in search of economic opportunity.[6] With the exception of minority groups such as southern blacks, they were an urban people who blended into western metropolitan areas with relative ease.

Americans have always been a restless people, and many observers—like De Tocqueville—ascribed this characteristic to the westward moving frontier. Whether the frontier was a major determinant in stimulating this trait is open to question, however. Economic opportunity may have been a stronger force. Of course, many individuals perceived economic opportunity as being directly linked to the frontier. Whether the frontier disappeared in 1890 is an assumption that can of itself be questioned. But census data after 1900 reveal that the percentage of native-born westerners living in states other than the one in which they were born rose steadily between 1900 and 1950 and reached its highest level just after World War II. This occurred in a period when the frontier had supposedly disappeared. Yet the mobility of Americans moving westward increased. In other words, the westward flow of population in the twentieth century was more significant in terms of numbers than it had been in the nineteenth century. As an example, while in 1860 more than one-half of the migrants to California were born on the East Coast, in 1950, 60.7 percent were born west of the Mississippi River.[7]

The restlessness of the migrants did not cease even after they reached the Pacific Coast. Many large employers, such as the Martin Aircraft Company, complained of the high turnover of workers in their plants. In 1941 and 1942 it exceeded 100 percent annually. Their personal experience was also borne out by the census data. Thus, workers in the Los Angeles and San Francisco areas shifted their jobs more frequently than workers in similar jobs elsewhere. This may have been due partly to the restlessness of the people who moved west and the abundance of job opportunities they found there. But the boom town atmosphere added to the mobility. "We have hundreds of thousands of women who are working in our war factories," said California's U.S. Senator Sheridan Downey, "who are also keeping homes for their husbands and children. . . . They may be able to stand the gaff for 60 days or 6 months, but then they are exhausted and quit. . . . Many of the workers are living in such deplorable conditions that they do not have the proper school facilities . . . shopping facilities, or recreational facilities and they just move around attempting to better their conditions."[8]

The war accelerated the growth of suburbs in western metropolitan areas. That trend had already been noticeable before 1940 in the more heavily congested eastern cities. In this as in other demographic patterns, the West was already emerging as a pace-setter for the nation. California was far ahead of other states in spawning suburban areas which emerged after the First World War. By 1950 31.1 percent of California's population lived in suburbs—compared to a national average of 13.9 percent. But these statistics probably do not reflect the extent of suburbanization accurately, since until 1940 the census takers classified suburbs as rural non-farm areas. Only in 1950 did the U.S. census develop a more realistic classification which defined suburbs as attached to urban areas.[9] It is quite likely, therefore, that the official census data distorted and underestimated the urban characteristics of western settlers before 1950.

In comparison to earlier twentieth-century western migrations, that of the 1940s was characterized by youthfulness, by people who were under 30 and thus of prime child-bearing age. This was not surprising since it was this age group that was attracted by new jobs, rather than the very young or retirees. Although these migrants had a variety of talents, the typical newcomer to the West in World War II tended to be an unskilled worker with aspirations for improved economic status.[10]

Another striking characteristic of the World War II migration was its racial and ethnic diversity. In a not-untypical Oakland shipyard one could find Slavs, Russians, Portuguese, Germans, Irish, Chinese, Greeks, Italians, and large numbers of Okies among the milling throng of workers. But perhaps most remarkable of all was the increase in the number of black Americans. In 1940 they had constituted 1.8 percent of the population in California. By 1950 this had increased to 4.4 percent. The trend was similar in Washington, Oregon, Arizona, New Mexico, and Colorado. New job opportunities and a network of friends and relatives brought more than 250,000 blacks westward, most from the rural South. In addition, the number of Mexicans who visited the United States after 1942 to alleviate desperate labor shortages in the West came to constitute about half a million people. Precise statistics are difficult to determine because of the high rate of illegal immigration. The westward movement also affected Native Americans. From reservations in Oklahoma, New Mexico, Arizona, Utah, and other states, about 25,000 Indians moved to take up war jobs on the Pacific Coast, also establishing an Indian urban enclave in Los Angeles.[11]

One of the most significant changes in the western labor force during World War II was the large-scale infusion of women. In the aircraft and shipbuilding industries on the Pacific Coast at various times they constituted at least one-third, and sometimes more, of the active workers. The role of women in the West during the war is a subject so vast, and so important, that it merits detailed book-length studies in its own right. No brief mention can do it justice, except to call attention to the need for intensive study. The situation in the Pacific Northwest was not atypical. In Seattle, women came to be an important part of the labor pool. The Puget Sound Navy Yard, for example, in 1941 employed virtually no women, apart from a few office workers. But by the middle of 1943 women comprised 21 percent of its 30,000 employees. The commander, Rear Admiral C. S. Gillette, noted that women worked very well indeed in the Yard, but that he had problems with sending them on board fleet vessels at night to make repairs because of harassment. "Our bluejackets don't mix too well," he said. Although Gillette felt women were superior workers, he was concerned about their high rate of turnover. Special pressures stemming from the need to care for households, husbands, and children, he surmised, often interfered with their wartime jobs.[12] The problem of turnover with respect to women was endemic during the war years because in many cases the pressures on them were greater than those on men, in view of their traditional responsibilities as homemakers and mothers.

As the pace of mobilization increased in 1940 and 1941, severe labor shortages developed in the new war production centers. Until Pearl Harbor, the residue of unemployed left by the depression provided a pool of workers upon which employers with defense contracts could draw. But by the middle of 1942 the available local labor supply in most areas of the West was being exhausted. It was then that war contractors embarked on a frantic search for workers, whether skilled or unskilled. The shortage was most pronounced in the urban centers of the Pacific Coast, but was also evident in Phoenix, Denver, and many smaller cities. As Frank Roney of the War Manpower Commission said on September 9, 1943: "The entire West Coast economy is completely dominated by critical war industries. The economy of the West Coast centers around . . . aircraft, shipbuilding and repair, military installations of all types, non-ferrous mining, logging and lumbering, high value agriculture, and fishing. . . . That means that all major production areas on the West Coast today are . . . now facing a serious labor shortage."[13]

By 1943 the depletion of the available labor pool was threatening to disrupt production. The situation was critical and led U.S. Senator Sheridan Downey of California to inaugurate an investigation into the problem. He estimated in January 1943 that California would need at least 123,000 additional shipyard workers and another 55,000 individuals to work in the expanding aircraft industry. Anxious to promote the industrial expansion of his state, Downey hoped that the federal government might inaugurate a program to encourage available labor outside of California to migrate there. But as Americans elsewhere heard of congested housing and living conditions, they were increasingly loath to relocate on the West Coast. Downey hoped to change the then-current California image.[14]

The lack of housing on the Pacific Coast was a major impediment to the recruitment of new workers. "Housing is almost non-existent in most of the major areas of the West Coast at the present time," noted Frank Roney, "despite the fact that programs of housing developed for the West Coast have been the largest of any equivalent area in the country."[15] Donald W. Douglas, the president of Douglas Aircraft Company, stated even more bluntly that the major obstacle to increased production at his plants was the housing shortage. In his estimation, it could be remedied only with federal aid. Roney speculated that sizable numbers of war workers were returning to their homes in the South and Middle West simply because they could not find suitable homes. Of their decision, "part of it is undoubtedly attributable to housing, and I would say, a large part of it; what proportion no one knows. Community facilities account for a large part of it. The general lack . . . of adequate shopping, recreation, and other facilities . . . means that many of those workers who come out with their families are forced to live on a substandard scale. As a result, after a month . . . many of those workers decide, while wage rates might not be as attractive back where they came from, at least they get a little more pleasure in living back there, and they consequently return." To remedy the situation he recommended the expansion of federal housing programs.[16]

These views were amplified by others directly involved in man and womanpower procurement. Henry T. Kranz, Regional Director of the U.S. Civil Service Commission, related, as an example, the problems of the Salinas (California) Army Air Base in securing skilled mechanics because there was absolutely no housing in the area. "The difficulty of supplying . . . or keeping personnel ties in with the insufficiency of housing," he said. "Housing shows up as the crucial factor." In his estimation private employers had done much better than federal agencies in supplying housing for the new workers whom they hired. By mid-1943 the situation had worsened. "We certainly are not making work in quite a number of [western] areas attractive for the immigrants," admitted Charles E. Wilson, Executive Vice-Chairman of the War Production Board. "[They] have been attracted to the jobs but do not want to stay on them for any length of time under the existing poor housing conditions . . . particularly in connection with the aircraft plants." The War Production Board attempted to meet the crisis by creating five area production urgency committees (in San Diego, Los Angeles, San Francisco, Portland, and Seattle). These groups were composed of representatives from the armed services and federal civilian agencies. Their task was to determine job priority ratings to discourage nonessential workers from coming into these localities and causing further housing shortages.[17]

Transportation problems also contributed to the labor shortage on the Pacific Coast. As Senator Robert Reynolds (N.C.), chairman of the Senate Committee on Military Affairs, complained, in California, Oregon, and Washington workers had greater difficulties in getting to and from their plants than in the East because of the distances involved. In the San Francisco Bay Area, for example, it took many workers more than two hours to travel from San Francisco to the Richmond shipyards in the East Bay. In Los Angeles major factories were located on the periphery of the city—accessible only by automobile. The average worker in the California shipyards, Frank Roney estimated, traveled to and from work at least 52 miles daily. Many labor problems that slowed production, such as absenteeism and fatigue, were largely due to commuting difficulties. Whenever production schedules were impeded by transportation problems, the War Manpower Commission turned the problems over to the Office of Defense Transportation. But that agency often lacked the means to correct local situations. Transportation was closely tied to housing because even if workers located suitable housing, it was often too far from the shipyards and factories where they worked.[18] So the problems leading to labor turnover, absenteeism, and fatigue persisted.

Related to housing and transportation bottlenecks were inadequate service facilities for thousands of newcomers. For many, mundane shopping became a nightmare. After working full shifts workers were often forced to stand in line for hours in grocery stores, frequently distant from factory or home. More often than not the supply of scarce food items was exhausted by the time they were able to do their shopping. As Charles E. Wilson said succinctly: "Where you have a condition where you are losing, as in the aircraft industry, over 8% of the total number of people employed per month, and in the shipbuilding yards considerably more, you very obviously have a practical problem . . . because I cannot think of anything more wasteful of manpower than a 100 percent turnover a year."[19]

The profusion of federal agencies attempting to deal with production bottlenecks was often more of a hindrance than a help. The Office of War Mobilization and Economic Stabilization, the Coordinator of Defense Housing, the National Housing Agency and the War Manpower Commission were only a few of the governmental bodies that attempted to deal with western production problems from

Washington. Far distant from these western localities, and often working at cross purposes, they were not particularly effective in improving working conditions in the frenzied activity on the Pacific Coast.[20]

By July 1943 the serious disruptions of production schedules in
shipyards and aircraft factories alarmed President Roosevelt. In an
effort to unsnarl the morass of conflicting federal programs, on April
9, 1943, he created, by Executive Order, the Committee for Congested
Production Areas in the Executive Office of the White House. Its
primary function was to cut through red tape and overlapping jurisdictions of the many war agencies involved in the mobilization effort
in order to achieve the primary objective—increased production.
Since a Congressional committee was already investigating glaring
inefficiencies of federal agencies in important production areas,
Roosevelt's move was undoubtedly also designed to forestall political
criticism.[21]

At the same time the Office of War Mobilization headed by
James F. Byrnes also attempted to remedy the situation by preparing a
West Coast Manpower Plan. Largely drafted by Bernard Baruch and
John Hancock, the program was designed to meet an estimate of the
War Manpower Commission for 500,000 additional workers required
in the three Pacific states in 1943 if production quotas set by the War
Production Board were to be met. Byrnes announced the comprehensive plan on September 3, 1943, to meet the urgent crisis. "We have
already fallen behind schedule for vitally important war items on the
West Coast due to manpower shortages," declared Byrnes. "The war
work scheduled for the West Coast this fall and winter would require
100,000 persons in shipbuilding . . . and 100,000 more in aircraft
construction. . . . Manpower and construction cannot be dealt with
separately for they are inseparable parts of a single, but complicated
problem."[22]

Based on a pilot program in Buffalo, New York, the program
encompassed fifty-seven main points. All responsibility for coordinating West Coast manpower needs was centralized in the War Manpower Commission. But the War Production Board assumed the right
to adjust war production schedules of all manufacturers on the Pacific
Coast, military or civilian, and created local advisory committees for
this function. To the dismay of many westerners the Plan limited
future industrial expansion requiring manpower on the Pacific Coast.
Some officials of the Selective Service System hoped that the mere
threat of moving production out of the area would serve as a spur to
increased productivity. At the same time the War Manpower Commission was instructed to establish priorities for all non-agricultural labor
on the West Coast. Workers were to select employment only from jobs
certified as essential by the War Production Board, while employers

were to hire only those who were certified by the U.S. Employment Service. Those engaged in critical occupations were to receive full consideration for draft deferment. And the Plan left open the possibility of shipping workers from other areas to the West Coast to fill the labor slack.[23]

Westerners were visibly upset by the promulgation of the Plan. Unfortunately, Byrnes had not consulted with them before announcing the formal proposal in Washington. California's U.S. Senator Sheridan Downey charged that the threat of withholding federal contracts from the West created confusion and demoralization in the western business community. Western labor leaders were equally alarmed. Senator Downey feared that nonessential and service industries could be severely hurt by the proposal.[24]

Western business leaders were likewise unfavorable to the proposal. Western members of an advisory group, the National Management Labor Committee, had urged Donald Nelson to defer implementation of the Plan. Many of these western businessmen felt that the geographical isolation of the Pacific Coast made it unique since it was still seeking to develop an industrial economy. Like Downey, they felt that Byrnes should have discussed the program first with westerners before undertaking its promulgation. Moreover, Chairman Andrew J. May (Ky.) of the House Military Affairs Committee, who had made an extensive inquiry into western labor conditions, also expressed his hesitancy about implementation of the Plan because he objected to the regimentation of workers. Like westerners, he felt that the allocation of labor could best be handled by local authorities rather than from Washington. Officials on the ground were far more knowledgeable about using available labor, he felt, than federal bureaucrats in Washington trying to relocate thousands of individuals by shipping them from one region to another.[25]

Much of this discontent was crystallized in the strong critical report made by Downey's Congressional subcommittee. His investigation revealed "most unhappy living conditions for hundreds of thousands of war workers," the committee noted. "Indeed . . . many thousands of workers on the Pacific Coast with their families are living under conditions that must be characterized as abominable." Although the committee approved federal efforts to maximize production, it sharply criticized the Byrnes Plan. Any effort to restrain workers from leaving their jobs, they felt, was bound to fail since it did not really address itself to underlying causes. "It must be understood that workers are absent from their jobs," the committee said, ". . . chiefly because of inadequate housing, transportation, shopping, schools, and other municipal facilities. How, under these conditions, compulsion or coercion of the worker can seriously reduce labor turnover or

absenteeism must remain a foremost problem." Instead, the committee recommended the importation of workers and more federal aid to
improve housing conditions. It also urged the use of 150,000 men
and women to service military installations on the Pacific Coast, the
use of Italian prisoners of war, and the accelerated importation of
Mexicans. But it strongly opposed the mandatory labor restrictions
contained in the Byrnes proposal or the curtailment of civilian and
military production in the Pacific states by federal fiat.[26]

Downey's report underscored the fact that the federal housing
program for war workers had been less than a full success. Although a
Coordinator of Defense Housing had prime responsibility for the
program, a number of other federal agencies were also involved, and
confusion and inefficiency were the norm. By 1943 the problems
aroused the attention of Senator Harry S. Truman and his Committee
to Investigate Defense Expenditures. Truman was particularly concerned about the Coordinator's construction of 750 dormitory units,
designed for aircraft workers, in San Diego, built in 1943 in only
thirty days. The seventeen structures were so unattractive that only 44
of the 750 rooms were occupied. Moreover, the Coordinator did not
provide furniture when he first made them available.[27] Not all federal
housing projects were such unmitigated disasters, but problems
abounded.

As a result of such strong western opposition, the Byrnes plan was
not fully implemented. A proposal to limit war production on the
Pacific Coast was seen by businessmen and politicians there as another
effort by eastern economic interests—strongly entrenched in the War
Production Board—to limit western economic growth. The problem
was more complex, of course, but given more than a half century of
eastern domination of the western economy, such fears were understandable. Thus, although the War Manpower Commission restricted
deferments for essential workers in West Coast industries, on the
other hand the War Production Board did not significantly reduce
priorities for western war industries.[28]

The severe labor shortage in the West affected not only the new
factories producing war materials but agribusiness as well. Already in
1942 crop losses due to labor shortages were considerable. W. E.
Spencer, chairman of the Agricultural Producers Labor Committee of
the California Citrus Growers Association, estimated that 50 percent
of that year's crop would rot for lack of harvesting help. At least
21,000 additional workers were needed, he claimed, if 75,000 car-
loads of citrus fruit were not to be lost.[29]

Several factors contributed to this farm labor shortage. Obviously,
the wartime draft was denuding rural areas of their traditional labor
supply. Moreover, the lure of higher paying jobs in urban industries

drew many workers from the farming regions of the nation. With a lessening of racial discrimination due to the increasing labor shortage, minorities such as blacks and Mexican-Americans pursued more lucrative job opportunities in industry. And in contrast to the depression years when farmers had decreased production in the face of shrinking markets, the enormous wartime demands now found farmers seeking bumper crops.[30]

Throughout 1942 various farm organizations mobilized their members to demand government help. Representatives from some of these groups met in San Francisco on November 6, 1942, to crystallize their grievances. They demanded occupational deferment for farm workers and draft exemption. They also urged that the U.S. Employment Service and private employers cease recruitment of farm workers for industrial jobs. At the same time they enthusiastically endorsed the importation of Mexicans for farm work, and the use of military personnel to augment the harvest labor force. Meanwhile, representatives of the California Farm Bureau Federation and the State Grange prevailed upon California's U.S. Senator Sheridan Downey to undertake a special Senate inquiry to investigate the farm labor shortage in the West.[31] Downey conducted hearings from November 30 to December 3, 1942, at which dozens of representatives of farm interests appeared. Although the producers of each specialty crop had unique problems, certain common complaints ran through the presentations of those who testified.

Many farm operators blamed the federal government for their labor shortage. Some of the large citrus growers in California and Arizona placed direct responsibility on the U.S. Employment Service for their plight. Instead of referring applicants to farms, they noted, the Service sent them to industrial establishments. One California cotton broker, R. V. Jensen of Clayton and Company, reflected the views of many of the big producers when he charged that the Employment Service and the Farm Security Administration were more interested in unionizing farm workers than in providing an adequate supply for the growers.[32] Such hostility between California and Arizona farm interests and the federal agencies had its roots in the bitter conflicts between the operators and migratory workers during the depression years in the 1930s, and the war did little to allay their mutual suspicions. But the feeling that the U.S. Employment Service was insensitive to the needs of farmers was not limited to the large operators, for smaller growers reflected similar views. A farmer who tilled thirty acres for vegetables in Los Angeles County was as vehement in his criticism as the proprietors of 30,000 acres.[33]

Of course, other influences contributed to the increasing seriousness of the farm labor shortage. Obviously the drain of the armed forces and of higher paying jobs in industry were major factors. This was a national as well as a regional dilemma. The West had special difficulties, however. Removal of all Japanese-Americans to internment camps left a major gap; they had been a vitally important factor in vegetable and fruit production. Those workers who were available often were inefficient, some growers charged. That was not entirely surprising since the level of farm wages was considerably below that of factory workers. And while western farmers were beset with a shrinking agricultural labor force, they also had to contend with an increasingly serious farm machinery and equipment shortage. To curtail the use of steel, for example, the War Production Board on October 20, 1942, issued its Limitation Order L-170, severely restricting the production of farm machinery. This constituted a heavy blow to western farmers, who were more heavily mechanized than those in other regions. Thus, while California farmers purchased 9,600 new tractors in 1941, they expected to secure no more than 800 in 1943; while they purchased 5,100 plows in 1941, they expected to secure no more than 600 in 1943. Whichever way they turned, or so it seemed to many agriculturists in the West, wartime mobilization created serious obstacles that impeded maximum production.[34]

During 1942 many farmers in California, Oregon, Washington, Colorado, and Arizona recruited students, women, retired people, and moonlighting white collar workers to help bring in their harvests. In the fruit-growing areas of the Pacific Northwest this auxiliary force worked well, in part because farmers had resorted to similar expedients in prewar days.[35] But in other types of specialized farming such an ad hoc labor force did not prove to be very practical. The more mechanized types of farming, particularly those dependent on irrigation, required people with some experience and skill. As George Sehlmeyer, master of the California State Grange, explained, for example, his efforts to train inexperienced workers in dairying were extremely frustrating. He had tried to teach young girls to operate milking machines, and gave them three weeks of intensive training. But the milking machines proved to be much more complex than the cows, and his efforts were unsuccessful.[36]

In California the State Department of Education became directly involved with supplying student labor for harvests and coordinated a statewide program, with special emphasis on recruiting young people in San Francisco and Los Angeles. Unfortunately, these expedients proved increasingly futile during 1942, particularly for large commercial operations. Already in September 1941 large farm operators in California, Arizona, and Texas petitioned the U.S. Immigration and Naturalization Service to allow the importation of 30,000 Mexican *braceros*. At the time that agency refused their request.[37] Instead, as the farm labor shortage worsened by June of 1942, the War Man-power Commission issued an order allowing for the systematic transportation of farm workers from one locality to another. The agency also urged employers to provide its farm workers with higher wages, better housing, and improved health care. Accustomed to a docile and poorly paid labor force, many western farmers disdained this directive, however, continuing to urge the importation of Mexicans.[38] To some extent, the situation was aggravated by a degree of insensitivity on the part of the U.S. Employment Service. Throughout 1941 and again during most of 1942 the Service belittled the requests of farmers for agricultural labor, for in the past growers had consistently overestimated their needs in order to attract a large labor pool and then depress the wages of their migratory farm workers. But the labor shortages of 1941 and 1942 were very real, unlike those of the depression years, and the forecasts of the Employment Service consistently wrong. On June 28, 1942, for example, the Director of the U.S. Employment Service in California, Ralph J. Wadsworth, declared that "there is no farm labor shortage at the moment . . . but we anticipate [one] in August." Meanwhile, farmers were claiming that the lack of help was critical. Yet under prevailing rules the Service could not certify a shortage until it actually occurred, and could not anticipate or estimate demand in the immediate future.[39]

Possibly Wadsworth's views were shaped by his opposition to the importation of Mexicans. In a letter to a California farmer, he said: "the reason I express doubt about the importation of labor from Mexico is . . . that there are already many Mexicans in this state who are unemployed." He also feared the opposition of social welfare organizations—still preoccupied with depression psychology—to the importation of *braceros*. The president of the California Grape Growers and Shippers Association, A. Setrakian, a very excitable and emotional man, recalled his encounter with Wadsworth. At a meeting in Fresno on July 6, 1942, Setrakian noted, he "told Mr. Wadsworth that we needed men, also where were we going to get them? He said, 'I don't know.' I said, 'We need Mexicans. When are we going to get them.' He said, 'I don't know.' I said, 'What have you come down to tell us?' He said, 'I came down to find out what kind of a solution you fellows can offer to the United States Employment Service!' Well, we thought that was a funny statement to make because, after all, the United States Employment Service was supposed to be the organization to furnish labor."[40]

By June of 1942 much of this discontent had crystallized into a proposal, supported by many western farmers, for the importation of Mexican farm labor. Governor Culbert Olson of California yielded to the pressure when on June 15, 1942, he sent an urgent telegram to

Secretary of Agriculture Claude R. Wickard, Secretary of Labor Frances Perkins, and Secretary of State Cordell Hull. "Without substantial numbers of Mexicans," the Governor pleaded, "the situation is certain to be disastrous to the entire Victory program." R. V. Jensen of Anderson, Clayton, and Company, a cotton broker, described the efforts of the California growers. "Early in this year [1942]," he noted, "there was formed a statewide war agricultural committee . . . [which] met from time to time and made surveys and recommendations with respect to the farm-labor problem which was beginning to be acute at that time. As a result of these surveys the committee came to the conclusion that the only solution . . . was the importation of Mexican workers and at a meeting held . . . on May 19 it was decided to send a subcommittee to Washington to confer with the State and other Federal Departments looking toward working out details with regard to importing Mexicans." In the nation's capital the group encountered the morass of the federal bureaucracy. The committee found it necessary to confer with at least ten different agencies and tried to develop a consensus among them. "It was necessary to bring about a meeting of the minds of ten Federal agencies and subagencies each with somewhat different axes to grind," Jensen said. "Various meetings were held . . . at some of which . . . the C.I.O. and the A.F. of L. were represented. At one of these meetings a tentative draft of the contract or agreement, under the terms of which Mexicans might be brought in, was presented." The California and Arizona growers objected to various provisions dealing with wages and bonding requirements. With the support of the War Manpower Commission, they succeeded in having objectionable features eliminated.[41]

Throughout the spring and summer of 1942 representatives of Mexico met with State Department officials to negotiate a formal agreement for the importation of Mexican labor. The Mexicans still remembered their World War I experience when more than 150,000 of their nationals had gone to work in western states as farm laborers. They had encountered miserable working conditions and less than adequate housing and sanitation facilities. They had usually received substandard wages; sometimes the promises of work did not materialize; and they were chronically threatened by deportation. Thus the Mexican representatives were cautious. On the other hand, State Department negotiators were subject to increasing pressure from agricultural interests. In addition to California and Arizona agribusiness, the beet sugar producers in western states like Colorado, Idaho, and Montana were among the most eager for Mexican labor, and it was in response to their requests that in April 1942 the Immigration and Naturalization Service established an interagency committee to investigate the possibility of importing *braceros.* This committee had representatives from the War Manpower Commission, and the Departments of Labor, State, Justice, and Agriculture, who met in May of 1942 to draft a preliminary plan.

At the same time Mexican President Avila Camacho on May 4 ordered his Departments of Labor, Interior, and Justice to form an interdepartmental committee to consider the *bracero* question. In the deliberations the U.S. State Department representatives were unenthusiastic because they feared that possible exploitation of Mexican workers could imperil the Good Neighbor policy. But on June 1, 1942, Mexico declared war on the Axis powers, and closer wartime collaboration between the United States and Mexico eased the way for a labor agreement. Final terms were suggested by U.S. Ambassador George Messersmith in Mexico City to Mexican Foreign Minister Ezequiel Padilla on June 15. During July and August the Mexican interagency committee pored over the proposals, sensitive to possible exploitation of Mexicans and ethnic discrimination. Yet many Mexicans hoped that workers might learn more about the technology of American agriculture and mechanization. And additional income for poverty-stricken peasants was not only desirable in itself but would benefit the nation's balance of payments. Such advantages overcame objections by the doubters. Thus, when Agriculture Secretary Claude Wickard visited in July of 1942 and conferred with Foreign Minister Padilla, they arranged a trial agreement. Between July 13 and 23, 1942, American and Mexican negotiators hammered out the formal details of what was to become the first of a series of *bracero* agreements. On August 4, diplomatic exchanges brought it into force.[42]

This *bracero* agreement of 1942 provided the basis for the importation of Mexican labor into the United States during the next five years. In the United States the Department of Agriculture had major responsibility for recruiting workers, using the U.S. Employment Service. In Mexico a bureau of migrant labor in the Ministry of Foreign Affairs was in charge of selecting workers. Mexicans in the United States were not subject to military service, and were guaranteed transportation, living expenses, and repatriation. To mollify U.S. labor unions the arrangement provided that Mexicans would not be used to displace American workers or to reduce wage rates. Negotiation of contracts between individual braceros and American employers were to be handled by the Farm Security Administration. Thus, the United States government now became an employer of *braceros,* in a modern version of the seventeenth-century practice of indentured servitude.

Contracts were to be made for a six-month period and were renewable. The United States was to pay all transportation costs. Although the federal government was authorized to seek reimbursement from employers, in practice it absorbed these costs. *Braceros* were assured of the same wage levels that prevailed for Americans, and to be offered similar conditions of housing, food, and health care. Possibly the Mexicans were unaware that American workers had no assurance of receiving such benefits. At Mexican insistence 10 percent of each *bracero*'s earnings were deducted to be placed in individual savings accounts in Mexico's Agricultural Credit Bank. Since Texans had developed a reputation for discriminating against Mexicans, the Agreement provided that no Mexicans were to be sent to that southwestern state.[43]

In view of the pressing need for farm labor in the United States American farmers lost little time in making the agreement operational. More than 4,000 Mexican workers came to the United States during the second half of 1942, 53,000 more in 1943, and 62,000 in 1944. Of a total of 309,538 wartime farm workers imported into the United States between 1942 and 1947, 219,000 were Mexican. Others came from the Bahamas, Barbados, Jamaica, Canada, and elsewhere. California used one-half of this work force while the remainder was scattered in the other western states.[44]

Braceros encountered problems on both sides of the border. In Mexico the Ministry of Foreign Affairs established a recruitment center at the National Stadium in Mexico City. But it created bedlam as many more Mexican peasants than could be hired streamed into the capital, adding to its already large population of urban poor. In 1944, for example, 50,000 applicants appeared although only 16,000 were hired. Even those who were selected often had to wait for weeks before work began. Meanwhile, they had no food, shelter, or sanitary facilities. Many walked about the streets, begging and scavenging, and sleeping on the sidewalks. As the situation became more chaotic, the Mexican government also established recruitment centers in the provinces at Guadalajara and Irapuato, but the process in Mexico was rarely orderly. Nor did the Mexican government carefully administer the remittance of monies sent to the Agricultural Credit Bank. Many *braceros* complained that they never received the 10 percent of their wages which had been sent to the Bank for safekeeping.[45]

Once in the United States, *braceros* encountered other problems. In the western states, wage rates were usually determined by county wage boards. These were appointed by the County Agents of the Department of Agriculture, and were usually composed of the leading local farmers. Quite naturally, these boards were more concerned about the interests of employers than of itinerant foreign laborers, and tried to keep wages as low as possible. Sometimes workers became ill due to different climatic conditions and earned nothing since they had no guarantee of minimum earnings. Only when a worker was unemployed for more than 25 percent of the period of employment was he entitled to a subsistence allowance of $3 daily.[46] Other disputes arose over quality of food and housing. Such controversies were often complicated by language barriers. The War Food Administration usually sought to mediate. It also held formal hearings to which the local Mexican consuls were invited. Many *braceros* felt, however, that they could not trust anyone, whether employers or representatives of the War Food Administration. Nor did they feel differently about a small force of labor inspectors hired by the Mexican government, or the Mexican consuls. On days when these outsiders visited the camps *braceros* were usually working in the fields. Mexican consuls were usually located in cities distant from agricultural areas, and, having many other duties, were largely ineffectual in monitoring the program.[47] Most labor camps in western states lacked educational and recreational facilities for the men after working hours. Numerous *braceros* also had spells of illness, since they were unaccustomed to American food. Initially, administrators gave little thought to the special dietary habits of the workers. California was the only state to enact legislation that provided minimum housing and sanitary standards for migratory workers. During the war the War Food Administration advertised for cooks in Spanish language newspapers, without great success.[48]

Although initially the *bracero* program was administered by the Farm Security Administration, it was soon transferred to the War Food Administration. Many American farmers were hostile to the Farm Security Administration, which they regarded as a pro-union, radical, social reform agency. Their attitude, part of a broader reaction against New Deal agencies during the war years, led the Secretary of Agriculture to transfer it to the War Food Administration which was more sympathetic to the labor needs of western agribusiness. That agency hired a field force of 2,400 men and women to administer the program. Financed by the President's Emergency Fund during its first eight months, the *bracero* program was regularly funded by Congress in its succeeding years.[49]

While the *bracero* program did much to alleviate the farm labor shortage in the West, an equally large Mexican migration came to work on the railroads of the region. Late in 1941 the Southern Pacific Railroad approached the Immigration and Naturalization Service about importing Mexican laborers, largely for track maintenance. Loud opposition from representatives of labor unions led the company to withdraw its request. By May of 1942 the labor shortage was so serious, however, that the railroad resubmitted its application. And to help the Southern Pacific fill 949 unfilled positions, the U.S. Railroad Retirement Board authorized it to recruit the necessary help.[50]

By the middle of 1942 the labor shortage on the railroads was more serious. Increased traffic wore out equipment more rapidly just as Class I railroads [major] were losing about 150,000 of their most experienced men to the armed forces. It was enough to alarm Joseph Eastman, Director of the Office of Defense Transportation. On October 20, 1942, he wrote to Paul McNutt, chairman of the War Manpower Commission, about the critical lack of track workers, and urged him to take immediate steps to ensure the safe maintenance of tracks and roadbeds. Since western railroads had utilized Mexican labor for decades, it was not surprising that they again looked southward in this new labor crisis. With the precedent of *braceros* for farm labor, western railroad officials pressed for a similar agreement on the importation of non-agricultural workers. On April 29, 1943, representatives of the United States and Mexico signed the necessary documents to bring the program into force.[51]

Under the plan the U.S. Railroad Retirement Board administered the recruitment of Mexicans for the War Manpower Commission. It was responsible for their transportation, for providing food and housing, and for distributing the workers to the individual railroads. In May of 1943 the recruitment drive began in the National Stadium in Mexico City. But the crush of applicants was so great—recreating chaotic conditions that had accompanied the call for farm workers— that the Mexican government also set up centers in San Luis Potosi and Queretaro. The rail program was about half as large as the farm labor operation. In 1943 the War Manpower Commission chose 20,000 Mexicans; in 1944, 40,000, and in 1945, 75,000. The Brotherhood of Maintenance of Way Employees—the major American union—reserved the right to review these import quotas.[52]

Western railroads eagerly availed themselves of the Mexican labor. Thirty-two rail carriers—almost all of the major lines in the West— requested *braceros,* from which the Mexican government excluded farm workers. The experience of the *braceros* in this program was similar to the farming operations. They could make their grievances known to Mexican consuls and labor inspectors who made regular tours, together with representatives of the Railroad Retirement Board. But as with farm workers, the labor camps were usually too distant for close contact with Mexican officials, while the representatives of the Railroad Retirement Board rarely understood the Spanish language.[53] Some workers were housed in freight cars, others in tent cities, and some were boarded in local homes. Neither the officials of the Railroad Retirement Board nor those of the railways gave much consideration to the educational and recreational needs of the men. Many Mexicans resented the enforced solitude and boredom in the camps. Often, they were frustrated in their expectations of learning something about American language and culture. In spite of these difficulties the behavior of most of these *braceros* was exemplary. By January 1, 1945, 80,273 Mexicans had been recruited for railroad work—more than half with the Southern Pacific and Santa Fe Railroads—in California, Washington, Oregon, Nevada, Arizona, and Montana.[54]

During the war the *bracero* program satisfied the mutual interests of the United States and Mexico. In the United States the *braceros* successfully alleviated a critical labor shortage in two vital industries, farming and railroading. Paul Scharrenberg, director of the California State Department of Industrial Relations, noted that the California farm crop in 1943 was valued at $1.5 billion, and Mexicans harvested about 15 percent of that crop. In 1944 Mexicans comprised 8.9 percent of farm workers on the Pacific Coast and 5.1 percent of those in the Mountain states. For Mexico the program helped to alleviate its chronic underemployment. The *braceros* brought $205 million of their earnings back to Mexico between 1943 and 1947, thus aiding their homeland's balance of payments. Moreover, some Mexicans viewed the program as a tangible contribution to the Allied war effort. Mexican Foreign Minister Ezequiel Padilla summarized official reaction when he said that the *bracero* program provided "an opportunity to earn high wages, a noble adventure for our youth, and above all, proof of our cooperation in the victory of our cause." Mexican President Avila Camacho, during President Franklin D. Roosevelt's visit to Mexico in 1943, was as effusive when he said that the wartime *bracero* program was "a symbol in which we understand the duties of reciprocal aid between people . . . a demonstration of the strong will which animates us."[55]

Wartime mobilization thus set a variety of forces into motion that resulted in another large population influx into the West. The expansion of production in almost every field created an unprecedented demand for labor that led to rising wage scales and acted as a magnet for those seeking economic opportunity in the United States and in neighboring countries. The surge of population was to affect the social structure of western communities and created new strains. Such stresses were evident in wartime urban communities throughout the West, and were particularly marked in the bustling metropolitan centers of California.

CHAPTER FOUR

Western Cities in Wartime: California

The overwhelming majority of newcomers to the West between 1941 and 1945 settled in towns and cities. Already by 1940 many western urban areas such as San Diego, Long Beach, Los Angeles, and San Francisco in California, and Portland and Seattle in the Pacific Northwest, were experiencing annual growth rates that exceeded 10 percent. Before the war the War Department was already consciously concentrating new military bases in the warmer areas of the nation, principally in the South and West. At the same time the Office of Production Management, the U.S. Maritime Commission, and other federal contractors for ships and aircraft awarded more than one-half of their orders to companies west of the Mississippi River.[1] Many western cities in the interior such as Phoenix and Tucson, Denver and Colorado Springs, Albuquerque, Tulsa, Dallas, and El Paso also grew, largely because of the proximity of nearby major air fields or other military bases. Between 1940 and 1943 metropolitan counties in the Mountain and Pacific states gained 920,000 residents—not to speak of an even larger number of transient military personnel. During this same period the metropolitan counties of the Northeast lost 1,023,000 people.[2] In the years from 1940 to 1947 the three Pacific Coast states increased 38.9 percent in population, measured against a national average of 8.7 percent.

But mere numbers alone do not tell the story of western cities in wartime. Throughout the West cities were more important than in other parts of the nation because the population of the region was so thinly distributed over vast areas. Thus, although Denver contained one-third of Colorado's population, it was the "capital" of a region 1,500 miles wide and 1,700 miles tall—sometimes also known as the Rocky Mountain Empire.[3] Even smaller towns and cities loomed large in relation to the territories which they served. The specialized urban services they provided for areas surrounding them often extended for several thousand square miles. As Carey McWilliams noted in 1949, in relation to their functions western cities were truly the capitals of their states—and of surrounding regions that usually transcended state boundaries. A good example was Reno, which between 1941 and 1945 had a population of only 23,000 but was the largest city in a state of 100,000 people. El Paso, with 110,000, was the biggest mountain city between Los Angeles and San Antonio on an east-west axis, and between Denver and Mexico City on a north-south axis. And Salt Lake City, with 150,000 citizens, was the focal point of a vast mountain empire encompassing not only Utah, but southern Idaho, eastern Nevada, and Mormon communities in Arizona, Wyoming and Colorado.[4]

Cities in the West had special problems, different from those in other regions of the United States. Some of these stemmed from their unique historical origins. Throughout the nineteenth century Congress—driven largely by motives of immediate political advantage or expediency—had approved boundaries for most of the western states without much regard for the interests or convenience of their inhabitants. By the twentieth century these artificial boundaries imposed special burdens on western state and city governments as they tried to develop transportation and water supply services, and to build social and cultural institutions. Another special difficulty was the high percentage of western lands owned by the federal government. In eight mountain states 54 percent of the acreage was under federal jurisdiction, and thus not directly under the authority of the states or the municipalities. Consequently, to a degree unprecedented in other regions, the urban communities of the West were federal cities—much more subject to the whim of federal policies than their counterparts in the East or South.[5]

The Second World War set in motion a boom not at all unlike the nineteenth-century mining and railroad booms which had brought large numbers of footloose people to the West within a short period of time. They came in search of fame or fortune, or perhaps just for adventure. As wartime mobilization gathered momentum during 1941 and 1942, it created millions of new jobs in the West which beckoned like a beacon to Americans in every section of the nation. Moreover, the dislocations wrought by the war in the lives of millions of Americans strengthened the rootlessness already stimulated by the the Great Depression. Always a restless and mobile people, Americans were even more disposed toward mobility under the influence of wartime stresses. Catherine Bauer, a housing expert and consultant to the Federal Housing Authority during World War II, commented on this trend when she noted in 1943 that "one-sixth of our population are in a state of flux, physically and psychologically. If you ask them where they expect to be five years from now, they shrug their shoulders." And she added cogently that "the waves of immigration and emigration dislocating the country today reflect, on the whole, trends and forces that have been operating over a long period. The war . . . [has] simply speeded them up."[6]

The resulting population surge consisted of more than 8 million newcomers west of the Mississippi River, not counting at least 3 million transient servicemen and women. They constituted the greatest population influx which the West had ever experienced in a similar span of time. No wonder that the migration created new social problems in western cities, problems of housing, health, transportation, education, and social services. And since the Great Migration of the years from 1941 to 1945 included significant numbers of minority groups, including blacks and Mexicans, the population boom also created new racial and ethnic tensions. Although conditions varied in particular localities, the war years subjected most western towns and cities to these strains. Most severely affected were urban areas on the Pacific Coast such as San Diego, Los Angeles, the San Francico Bay Area, Portland, Oregon, and Seattle. But other urban centers in the West, such as Phoenix, Tucson, Denver, and Tulsa, underwent similar stresses, even if their experience was not quite as traumatic. If the new problems brought by the large population influx varied locally, yet more striking was the similarity in wartime patterns of city growth. In most instances World War II left an indelible and distinctive influence on the urban West.

As the problems emanating from mobilization mushroomed in the first year after Pearl Harbor, congressmen from affected areas became increasingly concerned. By late 1942 the House Naval Affairs Committee expressed alarm over lagging production quotas due to urban and labor difficulties, and appointed a subcommittee headed by Congressman Ed Izak (California) to look into the problem. Its members, who represented important war production areas in every section of the United States, undertook a rather exhaustive investigation, primarily in major production centers in the West—San Diego, Los Angeles, San Francisco in the spring of 1943, Portland and Seattle in the fall. Although they found the Los Angeles and San Francisco areas particularly hard hit, the situation in Portland and Seattle was not much better. On the other hand, San Diego, although experiencing a phenomenal influx of people, and a doubling of the resident population in four years, experienced fewer strains and stresses. As an old Navy town, it had been accustomed to a large transient population for decades.[7]

In an effort to take the steam out of potential Congressional criticism of the mobilization program, Roosevelt acted quickly during the spring of 1943 to provide federal aid to the hard-pressed Western cities. On April 7, 1943, he issued an Executive Order to create the President's Committee for Congested Production Areas. The members of the committee, and their representatives in the local congested areas, were to cut through red tape—through the often conflicting policies of the various federal agencies operating in a particular urban locality. In addition, the committee coordinated the programs of diverse federal agencies and cooperated with state and local governments. So, in Portland, for example, committee representatives worked on the solution of housing problems, eased manpower shortages in aluminum, agricultural, and transportation industries, secured in-plant facilities such as lunchrooms, and aided in the expansion of hospital and fire services. Clearly, the committee had wide scope. As a result of its efforts labor turnover in the six principal shipyards of the area declined from 15 percent monthly in mid-1943 to 7 percent in March 1944.[8] Elsewhere, the committee achieved similar results, as it alleviated some of the worst wartime pressures before the end of 1943. Its work can best be appreciated by a closer examination of wartime conditions in San Diego, Los Angeles, San Francisco, and Portland and Seattle.

San Diego was transformed by the war from a sleepy Navy town into a major metropolitan region. As City Manager Walter W. Cooper said in 1943: "The war has revolutionized the economy of San Diego." And he added: "Its effect is not fixed or static, but it is a constantly changing factor in the life of the city."[9] Not counting military personnel, within three years its population increased by 75 percent. By 1945 its population had grown by 190,000, or a growth rate between 1941 and 1945 of 147 percent! In addition, an estimated 130,000 servicemen and women came into the area.[10] What had been a city of 202,000 in 1940 swelled to 380,000 civilians within the city limits by 1944 and 130,000 military people. "This unexampled growth," said Cooper, "has taxed the physical facilities, financial ability, and personnel of the city." And, perhaps welcoming an opportunity to air his frustrations, he poured his heart out to the sympathetic members of the investigating committee to acquaint them with the particular nature of the city's problems.[11]

Among those problems housing was a major issue. Between 1940 and 1943 San Diego increased its housing units by more than 30 percent—by a larger number than all of those built in the preceding thirty years. Most of the new dwellings to house war workers were constructed with federal funds. And still many housing needs remained unmet. The situation was well described by Robert Noonan,

Secretary of the San Diego County Federated Trades and Labor Council: "There seems to be little doubt that adequate housing is the most pressing problem facing the war workers in this area. Even a cursory inspection makes it evident that our facilities are woefully inadequate. . . . People have been compelled to live in crowded quarters under conditions which seriously impair health and morale with the consequent adverse effect on working efficiency."[12] Noonan believed that the chronic labor shortage in San Diego was in part due to the lack of housing. The Council's representative had succeeded in recruiting needed workers in Arizona, New Mexico, Texas, Colorado, and in other areas of California. But few of them were willing to come to San Diego unless they could be assured of living accommodations. Meanwhile, the labor turnover at a major aircraft plant such as at Consolidated-Vultee Corporation was a whopping 88.7 percent annually.[13]

That company was also typical in encountering special problems in housing single women, a major consideration, since more than 40 percent of its work force was composed of women. George Barton, a representative of Vultee's management, explained that individual landlords were more loath to rent rooms to single women than to single men, compounding the problem.[14] Consolidated-Vultee and the Ryan Aeronautical Corporation were hoping jointly to establish dormitories for women so as to provide them with minimal food and shelter.[15] In some cases as many as eight war workers slept in a single room, often in shifts around the clock. Such everyday frustrations contributed to the high rate of turnover in war related industries. Homer Kerr of the Civic Committee of the Loma Vista Housing Project articulated them well. By 1943 more than 16,000 people lived in the project yet "there were no stores or commercial facilities of any kind until the Safeway store was opened in February 2, 1943. This 1 store is inadequate to meet the shopping needs of 16,000 people and it often takes as much as an hour for the shopper to go through one of the 5 cashier's lines. This is the only commercial facility on the project." The project had no sidewalks along its older units. At least 1,845 units were equipped with kerosene stoves, but they were many miles away from stores where kerosene could be purchased.[16]

More than in many other cities, transportation became a pressing problem in San Diego because of extensive distances between residences and work places. As City Manager Walter W. Cooper explained, "Our war plants were not located . . . with respect to our transportation. . . . Many of the military establishments were not located with respect to our transportation or the housing establishments either. You will find our streets are crossed by canyons. You can't just go directly east and west. The grades involved are such they can't be traversed by motor busses."[17] Glenn Rick, San Diego's Planning Engineer, felt that the huge population increase had a profound effect on the city's street and transportation system by changing prevailing traffic patterns. Particularly striking was the increase of automobile registrations—from 121,663 in 1940 to 152,461 in 1942, and more than 178,000 by 1945. At the same time wartime restrictions on gasoline and tires placed an enormous burden on the streetcar and bus systems in the city. By 1943 their passenger loads were 442 percent higher than they had been in 1940.[18]

The wartime influx strained many other city services. Fire Chief John E. Parrish complained about a critical lack of manpower, a shortage of equipment, and vast new neighborhoods requiring protection. School Superintendent Will C. Crawford castigated the lack of cooperation from federal officials in accommodating tens of thousands of new children for whom school buildings had yet to be constructed. Moreover, the city had to assume the cost of educating children who lived in federal housing projects, but whose parents paid no local taxes.[19] Police Chief Clifford Peterson was more concerned with new traffic problems than with major crimes, for the crime rate did not increase appreciably during the war, although tens of thousands of servicemen roamed San Diego's streets at night creating somewhat of a carnival atmosphere. As Commander T. M. Leovy, District Patrol Officer of the Eleventh Naval District in San Diego, described it, "The mere gathering of persons of common classification has a tendency to produce a psychological condition similar to that which may be found at a convention of Legionnaires, Elks, or others."[20] Predictably, the large transient population aggravated prostitution and venereal diseases. Under pressure from Armstead Carter, chairman of the San Diego Citizen's Committee to Control Venereal Disease, the police department on October 8, 1942, instituted a system whereby all women arrested for prostitution or vagrancy were held under quarantine and examined for venereal disease. If infected, the police held them until they were cured.[21] But the shortage of skilled police personnel—men and women—and the financial inability of the city to expand its force to keep up with the population increase created serious problems of law enforcement.[22]

Considering the extraordinarily large influx of population, San Diego coped exceedingly well with its new wartime problems. Few other urban areas experienced as large an increase of people— measured in percentages—as San Diego. Yet, despite stresses, living conditions in San Diego between 1940 and 1945 reflected fewer strains than those in most other congested war manufacturing centers. In spheres such as housing, transportation, and education, conditions were more favorable than elsewhere. No doubt the mild climate and the availability of land and open spaces in the San Diego vicinity eased the burden of absorbing several hundred thousand newcomers. The prominent role played by the United States Navy in the municipal affairs of San Diego also contributed to the maintenance of order, particularly of the transient population of servicemen and women.[23] Thus, although the war brought a doubling of population in the area, San Diego weathered the shock with amazing resilience.

Further up the coast, Los Angeles was also experiencing severe growth problems due to wartime migrations. However, since Los Angeles had been accustomed to rapid growth for more than two decades, the shock of a new surge of population was not as great as elsewhere. Moreover, the increase of defense production in the area was reasonably gradual. Still, more than half a million people poured in during the war years. In 1940 the U.S. Census reported 2,904,596 people in the Los Angeles area (1,504,277 in metropolitan Los Angeles). By the end of 1943 Orville R. Caldwell, Executive Deputy to the Mayor of Los Angeles, estimated population to be 3,300,000 (1,750,000 for the city of Los Angeles).[24] One of every forty Americans in the United States lived in the Los Angeles area, which also produced 10 percent of all war goods in the nation. Since California secured 17 percent of all war production, Los Angeles garnered more than one-half of this total in the state. And somehow the city was able to cope with a flood of newcomers without serious breakdowns. As Eugene Watson, Jr., representative of the National Housing Authority (Region X), aptly noted: "The Los Angeles locality was perhaps better prepared than any other city on the west coast to absorb the shock of conversion from peacetime to wartime activities."[25]

A wide range of industrial activities drew the vast immigration. Most important, of course, were the huge new aircraft and shipbuilding plants. As the largest major plane manufacturing center in the nation, the Los Angeles area boasted of extensive factories owned by Douglas, Lockheed, North American Aviation, Northrop, and Hughes Aircraft. Henry J. Kaiser operated the vast California Shipbuilding Company at Terminal Island—and, to supply it with steel, built the new nearby Fontana steel mills. Of the 350,000 airplane factory employees on the Pacific Coast, more than two-thirds worked in southern California.[26] Aircraft and shipbuilding accounted for three-fourths of the manufacturing in the Los Angeles area. But in addition, hundreds of smaller establishments sprang up engaged in the fabrication of aluminum, synthetic rubber, machine tools, ordnance, petroleum refining, and tank assembly. No wonder, therefore, that the rise in the area's employment was more than four times the national average.[27] Southern California also boasted of numerous large military installations, including the U.S. Naval Drydocks at Terminal Island, the vast U.S. Naval Supply Depot at San Pedro, the Long Beach Naval Hospital, U.S. Marine Corps Air Stations at El Toro and Santa Barbara, and Wrigley Field—to name only a few. The southland emerged as a distinctive region with a population greater than that of 37 states.[28]

This tremendous influx created an increasingly tight housing market in Los Angeles. By July 1943 the vacancy rate was estimated at less than .4 percent. The housing problem was worst in the harbor area which embraced one-third of the total war workers in the area, including 100,000 shipyard workers. The topography and extent of the Los Angeles region made some of its housing problems unique. As Eugene M. Weston of the National Housing Authority noted: "The Los Angeles housing problem has been particularly difficult to isolate because of the complexity of the area with respect to geography, industry, and availability of manpower."[29] In theory, residents of the San Fernando Valley could commute to the harbor area, some forty miles distant. In practice, this was not very feasible in view of intervening mountains and canyons and the inadequacy of existing transportation arteries. Thus the National Housing Agency divided the Los Angeles area into six districts and sought to build new units near new production facilities. If the city was able to absorb the newcomers without complete chaos, this was partly because in 1941—at the start of the mobilization—Los Angeles was experiencing a housing slump due to overbuilding, with 68,000 unit vacancies. These were immediately available to in-migrants. And during the war, private and public housing provided 160,500 new housing units.[30]

Unlike most other cities rocked by wartime changes, Los Angeles had traffic problems more serious than its housing shortages. As the premier automobile city in the United States, its automobile congestion worsened considerably between 1941 and 1945. In a survey of 225,000 industrial employees in April 1942 the California State Railroad Commission found that more than 85 percent traveled to work in cars.[31] Moreover, most new housing projects were located without reference to mass transit, and their occupants added to the already large flow of vehicles. Even when the Pacific Electric Company, an important electric car line, established a special service from Los Angeles to Terminal Island and the vast shipyards of the California Shipbuilding Company there—providing special parking lots at stopping points along the way—the overwhelming majority of workers still traveled in their cars.[32] On other lines a shortage of operators prevented the company from using its available equipment. The *Los Angeles Express* in 1944 estimated that 43 percent of the city's streetcars were idle because of a lack of motormen and conductors.[33] A strike of streetcar operators in September 1943 did little to improve the mass transit situation. Service on the Pacific Electric Company cars steadily declined during the war period. Without a mass transit system the city grew even more horizontally and became increasingly dependent on automobiles.[34] The situation became so serious that the eight major aircraft manufacturers in the area appealed directly to Washington. In view of their annual labor turnover of 100 percent, they urged Joseph Eastman, Director of the Office of Defense Transportation, to treat the entire metropolitan area as a single administrative unit. The California State Highway Traffic Advisory Commission was too political, they felt, to provide effective solutions for the area's traffic problems.[35]

The enormous increase of automobile traffic during the war as well as increased industrial production created serious new problems of air pollution in the metropolitan area. The severity of this smog led the Los Angeles City Council to request Charles L. Senn, director of the sanitation section of the Los Angeles Department of Health, to make a special investigation in 1943. In a pessimistic report he noted that pollution covered a five-mile area off Broadway and 7th Street on four separate occasions (July 26, September 21, October 5, October 12, 1943).[36] Within a few days of receiving this report, on October 28, 1943, the Board of Supervisors appointed a five-member Los Angeles County Smoke and Fume Commission to confer with businessmen, and county and city department heads. One of their prime functions was to persuade public as well as private officials to utilize smoke abatement devices. Even so, the increase of smoke and smog during wartime was considerable. Los Angeles County Health Officer H. A. Swarthout complained in 1945 that on some days the smoke was so thick in the area as to endanger military air travel.[37] Late in 1945 an anxious Mayor Bowron wrote to Nobel Prize–winning physicist Robert Millikin at the California Institute of Technology to ask for his help in the solution of the smog problem. By that time the Supervisors had created an office of Director of Air Pollution to develop a more comprehensive control program because increasingly some wartime industries accentuated the air pollution. Manufacture of synthetic rubber, for example, brought unexpected odors and smog into the heart of Los Angeles. The Rubber Reserve Corporation had invested more than $59 million in synthetic rubber manufactures in the Los Angeles area in its crash programs. But the Southern California Gas Company, which was operating a butadiene plant under federal contracts, created such serious pollution problems that at one point in October 1943 the City Council considered legal action to close it down. Only after a direct appeal from Bradley Dewey, Director of the Rubber Reserve Corporation, did the city fathers reluc-

tantly desist. Instead, they demanded installation of special anti-
pollution devices. By the beginning of 1944 such equipment
succeeded in removing the most noxious odors.[38]

The population crush also placed burdens on police and fire protection systems. Police Chief C. B. Horrall noted that the 35 percent
increase in recorded traffic problems during the war was greater than
in most other cities, in view of the heavy reliance on automobiles by
Los Angeles area citizens. In contrast to San Diego, Los Angeles also
underwent a significant increase in violent crimes. Felonious assaults
and robberies rose by 50 percent during 1943. Horrall charged that
blacks were responsible for some of the increase in crime, perhaps
because of the severe overcrowding in black neighborhoods. The Los
Angeles Police also reported a doubling of arrests for juvenile delinquency between 1940 and 1943, which Horrall attributed to wartime
disruption of families. Consequently, the police imposed a 9 P.M. curfew for youths under seventeen years of age. Yet law enforcement was
plagued by a lack of police officers since the regular force of 2,547
individuals was chronically 500 short during the war.[39]

In fact, the city was unable to deal with juvenile delinquency with-
out appealing for state and federal help. Mayor Bowron established a
Los Angeles Youth Activities Committee which cooperated with the
California War Council in a statewide program. After a direct appeal
to federal authorities the Mayor secured funds from the Federal
Works Agency for fighting juvenile crime.[40]

The old western vigilante spirit reappeared briefly. Like other
West Coast residents, Angelenos had a case of war jitters, with many
expecting a direct Japanese attack or perhaps German sabotage. During 1942 talk about a defense or militia force was rife. In August 1942
Mayor Fletcher Bowron wrote to City Attorney Ray L. Chesebro inquiring about the legal basis for a local militia to guard defense installations since neither the U.S. Army nor the State Guard seemed interested. Local patriots offered themselves as a Citizen's Defense Corps.
But the evacuation of Japanese-Americans quieted fears, while flag-
ging concern about German spies dampened the plans for vigilan-
tism.[41]

Like other urban centers in wartime, Los Angeles experienced
considerable financial strains. As the city expanded services to the
rapidly growing population, its tax base and its municipal income
decreased. In part, this was due to the increasing decentralization of
industry in the Los Angeles area. New plants sprang up, primarily
outside of the downtown area. That section of the city went into
decline. Moreover, most new migrants were renters rather than property owners, but demanded city services. This trend profoundly altered the tax structure. Although in 1929 Los Angeles had financed

76 percent of its municipal expenditures through the general property tax, for example, by 1943 the city secured only 50 percent from
this source. During the war the Bowron administration was obliged to
impose new license and sales taxes to make up the shortfall. Even so,
the shift in population and tax bases imposed serious difficulties for
management of the city's wartime budgets.[42] This dilemma explained
an increasing tendency of city officials to look directly to Washington
for financial help. Mayor Bowron, for example, unable to provide
adequate fire protection throughout the area, negotiated directly with
the U.S. Navy to provide fire protection for Los Angeles harbor and
also appointed a representative to deal directly with the War Department on similar matters.[43]

Life in wartime Los Angeles had a hectic pace, and the peculiar
shape of the city and problems of transportation contributed to a high
rate of absenteeism in its war plants. During the first six months of
1943, for example, Pacific Coast aircraft plants hired 150,000 workers, and lost 138,000! This high rate of turnover was due to various
factors. The stress of living on wheels was too much for some mid-
westerners from rural areas who returned home after a stint of urban
life in southern California. Many women, who comprised 45 percent
of the work force in Los Angeles area aircraft factories, found the
challenge of maintaining a home, raising children, and commuting to
a full-time job too much over a period of time. This despite the
establishment of one of the most extensive child care programs in the
nation by the Los Angeles Area Committee of the Aircraft War Production Council—with federal aid.[44] The war therefore accentuated
population growth in Southern California, and in the process imposed new strains of urban living.

The war also left a deep imprint on the San Francisco Bay region.
That metropolitan area comprised nine counties which, although
closely interdependent, were not functionally organized to operate
with optimum efficiency. Conflicting jurisdictions of hundreds of
political entities within the area tended to impede the flow of people
and industrial facilities, and to make life harder for the hundreds of
thousands who worked in its war industries. In the decade before
Pearl Harbor jealousies and fears had impeded plans by the California State Planning Board to establish a regional planning commission
for the Bay Area and left the various governmental units divided and
uncoordinated.

The major impact of the war was not so much on the city of San
Francisco as on Oakland and the smaller towns around the Bay. That
was in part because the area was the number one shipbuilding center
in the nation, securing between $4 and $5 billion in shipbuilding
contracts from the U.S. Navy and the U.S. Maritime Commission. Of

course, scores of related industries in the vicinity also benefited from this boom. At the same time, American involvement in the Pacific accentuated Oakland's importance as a major supply depot as well as a port of embarkation. Blessed with a mild year-round climate, the Bay Area was also ideal for scores of military installations which made the San Francisco area, no less than southern California, a "federal city."[45] The Navy had vast facilities at Treasure Island, at the Marin County Naval Air Station, the Tiburon and Alameda Naval Air Stations, and Moffet Field, and large Navy yards at Hunter's Point and Mare Island. The Army's large installations included the Presidio, Forts Mason, Scott, Finston, and Miley in San Francisco, Hamilton Field and Forts Barry, Baker, and Cronkhite in Marin County, and Fort McDowell on Angel Island.[46] Few metropolitan areas in the West were as fully girded for a full-scale war as the Bay Region.

Geographical necessity imposed special burdens on the small cities around San Francisco Bay. With their deep water channels, towns like South San Francisco, Sausalito, Vallejo, and Richmond now became the major shipbuilding centers of the nation. But in 1941 they were totally unprepared to receive the more than 500,000 people who converged upon them from every part of the nation. The new migrants found little available housing, inadequate means of transportation, a dearth of shopping facilities for even bare necessities, overcrowded schools and hospitals. In some areas no sewers, roads, or parks, or even rudimentary law enforcement and fire protection were available. By 1943 utter chaos prevailed in the cities of the Bay Area and threatened a very real breakdown of war production. How they coped with this unprecedented crisis—and still met production records—makes a fascinating story of human endurance and determination. After 1943 conditions somewhat improved.

San Francisco buckled under the influx of more than 125,000 new residents, most of whom worked in Bay Area defense establishments. In addition, the city was host to tens of thousands of "war tourists," relatives or friends of servicemen departing for or arriving from Pacific battle areas. At the same time it continued to provide the traditional function as an entertainment capital in the West for thousands of servicemen and women.[47]

Such a situation placed great strains on San Francisco housing. "A great many of our hotels, both large and small, are operating at full capacity," reported Dr. J. C. Geiger, San Francisco's Health Director. "A great many of the smaller hotels are occupied almost entirely by shipyard workers who have come here from other parts of the country."[48] To accommodate some of the transients the San Francisco Housing Authority—with federal funds—built temporary housing projects at Hunter's Point near the San Francisco Naval Shipyard, and at Candlestick Cove. These instant slums housed about 35,000 people. The National Housing Authority also attempted to convert 5,000 to 10,000 existing properties for additional units but this program had only very limited success.[49] And the press of population tended to hasten the deterioration of older neighborhoods.

Congestion created increasing health hazards. In San Francisco the veneral disease rate in 1942 and 1943 shot up by more than 75 percent. The city's health department attempted to counter this rise by operating four of the fourteen veneral disease clinics available and by offering free diagnosis and treatment. Equally troublesome was the fact that many of the black newcomers had not received proper immunization in rural areas from which they came and required instruction in elementary health education and nutrition. "The unprecedented influx into the San Francisco schools," said Dr. Geiger, "has made it necessary to divert school physicians and school nurses to this group. . . . The new children have questionable health backgrounds; immunization histories are sometimes vague or non-existent . . . overcrowding and substandard hygienic conditions have played a part in the increased incidence of communicable diseases."[50] Such conditions made it impossible for the existing staff to provide adequate health care for either new or old residents.

To counter the upsurge in venereal diseases the Police Department mounted a campaign to curb prostitution. Mayor Angelo Rossi proposed several new city ordinances which made hotel clerks and taxi drivers liable for solicitation. The city also established a curfew for minors in public places. And on March 18, 1943, the city opened a new women's detention ward to examine women suspected of prostitution.[51]

Unlike Los Angeles, San Francisco did not experience serious transportation problems. Endowed with a good public transportation system, the city was able to absorb the new influx of population although it strained existing facilities to their limits. Mayor Rossi estimated that passengers carried by the two major streetcar companies increased by 43 percent during 1943 compared to the previous year. What was most urgently needed, he complained, was new equipment, and draft deferment for motormen and conductors.[52]

As war workers crossed the Bay to Oakland, they found conditions far more hectic than in San Francisco. City Manager Charles R. Schwanenberg of Oakland noted in 1943: "The impact of war activity in Oakland has revolutionized the economy of the entire east bay area. The magnitude of the problems and the complex relationships of one to the other has been beyond the capacities of the municipalities to solve on the local level. The federal government was forced into the picture in order to assist a solution. The result has been confusion since the solutions were predicated on the immediacy of the situations without any introduction of planning on a long-range basis." Between 1941 and 1945 at least 200,000 people poured in, increasing the population to about 700,000.[53]

The litany of problems in Oakland was typical of the war boom towns. Inadequate housing, a breakdown of city services, particularly transportation, a lack of schools, especially for residents of housing projects, crime, and health and sanitation problems. Schwanenberg felt that if a few federal agencies could centralize public policies rather than have these administered by scores of local, often overlapping, jurisdictions, the problems could be met much more effectively than under current practices.[54]

The small city of Vallejo in the East Bay, a major shipbuilding center, shared Oakland's woes. Mayor John Stewart estimated in 1943 that his city's population was at least 100,000—more than five times its size in 1940! The town's major employer was the U.S. Navy's Mare Island Shipyard, which increased its work force from 5,000 in 1940 to 45,000 two years later. In Vallejo people lived in shacks or stores; 4,000 lived precariously in trailer camps; some merely camped out; 25,000 moved into hastily erected temporary housing units thrown up by the U.S. Maritime Commission; and another 15,000 lived in Chabot Terrace, a 3,000-unit federal housing project which lacked sewers, streets, and schools. Even so, 14,000 Mare Island employees could not find any local accommodations. They lived within an 80-mile radius of the shipyard and often traveled more than five hours daily to and from their jobs. The Navy leased a fleet of buses from Pacific Greyhound lines to help provide necessary transportation. No wonder that absenteeism was a major problem at Mare Island and impeded its production schedules.[55]

But conditions in Vallejo seemed almost heavenly compared to the chaos prevailing in neighboring Richmond. That sleepy little town of 23,642 in 1940 was transformed into a city of more than 150,000 within three years. It was the quintessential war boom town in America. As Congressman George J. Bates (Mass.), a member of the subcommittee investigating congested areas, said: "Here is a community . . . which, I think is undoubtedly the worst that we have run across in the entire country in these congested areas. I don't think there is any comparison between your problems in Richmond and any other city even though the other cities are bad."[56]

More wartime contracts descended upon the city than it could absorb. Four major Kaiser-operated shipyards and fifty-five other war industries ranging from the manufacture of Jeeps to munitions were centered in the community. Contra Costa County, in which it was located, produced 3.5 percent of all war production in the United

States, and 70 percent of all the chemicals refined in the eleven western states.[57] "Richmond is one town in America that has been deluged by the federal government to such an extent that the civil government is about to break down unless we get some help," lamented City Attorney Thomas M. Carlson. Unlike Vallejo, which had the United States Navy as its advocate in Washington, the U.S. Maritime Commission left local officials entirely to their own devices. "We want the influence of Congress with the Maritime Commission," said Carlson, "so that they will adopt Richmond the same as the Navy has adopted Vallejo."[58]

The hordes of invading workers made Richmond's housing situation desperate. Former sheriff John A. Miller noted that people lived "in trailers, tents, tin houses, cardboard shacks, greenhouses, barns, garages, in automobiles, in theaters, or just fenced-off corners with the stars for a roof."[59] Private builders rapidly threw up 4,557 houses; local residents made 4,800 rooms available, many with "hot beds" in which people took turns sleeping around the clock. In one case the fire department forced a landlord to vacate 65 people from his house. And the U.S. Maritime Commission and the Richmond Housing Authority built 21,000 temporary emergency units for families and 4,000 dormitory units for single men (not women). This was the largest housing program in the United States at the time.[60]

Still, tens of thousands of war workers could find no shelter in Richmond and commuted from other communities in the Bay Area. For them transportation became a major problem, particularly because the region lacked a unified transportation system. People poured in by train, by car, and by bus—but the wartime shortage of equipment made it impossible to serve this vastly expanded population. In a desperate move the U.S. Maritime Commission rejuvenated old ferry boats which plied between San Francisco and the Richmond shipyards. In an even more dramatic move the Commission imported the old cars of New York City's Third Avenue Elevated Railway. Rechristened the Richmond Shipyard Railway, the cars wended their way on Oakland's San Pablo Avenue from 40th Street along a twelve-mile stretch to the Richmond shipyards. They also brought the rush-hour atmosphere of New York City, since many a time workers were unable to enter the crowded trains at intermediate stops between terminals. Life was difficult for Richmond war workers, and the difficulties of housing and transportation contributed to a high rate of absenteeism.[61]

Neither the efforts of the Richmond Chamber of Commerce nor the California State Railroad Commission in seeking to secure new equipment and to train women as train operators succeeded in easing the situation by 1944. "The lack of adequate and properly coordinated transportation facilities in the San Francisco Bay area is undoubtedly the primary factor in the failure to obtain the highest degree of efficiency from the available labor supply," concluded the Congressional investigating committee. "This same lack is unquestionably having an adverse effect upon the procurement of the additional migrant labor that is so badly needed. Because of traffic congestion and delays thousands of workers are forced to put in 12 or 13 hours a day in order to work 8 hours. The peculiar geographical situation in the bay area probably makes the transportation problem more acute than in any other section of the country."[62] And C. E. Miller, a production engineer at Kaiser Shipyard #2 in Richmond well summarized the effect of these problems when he noted that: "I have found in talking with thousands of men and women in yards and their supervisors that the principal cause for absenteeism is the transportation problem. [Those who] travel long distances to and from work . . . have no time for relaxation and no release for nervous energy. . . . We are losing about 4,000 people a month in just one yard who are quitting because they can't stand the strain."[63]

The municipal authorities of Richmond also found themselves unable to provide adequate police protection. "We put on 19 police officers," said City Manager James McVittie, "but that is about as far as we can go on that." And he continued: "We believe [that] since all these people come from all over the United States to Richmond the United States government has a responsibility . . . to see that these people are protected." But that protection was not extended. The city's jail, for example, had been constructed in 1919 with six cells. It was utterly inadequate to serve a community of more than 150,000 which usually had more than sixty prisoners at one time. In 1940, Police Chief L. E. Jones reported, his department had thirty-five men serving a town of 20,000 people. The nineteen additional officers hired in 1942 still could not cope with "increasing robberies, burglaries, holdups, thefts, juvenile delinquents and drunks." Since the city had no funds, it appealed directly to the United States government to build a jail commensurate with its population and to enable it to hire at least seventy-five additional police officers. According to the chief's annual reports between 1940 and 1943, complaints to the police more than quadrupled, the value of stolen property rose eightfold, as did rape, robbery, and assault, although the greatest increase was in petty theft and burglary.[64]

Fire protection became as critical as protection of life and limb. "Our fire situation is such that we were operating very successfully two years ago with the small city that we had," said City Manager McVittie, "but when you come along and 100,000 or more people come in, that is something to think about. You just have to do the best you can." The U.S. Maritime Commission did construct a fire house and provided three pumpers for the city, but demanded that municipal authorities pay for its operation. Since the hard-pressed city lacked the tax base and the revenues to operate the equipment it just stood idle. "We are going to have those pumping engines," said McVittie, "and the doors are going to be locked. If we have a fire . . . there are going to be three big pumpers lying idle because there is no money available, to put men on there." Although the city applied to the Federal Works Administration for operating funds, that agency rejected the request. This despite the fact that in addition to having to provide fire protection to the residential areas of the city Fire Chief W. P. Cooper also noted that he had "the responsibility . . . for the four shipyards, and also all the federally constructed housing units which . . . constitute a very serious conflagration possibility."[65]

At the same time, the influx of war workers created dire conditions in Richmond's schools. As School Superintendent Walter T. Helm reported, school enrollment between 1940 and 1943 more than tripled. Schools operated on double sessions with classes exceeding sixty students. Since the city lacked money for recreational facilities, it was unable to provide playgrounds or community centers for the many thousands of children not in school at a given time of day. Understandably, this situation contributed to a high rate of truancy, and also to juvenile delinquency. In desperation city authorities turned to federal authorities for aid in new school construction. The U.S. Maritime Commission, the Federal Housing Administration and the Federal Works Agency agreed to provide needed funds—but meanwhile the Richmond school system struggled under intolerable conditions throughout 1943 and 1944. Moreover, the city simply lacked the funds to operate an expanded system. Although the state of California was collecting increased revenues with a 3 percent sales tax, it was returning only 60 percent to cities to underwrite the cost of elementary schools. And since the state made such allocations on the basis of the previous year's enrollments, Richmond's situation was even more desperate. It had 3,000 pupils in 1940, and more than 35,000 in 1943.[66]

This population surge wreaked havoc with the city's finances. "The people coming to this city to work in the shipyards are requesting increased municipal services of all kinds," said McVittie. "But on account of not receiving taxes from the Government owned industries . . . and from tax-exempt housing units, we are unable to raise sufficient revenue with which to provide these requested increased services." Even though Richmond raised its tax rate in 1942 to 24 cents on each $100 assessment, this was still not enough to meet the crisis. Thus McVittie urged the federal government to pay for increased municipal services since most war workers were engaged on federal projects. Even the land which the United States Maritime Commission cleared for four new shipyards and for federal housing projects was federally owned and not subject to local taxation. Thus the city was deprived of the opportunity to increase its property tax base at the very time when the growing population forced it to expand its services.[67]

The population influx greatly increased water pollution on the Bay. As City Engineer Edward A. Hoffman told the congressional investigators, the shipyards "created a great need for increased sanitation. The problem concerned polluted water in the tide flats, the drainage canals, and the shipways. The water was polluted by the emptying of raw sewage onto the tide flats close to shore, and directly into the inner harbor." Additional sewers were needed to prevent pollution since the city had no resources for such projects. Hoffman appealed directly to the congressmen for federal aid.[68]

John Miller, the Area Coordinator of Civil Defense for Contra Costa County, expressed the feelings of many of his fellow citizens. "In 1940 Contra Costa County had a population of 100,230 happy souls. Her people for the most part were engaged in the manufacture and commerce of the nation. . . . These people, honest hardy Westerners, were happy with their homes, their jobs, and in the knowledge that they lived in the only county in California functioning without the benefit of a single Federal or State project. . . . Then came the rude awakening. . . . Things began to happen . . . population zoomed from 100,000 to 324,000 to 780,000. The pyramiding of war production and people influx brought with it many problems."[69] Miller's description was apt for Richmond; but Richmond was only a microcosm of many areas of the West—and much of the United States in succeeding decades.

The Congressional investigators were visibly shaken by the chaos which they witnessed in the Bay Area due to wartime disruptions. So serious was the crisis that the committee recommended against further expansion of war industries in the area. They also criticized the bewildering array of federal agencies operating in the area who worked independently of each other with little coordination, even when dealing with common problems. The committee recommended that President Roosevelt appoint representatives who—like ombudsmen—would coordinate disparate federal programs in the area. Moreover, many local problems could be met more effectively by state and municipal officials than by distant administrators in Washington.[70]

By 1944 the Committee for Congested Production Areas had appointed a coordinator for the Bay region who promoted more effective federal programs. In housing, education, and health the coordinator was particularly effective in easing the severe strains under which war workers were living. By the middle of 1944 new school buildings were completed in Richmond, San Pablo, Vallejo, and elsewhere. Also, new child care facilities were opened in South San Francisco, Oakland, Pittsburg, Richmond, and San Pablo. In Vallejo the Chabot Housing Project was equipped with sanitary sewers and a new hospital.[71]

But the Bay Area was a study in extreme contrasts. It contained some of the worst—but also the most efficient—congested war production areas in the West. The difference lay in the degree of planning for growth and expansion of localities. A fine example of careful planning by federal and local officials was in Marin County where the B. A. Bechtel Corporation—a Kaiser subsidiary—established the Marinship yard in 1942. With more than 25,000 workers during its first year, this also proved to be one of the most efficient in the West—and the nation. Near the yard the U.S. Maritime Commission built an entire new town—Marin City—for 6,000 workers. Conscious of the environmental concern of nearby affluent Marin County residents, the National Housing Authority built attractive redwood homes carefully related to the rolling contours of the meadow in which they were built. Unlike other federal projects, Marin City was built with schools, churches, and, within a few months, an ample shopping center. "We have visited hundreds of war housing projects in the United States," said Congressman George Bates (Mass.) after visiting Marin City in 1943, "and we have seen none that so ideally meets the requirements of a community of war workers. . . . It is the best administered and best organized war housing project that I have seen in our tour of the country."[72]

The wartime experiences of cities on the Pacific Coast were far-reaching, and created a context for their development during the second half of the twentieth century. In many communities the war accelerated the deterioration of old neighborhoods and the inner city. The war increased minority elements in the population and made their populations more heterogeneous. At the same time the war worsened the urban financial crisis, eroding the tax base at the very time when demands for city services were increasing because of growing populations. One major result of this development was increased dependence of the cities on federal funds and services.[73] And although it constituted a more intangible element, it could be argued that the war tended to decrease the quality of urban life in the West Coast cities, particularly in the inner cores.

CHAPTER FIVE

Western Cities in Wartime: The Pacific Northwest, Mountain States, and Southwest

Elsewhere in the West cities also experienced shock waves set into motion by wartime mobilization. Although the disruptions they experienced were not as severe as those in California, this was a matter of degree. Thus, the war brought an appreciable increase in population, including significant numbers of minorities, and accentuated urban social problems. And as the demands for municipal services increased, the tax base eroded. Moreover, the crush of people tended to hasten deterioration of older neighborhoods in metropolitan areas and to create new and serious housing problems, then and for years to come.

Extraordinary expansion of the nation's ship construction program also initiated unprecedented activity in Portland, Oregon. There the flow of population created boom town conditions not unlike those in California. While the U.S. Maritime Commission awarded major shipbuilding contracts in the area, the Defense Plant Corporation made large investments in extensive new aluminum processing plants. Availability of cheap electricity was a major reason for locating aluminum manufacturing in the region since the Bonneville Power Administration supplied more than one-half of its electric power. At the same time Congress poured more than $2 billion into the Bonneville Power Administration on a crash program to increase its generating capacity more than sixfold between 1941 and 1945. Ships, aluminum, and power were the three main ingredients that transformed Oregon's economy during wartime, diversifying its hitherto largely agricultural and natural resource economy.[1]

Much of this boom focused on the towns and cities of the state, of which Portland was the largest. During the war years the city gained 160,000 newcomers, boosting its population to 359,000. In addition, another 100,000 persons came to work in Troutdale, Oregon City, Vanport, and Vancouver. A majority of the new workers were hired by companies operated by Henry J. Kaiser. As his son, Edgar F. Kaiser, who managed the Portland shipyards, said in 1943: "The employment in the three Maritime yards under our management—Oregon Shipbuilding company, Kaiser Co., Inc., Swan Island, and Kaiser, Inc. Vancouver—. . . will be in excess of 100,000."[2]

With such a large influx, housing problems became a serious matter, although conditions were generally not as desperate as in northern California. Still, in 1943 the Kaiser yards were hiring workers faster than housing could be made available for them, leaving many literally out in the cold. Most workers at first came by themselves, but after a few months usually brought their families. Since rentals of private homes were rarely available, most were dependent on hastily erected trailer camps, and on public housing. More than 175 new trailer camps sprang up just outside city limits during 1943. Meanwhile, the National Housing Authority programmed 40,500 family housing units for Portland, of which 34,000 were financed with federal funds. In addition, the Agency provided 21,700 dormitory and barracks accommodations for single workers. Some of these facilities also served as reception centers for new arrivals. A prime function of the dormitories was to provide basic shelter for workers at the Kaiser and Oregon shipyards. Since these units were rather primitive, however, as in San Diego, they were usually not fully occupied.[3]

But hastily erected housing often did not solve many problems of everyday life. In the helter-skelter of wartime frenzy, inefficiency and lack of coordination were not uncommon. Although the National Housing Authority might throw up prefabricated housing, as often as not some of its administrators neglected to order necessary furniture! Thousands of housing units remained unoccupied for months because furniture was unavailable or had not as yet been delivered. That was true, for example, of the large Fairview housing project in Troutdale (14 miles from Portland), built to serve a new Alcoa plant. Hardly less serious was the absence of shopping facilities in the new housing areas. Workers often found it difficult to purchase food—not to speak of other necessities of life. When required to travel long distances to buy groceries in older parts of the city, many workers simply stayed away from their jobs, thus contributing to absenteeism. In fact, the absentee rate in Portland and Vancouver was considerably higher than in California. During 1943 it was also reflected in an astounding labor turnover rate of 150 percent annually. To a large extent it reflected low morale because of difficult working and living conditions in a congested area where, unlike California, the sun was obscured by rain during many months of the year.[4]

One of the most spectacular reflections of the wartime housing boom to be found anywhere in the nation was at Vanport, just north of Portland. In 1940 that area was completely empty, an unoccupied stretch of mudflats. Three years later it was a bustling city of 10,000 housing units peopled by 40,000 individuals, most of whom worked in the Kaiser shipyards. Those who lived there found it neither comfortable nor attractive. Most dwellings were heated by coal, which each tenant stored in a bin out front, for lack of space. Residents had ice boxes but no refrigerators. Drainage in the area was extremely poor, and the cold dampness of the houses was greatly worsened by their concrete floors. The contractor had installed these because of difficulties in securing priorities for lumber. For stoves most houses had two-burner hot plates which—they found after initial use—had an average durability of only 72 hours (less than one month). In fact, to keep Vanport's 12,000 stoves in operating order, and to keep the war workers eating, C. M. Gartrell, chairman of the Portland Housing Authority, ruefully reported that he employed twenty-two full-time electricians around the clock. Even so, the equipment was barely kept in operating condition and at least 300 units remained vacant each week because they completely lacked cooking facilities.[5]

Such living conditions understandably created difficult problems for the schools. James T. Hamilton, the school superintendent at Vanport, ascribed the low morale in his system to overcrowding and to inadequate construction of new buildings. Four thousand children in Vanport attended classes in two shifts of four hours each in five small buildings. At the same time, the houses in which children lived were too small for them to remain at home for any length of time, particularly when their parents were away at work, but on different shifts. Yet Vanport lacked recreational facilities or playgrounds. Thus, youngsters had nowhere to play but the muddy streets. And as Hamilton said, all these problems were complicated by the fact that "all people come to Vanport as total strangers [yet] children need group participation and leadership."[6]

Within Portland, school conditions were somewhat better than in Vanport. More than 6,000 new children came during the first year of the war, but since the Portland schools had considerable vacant classroom space in 1941, they were able to absorb them without undue strains. Only five schools required double shifts. That, Acting Superintendent J. W. Edwards felt, "worked a hardship on the pupils who are free half of the day. . . . Their educational opportunities are reduced . . . and delinquency problems mount because of their hours of leisure time." He complained that those who planned the housing projects either largely ignored the need for schools or built facilities that were impractical. The federal planners who constructed 2,000 houses in the Guild's Lake area near Portland shipyards, for example, made no provisions at all for schools, and yet the Portland school system had to provide for the 2,500 youngers who moved into the area.[7]

The crush of people also placed severe strains on the recreational facilities in the Columbia River area, although city authorities were operating recreational areas and swimming pools at maximum capacity. They simply lacked money and staff to keep them open sufficiently to meet demands. In newer neighborhoods such as Vanport, construction of recreational areas and playgrounds usually lagged many months behind occupancy and contributed to dissatisfaction of workers and the high rate of job turnover.[8]

Health care in the Pacific Northwest was far better than in many other congested war regions of the West. To a considerable extent this was due to the extensive health program of the Kaiser Corporation. Relying on their experience in California, the Kaisers organized Portland physicians into the Portland Physicians Service to provide prepaid medical and hospital care. In the Vancouver area the Kaisers formed a nonprofit foundation to build a new hospital and also to provide prepaid medical care for shipyard workers in the Kaiser organization.[9]

For Portland this was a blessing because like other western cities affected by war industries it was confronted with serious new financial problems. As elsewhere in the West, Portland's Commissioner of Finance, Cooper, noted the state of Oregon did not transfer its swollen tax revenues to the cities although the municipalities were hard pressed to accommodate the hundreds of thousands of newcomers. The urban areas thus came to look to the federal government rather than to the state capital for aid. In the words of Congressman George Bates (Mass.), in this dilemma "the Federal Government is compelled to come into communities like this and assist at least to some degree."[10]

Compared to other western cities, Portland's problems were less severe. Edgar F. Kaiser in 1943 perceptively evaluated the Portland scene:

> No community can expand as this one has done, without it being a strain on the entire population. . . . You may properly ask why, in our opinion, the condition of the Portland-Vancouver area is best of any congested area on the Pacific Coast. The reason for this is that . . . State and city officials, community organizations, Government agencies involved, and industry have met together and discussed each particular problem. . . . In other areas of the Pacific Coast there has been a considerable divergence of opinion. Industry has not been able to get together; city and State officials have had one program, por-

tions of industry another with the result . . . that what was finally done
was inadequate or too late.[11]

Further northward on the Pacific coast, Seattle also found itself
shaken by an unprecedented boom. In 1940 its population numbered
368,000; by 1944 it had 530,000 within its city limits, and 650,000 in
its metropolitan area.[12] Seattle's boom was triggered by many types of
wartime manufactures, but preeminently by shipbuilding and aircraft
manufacturing. Henry J. Kaiser's vast shipyards employed between
70,000 and 100,000 persons, and the Puget Sound Naval Shipyard in
Bremerton and other shipbuilders accounted for perhaps 30,000 additional employees. Meanwhile, the Boeing Company was virtually
making Seattle into a company town. In 1939 Boeing employed 4,000
workers and enjoyed annual sales of $10 million. But by 1944 the
company had more than 50,000 people at its Seattle plant alone and
produced more than $600 million worth of aircraft. And in its branch
plants in the region and among subcontractors Boeing employed almost as many individuals as at its main plant. The magnitude of this
growth is readily understood if one remembers that in 1939 the total
value of all of Seattle's manufactures was only $70 million.[13]

The urban problems experienced by Seattle as a result of an extraordinary influx of newcomers were not unique, according to D. G.
Shanahan, secretary to Seattle's Mayor William F. Devin. Shanahan
noted not only the congested housing situation, but also increasing
crime, fire hazards, and health problems, in what for decades had
been a rather stable community. Moreover, Seattle's transportation
system was being strained to the utmost by wartime conditions, also
adding to increasing problems for its overcrowded schools. The de-
creasing quality of life, particularly for recent immigrants, contributed to a high rate of labor turnover in the city and often impeded
production.[14]

Housing conditions for war workers in Seattle were among the
worst in the nation. During the war the Puget Sound region literally
bristled with shipyards which dotted Bremerton, Seattle, Tacoma,
Everett, Kirkland, and Bainbridge Island. Usually the yards were able
to increase the number of workers they hired faster than the government and private builders could provide the necessary housing, thus
creating a chronic backlog. In 1943 the National Housing Authority
planned 45,000 new family dwelling units for Puget Sound, and 6,300
units for single workers. But the housing agency's task was complicated by constantly changing estimates of needs. The Bremerton
Navy Yard, for example, in June of 1941 estimated a peak force of
12,000 workers. Its commander, Admiral Tefferton, frequently revised his estimates, however, and by the middle of 1943 the yard

actually employed 36,000 men and women. In addition to the rush of defense workers, an unpredictably heavy demand for housing was created by thousands of servicemen and women who milled about in the port city. Meanwhile, shortages of lumber and sheeting materials held up such new construction as was authorized.[15]

What was it like to live in a public housing project in wartime Seattle? One of the tenant representatives from the East Port Orchard Housing Project, near the Puget Sound Navy Yard, vividly described conditions there:

> Clothing must be washed by hand in the kitchen sink and dried above the kitchen stove. . . . Remember the kitchen and living room are actually one small unit. . . . Due to poor design adequate chimneys are not provided on buildings, causing stoves to fill the homes with smoke. . . . Many men on the project work night shifts, and the women do not feel safe with the windows open while they are gone. . . . Refrigerators in the apartments consist of a small built-in cupboard, with a metal pan for holding the ice. Food will not keep overnight . . . and the danger of eating contaminated food is always present. No playgrounds or recreational facilities [are] available, and the area even lacked a school. Only one doctor is provided for a community of approximately 4,000 people.[16]

The situation for aircraft workers was often not much better. As W. C. Patterson, administrative assistant to the president of Boeing, lamented, his company was hard pressed to find accommodations for its workers reasonably near its factory sites.[17]

The crush of population increased problems of law enforcement in Seattle. As H. D. Kimsey, the city's police chief, complained, his most pressing need was to get enough men and women for his force. Of 611 police personnel authorized for the Seattle department in October, 1943, he was able to maintain only 493, and faced further impending reductions. This was at a time when the population was increasing by 50 percent. The greatest need was for improved traffic control and the curbing of prostitution. Serious crimes such as homicides and rapes did not increase significantly in Seattle during the war years, not even juvenile delinquency—in contrast to most other bulging wartime areas.[18] The situation in Seattle was not duplicated in the smaller cities surrounding it, however. The population of Bremerton, site of the huge Puget Sound Navy Yard, grew from 15,000 people in 1940 to 75,000 four years later. Conditions there were similar to those in Richmond, as described in Chapter 4. The stresses which Mayor L. Kean described, particularly the increase of serious crimes, contrasted with less unsettled conditions in Seattle.[19]

Despite great strains, Seattle's municipal government valiantly coped to provide needed social services for its burgeoning population. School congestion in the city was far less severe than in other western cities. Most schools did not require double sessions but operated on normal schedules. The greatest problems were near the new housing projects. Samuel E. Fleming, the acting Superintendent of Schools, bemoaned the lack of school buildings to accommodate the children of war workers. He deplored unconscionable delays in building new schools because of problems in securing priorities for building materials.[20]

Health care facilities in Seattle were more greatly strained. Whereas the city had one physician for every 600 people in 1940, by 1944 that ratio had increased to one physician for every 1,400 people. As Dr. Ragnar D. Westman, the Acting Commissioner of Health in Seattle reported, people were lined up in doctors' waiting rooms for hours. Hospitals in the area were so crowded that they had long waiting lists. Some hospitals simply had to close off entire wings because they lacked doctors, nurses, and auxiliary staff. In such a situation it was not surprising that Seattle experienced a veneral disease epidemic during 1943. The city's Health Department staff was so depleted that it had to borrow personnel from the United States Public Health Service. With the opening of new treatment centers, however, they brought the situation under control before the year was out.[21]

As in other western cities, an important effect of the war was to worsen Seattle's financial condition and to sow the seeds of inner city decay. "The increase of population," said I. Comeaux, Seattle's Chief accountant, "and the necessary increase of fire and police protection and sanitation have added to our financial burden. The city received no additional revenue from the State, although the State benefited considerably from increased sales taxes."[22] In addition, the operation of extensive federal facilities in the Seattle area deprived localities of much-needed local revenues. "The payment in lieu of taxes by the federal government to cities and counties on Government-owned property is entirely out of line with the general tax structure," complained L. H. Unzelman, the mayor of Everett, Washington. "The same service is given to the housing areas as is required by the city at large, such as fire and police protection, street and sewer maintenance."[23] His complaint was echoed by mayors up and down the Pacific Coast.

Western cities in the interior were not jolted quite as severely by the wartime boom as those in the coastal areas, yet here too wartime mobilization left an indelible impact. The difference was more a matter of scale than of substance. In the interior, too, the war transformed economies, promoted rapid growth of population, introduced large numbers of ethnic and racial minorities, and hastened cultural development. At the same time the war created new patterns for urban growth, and new urban problems that provided a context for their development in the next forty years. Although much of the history of urban development during the war years still remains to be written, a brief analysis of cities like Denver and Tucson provides an illustration of these major trends.

One of Denver's major historians, Lyle Dorsett, has noted: "World War II left a wake of change as profound as anything since the silver boom of the 1870s and 1880s."[24] These changes included unprecedented economic expansion and a consequent increase of population, including also a significant growth of minorities. Colorado's total income soared from $617 million in 1940 to $1,317 million in 1945, and Denver garnered a significant portion of this total. The new jobs created by this frenzied activity drew 100,000 newcomers to Denver, boosting its population by 20 percent.[25]

Like the silver rushes of the 1870s, war mobilization provided extraordinary stimulus for Denver's economy. Older business establishments such as grain mills, sugar refineries, and meat-packing plants now came to work at capacity, as they had not during the previous decade. Foundries geared to the manufacture of mining equipment converted to war materials. But the most spectacular surge came with new industries. Remington Arms hired 20,000 people to manufacture munitions, and so employed 40 percent of all of the workers in the city's manufacturing complex. Henry J. Kaiser operated a portion of the Denver Ordnance Plant to make artillery shells; the Rocky Mountain Arsenal hired 14,000 people in the fabrication of chemicals and poison gases. Shipbuilding became another major industry. As the U.S. Navy shipyard on Mare Island, California, reached optimum production, the U.S. Maritime Commission stretched its capacity inland to Denver, establishing a large new facility which manufactured prefabricated parts for destroyer escorts and LCTs (landing barges) and sent them by rail to Mare Island, where the final product was assembled. All of the 31 destroyer escorts and 301 landing craft launched at Mare Island were built in Denver, perhaps the only ships in the United States to cross the Rocky Mountains.[26]

Probably Denver could have had even more war industries had its conservative business community made more aggressive efforts. But the caution and conservatism of its banking and business leaders in the generation before the Second World War was legendary. In 1941 Henry J. Kaiser had grandiose plans for Denver's industrial development yet was stymied by the city's banking and business leadership.[27] Even the shipbuilding venture was initiated by Mare Island Commander A. S. Pitre, not by the local business community. In September 1941 he began negotiations with the Office of Production

Management and select Denver businessmen. After extensive negotiations they reached an agreement on December 2, 1941, and the venture then got under way. Within a few months the first shipment of prefabricated hull sections left Denver. Cynthia Carr, daughter of Colorado's governor, christened the U.S.S. *Mountain Maid* with melted snow brought from Pike's Peak! A little later Miss Carr traveled to Mare Island where on August 8, 1942, she rechristened the assembled ship the U.S.S. *Bentinck.*[28]

All this economic activity resulted in a predictable influx of new people and the crystallization of new urban problems. As in other western cities, the coming of more than 100,000 new Denverites created a tight housing situation although the congestion did not approximate the crises on the Pacific Coast or in some eastern cities. More than most metropolitan areas, Denver had room to grow, and it spread horizontally rather than vertically. Already in the decade before Pearl Harbor suburbanization had begun to be a noticeable trend, and the war accelerated that tendency. Deterioration of the downtown area was accentuated by the war. Mayor Ben Stapleton was clearly aware of what was happening and tried to stem the decline. At his instigation the city adopted a new housing code in 1944 which facilitated the improvement of substandard buildings and became a model for urban renewal in its time.[29]

In addition to the civilians who poured into Denver during the war years the city was inundated by tens of thousands of servicemen and women, who flocked in on weekends. Just west of Denver the Army was training troops for mountain warfare, while Lowry Field and Buckley Naval Air Station became major installations. Vast new military complexes were also established at Colorado Springs, sixty miles south of Denver, where Fort Carson and other federal encampments contained large numbers of military personnel. Many of these young men and women fell in love with the beauties of the Denver area and returned to live there after the war.[30]

Wartime mobilization brought new industries to Tucson. A Consolidated-Vultee Aircraft plant opened up thousands of new job opportunities, and scores of smaller firms received federal contracts. At the same time the armed forces established new training facilities in the area, partly because of its year-round mild climate. One of the largest was the Air Force's Davis-Monthan Field, which became a major training school for bomber pilots. Not surprisingly, Tucson underwent a dramatic population boom in wartime; its population doubled from the 48,000 reported in 1940 to 92,000 in 1946.[31] Although these numbers were relatively small compared to the metropolises of the Pacific Coast, this increase brought urbanization to the Southwest, hitherto a sparsely populated area. Tucson did not experience urban problems such as congested housing, inadequacy of health and social services, and crime on the scale of larger metropolitan areas. But problems did develop as a result of the influx of new people which created strains that heralded the urban difficulties of the next generation.

The impact of the war in the Southwest was to transform sleepy towns like Tucson into bustling urban communities. To be sure, the pace of transformation was not quite as hectic as on the Pacific Coast. But the war left its mark on the region and initiated the process of urbanization on a hitherto unprecedented scale.

To the west of Tucson wartime currents were stimulating still another urban center to arise out of the desert, one which was to have a rapid rise as a major entertainment center for the nation. In 1941 few had heard of the obscure Nevada town of Las Vegas, which had had a checkered history and had vainly struggled to grow for more than half a century. Even Spanish explorers had avoided the forbidding wilderness of southern Nevada, and it was not until John C. Fremont and Kit Carson visited the area in 1844 that the first Mormon migrants established short-lived colonies there. But by 1890 the discovery of minerals such as zinc and copper brought a small nucleus of miners into Las Vegas and the construction of local railroads. Still, the town did not get a boost until 1909 when the Union Pacific Railroad established shops there. By then its population was about 2,000. Despite strenuous efforts by its boosters over the next thirty years, it grew very little.[32]

During the Great Depression Las Vegas boosters were encouraged by the construction of nearby Boulder Dam. That brought money and people to the area between 1929 and 1936. The construction of Lake Mead in conjunction with the dam created a new recreation area which was bound to attract some tourists who came to contemplate the world's largest dam. Although by 1941 the population of Las Vegas had grown to 8,000, few expected much further growth.

Yet, during these years an influx of Hollywood movie celebrities was beginning to give Las Vegas an aura of glamour, and was attracting tourists who hoped to mingle with the stars. In 1931 Rex Bell married Clara Bow, one of the most famous movie idols of the 1920s, and the couple moved to a large ranch near Las Vegas, then considered an unusual and exotic location. In subsequent years many Hollywood celebrities visited them there. After 1935 the newly paved highway to Los Angeles and the regular runs of the Union Pacific's "City of Los Angeles" made Las Vegas more accessible. For southern Californians it became more attractive for quick marriages and divorces than the more distant Reno. The most famous divorce of the 1930s that served to publicize still-obscure Las Vegas was that of Rhea Langham Gable from Clark Gable in 1939 while he was filming *Gone with the Wind.* That event triggered new records for divorces in the county between 1939 and 1941. And to serve the famous and not so famous, several enterprising real estate developers now built the first luxury hotels in the area.[33]

World War II really transformed the sleepy little desert town, however. It tripled its population from 8,422 in 1940 to 24,624 ten years later. The completion of Boulder Dam also provided cheap power for new industries and suddenly made the Las Vegas area an attractive industrial site. Moreover, extensive brucite and magnesite deposits in nearby Nye County provided easy access to minerals needed for the manufacture of magnesium. Nevada's Congressional delegation in 1941 was keenly aware of this potential. It will be re-membered that Senator Pat McCarran (Nev.) in particular successfully lobbied for a basic magnesium plant there. It operated between January 1942 and November 1944 with 13,000 workers. Both the construction of the plant and its substantial payroll created an economic boom for Las Vegas and southern Nevada during the war.[34]

Wartime mobilization also led the federal government to establish extensive military installations in Nevada. Its proximity to the Pacific Coast, year-round good flying weather, vast uninhabited spaces, and remoteness were irresistible attractions in wartime. Thus, the Air Force established Nellis Air Force Base near Las Vegas in 1941 and Stead Air Force Base near Reno in the following year. The Navy chose Fallon for a naval air station and greatly expanded its naval ammunition depot near Hawthorne, employing more than 6,000 people there. For a state with as sparse a population as Nevada (100,000 in 1940) this influx of people and money was truly heady, for the newcomers were ready to spend freely to obtain rest, relaxation, and entertainment.[35]

With the increase of population in the state, and with its proximity to the vast military installations in California, Las Vegas became the great entertainment capital of the West during the Second World War. Its geographical location was an asset, for like the hub of a wheel it was accessible—by car or air—to many of the burgeoning metropolitan areas of the West. San Diego, Los Angeles, San Francisco, Denver, Salt Lake City, El Paso—all were within easy reach. Los Angeles in particular was only six hours away by car. By 1943 hundreds of thousands of prosperous war workers and servicemen and women were streaming to Las Vegas on weekends. Gambling had been legal in Nevada since 1931 but had not had an appreciable impact on its economy until the war. But then, with an entertainment package offering legalized gambling, liquor, and a tradition of red-light districts, Las Vegas drew the multitudes into its orbit.[36]

In the midst of a newly affluent population various entrepreneurs now prepared to exploit Las Vegas attractions. The originator of the Nevada "entertainment package" was Newton Crumley, Jr., owner of the Commercial Hotel in Elko, Nevada. In 1942 he engaged nationally known band leader Ted Lewis to play an eight-day engagement for $12,000. Most other hotel owners in Nevada were incredulous, for who would go to Elko to hear Ted Lewis? But to the surprise of many, Lewis packed them in and the milling crowds at the Commercial Hotel made the daring gamble a success. In ensuing months Crumley engaged other big-name entertainers like Paul Whiteman, Tommy Dorsey, the Andrews Sisters, and Chico Marx.[37]

Among the towns of Nevada, however, it was Las Vegas that was best situated geographically to become an entertainment center, and its business leaders quickly imitated Crumley's concept. The first large tourist hotel in Las Vegas, the El Cortez, opened its doors in November 1941. Within a year, Thomas E. Hull, a California hotel owner, opened the Hotel El Rancho Vegas, right on the road leading from Los Angeles into the little city. It was complete with swimming pool, bars, and a large casino. This was the first hostelry on what in later years was to become famous as the Las Vegas Strip, its main thoroughfare. Its success quickly attracted a Texas theater owner, R. E. Griffith, who in 1942 built the Last Frontier Hotel nearby. Both Hull and Griffith hired entertainment directors and provided patrons with big-name stars and variety shows, gambling, and other assorted pleasures. Meanwhile, during the war the gambling clubs with names like Pioneer, Golden Nugget, and Mint expanded on nearby Fremont Street.[38]

The potentials of Las Vegas, so vividly revealed in wartime, also attracted organized crime. One of the most enterprising entrepreneurs with connections to the Chicago underworld was Benjamin "Bugsy" Siegel, who came to Las Vegas in 1942 to establish racing wire services. Within a year he purchased interests in the Golden Nugget and Frontier Clubs and obtained a license to build a hotel-casino on the Strip. When his Flamingo Hotel opened in 1946, it was easily the most luxurious and opulent in the state. It provided a touch of glamour and chic for Las Vegas and now drew even more Hollywood movie stars and international celebrities. "To the entertainment package idea of Crumley, Siegel added the basis for a tradition of opulence and luxury in Las Vegas," commented a later observer, Dean Jennings, "even if some critics felt it to be decadent or jaded." Nevertheless, some local citizens felt that he put Las Vegas "on the map." Bugsy did not live to enjoy the success of his enterprise, however, for in 1947 he was shot down in his hotel in a not untypical gangland execution.[39]

The war experiences thus constituted a metamorphosis for Las

Vegas. In 1941 it was still a sleepy railroad town, hoping for a modest increase of family tourist traffic. Five years later it was already on the way to becoming the entertainment capital of the new affluent society in the West, and indeed, of Hollywood and the international set. It added still another dimension to the emergence of an urban civilization in the wartime West.

CHAPTER SIX

Blacks in the Wartime West

Wartime mobilization brought rapid changes in the relations between minorities and their fellow citizens in the West. The acute labor shortage now opened job opportunities for blacks in spheres from which they had been excluded for many decades. Involvement in the war and a greater consciousness of the democratic ideals for which Americans were fighting against the Axis also began to dampen discrimination. Thus, the wartime experience gave a decided impetus to diminution of racial and ethnic prejudices on the part of the majority of Americans. At the same time, it gave new self-confidence and self-consciousness to blacks in the region. Their hopes and aspirations were heightened by the war and they themselves took a more active role in achieving equal rights. Of course, racial and ethnic attitudes do not change abruptly within a short time span. Such changes are usually gradual and are accompanied by tensions. These strains were certainly reflected throughout the West during World War II.

Nevertheless, the changing situation of minorities in western society wrought by the wartime experience was remarkable. In 1940 minorities in the West were passive and subdued, excluded from many spheres of the region's activities. But by 1945, the minorities were actively striving for equal rights, and had won some economic and social gains. For them the war had been a liberating experience. This is not to say that equality had been achieved, nor that many problems involving racial tensions and accommodation had been resolved. That was certainly not the case. What is striking in surveying the course of minorities in the twentieth century West, however, is the crucial impact which the Second World War had in stimulating the movement for equal rights.

The large-scale influx of black Americans into the West between

1942 and 1945 was one of the significant changes in the region's population pattern wrought by World War II. In 1940 the black population west of the Mississippi River was insignificant—only 171,000, less than 1 percent of the population. By 1945 it was about 620,000. Most of these were migrants from the deep South, lured by hitherto undreamed of employment opportunities. Geographical conditions, available arteries of transportation, and economic opportunities made Los Angeles in particular a Mecca. The majority of blacks who migrated westward first came there. Many remained, but others moved onward up and down the Pacific Coast and smaller numbers went inland.[1] As the nineteenth century had seen the first great white migrations into the trans-Mississippi West, so the twentieth century witnessed the first great black migrations into the area.

In the initial stages of mobilization, from 1940 to 1942, relatively few blacks came to Los Angeles. At that time the pool of unemployed whites was still large, perhaps numbering two million. Moreover, the volume of defense contracts in California was still moderate. Consequently, discriminatory barriers were still rigid. At the same time it was not clear to many blacks in the South whether rigid discriminatory policies would be followed in their native region, where new defense-oriented jobs were also opening up. By 1942, however, it was evident that southern whites were determined to confine blacks to the most menial jobs in Southern defense industries. A decline of cotton prices and increasing mechanization of southern agriculture provided additional motivation for migration outside the region.[2] By late 1942, therefore, the stage was set for a massive exodus of blacks from the South. The majority went north, but a significant number made the westward trek.

Of the 131,000 newcomers to Los Angeles between 1940 and 1942 perhaps only 3,000 were black. During this period job discrimination was rife. As in the South, most technical training schools refused to accept blacks into their programs. In August of 1940, for example, the manager of Industrial Relations for Consolidated-Vultee Aircraft in San Diego wrote the Los Angeles Council of the National Negro Congress: "I regret to say that it is not the policy of this company to employ people other than that of the Caucasian race. Consequently we are not in a position to offer your people employment at this time."[3] The president of North American Aviation Company echoed this statement in the following year: "Regardless of their training as aircraft workers we will not employ Negroes in the North American plant. It is against company policy."[4] And the distinguished black economist Robert C. Weaver told a Congressional committee in July 1941 that "there were exactly four Negro production workers in the aircraft industry in southern California a month ago. . . . In the Los

Angeles area . . . several thousand trainees could have been recruited and that population has been completely untapped to date."[5] In the shipyards of Los Angeles—as in Oakland—AF of L unions such as the International Brotherhood of Boilermakers resolutely refused to accept blacks as full-fledged members. On the other hand, the CIO unions insisted on nondiscriminatory clauses in industrial contracts and gave encouragement to blacks.[6]

In California black workers were particularly active in utilizing the services of the Fair Employment Practices Committee (FEPC) to break down discriminatory barriers. Region 12 of the FEPC embraced California, Nevada, Washington, and Oregon and was under the direction of Harry Kingman, an able public servant who gathered a devoted group of field representatives and examiners about him. An examination of the more than 600 complaints that came up before Region 12 in the years from 1941 to 1945 reveals that Kingman usually sought to secure voluntary compliance through negotiations rather than resort to further legal action. In most instances he secured a satisfactory settlement for both employers and employees— except for the crank charges of some individuals who made unsubstantiated allegations. The glare of publicity—real or threatened— and extended public hearings usually sufficed to persuade employers to abandon discriminatory practices.[7]

Leaders of the black community vigorously protested the pattern of discrimination. Professor Rayford Logan, a prominent black historian at Howard University, chaired a committee to secure greater participation of Negroes in the national defense program. With some bitterness he confronted Senator Harry S. Truman, chairman of the recently established U.S. Senate Committee to Investigate the National Defense Program, arguing that the aircraft and shipbuilding industries were particularly guilty of discrimination, largely due to the refusal of AF of L unions in those industries to accept blacks. He felt that inclusion of a clause in all federal contracts barring discrimination would most likely break down such racial barriers. But Logan readily admitted that black leaders themselves were split over the best strategy to follow in attacking racism. Some were willing to accept segregated employment in industries which had excluded them, while others demanded unrestricted integration.[8] Among those who supported Logan's position was John Davis, secretary of the National Negro Congress, who claimed to represent three million blacks. Davis estimated that 70,000 skilled Negro craftsmen were at that moment available for the shipbuilding and aircraft industries. As Davis wrote to Senator Truman:

> The situation confronting Negro skilled workers seeking employment in defense industries has become extremely acute. Industrial estab-

lishments which have received millions of dollars in government contracts for defense materials have adopted policies of total exclusion of
Negroes from jobs.

As examples, he cited the Glenn L. Martin Aircraft Corporation,
which flatly refused to hire blacks, and noted the statement of
W. Gerard Tuttle, manager of industrial relations for Consolidated-
Vultee Aircraft Corporation, that their policy was one of "Caucasians
Only." "More than one hundred other industrial concerns approached by us have adopted a similar policy," Davis noted. "Of the
more than 103,000 new workers employed in this [aircraft] industry
during the last ten months less than one hundred have been Negro.
Thus, side by side with our expanding defense program we are completing the ceremony of burying alive thousands of skilled and semi-
skilled workers in an economic graveyard, solely because of the color
of their skins."[9]
Some of the most effective evidence of discrimination against
blacks by western defense industries was that of Robert C. Weaver, the
economist who was a former member of Franklin D. Roosevelt's Black
Cabinet. In May of 1941 he was the chief of the Negro Employment
Branch of the Labor Division in the Office of Production Management. "Restrictive employment patterns operate against Negro workers in practically all defense industries," Weaver wrote Truman.
"Many factors contribute to this wide-spread exclusion of Negro
workers. . . . One important factor is the attitude of management—
both top and supervisory. . . . Another is the attitude of organized
labor . . . a third factor . . . is the general attitude of white employees
toward the introduction of Negro workers. . . . I do not believe that I
can stress too much the economic waste, and the dangers of our
national unity which result from the widespread discrimination
against Negroes."[10]
By 1942, however, the growing labor shortage in Los Angeles was
beginning to break down discriminatory barriers. At the same time,
establishment of the Fair Employment Practices Committee by President Roosevelt in July 1941 gave moral sustenance to those seeking
equal opportunities, although the committee was slow in organizing
its operations. In July 1942 for example, a group of black women
marched on the U.S. Employment Service offices in Los Angeles and
demanded production jobs.[11] By August 1942 the Los Angeles Board
of Education also established training courses in black and Mexican
neighborhoods to equip minorities with special skills.[12] News of these
changes spread like wildfire in the black community—by word of
mouth and by letter to relatives in the South. Thus, the war triggered
the largest westward migration of blacks in the nation's history, a
veritable exodus. Between the spring of 1942 and 1945, 340,000

blacks poured into California. Most stayed in Los Angeles; a substantial number (125,000) went to the San Francisco-Oakland Bay Area; and smaller numbers went to Portland, Seattle, Denver, Phoenix, and smaller towns.[13]

The first sizable waves of blacks began to arrive in Los Angeles by March of 1942. At that time the Southern Pacific Railroad was transporting southern blacks to Los Angeles free of charge to work as section hands on the western lines. About 3,000 men arrived in March 1942, but few of these individuals actually went to work for the railroad. Hearing of higher wages in the shipyards and in service industries, they disappeared in the anonymity of the big city. Southern Pacific made no strenuous efforts to retain them, since railway executives were in the process of securing Mexican *braceros* for track maintenance work. Many of the newcomers were temporarily homeless and unemployed and became dependent on city and state relief programs. In fact, during July 1942 Carey McWilliams, California Commissioner of Immigration and Housing, established a committee to investigate the alleged "dumping" of the black migrants. Meanwhile, in the ensuing twelve months, blacks continued to arrive at the rate of about 10,000 monthly.[14]

The increasing labor shortage opened new opportunities for blacks. Industrial expansion of the area and conscription combined to create a critical need for workers. Shipyards were among the first enterprises to remove discriminatory barriers. The California Shipbuilding Company and Consolidated Steel Yards began hiring more than 7,000 blacks beginning in mid-1942. Lockheed Aircraft started to break the color barrier in August 1942 when it hired the first of its 7,186 black workers who constituted 7.2 percent of its labor force.[15]

In smaller industries and businesses resistance to hiring blacks was stronger. Thus, the Association of Street, Electric Railway and Motor Coach Operators (AF of L) threatened the Los Angeles Railway Company with strikes and walkouts if it hired black men or women. In August 1944 the Fair Employment Practices Committee, heeding a formal complaint from black employees, ordered the promotion of black janitors to operators. A similar order in Philadelphia had led to a walkout of 5,000 transit workers and a small race riot. The FEPC held hearings on the Los Angeles controversy just one week after the Philadelphia disturbances. Officers of the Los Angeles Railway Company warned of possible violence in Los Angeles as well. Fortunately cooler heads prevailed.[16]

Many of the AF of L unions dropped their racial barriers only gradually during the course of the war. The International Association of Boilermakers forced blacks to join segregated auxiliary locals. These kept blacks "in their place," usually as common laborers. In

July 1943 three hundred black workers protested the practice and refused to pay their dues. The FEPC investigated their complaint but was powerless to make changes. The case was then taken to the California Supreme Court which in *James v. Marinship* (1944) declared segregated unions in a closed shop unconstitutional, and forced abandonment of the practice.[17]

Invariably these confrontations increased racial tensions. The conflict over streetcar conductors and operators led one observer, H. C. Legg, the Los Angeles representative of the Committee for Congested Production Areas, to report in April 1944: "For several months there has been a bad racial problem seething beneath the surface in this area. . . . This feeling has come to the surface several times in the past, and at the moment is out in the open because of the unwillingness of our local transportation company to employ negroes [*sic*] as platform workers on their streetcars."[18]

Both blacks and whites also charged that the influx of southern blacks bred problems since some behaved boisterously, spent conspicuous sums on liquor and narcotics, and contributed to a dramatic increase of crime. As Los Angeles Executive Deputy to the Mayor Orville R. Caldwell said: "The Negro who was born and educated here . . . fits into our picture, but these Southern Negroes are a serious problem. They don't get along with the Negroes who were born and reared here, nor with the white residents. . . . If in-migration is not stopped, until such time as these people can be properly absorbed into the community, dire results will insue [*sic*]."[19] As if to underscore his statement, in May 1944 a band of more than 100 black youths stormed a trolley car and beat white passengers.[20] A black official of the National Association for the Advancement of Colored People, in contemplating the newcomers, noted that "The influx of southern whites here, who bring with them their provincial and distorted racial views, in my opinion is directly the cause of this new friction. Secondly, southern Negroes, who have moved here in large numbers, haven't helped the situation any. Generally speaking, they have gone from one extreme, that of being almost completely suppressed in the south, to the other extreme, that of taking advantage of comparative freedom by unnecessary bulldozing tactics in their relationships with other groups."[21]

Most blacks who came to Los Angeles faced housing discrimination. Restrictive real estate covenants in the Los Angeles area severely limited black housing. Thus the newcomers poured into the established black neighborhood in the central city which, by 1950, held 78 percent of the city's blacks. Others sought accommodations in federal housing projects. During 1943 the crush was so intensive that the National Housing Authority in Los Angeles considered controlling the migration and limiting it to essential workers.[22] But the congestion in black neighborhoods during wartime was intense, for while the black population of Los Angeles doubled between 1940 and 1944, it was still limited largely to the same area. Some blacks did move into Little Tokyo, the neighborhood vacated by the Japanese and rechristened Bronzeville, soon to become the city's worst slum area.[23] Room for expansion became available only in the decade after the war. At that time more whites moved from the inner city to the suburbs, thus vacating older houses. Not until 1948 did the U.S. Supreme Court, in the case of *Shelly v. Kramer*, declare restrictive real estate covenants to be invalid and unconstitutional, thus easing the housing pressures on the black population.[24]

During 1943 and 1944 the housing situation became more critical. Orville R. Caldwell, executive deputy, City of Los Angeles, in 1943 estimated that at least 120,000 blacks had poured into the area, with as many as 6,000 to 10,000 arriving monthly that year.[25] Caldwell urged limitation of this migration. "I urge that your committee take enough time . . ." he said, "to walk through the former Little Tokyo. Here you will see life as no human is expected to endure it. Conditions are pitiful, and health problems are prevalent. As the colored representative on the Los Angeles Women's War Chest Committee said: 'These conditions almost require the help of missionaries.' If inmigration is not stopped until such time as these people can be properly absorbed into the community, dire results will ensue."[26]

But by 1944 wartime conditions very slowly began to break down segregation patterns that had been prevalent before 1940. Thus, the Los Angeles Housing Authority for years had followed a policy of maintaining a ratio of one black to ten whites in federal projects. The influx of blacks during the war was so great, however, that the Authority removed that restriction in the middle of 1943, and provided housing for war workers irrespective of race.[27] At the same time older black residents of Los Angeles sometimes resented the newcomers. In Venice (in the Los Angeles area) two mass meetings of black residents protested against the construction of a new housing project for blacks (in a black neighborhood).[28]

Inevitably congested housing conditions created health problems for the new black arrivals. Dr. George M. Uhl, Health Officer of the Los Angeles Department of Health, was particularly concerned about the large numbers of the new migrants who had not been vaccinated against smallpox and diphtheria. He also felt that many had little knowledge of health education or sanitary practices needed in a large city. But they had a willingness to learn and so he proposed creation of district health centers in black neighborhoods. In particular, immediate action was needed to control the venereal disease rate among the black population which comprised 25 percent of all venereal disease admissions in Los Angeles.[29]

In part to calm tense feelings in the black community, Mayor Bowron issued a statement on July 31, 1943, concerning his administration's policies on Negro rights. "The right of colored men and women to work in defense plants on the basis of equality with white workmen was early recognized in the Los Angeles metropolitan area," the mayor noted, with some exaggeration. That migration also created a major housing problem in the city, both for those who intended to stay there and for those who were just passing through on their search for jobs somewhere along the Pacific Coast. Bowron felt that city authorities by themselves could not cope with the problem. "Since the migration here of negroes [*sic*] is caused entirely by the demand for war workers, it is believed that this is a federal and not a local problem, and the situation should be met by the construction of adequate housing facilities for negro [*sic*] families at federal expense. . . . We simply cannot throw these people into the streets." Bowron formed a local committee including black civic leaders to advise him on the needs of the black community and also appealed directly to President Roosevelt to provide federal aid for war housing.[30]

Despite Bowron's attempts to assuage racial tensions, the influx of southern blacks into Los Angeles during the last half of 1943 brought increased friction and numerous racial incidents. On September 15, 1943, for example, a fight between blacks and whites took place at 5th Street and San Pedro Street. On the next day two policemen were knifed at North Broadway and College Streets as they were investigating a racial disturbance there. On September 17, 1943, a policeman critically wounded a black man who allegedly threatened him with a knife at 7th Street and Central Avenue.[31]

At the same time anxieties heightened in neighborhoods into which blacks were pouring in increasing numbers, such as the Central Avenue district. There white cafe owners often refused service to blacks, accentuating the potential for violence. On October 10, 1943, for example, a small crowd of twenty-five blacks wrecked the Paramount Cafe whose white owner had refused them drinks. They were prevented from destroying other cafes in the area only by swift police action. The white proprietor allegedly had struck a black patron on the nose with a wine bottle, and his black bartender then used further force. According to an informant for the Navy Shore Patrol, some of the disturbances in the area were prompted by one Ephraim Lincoln, a black pool hall operator (Lincoln's Pool Hall at 723 E. 5th Street) who hoped to buy out the establishments owned by whites. But the chief petty officers of the Shore Patrol felt that racial discriminations kept tensions bubbling.[32]

During October 1943 disturbances increased. A small riot ensued at a dance hall at 1480 West Jefferson Street on October 15. It appeared that three white soldiers—unaware that they were intruding upon a black social event—became involved in fist fights. Soon more than 500 people became embroiled in a wild melee. Some of the demonstrators boarded streetcars passing through the area and robbed white passengers. It took a large force of Los Angeles police and riot squad officers to curb the disturbance, which ended with the arrest of 42 blacks. Three days later, a deputy marshal attempted to serve dispossession papers on a black resident at Holmes Avenue and 53rd Street. The man waved a gun and threatened to kill the sheriff's deputy, a crowd gathered, and the officer shot the man. As excitement heightened, a force of Los Angeles police and riot personnel rushed to the area to quell the unruly spectators.[33]

Black community leaders hoped to calm the tensions. Some were members of Mayor Bowron's Negro Victory Committee, established in July 1943. The group included Norman C. Houston, Secretary-Treasurer of the Golden State Life Insurance Co., Floyd Covington, Executive Secretary of the Los Angeles Urban League, Thomas L. Griffith, President of the Los Angeles branch of the NAACP, Edwin L. Jefferson, Municipal Court judge, and various labor leaders. Bowron also created a Committee on American Unity to aid in alleviating housing discrimination. Smaller groups tried to do their part. Thus, the Reverend Clayton D. Russell, who was also chairman of the Negro Victory Committee (and pastor of the Independent Church at 18th and Palomas Streets), organized a Protective League for Colored Women in Defense Plants. At least two hundred of the women who worked at the North American Aviation plant in Inglewood were members of this group.[34] Many blacks understandably feared violence. The militant black newspaper, the *California Eagle*, wondered about the growth of the Ku Klux Klan. "We perceive," it editorialized on October 2, "a somber and dangerous connection between the freshly launched KKK organizing drive here . . . the National Club ammunition build-up and the continued anti-Mexican and anti-Negro incitement of the Hearst press."[35] As a matter of fact, the publisher of the *California Eagle*, Charlotta Bass, on October 12, 1943, led a group of black leaders on a visit to Mayor Bowron's office. They demanded an expansion of the Mayor's Committee on American Unity, more public mass meetings to promote interracial unity, and an end to the discriminatory hiring practices of the privately owned Los Angeles Railway. The mayor listened, but agreed to do no more than to expand his committee. A week later Walter White, national executive secretary of the NAACP, addressed a meeting of more than one thousand people at the Second Baptist Church on the race issue.

Within a month a group of black protesters picketed a meeting of the Los Angeles City Council demanding that it take action against anti-Negro property restrictions which were proliferating in the area. Even the *Los Angeles Sentinel,* a moderate black newspaper, expressed fears of a major race riot.[36]

Despite strains and pressures, Los Angeles did serve as the land of opportunity for blacks who migrated there in wartime. Many improved their economic status; despite discrimination, they experienced a greater degree of personal freedom there than in their native South; educational opportunities were more accessible than in rural areas; and urban social services and health care were readily available. The war thus accentuated the transformation of blacks from a rural to an urban people. That transformation was especially significant in Los Angeles to which the war brought its first appreciable black population.

The San Francisco housing situation was also difficult for the approximately 15,000 new black migrants. Most of these immigrants congregated in the western district just vacated by the Japanese. Into this area moved "the majority of our increased colored population," said Dr. J. C. Geiger, himself a Louisianan. "These people have occupied stores, rear porches, in fact practically any space available in this area. . . . Some of the premises so occupied are lacking in proper light, ventilation, plumbing, and cubic area. Many of these units were previously considered substandard and the individuals now occupying them have certainly not added to the desirability of the dwellings. Careless housekeeping and generally insanitary conditions prevail. The majority of the individuals housed in this section seem perfectly content with the accommodations and apparently are not interested in obtaining more desirable quarters. They do not seem to have any particular idea as to proper housing facilities, nor do they seem interested in the danger to health through improper ventilation of stoves [and] gas appliances."[37] Geiger did not mention that many of the black migrants came from poor rural sections of the South and were largely unfamiliar with the requirements of urban living—whether they involved the operation of gas stoves or applying for a job.

The wretched conditions in San Francisco's black neighborhoods were strongly condemned by Wesley Peoples, secretary of the Negro Chamber of Commerce. Although aware that housing conditions were poor for most of the newcomers, Peoples told visiting congressmen that "you may appreciate that the housing situation of Negroes is three times as great." He complained that the San Francisco housing location service refused to make its lists available to blacks. "Our people are living in stores and all kinds of places," he said, [and] "this brings the question of health. . . . Here in San Francisco I know there are a number of places which should be made available for our people. It makes a terrible blot on democracy if that practice [discrimination] continues."[38]

Housing conditions were no better for blacks across the Bay in Oakland. Katherine Legge of the Oakland Housing Authority noted that "We have a decided housing problem with respect to the Negro civilian war worker. You nor anyone has any idea of the living conditions of the Negroes working in defense industries. I can take you to see numerous families where 14 people live in 1 room."[39]

In the Bay Area, like many boom towns in the war, Richmond now for the first time attracted significant numbers of black Americans. In January of 1941 only 150 non-whites worked in Richmond, but by September 1943 that number had increased to 9,500. As Arthur Hall of the United States Employment Service noted in 1943: "Because they constitute the last remaining source of supply every effort has been made to promote the full utilization of minority groups in the war-production program. . . . It should be emphasized that there still exists in this area a large reserve of women and non-whites who have been virtually excluded from employment because of restrictive hiring practices of employers and unions. It is imperative that this group, already housed and established in the community, be used." Hall believed that the opposition of AF of L unions to the hiring of blacks explained why, despite the critical labor shortage, at least 5,000 blacks in the Bay area were unemployed. This was true of the boilermakers, machinists, painters, and shipfitters locals. But the pressures to break down discriminatory barriers were too great for lengthy opposition. By March 1943 the electricians' union reluctantly began to admit blacks.[40]

Housing for black workers in Richmond presented problems. Some lived in neighboring Vallejo where the housing authority followed a practice of integration. That policy upset Mayor John Stewart of Vallejo who noted that "there is much objection to the Negroes and Filipinos being indiscriminately placed in these housing projects alongside of white workers." He felt that this policy accentuated racial tensions. "Surely, where we have southerners by the thousands in our community at the present time . . . the fact that Negroes are being allowed to come in is creating a dangerous problem," he said. "We have trouble between the blacks and whites."[41]

Racial tensions in the northern California area were heightened by the worst domestic disaster in the nation's war production program, the explosion at the Port Chicago Naval Ammunition Depot (near Vallejo) in which more than three hundred people lost their lives. On July 17, 1944, hundreds of Navy stevedores at the Port Chicago Annex of the Naval Ammunition Depot were loading ammunition on two merchant ships, the S.S. *E. A. Bryan* and the brand-new S.S. *Quinault Victory*. One of the ships had already been loaded with ammunition bound for the Pacific fronts, and a stevedoring crew was loading thousands of tons on the other vessel. Most of the ships' crews were ashore, with only a few left aboard to ready the ships for an early departure. Nearby, two Coast Guard vessels were tied up to keep an eye on the proceedings. About 10 P.M. a locomotive hauling cars loaded with ammunition wended its way slowly to the dock. After that no one was quite sure what happened. At about 10:20 P.M. reporter Jack McDowell of the *San Francisco Call-Bulletin* saw a flash that filled the sky with flames. Then two tremendous blasts shook the entire area and the entire coastal strip of California for one hundred miles from Sacramento to San Jose. Even a C-46 cargo plane flying in the vicinity at 7,000 feet was showered with debris. On the docks, three hundred men vanished within ten seconds between the two blasts produced by 10,000 tons of ammunition. The two big cargo ships also disappeared without a trace—blown to bits—as did the two Coast Guard vessels. Most of the dock and the ammunition train were also gone. In the explosion 327 people were killed, although searchers found only 25 bodies. Two hundred forty sailors were injured, as were hundreds of inhabitants in the nearby town of Port Chicago—a mile away—which was largely destroyed.[42]

The tragedy had racial overtones because most of the stevedores who had loaded the ammunition and who lost their lives were black. Within a few weeks after the disaster the Navy assigned 277 black sailors who had survived to stevedoring duty at the Mare Island Ammunition Depot (in Vallejo). But these men now refused to handle any more ammunition. Rear Admiral Carleton Wright, District Commandant, personally talked to the men about the situation and persuaded 227 of them to return to work. But the other 50 refused and were consequently tried by a general court-martial. The trial was the largest mass trial in Navy history. Held at Yerba Buena Island, it took thirty-three days. The naval court found all of the men guilty of mutiny or unbecoming conduct and sentenced them to prison terms ranging from eight to fifteen years.[43] Inevitably, the racial aspects of the entire episode inspired mistrust and hostility.

In the Pacific Northwest the coming of black migrants also brought increased racial tensions and discrimination. According to the census of 1940 Portland had 1,800 black residents. But by 1945 that number had increased perhaps tenfold as an estimated 15,000 black Americans streamed into the city, most of them from the South. The Kaiser shipyards absorbed the majority of these individuals while others filled unskilled jobs in the local service industries.[44] As they poured into the metropolitan area, they confronted discrimination hardly less severe than in the lower South from whence they came, for many of the migrants to the Columbia River area after 1940 were poor Southern whites who came to take jobs in the timber industry and brought their racial attitudes with them. Blacks in Portland experienced widespread housing discrimination and were rigidly excluded from public places of amusement or recreation. In fact, in some areas, such as at Albina (the black section), Acting Mayor William S. Bowes lamented the complete absence of any recreational facilities. Virtually all blacks were forced to live in the black district (east of the Columbia River, between Holladay and Russel Streets to Union Avenue), or in segregated public housing projects, including a portion of Vanport. Even black service personnel met strong hostility. Thus, Lt. R. K. Miller, Acting Captain of the Port of Astoria, wrote on October 29, 1943, that "the colored . . . Coast Guard beach patrol units in this area find it impossible to secure quarters or recreation in Astoria while on liberty." State Senator Jenkins reflected the mood of many when he charged that blacks were responsible for the growth of juvenile delinquency in the area.[45]

Despite these hardships, however, the wartime economy of Portland presented blacks with new opportunities. Black churches as well as the National Association for the Advancement of Colored People gained new members and enlarged their activities. The Urban League was similarly affected. Thus, the war years laid the basis for demands for greater racial equality for blacks and led some blacks as well as whites to work for improved interracial relations in the ensuing decade.[46]

In Seattle blacks were not particularly welcomed, either. From a small handful, just 3,789 in 1940, the black population increased to almost 30,000 by the end of the war.[47] Whites in the Seattle area did not take kindly to this influx, and discrimination against blacks was rife, far more so than in California or most other areas of the West. That discrimination extended to most aspects of daily life.

Even black servicemen were exposed to rigid discrimination. "The influx of colored naval personnel as well as colored civilian workers," said Rear Admiral S. A. Taffinder, Commander of the Puget Sound Navy Yard, "is creating housing and community service difficulties. People in the Northwest are not used to colored people in any numbers and do not accept them willingly. They must, of course, be treated with full regard to their rights as citizens." One of his subordinates, Captain C.A.F. Sprague, Commandant of the Naval Air Center in Seattle, amplified this impression. "In several instances the civilian population in the Pacific Northwest has imposed widespread and stringent regulations upon [Negro naval personnel]. The Pacific Northwest seems wholly unprepared for the influx of any substantial numbers of them. Extended liberty has had to be given Negro personnel in small communities to give them an opportunity to visit Portland or Seattle where small colored civilian communities exist. This may not be an ideal solution, but seems designed to minimize intramural frictions . . . I would say definitely that if the influx of Negroes continues, it is going to raise serious recreational problems."[48]

Black civilians experienced even more discrimination. Large numbers of blacks went to work in the Bremerton, Puget Sound shipyard, where the black population shot up from 28 in 1939 to 2,400 in 1943. Although at first the Bremerton Housing Authority did not discriminate against blacks, assigning them living quarters next to whites, it changed that policy by 1943, segregating Negroes in a separate project (Sinclair Park). Since it was eight miles outside the city limits, the Authority virtually had to force people to live there. Meanwhile, discrimination in public places became firmly established. "There are many places that cater to white trade only, and I have felt sorry for these people," said Mayor L. Kean of Bremerton. "The city is trying to set aside a commercial center where the colored people can have a barber shop, beauty shop, restaurants, and shops. There is no colored section in Bremerton, and the only place where they have been made more or less welcome is the Filipino pool hall." Medical and dental services were also denied to blacks.[49]

Such widespread discrimination did much to lower morale among blacks in the Seattle area. With some bitterness J. R. Lillard, a black representative of the United Service Organizations Industrial Services in Bremerton, recounted the discrimination that met blacks on and off the job. Within the Navy Yard he castigated the practice of assigning blacks to jobs other than those for which they had been recruited. He also deplored the exclusion of blacks from some shops in the Yard and discrimination in placement and promotion. He strongly denounced the fact that no supervisors were black, although some blacks had been in their jobs for as long as nineteen years. Nor were blacks represented in the personnel department. In more general terms he criticized the "tendency of the plant to practice and promote segregation and discrimination [and] the apparent inclination of all concerned to pity the plight of the Negroes yet to do nothing to remedy same." Under such conditions, Lillard said, "the workers feel as though these facts are either unknown to the commandant and higher officials or that they are known and endorsed. . . . In view of this their interest is practically gone and there ceases to be a united effort to exert themselves to the fullest."[50]

Lillard also described black grievances off the job. "At first it was inadequate housing facilities," he said. Then came "the tactful segregation and discriminatory practices on the part of the housing officials." Thereafter, housing officials were "tactfully placing . . . a majority of the Negroes in a particular housing project and then as per custom, running out of money before the project was complete." Once segregated, blacks lacked public transportation, recreation, shopping, and medical care. Anti-black signs throughout the community further fanned racial tensions. "Since these facts are no hidden secrets to local officials, the Negro workers are beginning to question the sincerity of each in reference to the war effort. . . . Negroes do not expect race problems to be solved over night [but] neither do they expect racial tensions to be fostered and promoted by individuals in authority. . . . Now we are beginning to ask ourselves this question: 'Why are we losing our loved ones? Why are we fighting?' "[51] The war thus accentuated racial consciousness among blacks, and confronted whites starkly with the issue of discrimination. The civil rights issues of the postwar era were a direct outgrowth of new racial confrontations spawned by the wartime experience.

The FEPC sought to combat discrimination against minorities in the Pacific Northwest. The Kaiser shipyards were especially cooperative. Still, various complaints by Kaiser workers reached the dockets of the federal agency. In Portland, Kaiser housed some of its black workers in barrack-style dormitories. Two enterprising residents, C. Simpson and J. J. Brewster, inaugurated lucrative gambling games there, arousing the ire of some of their fellows. One of these, Walter C. Carrington, complained to Edgar F. Kaiser himself, the general manager of the Portland yard. Kaiser issued an order stopping all gambling on shipyard premises. That led a group of black workers to draft a petition urging continuing of the segregated gambling operation. "We know from past experience that mixing up with white folks in our games will make troubles . . ." the complainants noted, placing Kaiser in a difficult position. Eventually, however, the FEPC supported management in eliminating open gambling in residential quarters.[52]

Blacks also complained about discrimination in the shipyard's mess halls. At Swan Island some blacks complained about being excluded from tables with white workers. Anxious not to disrupt production, Edgar Kaiser wrote the FEPC that "I agreed . . . that we would provide tables for colored workers only, tables for white workers only, and tables for mixed groups."[53]

The effort to provide integrated housing facilities sometimes created problems. Most blacks at Swan Island, for example, were housed in large dormitories containing twelve to twenty-four people. Most whites, on the other hand, occupied buildings which had double rooms. Edgar Kaiser thus appealed to Harry Kingman, Regional Director of the FEPC, to use his influence with the U.S. Maritime Commission to provide funds for converting the dormitories into double rooms. Kaiser made his request "not only [to] prevent any possible discrimination but also [to increase] production." Kingman himself was cautious on integration and wrote for advice to Milo Dempster at Marinship in Sausalito, California, who had accomplished the most successful housing integration of any western shipyard.[54]

Yet the shipyards provided the major source of entry into the western labor market for most blacks. Of the 7,541 non-white workers in the city of Portland on September 1, 1944, 7,250 had jobs in the shipyards! Except for 260 in steel fabrication, only a very small fraction was able to find work in other industries—whether aircraft, food processing, paper mills, or furniture manufacturing. Consequently the FEPC investigated alleged discriminatory practices of a diverse array of businesses such as the Shell Oil Company, the Portland Chain Manufacturing Company, and others. In many cases the experience of the Rath Packing Company was typical. Its employees claimed that they would not work alongside black workers, and management used this threat as an excuse to defend its discriminatory policies. At the same time the local AF of L. union refused to admit blacks as full-fledged union members, thus making it more difficult for the employer to hire blacks. In such an impasse even the FEPC could rarely have an immediate impact, but airing of the charges by complainants usually brought about some initial movement that was accelerated by worsening labor shortages.[55]

Not only management but also organized labor harbored discriminatory feelings. In the Portland shipyards the Boilermakers Union as late as 1944 refused to admit blacks. The union created a separate auxiliary local exclusively for blacks who were required to pay dues but were not allowed other rights of union members, including voting rights. Thoroughly demoralized, on September 1, 1943, a group of black shipyard workers protested and withheld their dues. At that point union leaders insisted that Kaiser management discharge the dissidents. It was then that the aggrieved black workers filed their complaint with the FEPC, which ordered their reinstatement. Although Kaiser and his executives strove to break down discrimination, the Boilermakers Union continued to be obstructionist.[56]

Blacks were not successful in securing jobs with the Portland Traction Company. Even in late 1944 the company refused to hire blacks, although the color barrier in the Los Angeles transit system had been broken. FEPC Examiner Ed Rutledge was still hoping to persuade the Portland company to relent. Meanwhile, he urged the Reverend James Clow, president of the Portland chapter of the NAACP, to continue to make job applications so that individuals could make formal complaints to the FEPC. He also hoped that support from Edgar F. Kaiser, with whom Clow met on various occasions, would help to break down discriminatory barriers.[57]

Rutledge well summarized the Portland racial situation in November 1944. Except for the Kaiser shipyards, it was virtually impossible for blacks—skilled or unskilled—to find employment in Portland business enterprises. Fewer than 250 of approximately 9,000 black workers had jobs outside the shipyards, and in most of those instances they occupied menial positions, usually confined to janitorial duties. Rutledge hoped that publication of such facts would induce white employers as well as employees to change their discriminatory attitudes.[58]

Racial barriers outside the Kaiser shipyards also characterized the labor situation in Seattle. Unlike the aircraft factories in California the Boeing Company did not hire significant numbers of blacks during the war years. The discriminatory patterns became apparent as early as January 1942, when Robert Weaver sent a telegram to company officials to call attention to their racial exclusion. After conferences among Boeing officials the company sent notices to four Negro applicants inviting them for interviews. The two who responded were considered for janitorial work. But the company assured the FEPC that it would not discriminate against black applicants. Yet no blacks were enrolled in training classes at Boeing, nor did the U.S. Employment Service refer blacks to the company. At the same time the International Union of Machinists resolutely refused to certify blacks. James Duncan, regional representative of the union, repeatedly rejected FEPC requests to modify the policy. As for Kingman and the FEPC, they decided not to press the Boeing case since the Seattle shipyards provided blacks with ample employment opportunities.[59]

Discrimination also met blacks who moved to interior cities. Denver's black population, concentrated in the Five Points area, increased to 15,000 in wartime. Black servicemen usually could not find rooms in hotels or boarding houses while on leave. Their situation was so desperate that Ben Hooper, a successful black tavern owner, turned some of the rooms in his Casino and Ex-servicemen's Club into a dormitory for them. When the Denver Police raided the establishment because it did not have a license to rent sleeping rooms, Hooper appealed directly to Mayor Ben Stapleton to end such harassment.[60] Those blacks who came to seek new jobs often improved their lot. Their income continued to be less than that of whites, but more than that of Hispanic-Americans. At the end of the war prosperous blacks were beginning to move out of the congested Five Points area and expanding into better homes eastwards.[61]

The experiences of blacks in Denver were not at all unlike those in

Tucson where the black community almost doubled during wartime. Most of the newcomers came from the South. According to a survey made in 1945, the majority worked as domestics or janitors. Initially, their coming led to increased discrimination. As one black Tucsonian who had lived there since the First World War noted: "There wasn't no discrimination against them [Negroes] then. Then, later . . . they began living in bunches."[62] Blacks lived in a segregated slum area of Tucson and their children went to a largely black elementary school. Like many Southern states, during World War II Arizona still had a law prohibiting intermarriage of blacks and whites. The plight of blacks was well described by June Caldwell, wife of writer Erskine Caldwell and a contemporary Tucson resident, who wrote just after the war that "they attended separate grammar and junior high schools; Negroes were not welcome in public parks but the city provided a "Negro" park with pool. Residential segregation was strict. Although the public buses were not segregated, blacks were not served at drug counters. Employment opportunities were restricted to menial unskilled jobs. Unions in Tucson rigorously excluded blacks."[63]

But blacks met some of the most strident hostility in Nevada where black employees at the Basic Magnesium plant near Las Vegas (Henderson) experienced chronic discrimination. FEPC Examiner Robert E. Brown reported from the scene that black workers faced discrimination not only in the plant but in the community as well.[64] In desperation, in October 1943, 186 black workers staged a sit-down strike in the factory, demanding changes in the pattern of rigid segregation within the plant, in the canteen, and in housing. The company's reaction was to fire all of the men, an action abetted by local AF of L officials. Some of the black workers also claimed that they were beaten. Although the dismissed employees made an appeal to the War Manpower Commission, that body held that they had been dismissed for cause.[65]

The strong anti-black prejudice at Basic Magnesium was only a reflection of the racial situation in Nevada. Florence Mayberry, the FEPC's consultant in the state, reported that anti-black prejudice was rife throughout Nevada.[66] Black employees at the huge U.S. Navy Ammunition Depot in Hawthorne had many difficulties, too. During 1944 they filed at least four separate complaints with the FEPC. Thus, Albert Johnson charged that although he was a skilled typewriter mechanic, he was paid only a laborer's wages; August Mintz and Walter Wragg alleged that they were classified as laborers although they were qualified for skilled work. A more serious complaint came from Katie J. Kelly. She had been recruited by the Navy in Baton Rouge, Louisiana, as a Mechanic Learner. When she arrived in Hawthorne, Lt. Commander Johnstone ordered her incarcerated in the Mineral County Jail since he felt that no lodging facilities to accommodate Negroes were available in the town. Upon her complaint to the FEPC it sent its own examiner to the community to verify her accusations. Local hearings corroborated her account and led to a reprimand of Johnstone by his superiors.[67]

At the same time the commander of the 12th Naval District appointed a committee to investigate discrimination against blacks at Hawthorne, including a representative from the FEPC and one from the Civil Service Commission. The committee found that Negroes had few business establishments or recreational facilities in the area which were willing to provide them with services—whether integrated or segregated. The community center was open to blacks only on Wednesday evenings. The Navy Depot barber shop refused service to blacks, as did local restaurants and drugstore counters. The local movie house maintained a roped-off section for blacks. Most businesses in Hawthorne displayed "No Colored Trade Solicited" signs. The chairman of the County Commission, when asked to answer these charges, stated bluntly that the community did not welcome blacks and hoped that the exclusionary policies would discourage new migrants. The Navy investigators, when confronted with these rampant discriminatory patterns, recommended that Navy personnel urge townspeople to provide services for blacks—at least on a segregated basis. It also recommended the upgrading and reclassification of black workers at the Depot. This satisfied the FEPC, which took no further action in the matter.[68]

The experience of blacks in Nevada may have been extreme but unfortunately was not unique. World War II had for the first time brought a significant number of black Americans to the West, and everywhere they encountered discrimination and hostility, particularly in job opportunities, in housing, and in availability of public accommodations and services. Yet wartime conditions also hastened the breakdown of discriminatory patterns. Labor shortages opened up new employment opportunities; the FEPC clearly placed employers who practiced racial discrimination on the defensive; wartime congestion resulted in the first integration of public housing and some public accommodations. Black ghettos also aroused a black consciousness of voting power, and in many cities community groups opposed to racism organized to facilitate further integration. It would be too much to say that World War II ushered in a new era of race relations in the West. But wartime conditions accelerated the breakdown of discrimination patterns and crystallized conditions that generated the civil rights movement just a decade later.

CHAPTER SEVEN

Spanish-Speaking Americans in Wartime

World War II had a significant effect on the Spanish-speaking people of the United States. Few other events in the twentieth century did so much to sharpen their ethnic consciousness and to focus the attention of the federal government on their particular problems. These included economic deprivation and poverty, since the annual income of Hispanics fell below the general average for Americans. Most Spanish-speaking Americans were rural or had recently emerged from rural backgrounds and lacked requisite educational training or skills to compete effectively in an industrialized society. Moreover, in many parts of the West, members of this minority faced economic and social discrimination which further impeded their mobility in American society. These conditions were not new; they had characterized their lives for generations. But World War II dramatized the plight of groups such as Hispanics and opened up new opportunities. As Americans fought for democracy throughout the world they became more conscious of the inequalities within their own borders. And the massive war effort created hitherto undreamed of possibilities for jobs, education, and training. Invariably, these drew Spanish-speaking Americans to towns and cities, thus accelerating their urbanization. As it did for other minorities, World War II had a liberating effect on Spanish-speaking Americans, and resulted in the development of federal programs to improve their welfare.

At the outbreak of World War II, Spanish-speaking Americans constituted the largest minority in the West. In the area west of the Mississippi River (excluding Texas) lived about 1.5 million Spanish-speaking Americans who were concentrated in the Southwest, in the Rocky Mountain area, and along the Pacific Coast. Of the 354,432

Mexican-Americans in California in 1940, 219,000 lived in Los Angeles. That city's barrio was the largest concentration of Mexican-Americans outside of Mexico City. During the war the numbers increased significantly, although precise figures are not available due to problems with census enumeration and the flow of illegal aliens.[1] Until 1941 the great majority were unskilled workers, excluded by labor unions and largely outside the mainstream of American life.

The precise number of these people was in dispute. It was believed by the Coordinator of Inter-American Affairs (CIAA) that the U.S. Census had undercounted Spanish-speaking Americans in the Southwest. Some, because of their illegal status in the United States, had avoided census takers, while others had language problems or shrank from all government officials. Moreover, the census takers did not distinguish between rural and urban Spanish-speaking individuals, and missed some in outlying areas. Therefore, Dora Hettower of the CIAA staff in 1943 made independent estimates that were considered to be a closer approximation, which the agency used to develop its programs. Hettower noted:

> The following breakdown of the Spanish-speaking population in the Southwest into urban and rural dwellers is an estimate based on our knowledge of the social and economic situations in the Southwest. Census figures give a rural-urban breakdown only for the entire population; there are no such figures for the Spanish-speaking people. Our estimates consider the distribution of the total population and also the general social and economic conditions of the Spanish-speaking people and its special effect on their distribution.

	Urban	Rural
Texas	300,000	700,000
Colorado	30,000	120,000
New Mexico	75,000	225,000
Arizona	25,000	175,000
California	300,000	200,00

> All authorities agree that the census figures on the Spanish speaking are too low. . . .[2]

The problems of Hispanics were eminently visible on the Pacific Coast. Many of those in the barrio of East Los Angeles existed on a poverty level. The median income of a Mexican-American family in 1940 was $790 a year—compared to the federal minimum standard of $1,310 for a family of five. And in the barrio Mexican-Americans lived in a world apart: with their own values and institutions. To escape from this enclave was difficult. Financial stringencies alone were a major impediment. In addition, restrictive real estate covenants prevailed throughout Los Angeles. Thus, when Alex Bernal, a California-born Mexican-American, moved into a "restricted" part of Fullerton in March of 1943, three of his neighbors objected, claiming that Mexicans were dirty, noisy, and lawless, and went to court to enforce a 1923 deed restriction. Although the Superior Court declared such deed restrictions to be unconstitutional, the case demonstrated one common American image of Mexicans as lazy, dirty peons.[3]

In Southern California, job discrimination was not uncommon in the early stages of the war. "Any United States Employment Service office in California could testify that the placement of even well qualified Mexican youths necessitated a struggle with prejudiced employers," reported a contemporary observer. Most defense plants and citrus packing operations refused to hire Mexican-Americans, claiming that whites would not work beside them. A survey of the Los Angeles City and County Civil Service Commission in 1944 revealed that although Mexican-Americans constituted 10 percent of the population, they held only 2.5 percent of the jobs in local government.[4]

If discrimination against Spanish-speaking Americans was not as vehement as against blacks in the West, nevertheless enough injustices occurred to arouse concern. The Rocky Mountain minority representative of the War Manpower Commission reported in 1944 about Denver employers who refused to hire "Mexicans" (in the particular case the young man was descended from an old New Mexico family), of the segregation of Spanish-speaking laborers in a Colorado war construction project, of differential wage scales. But the extraordinary shortage of labor during the war and the concerted efforts of the Fair Employment Practices Committee and the War Manpower Commission to break down discriminatory practices were yielding more results, he believed, than individual efforts of the previous eighty years.[5]

The problems of Spanish-speaking Americans in Denver were not unique. By 1945 at least 30,000 resided there, most of them unskilled workers. Some were migratory Mexican field workers who had come to labor in sugar beet and vegetable fields of the Rocky Mountain area and who sensed greater opportunities in an urban environment. As the newest large minority in Denver they lived under undesirable conditions. A contemporary estimated that 88 percent lived in substandard housing. Their infant mortality rate was twice the city's average. Employment opportunities were limited. In a sample survey of employment opportunities in Denver, of 189 business establishments Charles Graham and Robert Perkin reported that 107 employed no blacks and 80 no Hispanics. Clearly, employment opportunities for minorities were restricted, but World War II began to open up new fields that drew increasing numbers of Spanish-speaking Americans to Denver in succeeding years.[6]

In the more urban areas of the Southwest such as Tucson, conditions for Spanish-speaking Americans approximated those in Los Angeles. In 1940 the U.S. census had recorded 34,000 Anglos, 12,000 Mexicans and Mexican-Americans, 1,678 blacks, and 417 Indians in Tucson. By 1946 the tallies showed 69,000 Anglos, 18,000 Mexicans and Mexican-Americans, 3,000 blacks, 1,500 Indians, and 500 Chinese. Minorities in Tucson were usually subject to various forms of discrimination. Most Americans in the area did not consider them as "white" and until 1941 excluded them from white collar occupations. A few business establishments were owned by Mexican-Americans, but the majority were unskilled workers. Most Spanish-speaking residents lived in dilapidated adobe apartments in the downtown neighborhoods, and knew they were not welcome in the city's better restaurants or hotels. Local business schools reported problems in placing Mexican-Americans in white collar or secretarial jobs. And the Southern Pacific Railroad, a major employer in the city, refused to hire Spanish-speaking individuals or Indians as firemen or brakemen.[7]

The responses of the Spanish-speaking communities to such problems varied. A majority, especially the older generation, endured their lot in silence. They had been culturally attuned to deprivation in and outside the United States for centuries, had limited aspirations, and reflected a conservatism often associated with people from peasant backgrounds. Many were strongly patriotic. The enlistment rate of Hispanics in the armed forces was well above the average for Americans. Their ethnic pride was strengthened during the war by the distinguished military records of Spanish-speaking Americans, seventeen of whom earned the Congressional Medal of Honor. In fact, the first draftee to win this distinction was José Martinez from Colorado. Others won a wide range of decorations for meritorious service and bravery under fire.[8] But not all Spanish-speaking Americans shared the same values, as is the case in any ethnic group. Some of those in their teens and twenties reacted against the conservative values of their parents. They seemed suspended between two worlds, half Mexican or Hispanic, and half American. On the one hand, they rejected the Mexican peasant culture of their parents, with its clear sense of rural values derived from a rural Mexican environment. On the other hand, they were aware that they were not fully accepted in the mainstream of American society. Half Mexican and half American, the young generation growing up in World War II sought its own identity.

Some of them found it by joining special gangs. These were not

unique to Mexican-American youths, of course, but they were especially drawn into this type of social organization because of their particular cultural background. Gangs that had a purely social function
became known as *palomillas,* while those who displayed some antisocial
tendencies became known as *pachucos.* The latter developed their own
language (patois), standards of behavior, and modes of dress. For
some youths the gangs provided a sense of status. Also, as one observer remarked, they relieved boredom with "smut sessions, dancing, gambling, and narcotic drug parties; gang fighting, raiding, rob-
bing, and committing acts of vandalism." Octavio Paz, a noted
Mexican writer and social critic, aptly noted about the *pachuco:* "Their
attitude reveals an obstinate, almost fanatical will-to-be, but this will
affirms nothing specific except their determination . . . not to be like
those around [them]. . . . [Their] whole being is sheer negative im-
pulse, a tangle of contradictions." Often, the result was to engage in
exaggerated forms of behavior, whether in dress, language, or personal interaction. Those *pachucos* who rejected their parents, a contemporary sociologist observed, and aspired to become full-fledged
Americans frequently exaggerated what they considered to be
"American" characteristics. They rebelled against their fathers and
their families and often drifted into juvenile delinquency. Although
wartime jobs boosted family income, they loosened ties in the tradi-
tionally close-knit Mexican-American family.[9]

The origins of the *pachuco* movement are unclear. According to
one account, it began in El Paso, Texas, during the 1930s (*Pachuco* is a
slang name for El Paso). There a group of members of the 7X gang
congregated in the area of Florence and 8th Streets in that city's
barrio. Involved in the local drug culture, they popularized a distinctive style of speech adapted from the Calo of the Mexican underworld. It remained a local El Paso dialect until 1942 when a large
group of El Paso youths of Mexican-American descent migrated to
Los Angeles. Most of them hopped Southern Pacific freight trains on
this migration, and numbers of them scattered in towns along the way,
such as Tucson. This wholesale migration of 1942 was prompted by
the police chief of El Paso who threatened to arrest the youths on
various charges unless they left the city. Once in Los Angeles the
pachucos adopted the zoot suit as a distinctive style of dress. This was
marked by a long coat, pancake hat, pants with narrow cuffs, and
thick soled shoes. Heavy gold chains adorned the suits. *Pachuco* men
wore their hair long, slicked to a ducktail effect in the back of the
head. By late 1942 these self-styled *pachucos* had formed distinctive
gangs in Los Angeles and other Southwestern cities like Tucson and
became an increasing problem for law enforcement authorities in the
region.[10]

Most Mexican-American youths were law abiding. As Karl Holton of the Los Angeles County Probation Department said in wartime: "The great majority of Mexican children are not involved in these delinquent activities . . . [but] there is a specific problem of gang violence that must be, and is being dealt with." But the minority who were in *pachuco* gangs increasingly attracted attention in the newspapers since they contributed to increasing crime in the Los Angeles area during 1942 and 1943. Arrests for juvenile delinquency, burglary, and theft rose significantly during these years.[11]

Throughout 1942 ethnic tensions mounted in the Los Angeles area. The Hearst newspapers in particular sensationalized what their editors perceived as a Mexican crime wave. The Chandler-owned *Los Angeles Times* was equally strident, as indicated by the tone of the following account on August 10, 1942:

> City and County authorities last night continued their relentless drive against youthful "pachuco" gangs, arresting 30 additional suspects to boost the two-day total of arrests to more than 300 in what was termed the biggest roundup since prohibition days. . . . Captain Joe Reed . . . who directed the roundup of the youthful terrorists, announced the following "breakdown" of charges against the suspects: suspicion of robbery, 48, suspicion of assault with deadly weapon, 39, violation of selective service registration, 20. . . . The law enforcement officials stationed themselves at scores of intersections throughout the eastern edge of the city and nearby points in the county, checking all automobiles that passed and arresting suspicious youths. Police seized more than 100 knives with blades ranging from 3 to 6 inches in length, half a dozen butcher knives, three revolvers, several daggers and stilettos, several lengths of steel chain, which the police said the youths wrap around their hands to slug opponents in their gang fights.[12]

During the first half of 1942 the Los Angeles Police Department became more nervous about the *pachucos* and tended to view perfectly innocent Mexican-Americans on the streets as potential criminals. That was reflected in their arrests of groups of Mexican-American youths for alleged crimes, for loitering, gambling, or merely on suspicion of possible illegal activities.[13] Increasing tensions, exacerbated by the hectic wartime pace, created conditions for overt violence.

The violence came in August 1942 in the well known case of the Sleepy Lagoon. On Saturday evening, August 1, 1942, a brawl took place between two rival Mexican-American gangs near an East Los Angeles watering hole known as the Sleepy Lagoon, in the vicinity of Slauson and Atlantic Boulevards. A member of the 38th Street gang, Henry Leyvas, had taken his girl friend to the Lagoon, where he was set upon by a rival gang, the Downey Boys. Intent on revenge, Leyvas returned a few hours later with his buddies. Eventually they found their rivals, and a free-for-all ensued. No one could testify just what precisely happened on that night. But on the next morning the Los Angeles police found the unconscious body of Jose Diaz, a Downey Boy. He appeared to have been drinking and had repeatedly fallen. Although rushed to a hospital, he died a few hours after he had been discovered. Despite the fact that the police could find no murder weapon they speedily rounded up 22 gang members. Soon thereafter the youths were charged with the murder of Diaz. At the same time the police arrested 300 other Mexican-Americans on a variety of lesser charges.[14]

During the fall of 1942 the much publicized trial of the accused took place. One of the defendants' lawyers, Anne Zacsek, charged that the police beat one of her clients, and that deputy district attorney Shoemaker denied them a change of clothes and a haircut before their appearance in front of a jury. Moreover, the California Appellate Court later found that the trial judge, C. W. Frick of the Los Angeles Superior Court, had conducted the proceedings in a prejudicial manner. On January 12, 1943, the jury in the Superior Court rendered its verdict. It convicted three of the defendants of first-degree murder, nine of second-degree murder and assault, held five guilty on lesser charges, and acquitted the five remaining gang members. Judge Frick sentenced the three accused of first-degree murder to San Quentin Prison while the others were remanded to the Los Angeles County Jail.[15]

The conviction of the Sleepy Lagoon defendants aroused high emotions in the Mexican-American community. While the initial verdict was on appeal a group of interested citizens formed a Sleepy Lagoon Defense Committee. Its organizer was La Rue McCormick, accused at the time by the California Legislature's Un-American Activities Committee (headed by Jack Tenney) of being a member of the Communist Party. Its indefatigable executive secretary was Alice Greenfield, a young activist reformer. Its chairman was Carey McWilliams, a socialist who was a well-known writer on California, a strong advocate of civil rights, and chief of the Division of Immigration and Housing of the California Department of Industrial Relations in Governor Culbert Olson's administration. Los Angeles Police Chief C. B. Horrall accused the group of being a Communist Front although its members were of various political persuasions.[16]

Some members of the movie colony and Hollywood celebrities rallied to the cause of the defendants and raised money to help pay legal costs for an appeal. A prime source of income was a pamphlet by a noted screen writer, Guy Endore, *The Sleepy Lagoon Mystery* (Los Angeles, 1944), which did much also to publicize the case. Benefit dinners and concerts headlined by such stars as Henry Fonda and Anthony Quinn brought in additional funds. Orson Welles succinctly summarized their prevailing mood when he told the Parole Board at San Quentin Prison that "After a very careful examination of the records and facts of the trial, I am convinced that the boys in the Sleepy Lagoon case were not given a fair trial, and that their conviction could only have been influenced by anti-Mexican prejudice. I am convinced, also, that the causes leading up to this case, as well as its outcome, are of great import to the Mexican minority in this community." The committee collected about $100,000, enough to hire lawyers who filed the case with the District Court of Appeals. In October 1944 that tribunal reversed the guilty verdict and ordered all the accused freed. The court cited a lack of evidence and condemned the prejudicial conduct of Judge Frick in rendering the decision.[17]

In 1964, Guy Endore, who during the McCarthy era had been blacklisted by Hollywood studios because of his alleged Communist affiliations, reflected on the case. Endore thought that Judge Frick had been particularly hard on the Sleepy Lagoon Boys because he was known to be harsh with first offenders, and hoped to dissuade them from a life of crime. As he reminisced, Endore said that he did not think the Sleepy Lagoon Boys were "nice," although he did not condone the rather strident anti-Mexican prejudice fomented by the Los Angeles newspapers in 1942 and 1943. Perhaps Carey McWilliams, one of the most ardent champions of the Sleepy Lagoon Boys and of zoot suiters in World War II, summarized the situation most aptly when he said in 1978 that "I wouldn't say the zoot suiters were mother's angels but they weren't devils, either. The papers were dreadful. The officials were no better."[18]

The significance of the Sleepy Lagoon case was to heighten tensions between the Mexican-American community and others whom they regarded as Anglos. In a sincere effort to improve intergroup relations the Los Angeles Grand Jury appointed a Special Committee on the Problems of Mexican Youth. This group contained a variety of viewpoints, and numbered among its members not only Carey McWilliams but Mexican Associate Consul Manuel Aguilar, UCLA Anthropology Professor Harry Hojer, Guy Nunn of the War Manpower Commission, and others. On December 22, 1942, this committee made a report to the Grand Jury in which it noted that "young people of Mexican ancestry have been more sinned against than sinning, in the discriminations and limitations that have been placed on them and their families." It recommended the abandonment of discrimination against Mexicans in public places such as playgrounds and swimming pools (open to Mexicans only one day a week), and in defense industries. It also urged more vocational training as well as an increase in the number of Spanish-speaking police.[19]

Although the report aroused some attention, it had little immediate impact. The Los Angeles newspapers continued their extensive coverage of *pachuco* gangs; city officials remained passive; and a local coordinating council organized by Manuel Ruiz to increase Mexican enrollment in trade schools made little progress.[20]

As 1943 began, therefore, ethnic tensions were even more strained than they had been in the previous year. By this time the zoot suit had gained considerable popularity among Mexican-American youths. Zoot suits appealed to lower class youths of different ethnic or racial backgrounds, but enjoyed special favor among blacks in New York and the *pachucos* of the Southwest and Los Angeles. A contemporary sociologist, Beatrice Griffith, estimated that two-thirds of the Mexican-American boys in Los Angeles wore zoot suits although perhaps only 5 percent were members of the *pachuco* gangs that engaged in criminal behavior. In the popular mind, however, most zoot suiters were stereotyped as *pachucos* and as common criminals.[21] And just as the zoot suit was a symbol of Mexican-American identity to Anglos, the uniforms of servicemen became symbolic as a badge of the dominant Anglo society.

Such a sharpening of ethnic consciousness triggered numerous incidents that created a tense atmosphere. During the spring of 1943 zoot suiters often attacked servicemen, whom they saw also as rivals for the affections of their girl friends. Servicemen in the barrio were subjected to beatings, robberies, and harassment at the hands of *pachucos.* The uniforms of each group provided instant visibility—and instant conflict. And the situation in Los Angeles was duplicated in other western cities, if not as pronounced. In April 1943 a group of sailors and Marines attacked Mexican and black zoot suiters in Oakland. A month later servicemen in Venice (just south of Los Angeles) became involved in a disturbance with zoot suiters at a dance hall. By the middle of May 1943 the attacks by zoot suiters on servicemen had increased both in volume and in intensity. A special report made by Lt. Glenn A. Littin to the commander of the Eleventh Naval District detailed 83 separate incidents involving Navy men only in the Los Angeles area during the last week of May.[22]

In many cases zoot suiters did not go beyond name calling and verbal abuse, harassment, and some shoving. Thus, "on Saturday, June 5 about 2200 [Radio Man 3d Class Chauncey A.] Bengiveno was on a Pacific Electric car with several sailors, going to Long Beach. When the car stopped at Compton, several zoot suiters appeared by the car and dared the sailors to come out. At the same time a group of other zoot suiters came from behind the station and attempted to break into the car, but the door was closed and they were not able to enter." Another reputed incident involved Seaman 2d Class Cecil Maggard. "On Sunday morning, May 29 at 0600 Maggard and G. C. Lee were walking passed [*sic*] New Depot Street on Figueroa, coming to the Armory," wrote Littin. "A group of Mexican zoot suiters, about ten or fifteen in number, ran after the sailors, throwing rocks at them and cursing them. No provocation of any kind for the assault was given by the sailors. No injuries resulted."[23]

In some cases the zoot suiters reportedly harassed the families of servicemen. Littin noted the case of George R. King, whose wife worked at Lockheed Corporation. For several nights after May 27, he charged, groups of zoot suiters accosted her on the way to work, seeking to pick her up on the corner of Euclid and Whittier Streets where she usually boarded a streetcar. In the following week King had to arrange an escort for his wife. Then, "on Sunday, June 6 while sitting on his front porch with his family, zoot suiters began to appear in increasing numbers, cruising back and forth in front of King's house. They began cursing him and threatened to 'get him.' It became necessary for King to telephone the police. . . . The zoot suiters have on several occasions pushed King's children from the sidewalk into the street and fear for their safety made it necessary for him to send them to Sacramento."[24]

Various incidents resulted in more serious injuries to Navy men, however, according to the Navy version. Thus, "on the 31st of May Seaman 2d Class Homer C. Draper, along with several other service men, were on their way downtown about 2030. Very suddenly, without any warning of any kind, zoot suiters attacked the service men from all directions, throwing rocks and bottles, and a general fight ensued. . . . Someone hit Coleman on the head from the rear. Coleman was knocked unconscious and remembers nothing further. . . . His jaw was broken in two places. Coleman is receiving medical treatment from the Navy doctor." And, the report continued, "About the middle of April, Seaman 2d Class Robert J. Short and W. H. Bushman were returning to the Armory from downtown Los Angeles, about 2145. Just south of the viaduct on Figueroa three men dressed in zoot suits approached from the opposite direction and blocked the sidewalk. Short and Bushman stepped off the sidewalk in order to pass, and as they did so one of the zoot suiters hit Short in the jaw, and then all three ran, calling the sailors 'suckers.' Short's jaw was considerably swollen. He was given treatment at Sick Bay."[25] In another of the scores of incidents Seaman 2d Class Dale C. Henderson, "coming off liberty on Saturday night, May 22, about 2230, was crossing Pershing Square when two zoot suiters walked up and one hit Henderson in the eye. Two service men came to the rescue of Henderson and the zoot suiters left. The one that hit Henderson said, 'Oh, the Navy!' as he struck him. Henderson reports that on several occasions before, he had been cursed by Mexicans in passing cars and in restaurants."[26]

Hostile feelings between zoot suiters and servicemen mounted steadily during the second half of May. By that time taxis filled with men from military bases were cruising the city streets in the barrio of East Los Angeles to harass zoot suiters.[27] Meanwhile, attacks by *pachucos* on servicemen increased. As Captain Martin Dixon, Commander at the Chavez Ravine Naval Base in the heart of Palo Verde, a Mexican district, later said: "We had about ten of our boys insulted or attacked in April, and double that amount in May." Then, on Sunday, May 30, eleven soldiers and sailors walked along the 1700 block of North Main Street—in the worst slum area in Los Angeles. They were attacked by 35 zoot suiters but fought off their assailants. The Los Angeles police did little, aware that their civilian authority over military personnel was limited.[28] But the sailors who had been attacked were furious and sought to take the law into their own hands. "We're out to do what the police have failed to do," said one petty officer among them. "We're going to clean up this situation. . . ." And another added angrily: "We don't intend to be beaten and seriously injured while on leave here. If the police can't handle the little gangsters then we will."[29]

During the first week of June the pent-up emotions erupted in a full-fledged riot. On Thursday evening, June 3, 1943, several hundred servicemen left the Chavez Ravine Armory armed with rocks and sticks and rampaged through the barrio. Ironically, some of their first victims were members of a Mexican-American crime prevention group known as the Alpine Club.[30] Through the streets they went, on foot and in taxis, sometimes invading buildings such as movie houses and dragging out such hapless zoot suiters as they could find. Most of the violence was directed against Mexican-Americans, but blacks were also attacked. The Los Angeles police found itself unable to contain the rioters. On successive nights, on Friday and Saturday in particular, the rioting worsened as thousands of servicemen poured into East Los Angeles to strike at zoot suiters. The *Los Angeles Times* of June 8, 1943, described the battle zone:

> Thousands of servicemen joined by thousands of civilians last night surged along Main Street and Broadway hunting zoot-suiters. Chief of Police Horrall declared riot alarm at 10:30 P.M. and ordered every policeman on duty. More than fifty zoot-suiters had clothing torn off as servicemen and civilians converged on bars, restaurants, penny arcades and stores in downtown areas searching for zoot-suiters. Streetcars were halted and theaters along Main Street were

scrutinized for hiding zoot-suiters. . . . Police were handicapped by the
tremendous crowds of civilians who apparently had listened to the
police riot calls on the radio and had rushed into downtown. . . .
Traffic blocked as groups raced into streets after victims.[31]

According to the records of the 11th Naval District (San Diego),
the military authorities in the area made deliberate efforts to restrain
their men. Rear Admiral David W. Bagley, commander of the 11th
Naval District, sent a memo to those under his command on June 9,
1943, noting that "irrespective of what may have been the original
cause of these disorders the enforcement of laws rests in the hands of
the civilian police and is not a matter which should be undertaken by
any unauthorized groups of Navy personnel." He urged "the enlisted
men concerned . . . [to] refrain from such disorders."[32] At the same
time Bagley wrote to Señor Alfredo Elias Calles, the Mexican consul
in Los Angeles: "I deeply regret that individual incidents of hoodlum-
ism in Los Angeles have been interpreted as acts specifically involving
nationals of either Mexico or the United States." Admiral Bagley
stated, "You and I are sympathetic to each other's position in a situation which should have been classified as simple rowdyism." By June
10, 1943, the Los Angeles police had reestablished a semblance of
order, aided by military police and a military curfew, and the worst
race riot in Los Angeles history came to an end.[33]

Army commanders were concerned that such incidents be prevented in the future. On June 11, 1943, Major General Maxwell Murray of the Southern California sector of the Western Defense Command sent a release to his subordinates urging them to inform the
troops "of the serious nature of riot charges," which could result "in
sentences to death or long confinement. Military personnel of all
ranks must understand that no form of mob violence or rioting will be
tolerated."[34]

Within a month after the zoot suit riots the Eleventh Naval District
was also developing plans for more effective control of possible large
scale mob actions in the future. By August 2 Commandant S. F. Heim
of the Naval Operating Base on Terminal Island had formulated
standardized instructions for Riot Duty Personnel. He also worked
out cooperative arrangements for securing additional Army troops
for the Southern California sector. At the same time detailed instructions for riot control were also formulated by J. D. Colodny, the Commanding Officer of the Marine Detachments stationed at Terminal
Island.[35]

Immediately after the June zoot suit riots not only the military but
also civilian officials were anticipating further racial disturbances during the summer of 1943. "A tense situation is existant [sic]," noted the

Senior Patrol Officer of the Navy Shore Patrol on July 29, 1943, "and serious racial disorders may break out in this area at any time."[36] Mayor Bowron held an "off the record" conference on the race problem on July 20 with police officials and representatives of minority groups in the Los Angeles area. The mayor noted that he expected more racial violence and was particularly worried since the Los Angeles Police Department was short 500 men. Thus he requested the use of Army troops, if needed. Meanwhile, representatives from the black community argued that while tensions might be high, they could be relieved by relaxation of discrimination in housing and recreation. Mayor Bowron promised to look into the suggestions and to establish community action and educational programs to ease racial strains.[37]

Bowron and business leaders in the Chamber of Commerce were greatly concerned about the national and international image of the city of Los Angeles as a result of the riots. Bowron's correspondence reveals numerous efforts on his part to dispel the image of Los Angeles as a city beset with racial strife. One of his efforts was directed at Elmer Davis, Director of the Office of War Information:

> I do not question either the right or advisability of representatives of your office getting the facts and we would greatly appreciate anything that could be done in the ascertainment and declaration of the truth in order that the garbled, highly colored, wholly misleading and detrimental news accounts that went out to the entire country and relayed to the people of our neighboring American Republics could be corrected.

And then he leveled his shafts at "Mr. Allen Cranston of your office who rushed here from Washington, ostensibly to get information, but who has busied himself with many things that are not appreciated either by myself or others who feel that the responsibility for local conditions is our own." Cranston had publicly blamed city authorities for the disturbances and had organized a local committee allegedly to investigate the situation.[38] The mayor's sensitivity to negative publicity was also noted by Captain Heim of the 11th Naval District. After attending a meeting in Bowron's office with other military and community leaders, Heim reported to his superior, Rear Admiral Bagley, by telephone: "Admiral, what they are hurt about the situation—and oh, how they are hurt—is the City of Los Angeles being placed out of bounds and the publicity they are getting."[39]

In Washington, Nelson Rockefeller's Office of the Coordinator of Inter-American Affairs was similarly concerned about the impact of the riot on America's Good Neighbor policy and sought to take direct action to ease racial tensions in Los Angeles. (Ironically, the regional office of the CIAA in Los Angeles opened its doors on the same day that the zoot suit riots began.) As John Clark of the CIAA noted, "Mr. Rockefeller is personally greatly concerned with the problem."[40]

One of the major results of the zoot suit riots was to focus greater attention of many Angelenos on the Mexican-American community in its midst. For many, the disturbances had a shock effect, and much soul searching commenced to ascertain the reasons for the troubles. The Los Angeles County Grand Jury undertook a thorough investigation, and concluded rather curiously that racial and ethnic tensions were not a primary cause.[41] California Governor Earl Warren also established a special committee headed by Attorney General Robert Kenny to investigate the riots. In their report they dealt with a variety of influences without stressing ethnic tensions as a major factor. Public resentment of zoot suiters continued. In fact, the City Council passed an ordinance outlawing zoot suits.[42]

But various city and voluntary groups went to work to ameliorate bad feelings. Thus, the city of Los Angeles increased its budgets for education and recreation in the East Los Angeles area and embarked on a five-year community development program for Mexican-Americans. Mayor Bowron appointed a new Committee for Home Front Unity to facilitate communication between city officials and the Mexican-American community.[43] Rockefeller's Office of the Coordinator of Inter-American Affairs activated its new Los Angeles office to develop improved cultural relations between Mexicans and Americans. During the summer of 1943 the city and county of Los Angeles sponsored teacher workshops dealing with Mexican culture and developed adult job training programs.[44] The Los Angeles County Probation Department meanwhile developed a Group Guidance Program in 1943 designed to diminish violence among juveniles. And in the following year the Los Angeles County Board of Supervisors created a Committee on Human Relations. Composed of county government department heads and community leaders, the group was designed to develop intercultural programs for better mutual understanding.[45] Meanwhile, voluntary groups like the Catholic Youth Organization provided special counseling for Mexican-American juvenile delinquents and established a scholarship program for Spanish-speaking graduate students who promised to return to work in the home communities.[46]

Whether all of these activities did much to defuse tensions in wartime Los Angeles is difficult to judge. What can be said with greater certainty is that they represented efforts to prevent the outbreak of violence such as had disrupted the city during early June 1943.

The Los Angeles zoot suit riots had reverberations throughout the

West in communities where Spanish-speaking Americans resided. In Tucson, for example, throughout 1943, 1944, and 1945, street fights and public brawls revealed the increasing militancy of the Mexican-American community. In one incident—a reflection of the zoot suit riots in Los Angeles—a group of Anglo high school boys paraded through the Mexican areas of downtown Tucson to harass *pachucos,* and minor scuffles ensued. The end of the war lessened, but did not end, such tensions.[47] But the emergence of *pachucoism* during the war heightened ethnic consciousness and a sense of identity of Mexican-Americans in Tucson as elsewhere.

The long, hot summer of 1943 convinced not only city but also state and federal officials of the need to redouble their efforts to cope with some of the special problems of Hispanics. States like California and Texas began educational programs to train teachers to be more aware of cultural and language problems of Spanish-speaking students. At the federal level the Fair Employment Practices Committee (FEPC) and particularly the Coordinator of Inter-American Affairs (CIAA) developed policies designed exclusively to help this minority. The activities of these agencies in wartime were to be a prototype of public policies developed in the ensuing four decades.

The FEPC had been seeking to thwart discrimination in employment since it was created by presidential order in 1941. Although nationwide many of its energies were devoted to investigation of complaints by blacks, regional offices in the West paid increasing attention to cases brought by Hispanics outside California. One of the major supporters of the FEPC in Congress during the war years was Senator Dennis Chavez (N.M.), who sponsored a succession of bills to give it legislative sanction. Although President Roosevelt liked Chavez and viewed him as a spokesman for Hispanics in the United States, full White House support for such legislation was not forthcoming during wartime. As the only Spanish-speaking American in the United States Senate Chavez frequently urged his supporters to speak out against discrimination.[48]

But by 1942 the increasing breakdown of discrimination due to a growing shortage of labor was making job opportunities available for Mexican-Americans. Surprisingly, however, the Spanish-speaking population of the Pacific Coast made little effort to utilize the help of the FEPC, in direct contrast to blacks. A reading of the complete files of the more than 500 cases that came before Region 12 of the Fair Employment Practices Committee reveals that only one discrimination complaint was made by a Spanish-speaking person, despite the fact that Director Harry Kingman appointed a special agent in Los Angeles for Hispanic-Americans in the hope of publicizing the work of the commission and facilitating the use of its good offices. Many of the Spanish-speaking population in California were Mexican-Americans with little education who as yet were not well acquainted with the workings of the American governmental system. Sociologists have noted that they depended more on community or family leaders than on unfamiliar American institutions. It was hardly surprising, therefore, that the special examiner, Ignacio L. Lopez, was quite disappointed with the results his efforts brought. "The need for information about FEPC and its functions to the Spanish-speaking Americans is great," he wrote to Kingman. "Very few of these people know that such an agency as FEPC exists, and still fewer understand how it works. This is true of those living in California as well as those from Texas, Colorado, Arizona, and New Mexico." He contacted Maurice Hazen in the Office of the Coordinator of Inter-American Affairs to suggest that a publicity program regarding FEPC be developed in cooperation with the Mexican Affairs Committee of the Southern California Inter-American Council, but he found this group positively hostile. He also suggested a series of radio programs aimed at the Spanish-speaking community in the West because "radio is by far the best medium available in reaching the Spanish-speaking public."[49]

Although some discrimination against Spanish-speaking Americans undoubtedly occurred in Colorado and the Northern Rockies, the regional office of the FEPC (Region 10) received more complaints from Texas, Arizona, and New Mexico. The regional director for the Rocky Mountain and Southwest Region was Carlos Castaneda, who heard a wide range of cases, such as that of W. H. Ural, who charged that he had been a laborer with the Santa Fe Railroad in Albuquerque for twenty-five years and had not received a promotion because he was a Spanish-speaking American.[50] If the number of cases handled was fewer than those on the Pacific Coast, yet the complaints revealed some discriminatory patterns.

The FEPC made extensive investigations of discrimination in the Southwest and in the Rocky Mountain area. The Washington office sent one of its examiners, E. G. Trimble, into the Southwest in 1943 to gather evidence concerning discrimination against Spanish-speaking Americans. In El Paso, Texas, Trimble received complaints about discrimination by workers in the copper industry, particularly by employees of the Phelps-Dodge Corporation and Nevada Consolidated Company (a subsidiary of Kennecott Copper Company). About one-third of the 15,000 workers in the region's copper mines (New Mexico, Arizona, Nevada) were New Mexican, Mexican-American, Indian, or black. But the complainants to the FEPC were almost all Hispanic-Americans. They charged that their wage rates were lower than those of whites for similar work and that they were not advanced as rapidly as whites. Most also complained about being frozen in the lowest category of ordinary laborer. Trimble concluded that a general pattern of discrimination against Mexicans existed throughout the copper industry of the Southwest and that better paying jobs were simply out of reach for them on purely ethnic grounds. Moreover, within the industry Trimble felt that it was characterized by segregation, on the basis of patterns that had grown over the previous half century. Change would come only slowly, and so he recommended that the FEPC hold public hearings to expose these practices since the fear of publicity would induce most employers to abandon their discriminatory policies.[51]

More extensive in its programs for Spanish-speaking Americans than the FEPC was the CIAA, which embarked on a wide range of activities throughout the West. The primary aim of this agency, headed by Nelson Rockefeller during the war years, was to improve the Good Neighbor policy of the Roosevelt administration. One means of strengthening the ties between the United States and its neighbors in the Western hemisphere was to extend more direct aid to the Spanish-speaking people within the United States and to use them as a bridge to more cordial relations with Central and South America. In a very real sense, wartime pressures led Rockefeller and his staff to point to Spanish-speaking Americans as a model of American attitudes toward Hispanics. It was toward that end that the CIAA sponsored programs that anticipated most federal policies toward Hispanics during Lyndon B. Johnson's Great Society era and in the two decades thereafter. These included establishing institutes at colleges and universities to develop greater sensitivity to Hispanic culture and to train community leaders. The CIAA also sponsored conferences to deal with the issue of bilingualism and the educational problems of Spanish-speaking school children, and awarded scholarships to Hispanic college students. In many cities the agency provided direct aid for local governments engaged in community action programs in the barrios. It also made grants to states and localities to stimulate vocational training programs designed to aid Spanish-speaking Americans in acquiring skills which would qualify them for newly emerging wartime jobs. In their entirety, the CIAA wartime policies constituted the most comprehensive federal effort to deal with Hispanic problems yet made during the first half of the twentieth century.[52]

CIAA official Joseph E. Weckler clearly summed up the major goals of these programs:

> The Division of Inter-American activities in the United States is in part concerned with the problem of securing a higher degree of integration between the Spanish speaking residents and citizens of this country and the Anglo population. Our program is directly related to

the war effort. . . . If the Spanish-speaking people in this country are given the proper training and opportunities, they will be able to aid considerably the war production. To achieve this end considerable social rehabilitation needs to be done in many sections of the country. It will also be necessary to break down, so far as possible, Anglo prejudices against resident Latin Americans which have done so much to prevent them from securing training or jobs. This discrimination is also directly injurious to our relations with the other Americas, particularly Mexico.[53]

The CIAA made a conscious effort to stimulate cultural awareness through a variety of programs, including a Cultural Relations Division and a Radio and Motion Pictures Division. By 1943 Rockefeller had created a full-fledged Division of Inter-American Activities. That group prepared materials for teachers concerning the Hispanic heritage of the Americas and encouraged the teaching of Spanish in the United States. In Texas it inaugurated a statewide program to train teachers for Spanish-speaking communities while at Claremont College in California it conducted a workshop to train community leaders. It also sponsored Inter-American Centers in Denver, Salt Lake City, and Los Angeles which involved community, business, and educational leaders in activities relating to Hispanic-American culture in the United States and in Latin America.

One of the CIAA's key programs was involvement with Spanish-speaking minorities in the United States, particularly in Texas, New Mexico, Arizona, and California. "Among these groups it was found that problems arising from discrimination and lack of understanding offered fertile ground for the development of movements which would hinder the war effort and weaken hemispheric solidarity," wrote the agency's historian. The CIAA made grants to universities and chambers of commerce in the Southwest to ameliorate discrimination and improve teaching among Spanish-speaking minorities.[54]

Of the CIAA's numerous conferences on the condition of Hispanic-Americans in the Southwest one of the most important was held in Washington in July 1943. Attending were various government officials, the agency's field representatives, and numerous educators. In focusing on the importance of bilingual education the Conference agreed on the primacy of the Spanish language in any broadly gauged effort to improve the conditions of Spanish-speaking Americans in the Southwest. "The Conference agreed emphatically upon the importance of a knowledge of the Spanish language," the reporter noted, "so as to aid in the elimination of attitudes unfavorable to an understanding of the problems of the Spanish speaking minority."[55]

One example of the manifold activities of the CIAA was the sponsorship of a Conference on the Educational and Community Problems of Spanish-speaking People in the Southwest in cooperation with the University of New Mexico and New Mexico Highlands University in Santa Fe, New Mexico, August 19–24, 1943. Participants were educators and public officials from the region, including representatives of Spanish-speaking peoples, such as Professors George T. Sanchez of the University of Texas and Joaquin Ortega from the University of New Mexico. "The presence in the area of some two and one-half million Spanish-speaking people," noted Rockefeller's representative, historian Harold E. Davies, "a large proportion of them falling into the ranks of the low income groups, gives rise to many problems which are peculiar and common to the region."[56] That region included California, Arizona, New Mexico, and Texas. The conference discussants approached five major issues, issues that had a familiar ring even four decades later. These included problems involved in teaching the Hispanic cultural heritage in the schools and the special conditions surrounding bilingual instruction. The conferees also devoted time to bettering school-community relations. Another major concern was occupational training for Spanish-speaking Americans, especially in mechanical, agricultural, and manual industries. As a committee of the conference noted, however, it was "especially careful to guard against using manual industries as a means of perpetuating the low income status of the Spanish-speaking people." The group estimated that 800,000 Spanish-speaking people were available for the labor market, but urged special training "to give the Spanish-speaking individuals full opportunity to acquire the skill and knowledge necessary to raise their standard of living to those prevalent in the nation."[57]

The CIAA used federal funds to train Spanish-speaking Americans for wartime jobs. One example of its multifaceted programs was that of the New Mexico State Department of Trade and Industrial Education. Henry A. Gonzales, acting supervisor of the agency, reported in 1943 that while his department made some effort to train Spanish-speaking people in traditional crafts, "we have now shifted from crafts work to the metal working trade, to train people for defense jobs. . . . The boys and girls who two years ago were doing artistic tin work are today still working on metals, as riveters and airplane engine mechanics in war industries. . . . Similarly, our master wood carvers and joiners are constructing airplanes. . . . Girls from isolated communities who have had training in weaving and spinning . . . will make good workers in the fabrication and covering of airplanes. . . . This department [hopes] to bring these girls to our defense centers for training and subsequent placement."[58] The New Mexico agency taught classes in aircraft engine manufacture, riveting, oil field technology, and other subjects directly related to the war effort. Gonzales' brief report hinted at the far-reaching economic and social changes which the war had brought to the rural Spanish speaking villagers of the Southwest.

For many Spanish-speaking people of New Mexico, Joaquin Ortega of the University of New Mexico explained, the major problems related not so much to discrimination as to poor economic and health conditions. The key to solving their problems, he believed, was further educational and vocational training. Improvements in nutrition were bound to lead to increased productivity. Ortega also hoped the CIAA could involve Hispanic Americans more closely in community groups like the Boy Scouts, the Red Cross, and similar organizations to achieve greater social integration.[59]

Although the primary functions of the Inter-American institutes were educational, they often entered upon the administration of local action programs. The CIAA's Spanish and Portuguese Section approached Ben Cherington of the University of Denver and asked him to develop projects to increase participation of Hispanic Americans in community activities, particularly those that promised to improve their economic, educational and health milieu. Joseph Weckler of the CIAA was especially concerned with reaching the migratory beet sugar field workers of northeastern Colorado, city slum dwellers in Denver, and poor rural Hispanic-Americans in the San Luis Valley.[60] In Albuquerque, New Mexico, the CIAA was involved in a similar program with Joaquin Ortega of the University of New Mexico and the local chapter of the League of United Latin American Citizens to improve conditions in Barelas, a depressed barrio in that city. Similar programs were sponsored by the CIAA in Texas, where the University of Texas served as a major focus for its programs and where the CIAA also maintained a full-time field representative.[61]

The Second World War wrought great changes in the lives of Spanish-speaking Americans in the West, changes no less profound than the Mexican War of 1848 which had brought the transfer of the Southwest from Mexico to the United States. The war tended to uproot them from their placid rural environment and thrust them more directly into the mobilization effort. Fiercely patriotic, the high percentage who served in the American armed forces came back with an enhanced self-image and sometimes with new skills. Eager for economic betterment, young people especially migrated to towns and cities to take advantage of new job opportunities. Military service and urbanization tended to break down traditional values and life styles, and accelerated social and cultural integration into American society. At the same time Spanish-speaking Americans became more conscious of their own identity and of such discrimination to which they were subjected.

Discriminatory practices against Hispanics weakened during the wartime years. In a city like Tucson, for example, Spanish-speaking Americans now began to have access to white collar jobs, while the Southern Pacific Railroad abrogated its discriminatory hiring policies in the midst of war. An inventory of occupations in which Spanish-speaking Americans were engaged in 1946 revealed a broad range, reflecting the impact of the war. Meanwhile, Tucson's school superintendent between 1941 and 1945 made conscious efforts to integrate schools where there was evidence of *de facto* segregation.[62] Thus, the war changed the aspirations of Hispanics, heightened their ethnic awareness, and accelerated their assimilation. As few other events, it changed the direction of their lives. And at the same time it prompted federal and state governments to inaugurate programs for Spanish-speaking Americans that created important precedents for succeeding decades.

CHAPTER EIGHT

Western Indians and Japanese-Americans

World War II had a profound influence on Native Americans and on federal and state policies that affected them. In the words of John Adair, an anthropologist who made a special study of Indians in the Second World War, "There was a long continuum of change on these reservations caused by events going back some years before our entry into the conflict: the initiation of the Selective Service Act, the rationing of food, the building of war industries. . . . The superintendents of the different reservations had seen not only the steady flow of young men leaving for duty in the armed service, but they saw whole families pick up their most essential possessions and leave the reservations for war work. . . . The cash income of the Navajo tribe more than doubled; great quantities of store goods were purchased and most of the weavers laid aside their wool cards and spindles until after the war work and allotment checks dried up. . . ." And, Adair noted, with emphasis, "It is my conclusion after having interviewed over a hundred veterans . . . and observing many more at various ceremonials and other large gatherings, that the period of this Second World War has exerted a great impact on the cultures of these peoples, perhaps the greatest since the arrival of the Spaniards 500 years ago."[1]

The currents loosed by the war were many and varied. Clearly the mobilization of America's resources had a decided economic influence on the tribes by opening up hundreds of new job opportunities. For many reservation Indians, the war ended the isolation in which they had lived for centuries by providing opportunities for travel and for interaction with peoples from other cultures. Such social contact left a deep cultural imprint that was reflected in changing beliefs and ceremonials. Perhaps the revolution in Indian attitudes toward education between 1940 and 1946 was one of the most notable manifestations of such changes. To a considerable extent war-time experiences widened cleavages within the Indian community, between assimilationists (modernists) on the one hand and tradi-tionalists on the other. Such cleavages had been rampant since the beginning of the century and were now exacerbated by the war. Meanwhile, the training of thousands of Indians in special trades led to a slow decline of employment in agriculture and stock grazing and thus had an indirect effect on Indian environmental policies. And the war accelerated the urbanization of Indians as they, like other people, moved to cities to take advantage of new job opportunities. In short, one of the significant results of the war was to accelerate the accultur-ation of Indians into American society. To be sure, the road toward that goal in succeeding decades was often rocky—and for some no less a trail of tears than it had been for their ancestors.

Most Indians in the United States responded enthusiastically to the call to arms. "The Indians are a Mongoloid race," noted John Collier, Commissioner of the Office of Indian Affairs, shortly after Pearl Harbor. "Hitler's plan dooms them to eternal slavery if they do not resist. . . . They are not Aryans."[2] Thus, American entry into World War II elicited a genuine groundswell of sentiment among most Indian tribes, especially those in the West. Although some histo-rians have maintained that warlike tribes were more supportive than those inclined to peace, such a view is difficult to sustain with evi-dence. Many of the most peaceful tribes—people like the Isleta, Cochiti, or Zuni—rose to the occasion with a fervor that was un-matched, and contributed men and money far beyond their num-bers.[3] At least 25,000 Indians served in the armed forces; another 40,000 went into wartime work or seasonal farm labor. The war dem-onstrated that Indians were willing to leave their reservations to learn skills and were able to make adjustments to varied life styles in Ameri-can communities. Theirs was a notable record.[4]

Like few other events in the twentieth century Pearl Harbor stirred the passions of many Indian tribes. The noted writer on In-dian affairs, Pulitzer Prize winner Oliver LaFarge, reported that on Pearl Harbor day he was visiting the pueblos of New Mexico. "On Sunday, December 7, I went to Santa Clara Pueblo. There were ex-pressions of regret for the many boys in general, who were going to be killed. There was an unexpectedly keen sense of Hawaii and the Philippines, where a New Mexican anti-aircraft regiment has been stationed. There was a general acceptance of the war as their own, deriving from a definite feeling that they were sharers in America and democracy."[5] One of the most peaceful tribes, the Taos Indians, gathered around the flagpole soon after Pearl Harbor to pledge al-legiance to the United States. Tony Mirabal, representing Taos governor John Concha, reflected the prevailing mood when he said: "If they do not believe that the Taos Indians can fight just ask the old timers how we fought the Navajos and the other Indians in the early days."[6] One story made the rounds early in 1942 about a band of Apaches who collected their weapons and went to their Agency Superintendent to tell him they were ready for war. "Why do Apaches need training to make war?" they asked incredulously. The Marines were so impressed by young Navajos who could not speak English, however, that they established special language classes for them on the Navajo reservation at the Fort Wingate Boarding School to ready them for combat.[7]

On the home front, too, western Indians gave strong support to the war effort. The United Pueblos Agency—a branch of the Office of Indian Affairs supervising the Pueblos—collaborated closely with the New Mexico Civilian Defense Council. They made staff, equipment, and buildings available. All of the Agency's trucks, for example, were registered to prepare for a possible evacuation of West Coast cities. It also offered special courses for Pueblo youths to train them as hospital attendants. Throughout the West, Indian tribes contributed generously to successive war bond drives. Eight dancers from Jemez Pueblo were sponsored by the Santa Fe Railroad in a tour of eleven eastern states where they raised more than one million dollars for war bond sales.[8]

In the armed services the Indian contribution was notable. As of May 1945, 21,767 Indians served as enlisted men in the Army, 1,910 in the Navy, 121 in the Coast Guard, and 723 in the Marines. They garnered two Congressional Medals of Honor, 71 Air Medals, and a long list of other decorations. The majority were attached to the 200th Coast Artillery in the Philippines at the beginning of the war and the 45th Division from Oklahoma, which saw extensive action in Sicily and Italy. The first American soldier to ride into the center of Berlin in May 1945 was Harvey Natcheez, a Ute Indian. In the Pacific Pfc. Ira Hayes, a Pima Indian, became a national hero as one of the six Marines who raised the American flag on Mount Suribachi on Iwo Jima.[9] The highest ranking Indian in the armed forces was Brigadier General Clarence Tinker, an Osage from Powhuska, Oklahoma. Born and educated in the Osage Nation, and a graduate of Haskell Institute, he was a career Army officer who in 1941 was appointed Commander of the Third Air Force in Hawaii. At his own insistence he personally led an American bomber attack on the Japanese at the Battle of Midway where he was shot down and killed in action.[10]

Most western Indians were integrated into regular units, although some performed special services in separate detachments. At the beginning of the conflict the War Department considered the formation of separate Indian regiments, but after some consideration abandoned the idea.[11] But if the plan for distinctive Indian units did not materialize, the Marines did organize a very unusual detachment of Navajos for the Signal Corps. These Navajo "code talkers" saw extensive action in the Pacific where their special knowledge of the Navajo language added a distinctive touch to the codes used by the American armed forces.

Soon after American entry into the Pacific war the Marine Corps faced the problem of developing more extensive codes to provide communications in the guerrilla-type war that was developing there. The idea of using Navajos on the front lines was not entirely novel, for a few had rendered services during the First World War. Between 1918 and 1939 German anthropologists, ethnologists, and art students had visited most Indian tribes in the United States and had some acquaintance with their languages. The only large tribe that had not had contact with the Germans were the Navajos. Thus, American intelligence officials felt that this was perhaps the only Indian language in which neither Germans nor Japanese were proficient.[12]

The impetus for utilizing the special language skills of the Navajos came from Philip Johnston, in 1941 an engineer for the Bureau of Engineering of the city of Los Angeles. The son of a Protestant missionary of the Navajo Reservation, Johnston had spent his childhood there and was himself fluent in the language. Soon after Pearl Harbor he read a newspaper account of an armored division on maneuvers in Louisiana which was using several Indians for secret communications. That story led him to develop the idea that perhaps a secret code could be developed on the basis of the Navajo language which would be incomprehensible to the Japanese. Early in 1942 he presented his plan to Lieutenant Colonel James E. Jones, the Marine Corps Area Signal Officer at Camp Elliott near San Diego. Jones agreed to conduct a demonstration before Major General Clayton B. Vogel, the area commandant. At the same time Johnston prepared a detailed memorandum outlining the establishment of a separate unit of Navajo code talkers for General Vandergrift, Commandant of the U.S. Marine Corps. Despite General Vogel's enthusiastic urging Vandergrift and his staff were somewhat dubious about this unorthodox scheme, but did authorize a pilot project with a group of thirty men.[13]

Within a few months Johnston's plan had become a reality. The first contingent of twenty-nine Navajos arrived at Camp Elliott where—organized as the 382nd Platoon—they received special training in radio communications and in developing a special code based on Navajo. With the initial success of the pilot program the Marine

Corps recruited 300 additional Navajos to serve as code talkers. Philip Johnston, although he was by then forty-two years old—agreed to enlist in the Marine Corps to direct the program.[14]

In New Guinea and the South Pacific the Navajo Code Talkers performed important services, particularly in providing communications on the front lines at the battalion level. They were with the vanguard of the Marine assault waves on hundreds of Pacific beaches. Usually they were among the first to land, although their commanding officers used great care in deploying them since they were not as easily replaceable as regular troops. When not serving as scouts with the first assault contingents, the Navajos would quickly set up their radio gear and began transmitting information. That might concern communication between advance units, between support units and headquarters, spotting of Japanese artillery, or directing shelling by Marine detachments. As one of the Navajo signalmen later recalled:

> We used several types of radio sets. The TBX unit we used the most. It weighed about 80 pounds—very heavy to lug around. We had two sets; a transmitter and a receiver, connected with junky cable. We tried to set the generator on a bench of some kind when we could, so we could straddle the bench and crank the thing. But this didn't work on a location that was sandy. So the coconut tree came in very handy. We hooked the generator to the trunk, straddled the tree, and cranked. It took two men—one to crank the generator and get the juice going into the mike, and the other to transmit the message. We got information off the ship after a landing and kept those in charge of the operation informed.[15]

Whether integrated or separate, Indians often found their war service enlightening. Most experienced little or no discrimination in the armed forces. The letters written by Indian servicemen and women to those at home reveal that their impressions were similar to those of other Americans. Many would have preferred to remain at home, but they were determined to do their jobs and to take advantage of new opportunities before them. "So far I'm fine and alright still enjoying things as they come," wrote Pvt. José M. Tafoya (Santa Clara Pueblo) from New Guinea on January 8, 1944. "The things here is lots of difference from other places I have been. . . . One thing there is plenty of coconuts to eat. The other day I give a native a cigarette to get me a coconut, so he climed up the palm tree and got two for me."[16] Wade Hadley, a Navajo, greatly enjoyed his travel in Australia. "It's quite interesting," he wrote "to know how some people live in some parts of the world." Pvt. Stephen Herrera, a Cochiti, was enchanted by his tour of London's historic sites. From Italy Pvt. Simon

Archuleta from San Juan Pueblo reported that "Before coming here I was at North Africa and then to places like Corsica, Tunis, and Sardinia. . . . I hope to speak [Italian] language before long."[17] Pvt. Alfred Kayitah, a Mescalero Apache, was enthusiastic about his visit to Rome. "I had the most wonderful experience in all my life, while back" he boasted. "I got to see the city of Rome."

From Iran PFC Wilson-Guerrero, a Navajo-Apache, wrote a number of letters describing his experiences. He took special pride in his guard duty of President Franklin D. Roosevelt at the Teheran Conference in November 1943. "A few weeks ago we have an honor of guarding our president here in Iran," he reported on December 17, 1943. "I was guarding the backdoor where they have the conference. And saw a few of the big mens that got together. I also have an opportunity of seen Stalin."[18]

Some were so enthusiastic about their travels that they induced others to volunteer. Miguel Guiterrez, a Pueblo Indian, wrote home with such effusive words of praise for the Navy, for the training he was receiving, and for his travels that sixteen of his friends at the Pueblo also enlisted in the Navy.[19] Such experiences provided many Indians with new perspectives on themselves and on their place in the world. "One really never appreciates his homeland until he's elsewhere for a while," wrote Delray Echo Hawk, a Pawnee, from the Pacific area. On the other hand, men like these who had traveled about the world and who had immeasurably broadened their cultural horizons could not be expected to accept a passive role as non-voting wards of the United States government upon their return. In later years Raymond Nakai, a World War II Navy veteran and later chairman of the Navajo Nation, looked back on his war experiences and concluded that "from the service, the Navajo got a glimpse of what the rest of the world is doing. The Marines particularly did a great deal for him, not only in giving him a view of the outside world, but in giving him a glimmer of hope and the necessary vision of the benefits that can be derived from certain things he has seen throughout the world."[20]

Most Indians did not experience discrimination in the armed forces, unlike blacks. "The people here are very friendly to me and treat me mighty fine," wrote Pvt. Amaldo Pino (Tesuque) from California in 1942. Pvt. Ben Quintana, a shy and sensitive young man from Cochiti, reported from Fort Bliss in Texas that "The boys here seems friendly." "Getting along fine with men from different nationality," said Pvt. Rafael Roybal from San Ildefonso, an Army Technical School instructor.[21] "I am the only Indian in this camp," noted Pvt. Johnny Cata, Jr., a barrage balloonist from San Juan Pueblo, "But so far all the white boys are treating fine, but only they always call me chief." That was common throughout the armed forces and most Indians felt flattered.

What was true of Indian-white relations in the Army was also true of the Air Force. Sgt. Salvadore Romero from Cochiti, a tail gunner and radio operator on a B-17 Flying Fortress, commented that "members of the crew are swell to me, they are the best fellows after a guy gets to know them."[22] And although only a small number of Indians served in the Navy, they had few racial problems. Seaman George Lente from Laguna Pueblo, a deep sea diver, wrote, "I am doing fine on my ship, the mates are all nice to me." From a South Pacific island Ellison Bowman, a Navajo Marine, recorded that "I am ok here with these people over at South Sea Island. I am swell friend of white soldiers. I am the only one red skin with this outfit. I and them just like a brother now."[23]

Although not many Indians in the armed forces encountered discrimination, a few dark-complexioned Navajos in the Pacific had occasional difficulties with Americans who mistook them for Japanese. On the other hand, the Japanese often mistook them for Eskimos. One Navajo code talker was almost killed by fellow Marines and army men on New Georgia Island in New Guinea and told of his harrowing experience. "After we had hiked two or three days . . . the Japs hit our line. When we were under fire, one army officer pulled his .45 pistol on me, taking me for a Jap. You see, my beard grows like a Jap's, straight down. . . . So I had a hard time convincing that officer that I was an American Marine. They threatened to shoot me, but took me to headquarters at my insistence where I was identified."[24] Another Marine code talker had an even more frightening confrontation:

I had been on Guadalcanal for some time and was hungry for something like orange juice. The army usually had some and a transport had just come in close to where we were waiting on the beach to leave the island. I walked over to the army supplies and started digging for orange juice when somebody put an iron in my back. I thought whoever it was was just kidding and kept on digging. He finally said: "Get out of here, you damn Jap!" The sergeant standing there said, "He has Marine Corps identification and speaks good English." The man with the gun said, "I don't care if he graduated from Ohio State. We're going to shoot him. . . ."

Finally they took me back to my outfit. I had 15 men around me and the sergeant of the guard had a .45 cocked against my back all the way and I had my hands up all the way. When we got to the beach, they asked, "Is this your man?" and of course got the answer, "Yeah—that's our man. Hey—are you guys serious?" "You're damn right we are serious," they said. "If you guys don't make a positive identification we're going to take him back . . . and shoot him." After that they gave me a bodyguard.[25]

The war had a significant economic impact upon the Indian tribes. In simplest terms, it increased their cash income—and so further disrupted a simple pastoral barter economy found on some reservations. The average annual income of Indian families rose from $400 in 1940 to $1,200 in 1945. Ruth Underhill, a well-known anthropologist who was a student of the Navajo culture, put it more tersely. "World War II," she noted, "shook the Navajos out of the Middle Ages." Anthropologists who specialized in other tribes, such as Zuni and Cochiti, came to similar conclusions.[26] These gains came despite the phasing out of New Deal relief and employment projects by Congress, and severe cuts in Congressional appropriations for the Office of Indian Affairs. The abolition of the Civilian Conservation Corps was particularly hard for Western Indians. Commissioner John Collier of the Office of Indian Affairs was so furious about the demise of the CCC that he tendered his resignation.[27]

Nevertheless, new wartime opportunities compensated for the abandonment of some social programs. Indians found work near reservations, and in West Coast shipyards, aircraft factories, machine shops, railroads, naval installations, and as clerks. The war experience demonstrated that Indians could benefit from occupational training and perform well in industrial and technical jobs. At Fort Wingate, New Mexico, for example, the Army hired 1,500 Navajos to construct a huge supply depot there in 1942. Their performance was so good that the Army hired many to remain and operate the facility, in functions as varied as truck drivers, mechanics, electricians, stone masons, laborers, and clerks. Military authorities allowed them to live on the base so that they could be near their work and purchased hundreds of trailers, or "victory huts," to provide housing. The excellent job performance at Fort Wingate led the Army also to rely on several thousand Navajos to build and operate the huge Navajo Ordnance Depot at Bellemont, Arizona.[28] Significant numbers of Western Indians went to work in the shipyards of the Pacific Coast and in the aircraft factories of southern California—often as machinists, assemblers, or electricians. One Navajo who worked at the Moore Dry Dock Company shipyard in Oakland also continued his native trade as a silversmith, selling his Indian jewelry to delighted fellow shipyard workers.[29]

In the more sparsely populated non-urban areas of the West, Indian labor often played a significant role, as with the construction and operation of the vast new Naval Supply Depot established in May 1943 at Clearfield, Utah. When the Navy first began building the enormous facility it experienced serious difficulties in recruiting sufficient workers in the very thinly populated area. Meanwhile, some of the older Indian men and women living in New Mexico and Colorado pueblos had already placed advertisements in regional newspapers to offer their services for the war effort on a part-time basis, for many were still farmers and stockmen. The Denver office of the U.S. Civil Service Commission began to take advantage of these offers in mid-1943 and sent a representative to Santo Domingo Pueblo to recruit men with the understanding that they could go home to harvest their crops during the summer months. By December 1943 hundreds of Indians, including Pueblos from New Mexico and Colorado, Navajos, Shoshones, Apaches, Sioux, and Utes were bussed into Clearfield, where they proved to be excellent and dependable workers. As Oscar Carlson, the labor foreman at the Depot, said in 1945: "I have never had an Indian in my office for disciplinary action."[30]

Unlike blacks, Indians usually did not encounter discrimination in employment. As Superintendent L. E. Correll (of the Chilocco, Oklahoma school), wrote to Commissioner John Collier, he placed eighteen of the twenty men trained in sheet metal work in Wichita aircraft plants. "No trouble with labor unions has been encountered," he wrote, "and there has been no tendency . . . to discriminate against Indians." C. W. Spalding, the Superintendent of the Haskell Institute in Lawrence, Kansas, wrote to Collier in July of 1941 that "we have placed 61 Indians in productive national defense jobs during the past year." They work "at Columbian Steel Tank Company in Kansas City . . . and Navy shipyards. Very little difficulty has been found in placing well qualified Indian workers. . . . No employer has discriminated against Indians in our area." And George Trombold, personnel director of the Stearman Aircraft Company (a subsidiary of Boeing) noted: "We have been exceedingly well satisfied with the boys you have sent to us."[31]

The impact of the war on Plains tribes such as the Sioux was similar to that on Indians of the Southwest. Almost 2,000 Sioux served in the armed forces, where many developed leadership capabilities and talents which had not found outlets in reservation life. The broadening of their intellectual horizons which came with travel as well as closer mingling with non-Indians gave many a more positive self-image and also sharpened their racial consciousness and pride. A significant number of the tribal leaders in the next generation were World War II veterans, some of whom benefited from the educational benefits received under the G.I. Bill of Rights.[32]

Still, the immediate influence of the war on the Sioux reservation was disruptive. By 1943 the abolition of New Deal social programs had created severe dislocations. The Rosebud reservation, which counted 6,800 of the 32,000 Sioux in the United States, experienced increased privation and suffering. On the eve of war 95 percent of the population received public aid; the per capita income was $150 annually. The abolition of the Civilian Conservation Corps especially deprived most younger men of their sole source of cash income.[33] Within the general demoralization caused by the end of federal relief, most of the gardening and cattle cooperatives which Indian Commissioner John Collier had encouraged during the New Deal to supplement meager diets now disbanded. Shortages of canning equipment and the departure of young men for the armed sevices or war jobs elsewhere led to the abandonment of such self help programs during the war.[34]

The Rosebud Tribal Council viewed the war as an opportunity to press its claims for greater federal aid in the hope of improving economic conditions among the tribe. In a memorandum to the Sub-Committee of Indian Affairs of the House of Representatives on June 24, 1944, the Council gave vent to its concerns. Inadequate land utilization was one of their grievances. "Opportunities to engage in the livestock enterprise are available for . . . only about 25 percent of . . . our people," the Council noted. "The fact that not all of our land is being used by Indians is not the fault of our people. Certain unavoidable circumstances such as a series of drought years, lack of finances, checkerboarded pattern of land, and the fact that 60 percent of trust land is in heirship status are among the obstacles." The land base in Todd County, where the Rosebud lived, was inadequate for successful livestock raising. In addition, improvement in housing and health programs was also vital, the Council declared. The war had led to the abandonment of irrigation projects that the tribe considered essential for improvement of economic conditions. Central to any such improvement, however, was the need for better educational facilities, particularly opportunities for collegiate training.[35]

During the war the Rosebud Sioux experimented with various methods of land allocation in the hope of alleviating their desperate plight and in easing the problems of returning veterans. Some traditionalists felt that this could be achieved by returning lands to communal status rather than in individual allotments. This was the purpose of the Tribal Land Enterprise Program developed by the Council in 1943 and approved by Secretary Ickes in December of that year. The aim of the program was to sponsor intensive land management practices on consolidated land areas to realize greater returns and to benefit from economies of scale. At the time the Council expressed high hopes for the experiment, although these were not fully realized in later years.[36]

On the reservation the war spawned the organization of new

groups which publicized Sioux contributions to the armed forces. Among these were the Parents of Veterans of World War II. As Frank J. White, a representative of this group, noted in 1943, "the organization is appealing to Congress . . . to do something to safeguard our boys and girls who are in the armed forces. . . . They . . . should be . . . rewarded with pension, bonus, Sioux benefits; and many who are landless should get lands to rehabilitate them so that they would be the same as other citizens of this Nation."[37]

As in other tribes the war encouraged the Sioux to place greater emphasis on ceremonies and traditions. On the Rosebud reservation the tribe celebrated the Yuija ceremonial during 1943 to give encouragement and strength to their young men serving in the armed forces. Soon after the war the tribe celebrated the Dakota Indian Victory Dance in which Nazi flags were used ceremoniously to celebrate the defeat of the Axis.[38] The war brought a greater awareness of such traditions which had gradually atrophied in the half century after the demoralization of Wounded Knee. To some extent, war experiences contributed to greater cultural awareness which flowered in succeeding decades.

The worsening economic conditions on the Rosebud reservation during the Second World War led many Sioux to seek work elsewhere. Some migrated to distant war production centers while others found temporary work in surrounding areas. A contemporary sample revealed that only 20 percent left for more distant cities, largely because many lacked the necessary funds to travel very far. A larger number worked as seasonal farm laborers and ranch hands on the Plains, as in Nebraska corn and potato fields. A significant proportion of Rosebud Sioux also worked in nearby sugar beet fields, because some states like South Dakota greatly expanded production in response to wartime demand. Other Sioux worked on construction projects, particularly military depots and air training centers, as laborers, painters, carpenters, or plumbers. Those who had had some CCC experience usually made the best adjustments.[39]

The war had a varied influence on those Sioux who moved to cities. The minority with some education, often mixed bloods, found new job opportunities open to them and tended to move into the middle class. The greater majority of full blooded Sioux were unskilled, however, and congregated in urban slums. If they found employment, they usually worked as common laborers, and found it difficult to cope with new urban problems. Often they retained traditional habits and attitudes. Rosebud Sioux, for example, were suspicious of Pine Ridge Indians, and kept aloof from them in the cities. Thus, while the war accelerated the acculturation of a minority of Sioux who were skilled or semiskilled workers, it intensified the hardships of the majority who found acculturation and urbanization even more difficult under wartime conditions.[40]

The movement of a substantial number of Indians to cities and towns and into the armed forces tended to strengthen integration of some Indians into American society at the same time that it contributed to disruption of traditional life styles. The letters written by Indians in the armed services attest to this trend and also substantiate the conclusions of contemporary anthropologists. Certainly these letters need to be evaluated critically, but they reveal major themes which accord with those stressed by Indian leaders and organizations in succeeding years and thus have the ring of truth. One Indian observer noted that when Indian soldiers came home on furloughs, they had more self-confidence and ease in conversation. They appeared healthier than they had been in civilian life. Drunkenness was less pronounced even though access to liquor was much greater.[41]

An Indian commentator noted that "Indians today [1945] are taking more interest in newspapers and magazines. In order to keep up with world news, many of them purchased radios. They are interested because their sons . . . and relatives are serving our country in the various parts of the world."[42] Similar tendencies were observed by Mrs. Bernice Brode, wife of a Los Alamos scientist. Between 1943 and 1945 the Laboratories brought in Indians from nearby pueblos for a variety of jobs. Some of the Indian women came as maids to enable the wives of the scientists to take jobs on the site, since general policy was to let in as few outsiders as possible to preserve the secrecy of the atomic bomb project. "I think the Indians loved their daily trips to this other world," Mrs. Brode later reminisced. "The extra money was more than they had ever had, and new additions to houses, new furniture, and even a few inside bathrooms attested to the influence on them from Los Alamos." One young Pueblo mother complained to Mrs. Brode that the traditionalists in her pueblo [San Ildefonso] frowned on her desire for a new house after the war with a refrigerator, inside bathroom, and central heating.[43] In summarizing her impressions after more than a decade of reflection, and the perspective of time, Mrs. Brode noted that "No one planned any deliberate association of scientists and the Indians, but undoubtedly life at Los Alamos had its effect on the pueblos. For one thing, their reservation fields are still uncultivated. They work for wages on the Hill [town of Los Alamos] and buy food in stores. I got the impression in 1948 when I revisited the Pueblos that the Indians were eating far better. They certainly had new pieces of furniture [and] new appliances. . . . Their economy was tied to Los Alamos. The Indians, like . . . us, have to think and worry about the new atomic age. This, in itself, tends to broaden the life in the small Pueblo world."[44]

Indians themselves reflected similar sentiments. One of the Navajo workers at the Bellemont, Arizona military installation, Agnes R. Begay, looked back on her wartime experiences in 1977. She recalled that she especially appreciated the nice two-bedroom quarters in the trailers, the child care center, and the educational facilities provided by the Army. The experience, she noted, changed her life style as well as her expectations and aspirations.[45]

Of course, the war also disrupted established patterns of Indian social life. Certainly the conflict tended to break up the cohesiveness of Indian families, as it did those of other Americans. As Tonita Mirabal, an Indian student, reported in 1945: "Home is the basic unit of each pueblo family, but today a situation arises which threatened the continued efficiency of the family . . . due to the absence of the father and mother in war work or military services."[46]

If the war had an impact of hastening acculturation of some Indians, it also had the effect of strengthening various aspects of Indian traditionalism. As in American society as a whole, a feeling of patriotism, of nativism, or perhaps a return to ethnic or racial roots was as visible in the Indian community as among other minorities. This took various forms, as in the revival of traditional prayers and dances. At the very beginning of the war the people of Santa Ana Pueblo, like many other Indians, "left their homes and went secretly to their ancient shrine. There, in their former home, long since abandoned, the entire pueblo remained for one unbroken month in secret prayer."[47] In the summer of 1942 a revival of the ancient tribal dances was sweeping Indian country. By this time only the old men remembered the war chants and dances, and they generally took the lead in this revival. Thus the Sioux danced their first battle sun dance in fifty-two years on the Standing Rock reservation in South Dakota on August 7–8, 1942, praying for the destruction of Germans and Japanese and for the victorious return of 2,000 Sioux servicemen. Although the Office of Indian Affairs banned slashing of the dancers' chests, the dancers fasted for 48 hours while the singers ate meat before their eyes as an act of symbolic torture. The ceremony retained historical continuity since Henry One-Bull, a 97-year-old Sioux warrior who had participated in the Battle of Little Big Horn against General George Custer in 1876, witnessed the ceremonies.[48]

The return to traditional ceremonies was also evident in the tribes of the Southwest. Already by 1942 the annual Indian Tribal Ceremonial held at Gallup, New Mexico, reflected the emphasis on traditionalism. "War has aroused long dormant instincts in the First Americans of our Southwest," reported Ruth Kirk, a student of Indian lore, in the summer of 1943. "Old Jeff at Coolidge [New Mexico] is the only Navajo medicine man who remembers the war chants used anciently before sending the braves into battle, and Jeff had almost forgotten. But he revived his memories, rehearsed his rituals, and Navajo boys go off to war knowing they will have more courage, be safer, and more successful because Jeff has sung over them. So it goes in all the tribes . . . a renaissance of war dancing."[49]

Other ceremonies also enjoyed a revival. Among the rumors circulating in the Zuni reservation in 1945 was one about a number of unofficial contests that were being held on the reservation as to who could bring home the largest number of Japanese scalps. Two Navajo war veterans, Cozy Stanley Brown and Dan S. Benally, later recounted their scalping experiences in the Pacific and Germany respectively. And Pfc. Wilson Guerrero, a Navajo-Apache who was married to a Cochiti girl, wrote home with some embarrassment that "the little children of Cochiti day school . . . always ask for the scalp of Mussolini to make little Indian dolls out of it, so I don't know what to tell them, maybe a pig hide will do."[50]

One of the most significant effects of the war upon the western Indian community was to change attitudes toward education. From a sharp and understandable distrust of the white man's educational system before World War II most Indians involved in the war effort developed a strong desire for more training. Realizing as never before that they desperately needed education if they were to compete in the white man's world, Indian war veterans in particular became outspoken advocates of a wide range of educational programs.

Indians in the military services became aware of their educational deficiencies early in the war. Katie Jordan, a student at the Santa Fe Indian School, noted in 1944, on the basis of reading numerous letters from Indian servicemen, that "The first thing we usually realize in a soldier is his increased interest in education. As an example, the teachers here have received . . . letters from boys in the services saying they wished they had gone on to school. However, they are learning a great deal in Army life also. Indians in the military service, therefore, desire more education for Indian boys and girls. They say that a good education is really necessary in daily life."[51]

Katie Jordan's report was borne out by the letters which servicemen and women wrote home. Pvt. Felix Miller, a Navajo, reported from California in December 1942 that "we are getting along fine and enjoying this life and trying to get the best out of this training." A WAC, Pvt. Augustine Lovato from Santo Domingo Pueblo, who was in the Medical Corps, wrote on January 17, 1943, that the "Medical Corps is interesting and I enjoy going to classes and learn valuable things, which I wouldn't have the opportunity to learn elsewhere." Seaman George Lente from Laguna Pueblo said, on December 15, 1943: "I enjoy the work I am doing on the ship [U.S.S. *Oakland*] for I know I'll make good use of it when I get out of the Navy. I do plumbing, welding, and all kinds of repair work that needs to be done, still trying to learn something new every day." And a Navajo wrote regretfully from overseas: "I could be a technical sergeant only I haven't had enough school. Make my little brother go to school even if you have to lasso him."[52]

The service personnel's keen perception of the importance of education had reverberations among the Indians who stayed at home. Even older people on reservations were encouraged to develop greater literacy. Letters from soldiers in the armed forces were treasured by many Indians. At Picuris Pueblo, and probably on other reservations too, these letters inspired demands for adult literacy classes: parents wanted to read the letters from their sons and daughters, and to write them themselves without the interference of a third person.[53] Tonita Mirabal of the Santa Fe Indian School summarized the mood in 1944: "More than ever before, Indian parents are urging their children to go on to school . . . to receive a higher education. They are realizing how important education is to every individual. Letters from boys in the service have made parents realize more and more the need of education."[54]

Of course, merely to wish for more education was not enough in itself. But the G.I. Bill enacted by Congress in 1944 made it possible for the first time for many Indians to gain access to higher education. An Indian historian of the Pueblo tribes, Joe Sando, noted perceptively that World War II provided the first opportunity for the Pueblo peoples to seek college or university training.[55]

The economic and social changes loosed by the war on Indians of the West had a very decided impact on their political orientation. Before the war Indians had been excluded by many states from participating in the political process. Although Congress had granted citizenship to Indians in 1924 in gratitude for their contributions during World War I, even as late as 1940 states like New Mexico did not grant them the right to vote. Indians in the armed services particularly chafed under this deprivation. As Katie Jordan noted in 1944 about Indian soldiers, "Their interest in federal government has increased. . . . Above all, when this war is over, our Indian soldiers wish to be represented as citizens of their country which they have served very faithfully and loyally by being given the right to vote. All these things mean much to them and encourage them to do a better job fighting."[56] And Margretta Dietrich, president of the New Mexico Indian Rights Association, who corresponded with hundreds of Indian servicemen and women, noted perspicaciously that "Indians are already asking: 'If we are good enough to fight, why aren't we good enough to vote?' Indians who have proved themselves capable of being trusted as operators and teletypists in the control room of an airbase or as record keepers in a supply depot of North Africa, are not likely to be content, on their return, with the treatment given a minor child by the government. They will have earned the right to a greater share in the management of tribal affairs."[57]

Indians on the battlefields echoed these sentiments. Pfc. Wade Hadley, a Navajo, in a letter from the South Pacific wrote, "I am not bragging myself but I have been overseas 3 years now . . . I know I'm educated and grown-up man. I sometimes wonder what this is all about, when the going get tough. I wonder the people and the government will treat me the same way as they did before the war. . . . As far as the Army is concern, everybody is being treated the same. Being in the service that I can vote at the election. I can drink in the public bars any time I please. Because I risk my life in the front line for it. There for I should have the privilege. This deal should be continue after the war . . . I know the other nationality are not better human being that we are."[58]

Such an increasing consciousness of the white man's political institutions and of common Indian political interests stimulated organization among the various tribes. During the New Deal era efforts to organize a national Indian organization had repeatedly resulted in failure. But the Indian Reorganization Act of 1934 had given some Indians experience with the mechanisms of political power and state and federal government. The war accelerated this growing political consciousness and maturity. In the midst of the conflict a group of Indian leaders decided to make another effort to establish a national organization that could serve as a pressure group for Indian interests.

This attempt resulted in the formation of the National Congress of American Indians. From November 15 to 18, 1944, eighty delegates representing more than thirty tribes gathered in Denver to found a new organization to represent their interests. "We, the members of the Indian Tribes of the United States of America," they declared, ". . . in order . . . to enlighten the public toward a better understanding of the Indian race; to preserve Indian cultural values; to seek an equitable adjustment of tribal affairs; to secure and to preserve rights under Indian treaties with the United States . . . do establish this organization."[59] Conscious of other Indian rights organizations usually led by non-Indians, the National Congress restricted membership to individuals of Indian ancestry exclusively. Newly elected as President was N. B. Johnson, a Cherokee who was a state Supreme Court judge in Oklahoma. The Congress hoped to maintain a lobbyist in Washington, to promote scientific research bearing on special problems of Indians, and to provide scholarships for potential Indian leaders in colleges and universities.[60]

By 1945 Indians strove more aggressively to gain political rights of which they had been long deprived. One of their first efforts was to initiate litigation to secure voting rights. They won their victory in the 1948 federal decision in *Trujillo v. Garley*, which required the states to grant voting rights to Indians. And it was hardly accidental that in the immediate postwar years between 1945 and 1952 Indians initiated virtually a flood of legal suits over land and water rights as well as over civil rights. To a large extent the Indian rights movement was led by World War II veterans who actively involved themselves in tribal affairs after the war. Having seen the outside world, they gained a new perspective of themselves and their people.[61]

Congressional authorization for the establishment of the Indian Claims Commission in 1946 was a direct result of this outburst of political activity by Indians. The proposal was strongly urged by Secretary of the Interior Ickes and attracted bipartisan support during wartime. It easily won Congressional approval in the postwar era. Under the terms of the Act of 1946 tribes were given five years in which to file petitions concerning consideration of claims for compensation for lands they had once owned. The Commission was empowered with broad, rather sweeping jurisdiction to make awards which would, in its estimation, adequately compensate tribes in the light of mid-twentieth-century land prices. Appeals from the Commission's rulings could be taken to the federal courts which would be able to make final determinations.[62]

That Indian veterans returning to the reservations after the war would encounter cultural conflicts as they became embroiled with traditionalists was to be expected. Such controversies were not new, of course; they had permeated many Indian communities for decades. Wartime experiences, however, tended to sharpen these disputes in the immediate postwar era.[63] Just as global conflict strengthened the trend to traditionalism on reservations, so the veterans with their enlarged vision became instruments of change. In particular, the veterans as a group emphasized economic and social improvement for their people to a degree unprecedented in the prewar years. Thus, the war experiences spawned at least two trends—traditionalism and the focus on economic and social modernization—that became major goals both of the tribes and of the federal government in the period between 1950 and 1980.

Within particular tribes the reaction to returning servicemen and women varied. At Cochiti Pueblo, for example, the traditionalists in 1945 eyed the veterans with great suspicion. And yet, by 1961 veterans occupied all of the major positions in the government of the pueblo. At Santo Domingo, through their American Legion Post, the veterans pressed for policies of modernization. Among the Navajo, too, war veterans came to play a major role in tribal affairs. Once in a while, as among the Zuni, the traditionalists made a concerted effort to prevent veterans from introducing new ideas or practices. Although a few veterans conformed, most of those favoring modernization simply left the reservation. It was estimated that two-thirds of returning war veterans among western Indian tribes returned to their reservations while one-third took up residence elsewhere. Thus, in the three decades after World War II veterans played a key role in American Indian affairs and assumed leadership in seeking to blend traditional Indian values with a concerted effort for economic and social gains.[64]

Not all Indian veterans found the challenge of reconciling traditional values with those of a technological society easy. One who did not was Ira Hayes, a Pima who had become a national war hero as one of the six Marines who hoisted the American flag on Mount Suribachi on Iwo Jima early in 1945. The feat was recorded in a famous photograph taken by Joe Rosenthal which immortalized the spirit of America's fighting men in the Second World War. Not long thereafter the U.S. Treasury Department brought Hayes back to the United States to publicize the Seventh War Loan Drive. A rather shy man, Hayes dreaded to come home as a war hero. Inevitably he was asked to participate in innumerable parades and speaking engagements. The strain was great, and within a year he returned to the Pima reservation in Bapchule, Arizona where his family was desperately trying to eke out a bare subsistence on a few arid acres. But Hayes found adjustment to this life as difficult as adjustment to American society, and turned to alcohol. With the aid of federal Indian officials he was relocated to Chicago where he was employed by the Office of Indian Affairs. Yet his alcoholism became worse. Discovered as a derelict on Chicago's Skid Row, Hayes again became a public figure when the *Chicago Sun Times,* learning of his plight, raised a fund for his rehabilitation. Even relocation to Los Angeles did not cure him of his affliction, however, and on November 12, 1953, the *Phoenix Republic* reported that Hayes had been arrested for drunkenness for the forty-second time. Once again he returned to the Pima reservation. There, in January 1955, he was found dead of exposure and alcoholism. It was a tragic anticlimax to a war hero's odyssey. It is doubtful, however, whether Hayes was in any way typical of returning Indian servicemen. Personal problems as well as the challenge of bridging the gaps between two cultures played a role in his decline. But in the public mind, as reflected by the mass media such as newspapers, television, and motion pictures (a movie Hollywood made about the life of Ira Hayes), he was symbolic as a casualty in the Indian's effort to bridge the gulf between his own culture and that of white America.[65]

A direct consequence of the World War II experience was the termination policy of the Truman-Eisenhower administrations which encouraged urban settlement by Indians and dissolution of reservations. With hindsight it appears that this disastrous policy, conceived with good intentions, ignored the strength of traditionalism among American Indians and the deeply rooted matrix of an ancient and venerated culture.

In the immediate postwar era policymakers expected the returning veterans to lead an exodus of their people from the reservations. That did not happen. The expectations of Dillon Meyer, Truman's Commissioner of Indian Affairs, that such rapid changes were imminent were highly unrealistic. He himself had served as Director of the War Relocation Authority during World War II, with jurisdiction over interned Japanese and Nisei. Some of Meyer's critics charged that he had been unduly impressed by this experience and expected the Indians to be as adaptable as the Japanese. Meyer denied these accusations, asserting that "over the years governmental programs for the Indians have nearly always been framed in terms of basic lands resources, and have had the effect of tieing [sic] the Indians to the land, perhaps more closely than any other segment of our population. The government has tried . . . to encourage the Indians to make productive use of their land resources and to acquire basic skills in agriculture. . . . However, there are and have always been large numbers of the Indians who have no desire to be farmers or stock-men and who would much prefer some other type of activity."[66]

The end of the war had a disastrous effect on many of the Indians who had just borne military as well as civilian responsibilities. The cessation of hostilities left a vacuum in their lives that was not filled by constructive federal programs. As Commissioner Meyer noted in 1946: "The termination of the war . . . brought new problems to the Indians. Old problems were accentuated."[67] A major difficulty was the sudden drop of cash income for the many who had become increasingly dependent on a wage economy. Wartime jobs disappeared and military dependency allotments ceased. Job opportunities at home shrank drastically. For Indians the situation was starkly reminiscent of the Great Depression of the 1930s. The veterans readily became disillusioned. As one of the former Navajo code talkers wrote to Philip Johnston on June 6, 1946: "The situation out in the Navajoland is very bad and we as vets of World War II are doing everything we can to aid our poor people. We went to Hell and back for what? For the people back here in America to tell us we can't vote? Can't do this!

Can't do that! because you don't pay taxes and are not citizens! We did not say we were not citizens when we volunteered for service against the ruthless and treacherous enemies, the Japs and the Germans! Why?"[68] The Navajo were particularly hard hit, and the Tribal Council decided to take action on its own initiative. In April 1946 it formed a delegation of twenty-six members to go to Washington to present the Navajo dilemma to the Bureau of the Budget, the appropriation committees of the House and Senate, and the Department of the Interior. Chee Dodge, the revered chairman of the Tribal Council, put it bluntly. "We are here for the purpose of seeking aid on behalf of our people," he told the Senate Committee on Indian Affairs. In the summer of 1947 a serious drought greatly worsened conditions on the Navajo reservation. President Truman was sympathetic to their plight and on December 12, 1947, authorized emergency relief for the Navajos and Hopis.[69]

World War II did not fulfill many of the hopes and dreams it kindled among Indians, but nevertheless it had profound consequences for most aspects of Indian life. Historical perspective provided by succeeding decades indicated that the conflict decisively altered the economic, social, and cultural status of Native Americans and catapulted them into participating in the American political process. In stimulating traditionalism and acculturation the war provided the framework for most of the major issues that concerned the Indian community during the next forty years. And in raising the hopes and aspirations of Indian peoples it set a new agenda for Indian programs in the twentieth century—for economic betterment, for access to education, for social mobility, for civil rights, for racial consciousness and a distinct identity, and for racial pride. If the war did not initiate these issues, it did more than any other single event in a century to crystallize an agenda for Indians in twentieth century America.

If World War II disrupted American Indian life, it had a shattering effect on Japanese-Americans, forcibly uprooted by deportation to detention camps, displaced from homes and possessions which they often lost, and transplanted to unfamiliar environments. For many it was the most traumatic experience in their lives and it seemed at the time that the world as they had known it was destroyed beyond repair.[70] No other minority group in the United States was exposed to a similar experience. And yet, in retrospect, it became apparent as early as 1945 that the wartime experience had much the same effect on the Japanese-Americans as it did on other minorities. Paradoxically, some of the Japanese-Americans themselves wondered about the unexpected positive impact of what in itself initially was a negative experience. For the war shattered the closely guarded introspective life of

Japanese-American communities before 1941 and ruthlessly deposited them after release from detention camps within the mainstream of American society. In the process, the war altered the economic aspirations of Japanese-Americans; it broadened their social contacts; and it hastened the blending of Japanese and American culture. The shame that many Americans felt about deportation of innocent people was manifest even before the war had ended and by 1945 led to the lessening of such discriminatory barriers as Japanese-Americans had met before 1941. In terms of the acculturation of Japanese-Americans into American culture the war accomplished more in four short years than the entire forty-year period before. That the detention of Japanese-Americans was a questionable decision cannot be denied. But at the same time the unforeseen and unexpected beneficial effects of that detention experience cannot be ignored either.

As tensions mounted between the United States and Japan in the fall of 1941, the status of Japanese-Americans on the Pacific Coast became increasingly tenuous. In a special report to President Roosevelt in early November 1941, advisor Curtis B. Munson noted that while the great majority of Japanese-Americans were loyal to the United States, even a handful of potential saboteurs could wreak great damage to dams, bridges, and power stations along the Pacific Coast. In fact, much of the West Coast was not guarded.[71] Once the bombing of Pearl Harbor occurred, on December 7, 1941, newspapers in western cities were rife with rumors about alleged sabotage and fifth column activities by Japanese-Americans. During the second week of December 1941 the Federal Bureau of Investigation rounded up more than 1,500 Japanese-Americans whom it considered potentially dangerous. Even so, the commander of the Western Defense Command, General John De Witt, felt that this was not enough and that nothing less than the internment of all Japanese and Japanese-Americans was necessary to secure the safety of the West. In this view he was strongly supported by many state officials in the region such as Governor Culbert B. Olson of California and his state attorney general, Earl Warren.[72] After extensive deliberations by federal and state officials President Roosevelt on February 19, 1942, issued his famous Executive Order #9066 giving the Army the right to exclude persons from military areas where they deemed it necessary. Although the order did not mention Japanese-Americans by name, in effect it authorized military authorities to evacuate Japanese-Americans from the Pacific Coast to detention camps in the interior.[73]

Between February and May 1942 the Army made plans for the mass evacuation of Japanese-Americans on the Pacific Coast to ten detention centers to be hastily built in western states. During February

1. Women war workers at Douglas Aircraft Company Plant, Long Beach, California, October 1942.

2. President Roosevelt visits Henry J. Kaiser in his Portland, Oregon shipyard, September 23, 1942.

3. Women at work: Painting a B-25 bomber at North American Aviation Plant, Inglewood, California, October 1942.

4. Assembly line, Douglas Aircraft Company, Santa Monica, California, in World War II.

5. Booker T. Washington's granddaughters christen a Liberty Ship named after their grandfather, at California Shipbuilding Company, September 29, 1942.

6. Going to work at Oregon Shipbuilding Company, Portland, August 1943.

7. Keeping them happy at the Kaiser shipyards in Portland, Oregon during World War II.

8. Shipbuilding by the assembly line: Kaiser yards in Vancouver, Washington in wartime.

9. Rosie the Riveter at Oregon Shipbuilding Company in 1945.

10. "While Mommy works": A child care center at Oregon Shipbuilding Company, Portland, December 1, 1944.

11. Women help with the Oregon harvest during the war.

12. Western industry at war: The Colorado Fuel and Iron
Company plant at Pueblo, Colorado, 1942.

13. Army training for black Americans in the West.

14. Mountain training for the U.S. Army in World War II: on the road to Camp Hale near Leadville, Colorado.

15. Winning honors: An Indian soldier receiving decorations.

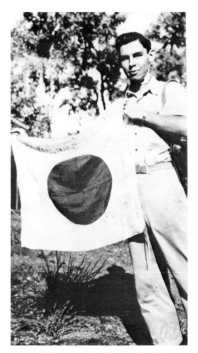

16. An Indian paratrooper in World War II.

17. The spoils of war: Indian fighter in the Pacific.

18. Indian communications specialist in action!

19. General MacArthur poses with Indian servicemen in the Pacific.

20. Army training for Indian soldiers.

21. Going off to war: Taking leave from the reservation.

22. Going to the American West: Mexican *braceros* on their way to work during the war.

23. *Braceros* in Oregon relaxing after work during the
war.

24. Denver in wartime.

25. Japanese-Americans en route to internment in Granada, Amache, Colorado, May 1942.

26. Western refugees: Japanese-Americans at Granada, Colorado rail station on their way to relocation center at Amache, May 1942.

27. Atomic city in the West: Los Alamos in 1945.

28. On the way to Trinity: Loading components of the world's first atomic bomb on the road to Trinity Test Site near Alamagordo, N.M., July 1945.

29. Science in the West: Readying the site for the first atomic bomb test near Alamagordo, N.M., July 1945.

30. The soldier and the scientist: General Leslie Groves presents Director J. Robert Oppenheimer with Certificate of Appreciation for Los Alamos Laboratories.

31. Atoms in the desert: The day after the world's first nuclear bomb explosion at Trinity Site, N.M., July 17, 1945.

32. A federal science city: Hanford, Washington.

33. Emigré scientist at work: Hungarian physicist Leo Szilard while at Los Alamos.

34. Distinguished émigrés: Writer Lion Feuchtwanger and his wife, Marta.

and March the House Select Committee on Defense Migration also held extensive hearings on the proposed removal in Los Angeles, San Francisco, Portland, Oregon, and Seattle, and found widespread public support. "So far as the Japanese are concerned," declared Earl Warren, "we have a tremendous problem in California to protect our state against fifth column activities. . . . It seems to me that it is quite significant that in this great state of ours we have had . . . no sabotage reported. It looks very much to me as though it is a studied effort not to have any until the zero hour arrives. . . . That was the history of Pearl Harbor. I can't help believing that the same thing is planned for us in California."[74] Consequently, on March 18, 1942, Roosevelt issued another Executive Order creating the War Relocation Authority, a new agency to administer the detention program. He transferred Milton S. Eisenhower from the Department of Agriculture to become the first Director. Meanwhile, western communities in the interior were hostile to detainees coming into their midst. In view of such strong negative feelings the Army decided to leave them where they were until the camps could be completed by June.[75]

Most of the Japanese were in California. That state had about 100,000 of the total number of 118,000 in the United States—60,000 in Los Angeles, 20,000 in the San Francisco Bay region, 8,000 in Sacramento, and others in smaller cities. Portland and Seattle each contained about 8,000 Japanese-Americans in their environs. In California, a public opinion poll in March 1942 reported that one-third of Californians wanted Japanese-Americans interned while 75 percent favored relocation of Japanese aliens to the interior.[76] Thus, in February 1942 the relocation of Japanese in Los Angeles began.

Elsewhere in California the process was similar, whether in San Francisco, Sacramento, or smaller towns.[77] The scale of Japanese-American evacuation was much smaller in the Pacific Northwest. Like Governor Olson in California, Oregon's Governor Charles Sprague fanned the fires of rising anti-Japanese feelings during the first months after Pearl Harbor. Although James Y. Sakamoto, editor of the *Japanese-American Journal* and past national president of the Japanese-American Citizen's League, pledged the absolute loyalty of his constituency, anti-Japanese sentiments grew.[78] Like the city council in Los Angeles, that of Portland decreed on January 13, 1942, that it would issue no further business licenses to Japanese-Americans whose annual licenses expired. And the council raised the question as to what measures it should take against Japanese aliens if neither federal or state government took punitive action. At the behest of the Insurance Commissioner of the state of Oregon, insurance companies cancelled the fire insurance policies of Japanese-Americans.[79] During February 1942 the Federal Bureau of Investigation began to search homes of Japanese-Americans in the Portland area as they were also doing in California. Meanwhile, Mayor Riley of Portland echoed the sentiments of Earl Warren in California, "The Pacific Coast is as wide open to fifth column attack as Pearl Harbor on December 7," he said. "I believe that the only reason the fifth columnists haven't struck so far is because their respective governments haven't given them the go-ahead."[80]

Before the Second World War Seattle had had a relatively homogeneous population with relatively few recent immigrants. It was therefore not surprising that Pearl Harbor aroused a virulent anti-Japanese hysteria in the city. In 1941 only about 7,000 Japanese and Japanese-Americans lived in Seattle (in a population of 350,000), and for years they had maintained a low profile. But the war with Japan changed all that. On December 7, 1941, the Federal Bureau of Investigation sent agents to arrest 100 important leaders of the Japanese community in Seattle although they had committed no crime.[81] This hysteria was fueled by a fear that Seattle lay defenseless against a possible direct onslaught by Japanese military forces. Wild rumors circulated about hostile planes over the Bremerton Navy Yard.[82] Under President Roosevelt's Executive Order #9066 authorizing evacuation of Japanese from the Pacific Coast, Seattle's Japanese community was ordered by the Army to leave on May 1, 1942, for detention camps in Idaho.[83] Just a month later the Japanese attacked the Aleutian Islands. In the opinion of one later observer, the evacuation prevented a race riot that might have taken place had the Japanese community still been in Seattle at the time of this offensive.[84] As in California, however, the evacuation was to lead Americans during the postwar decade to more intensive soul-searching about their racial attitudes.

Some Japanese-Americans in the Pacific Northwest sought in March of 1942 to settle in Idaho to escape internment. But their reception was no friendlier than elsewhere. "A good solution to the Jap problem in Idaho and the nation," exclaimed Idaho Governor Chase Clark, "would be to send them all back to Japan, then sink the island. They live like rats, breed like rats, and act like rats. We don't want them . . . becoming permanently located in our state."[85] But on March 30, 1942, the Army ended all voluntary evacuation and ordered Portland's Japanese-Americans to report to the Pacific International Livestock Exposition Building in Portland on April 28, 1942, for forceable evacuation. By the end of 1942 all of the Japanese-Americans on the Pacific Coast had been relocated in detention camps.[86] Their experience in the camps has been copiously described. None of the internees had been guilty of any wrongdoing to warrant suspicion of disloyalty. Their race was their only "crime." This realization became increasingly stronger with the progress of the war, and with the distinguished service of the Army's Nisei regiment in Italy. Beginning in 1944, therefore, the War Relocation Authority began the gradual process of deactivating the camps. Most communities in the United States were not particularly eager to receive the internees back into their midst. As late as December 1943 two-thirds of the Los Angeles residents polled believed that all Japanese should be deported.[87] But voluntary groups such as the Los Angeles Friends Committee and also the War Relocation Authority gradually created a more friendly environment for the Japanese-Americans which allowed them to return to their various localities, there to rebuild their lives.[88]

But strangely enough, this tragic experience also had an unexpectedly positive impact on the Japanese-American community. It accelerated its integration into American society. Even in the heat of war this positive aspect of the evacuation experience was clear to leaders of the Japanese-Americans. Writing in 1943, Larry Tajiri, editor of the *Pacific Citizen*, the major Japanese-American newspaper in the United States, noted: "The mass indignity of racial evacuation has sharpened a race consciousness born earlier of social discriminations and legal and extra-legal restrictions, and kept alive by the segregated nature of life in the Little Tokyos of the Pacific Coast. . . . But, more than anything else, detention in the monoracial world of the relocation camps has intensified the racial hyper-sensitivity of Japanese-Americans. . . . The train of circumstances set into motion by the evacuation now presents an opportunity to achieve, by strange contradiction, what they and other non-white groups have long sought— fuller integration into American life through dispersal of settlement. . . . This is the great paradox . . . that the evacuees in losing a part of America are having opened to them the whole of it. . . . The little Tokyos have been shattered . . . and will not be put together again."[89] And one of the internees from Sacramento, in reflecting on his experience in later years, came to similar conclusions, if in less eloquent language.

That's one good thing about human beings, after awhile, at least I, forget most of these bad feelings, recall only the funny and happy incidents. I used to have arguments with the authorities, but I seem to forget all those things. It's better, [otherwise you'll] have a miserable time living, so I always say there might have been something bad about relocation, legally speaking it was bad, this and that, but as a whole I think it did good to the Japanese people and Japanese community. It gave us a chance to disperse. Like I said, before the war we were in that little community all packed up as a unit, isolated, we were separate from the American community. After the war, we're right in there. That's one advantage.[90]

The Second World War thus had an extraordinary impact on minorities in the West. Although the experience of each was unique, although each had its own cultural context, yet the nature of the influences on them was remarkably similar. The war experience brought uprooting and dislocation—whether in military or civilian life. It also brought new economic opportunities, wider social contacts, and a heightened sense of ethnic and cultural identity. Viewed in perspective, World War II did much to hasten integration in the United States, acting as a catalyst to break down various barriers in the way of racial equality. This is not to say that the millennium was achieved in 1945. Obviously it was not. But in no other period of four years did such far-reaching changes take place in interracial relations. Naturally, the process of ethnic and racial accommodation created strains and set racial tensions into motion that accentuated conflicts. In the West these were not as bitter as in the Northeast and Middle West; there were no race riots as serious as those in New York's Harlem of 1942 or Detroit in 1943. But tensions there were, as newcomers to western war industries competed for jobs, scarce housing, and public services with white Americans from every section of the nation. Various positive influences emanating from the war also helped to break down discriminatory barriers. Most significant, perhaps, was the increasingly critical labor shortage which led war industries to a desperate search for willing hands, irrespective of age, or racial or ethnic background. As the propaganda campaign of the Office of War Information never tired of telling Americans, they were involved in a war to save democracy. Such an ideological commitment obviously did not mesh well with racial discrimination within the United States, and this was not lost on minorities, who, with a more developed consciousness, now intensified their striving for equal rights. Since most of those who moved westward settled in cities rather than rural areas, their sense of political and social identity was even further developed by concentration in urban centers. At the same time, President Roosevelt's action in establishing the Fair Employment Practices Committee in 1941 placed the power of the federal government behind their efforts to take advantage of new war-inspired job opportunities. These various influences coalesced during the war era to affect minorities in the West. Although the specific experiences of blacks, Spanish-speaking Americans, Indians, Japanese, and others varied, yet the ultimate impact of the war was similar for each.

CHAPTER NINE

Science in
the Wartime West

The vast influx of people in the West, which mirrored the extraordinary expansion of its wartime economy, provided an enormous impetus to the development of scientific activities in the region. The influence of the war on science in the West was profound and was to be felt for more than three decades after the conclusion of hostilities. The most visible effect was the extraordinary expansion of scientific activities west of the Mississippi River. Before 1941 the West occupied a distinctly secondary place in America's scientific establishment although institutions such as the California Institute of Technology and the University of California were rapidly gaining worldwide distinction. But the war wrought a notable transformation. Mobilization led to the establishment of new installations engaged in a wide range of scientific research. And, in turn, the new scientific facilites attracted significant numbers of distinguished scientists and technicians who now migrated westward. Between 1941 and 1945, these changes made the West one of the major science centers in the nation.

Since the large-scale infusion of federal funds was largely responsible for this flurry of intense activity, it was not surprising that a significant effect of war mobilization was to increase the dependence of western science on government. As the federal government had stimulated the western economy, as it had invigorated the growth of western cities, so too did it shape the direction of scientific activity in the region.

One of the federal government's principal instruments for expanding the scale of its scientific activities during the war years was the Office of Scientific Research and Development (OSRD). Created in 1941, it was ably directed by Vannevar Bush, formerly president of the Carnegie Institution for the Advancement of Science. Himself a distinguished scientist, Bush had wide contacts in the scientific community that enabled him to mobilize America's best scientific talents. The value of the contracts for scientific research awarded by the OSRD to universities west of the Mississippi River between 1941 and 1945 exceeded $99 million, more than the funds spent for scientific research in the West since its settlement. And that amount did not include the much larger sums Congress poured into the secret facilities at Los Alamos, New Mexico, and Hanford, Washington, which built the atomic bomb.[1] Nor does this accounting accurately portray the full extent of federal science activities in the West. Older agencies such as the U.S. Geological Survey and the Bureau of Standards, among others, were also instruments for the infusion of additional federal monies for scientific projects.

Of course, government support of science during World War II was not entirely without precedent. American involvement in the First World War had already touched the nation's scientists. Like most wars, that conflict skewed the nature of scientific research by bending the efforts of researchers toward weapons and other military needs. In recognizing the need for a central coordinating agency to supervise federal science programs President Woodrow Wilson on July 25, 1916, created the National Research Council whose task it was to coordinate government and private research agencies. Institutions like the Massachusetts Institute of Technology and the California Institute of Technology immediately expanded some of their research facilities. In this rather unobtrusive manner did government-sponsored research enter the universities. Some of those involved, such as the distinguished physicist Robert A. Millikan, were greatly impressed by the effectiveness of cooperative research on a large scale and in later years remembered the experience favorably.[2]

The World War I experiences were not entirely forgotten during the 1930s. President Roosevelt in 1933 appointed a Science Advisory Board under the jurisdiction of the National Academy of Sciences and the National Research Committee hoping that it might contribute to the solution of depression problems. But lack of funds and dissent among scientists led to its demise in 1935. At the time the National Resources Planning Board appointed a science committee to provide advice to federal agencies. Yet, when World War II broke out in Europe (1939), the United States still lacked a central science agency to coordinate various programs. Only as war clouds darkened in 1940 did Roosevelt create a National Defense Research Committee whose prime task was to recommend policies that bore directly on improved research to facilitate armaments.[3]

Somewhat more indirectly the war furthered the expansion of science in the West by bringing an extraordinarily gifted group of scientists to the region including some who were war refugees, political or religious exiles from Nazi Europe. The timing of their arrival was particularly significant. They came at a crucial juncture in the development of western science, at a time when it was ready for a big leap forward. The émigrés provided that special stimulus that transformed the quality of scientific research in the West. In four short years of war western science gained a distinction that gave it undisputed international renown, a renown which would have taken more than a generation to attain during peacetime.[4] To be sure, science had always been an international enterprise. Even between the wars small numbers of foreign scientists had found their way west of the Mississippi River. But between 1941 and 1945 the erstwhile trickle became a flood, to the everlasting benefit of western science.

The expansion of scientific research in many parts of the West during wartime was startling. Southern California became one of the nation's leading science complexes. The California Institute of Technology's Jet Propulsion Laboratory emerged as the nation's chief center for rocketry research under the deft guidance of rocket expert Charles C. Lauritzen. It served not only as a research facility, however, for during the war the Laboratory also manufactured thousands of rocket motors in Pasadena as well as tens of thousands of projectiles. Many of the scientists at the Institute, such as Nobel Laureate Linus Pauling, made fundamental contributions to other types of weaponry.[5] Nearby, in La Jolla, researchers at the Scripps Institute of Oceanography provided the armed services with fundamental information on ocean currents. The data they supplied not only helped in the development of new weapons but greatly aided the operations of U.S. naval vessels in the Pacific. To augment the work of the Scripps Institute, Frank Jewett, president of the National Academy of Sciences, helped to establish a new laboratory facility at Point Loma, in San Diego, operated by the University of California. That laboratory's prime objective was the improvement of submarine detection in the Pacific. Much of its work proved to be of a practical nature. But it contributed significantly also to the improvement of sonar devices and training men for underwater operations. During these years it did much, too, to increase basic knowledge of underwater reverberations and sound ranging conditions in the Pacific area.[6] Aviation medicine was stimulated in the West by the importance of the new aircraft manufacturing facilities there. At the University of Southern California in Los Angeles a group of scientists specialized in aviation medicine—of immediate relevance to the manufacture and testing of aircraft. Eager to conquer distances, westerners since the 1920s had consistently expressed a special interest in aviation.[7]

Other clusters of scientific research stimulated by the war were located in the San Fransisco Bay Area. The Radiation Laboratory at the University of California was gaining a reputation as a major center of nuclear research during the 1930s. On the eve of World War II when its director, Ernest O. Lawrence, received a Nobel Prize (1939) for his work in developing the cyclotron, it had become one of the world's major training facilities for nuclear physicists and technicians. As a contemporary science historian, Bernard Jaffe, noted at the time, "From Lawrence's laboratory streamed an army of young researchers who were put in charge of construction or maintenance of new cyclotrons built by other universities and . . . laboratories."[8] Although Stanford University was not a principal government contractor in World War II, it provided some able talent. The director of the Radio Research Laboratory at Harvard University, for example, which conducted extensive radar research, was Stanford's Professor F. E. Terman, who selected more Californians than easterners for his staff of 600. And Stanford physicist Felix Bloch, a future Nobel Laureate, found the restrictions of Los Alamos too confining and preferred to work at the Harvard facility during the war years.[9]

The Pacific Northwest region also witnessed the spawning of new scientific research. In Seattle federal contracts stimulated the establishment of highly sophisticated aeronautical research groups at the Boeing Corporation. The Applied Physics Laboratory at the University of Washington devoted itself to work on torpedoes. Meanwhile, the relatively cheap electric power available in the Pacific Northwest with the completion of Bonneville and Grand Coulee Dams was a major factor in the OSRD's decision to construct the world's largest plutonium production plant at Hanford, Washington. By 1944 that facility employed almost 20,000 persons in the fabrication of fissionable materials that were needed for the successful production of the atomic bomb.[10]

Increased federal support of science stimulated a quickened pace of scientific activity in the Southwest. In wartime the University of Texas was working on the development of airborne fire control testers while researchers at Rice Institute worked on special problems of nuclear chain reactions. At the University of New Mexico, a principal nonindustrial contractor of the OSRD during these years, researchers conducted extensive tests with V-1 rockets, also establishing new rocket proving grounds in the region. A major industrial contractor in the area, the Zia Corporation, created a vast new nuclear research and rocket experiment facility that was to play a major role in military research then and in postwar years (when it changed its name to Sandia Corporation, a subsidiary of Western Electric).[11] The Lovelace Clinic in Albuquerque specialized in aviation medicine. Of course, the most significant new science research facility in the Southwest was the new "science city" of Los Alamos, operated by the University of California, which produced the atomic bomb. During the war years it gathered a greater array of scientific talent in one location than had ever been gathered in any one place in the entire history of mankind.[12]

On a lesser scale the OSRD sponsored scores of new scientific projects throughout the West. The total impact of these varied activities was to bring distinction to science in the West. True, this was not a totally new departure. A contemporary scientist noted in 1944 that already in the 1930s "the center of gravity of scientific talent in the United States had definitely gravitated westwards."[13] But the war immeasurably hastened this development and accelerated it by at least one generation.

The war speeded further specialization in many spheres of science, and this increased complexity hastened the involvement of the federal government. Specialization and the pressures of the wartime emergency did much to foster the interdependence of many fields of science. Before 1941 research by individuals was still characteristic of most laboratories in Europe and the United States. But World War II fostered teamwork and large projects on a hitherto unprecedented scale, drawing the scientific community together in new interdependent relationships. That in turn fostered the need for expensive equipment and laboratories which only the federal government could provide. It was almost as if science in a technologically oriented society was assuming many of the characteristics of a public utility. Just as public works programs (such as road or railroad construction) in the West during the nineteenth century had been too vast for private enterprise to undertake unaided—leading to demands for government support—so by 1941 scientific projects were similarly engendering demands for public assistance.

Nevertheless, in 1939 many American scientists still had reservations about close government involvement with science. One of the most eminent was Vannevar Bush, president of the Carnegie Institution, who feared that the intrusion of immediate problems would divert scientists from long-range basic research.[14] Even so, he was aware that American scientists really had few options other than to collaborate with government once war broke out in Europe.

Still, some scientists in the West continued to be concerned about their relationship to the national defense program. In a long letter to Bush, Professor George H. Hildebrand of the Chemistry Department at the University of California expressed his fears that scientists would abandon basic research in favor of hastily contrived and impractical military projects. "My experiences during the World War in the Chemical Warfare Service," wrote Hildebrand, have "given me some familiarity . . . with the problem of coordinating scientific effort with military problems. . . . We should encourage members of the faculty . . . to stay on the job rather than to rush impulsively into some governmental . . . activity." In urging continued adherence to the basic research function of universities, Hildebrand wrote, he was expressing views shared by other leading scientists at the University of California such as Alsberg, G. N. Lewis, B. M. Woods, and H. B. Walker, with whom he had met to discuss his fears.[15]

By 1941, the OSRD was becoming more directly involved with the sponsorship of scientific projects throughout the nation, Bush gave increasing attention to locating new projects in the West. The reasons for such consideration were varied. Some of his concerns, however, were similar to those that determined the selection of the site ultimately chosen for the atomic laboratory in Los Alamos, which was typical of defense facilities in the West. Certainly one major consideration that swayed its planners was its inaccessibility, which provided the project with a high degree of secrecy. On the other hand, some access to transportation by rail or road was essential. Also needed was proximity to services, whether shopping areas or medical care. Decentralization of scientific research operations was another conscious objective to wartime planners in Washington, fearful as they were of possible enemy air attacks or sabotage. In addition, many of the scientific projects required extensive open spaces to allow for the testing of machinery or weapons. In general, federal officials preferred to establish new installations on government-owned lands, since this was not only less costly but did not necessitate long and often involved negotiations for the purchase of private properties. More than any other region in the nation, the American West provided favorable conditions for new scientific laboratories.[16] In 1941 the West still contained many isolated areas; its geographical extent spanned half a continent, with extensive inland regions; it still harbored vast open spaces that were unpopulated; and almost all of the public lands still under federal ownership were located in the West. The region thus offered a logical arena for the expansion of American science.

In addition, Bush was aware of the increasing stature of science in the West. That growing eminence was illustrated by the pioneering work of the Radiation Laboratory at the University of California. Since 1928 when the physicist Ernest O. Lawrence had arrived in Berkeley, that institution had been establishing itself as the nation's pioneer in high energy research. As Lawrence later recalled, the idea for the cyclotron came to him shortly after his arrival in Berkeley with a fresh Ph.D. from Yale:

When I came to California in 1928, it seemed to me that the most promising field on the horizon was nuclear physics. Accordingly, I gave considerable thought to ways and means of attacking the nucleus, and of course first of all I considered the general problem of accelerating ions. . . .

In those days I spent a good deal of time reading the current literature, and one evening about this time, eleven years ago, I was sitting in the main Library looking over some German electrical engineering journals and came upon an article by R. Wideroe on the acceleration of potassium ions. Reading German with some difficulty, I contented myself with looking at diagrams of the apparatus and immediately realized his [Wideroe's] method. . . . I immediately thought to myself, "Why, of course this is the way to overcome the problem of high voltages in accelerating atomic projectiles." Then and there I thought about various ways and means of extending the idea. . . . I wrote down the necessary equations . . . I suppose within an hour or two of reading Wideroe's paper I had come upon the principle of the cyclotron.[17]

By 1938 when Enrico Fermi's atomic discoveries in Rome won him the Nobel Prize, the Radiation Laboratory at Berkeley was already engaged in parallel lines of research. Lawrence recalled in 1945 that his laboratory was then attempting to explore the so-called transuranic elements. In particular, staff physicist Philip Abelson set himself the task of identifying the elements discovered by Fermi. Lawrence noted:

At that time, there was a complete muddle of understanding all the various radioactive products resulting from the bombardment of Uranium with neutrons; there was great difficulty in interpreting them in terms of transuranic elements and successive decay products. . . .

There is no doubt had this great discovery . . . of fission by [Lise] Hahn and [Adolph] Strassman (1938) been delayed a few weeks Abelson would have made it himself.

The circumstances as I recall them are interesting. Abelson had been detecting x-radiation with his little spectrometer for several weeks and was having difficulty in reconciling the observed wave lengths with those expected on the basis of what was thought to be the transuranic atomic of the products under observation. . . . But Luis Alvarez was one morning sitting in the barber chair in Stephens Union having a haircut and reading the [San Francisco] *Chronicle* when he came across the news item announcing the discovery of fission . . . and he bounced right out of his chair (he almost got wounded by the barber's razor) and went right over to tell Phil Abelson. From then on there was intense activity in our Laboratory, as elsewhere, on the multitudinous aspects of fission phenomena.[18]

As director of the Radiation Laboratory, established by the University in 1936, Lawrence built the nation's first cyclotron, and attracted some of the best young scientists in the United States, including J. Robert Oppenheimer, Glenn Seaborg, Emilio Segrè, Edwin McMillan, Joseph W. Kennedy, Philip H. Abelson, and Arthur L. Wahl.[19] The experiences of Lawrence at his Radiation Laboratory between 1940 and 1941 well illustrated the gradual shift from private to government support of science during these years. By 1945 the federal government was intimately involved with most science projects in the region as it had not been before. Lawrence was not only a brilliant theoretician and researcher, but he was also adept in securing funds for his enterprise. It was noteworthy that before 1940 he was able to pursue his impressive breakthroughs without federal financial aid. His prime source of support was President Robert G. Sproul of the University of California who provided him with modest but adequate budgets and wholeheartedly supported his plans to build larger cyclotrons.[20] In addition, Lawrence was effective in soliciting grants from private foundations of which the Carnegie Institution and the Rockefeller Foundation were important. In the process of dealing with private foundations he made personal contacts which stood him in good stead once greater federal financial aid became available after 1940. The network of individuals who moved from private foundations to government agencies and back constituted a veritable government-foundation complex which controlled most available funds for scientific research from private and public sources. Lawrence knew them well.

Early in the defense effort the Carnegie Institution was one important source of outside funds for Lawrence. Its president, Vannevar Bush, who was to direct the federal Office of Scientific Research and Development during World War II, was a distinguished scientist—and Lawrence's good friend. Lawrence maintained a running correspondence with him and kept him closely informed of his activities. In 1939 Bush and the Carnegie Institution were providing significant supplementary funds to Lawrence to enable him to build a larger cyclotron. In a typical informal report on his work, Lawrence wrote Bush on June 8, 1939:

I am dropping you this note to say that last night we observed for the first time a beam of 15 million volt deuterons emerging into the air from the window of the 60 inch cyclotron. Although there are yet, of course, some wrinkles to be ironed out, we are very gratified at the way the new outfit is performing.

And then he added rather coyly: "I am sure now the only difficulty in the way of going on to a hundred million volts is the financial one."[21] His relations with the Rockefeller Foundation were also good. "The work has been moving along splendidly," he wrote to Director Warren Weaver in 1939, "almost better than we might have hoped. Significant advances in cyclotron technique have been made." During the summer of 1939 Lawrence was already envisioning the building of increasingly larger cyclotrons. "We know that now we are over the top and it won't be long before we will be having deuterons and alpha particles of very high energy," he wrote to Weaver in April 1939. "You can well imagine the excitement around here."[22] That September he wrote to Weaver again, noting that "I am coming east for the National Academy meeting at Providence next month to give a paper describing the sixty-inch cyclotron and discuss the feasibility of building a larger one for the region above 100,000,000 volts. . . . The only practical difficulty is the financial one."[23] Although the University of California was strongly supportive of Lawrence's researches, it could not provide all of the capital funds that he needed for his ever more expensive equipment. Thus, the need for outside sources of funding became more pressing than ever. "President Sproul is wholeheartedly behind me in wanting to go ahead as soon as possible with the 100,000,000 volt cyclotron project," Lawrence wrote Weaver in October 1939. . . . He apparently foresees no difficulty in financing an operating budget for the great cyclotron once the laboratory is established."[24] Weaver and the Rockefeller Foundation were impressed, and willing to grant very substantial sums to Lawrence. "To put it mildly," wrote Lawrence to Weaver, "It was thrilling to hear that the Foundation has a 'lively' interest in the plans for the great cyclotron." When in late 1939 Lawrence received the Nobel Prize for physics, the prospects for the grant appeared even greater and Weaver gave him unqualified encouragement. "You can imagine my feelings," wrote Lawrence to him, "what with the Nobel Prize two weeks ago and then your letter Monday morning. It is almost too much to happen and maintain one's balance."[25] During the spring of 1940 he submitted increasingly detailed plans to the Foundation. Finally, on April 3, 1940, Weaver called Lawrence to tell him that the Trustees had voted him $1,400,000 for the new cyclotron. "It's hard to tell you how I feel," Lawrence told him over the telephone. "This is the most wonderful thing that ever happened."[26]

But the increasing complexity of research in physics, and the need for more costly equipment, led Lawrence gradually to look to financial help from the federal government. Some of the activity of the cyclotron was directly related to the increasing volume of scientific research dealing with atomic fission. Europeans were particularly aware of its value a year or two before most American scientists. As R. H. Fowler of the British Purchasing Commission wrote to Lawrence in January 1941, enclosing a letter from the eminent British physicist, John D. Cockroft, "The questions raised by Cockroft which more immediately interest you are clearly in the 93-94 field, and obviously Cockroft's mouth is watering at the thought of the strength of the source of 94 which you ought to be able to produce for experiment." And Cockroft himself wrote that "it would seem, therefore, that the uranium investigation deserves more vigorous attack in North America than it is now receiving."[27] Lawrence himself felt that greater federal aid was necessary if sagging nuclear research in the United States was to be stimulated. He hoped to give greater impetus to the American program by underscoring recent British experiences. In his own recollection of events, recorded in 1945, he wrote:

> I obtained some very powerful ammunition from Oliphant [an eminent British physicist] who visited the Laboratory for a day or two in the fall of 1941. . . . Oliphant dropped by to see me and told me that although he was not a member of the Maud Committee in England, he knew that the uranium matter was being taken seriously in England, and that on the other hand in this country where the work really should, and indeed only could, be done on a sufficiently large scale the Briggs Committee was not functioning properly.

And Lawrence continued:

> I told Oliphant that . . . the fact that the British were going ahead on this enormously larger scale than we were undertaking at the present time in this country, was just the ammunition that I needed to persuade our people to expand the program. I therefore asked him to prepare for me a short statement on the subject which I could show to certain people.[28]

Within a few weeks Lawrence approached the leading American scientists who had access to federal funds. "I took the statement with me to Chicago," Lawrence remembered, "where I was the guest of the University for several days in connection with their anniversary celebration, and showed it to Arthur Compton and enlisted his aid in stirring up action. Also, Conant was at the Chicago celebration, and Conant, Compton, and I got together one evening in Compton's house after a meeting, and I showed him Oliphant's statement and talked the whole matter over with him. I think it was this meeting that got the ball rolling."

Lawrence firmly believed that his action invigorated the Manhattan Project. "At that time also, . . . I suggested to Compton that perhaps the best way to get action would be for him to go down to Washington and show this statement of Oliphant's to Vice President Wallace and see if he couldn't stir something up. This Compton did; I believe he went down on the train the next day and had a talk with him. I know that Bush was very much annoyed that Compton had done this, and some day I will have to confess to him that I was the rascal that put Compton up to that trick. I am sure now that Bush would agree that it was the right thing to do, that it was important somehow to get the uranium program going full steam ahead."[29]

The increasing awareness of American scientists about the importance of fission research was heightened in the spring of 1941. Then Vannevar Bush asked Frank Jewett, president of the National Academy of Sciences, to appoint an advisory committee under the chairmanship of Lyman Briggs, an American physicist, to consider the possible military aspects of atomic fission. Lawrence was appointed a member of the group.[30] Within two months the National Defense Research Committee offered a contract to the University of California for the production of unnamed elements with the cyclotron. The Regents accepted with alacrity. Lawrence reported to Briggs that summer that "the uranium work [is] going forward very satisfactorily. A long cyclotron bombardment extending over several weeks has just been completed. . . . The result is of greatest importance in connection with the possibility of an explosive chain reaction."[31]

Later that fall Lawrence felt the world situation to be so serious that he advocated exclusive concentration on nuclear research. "It seems to me so clear now," he wrote to A. H. Compton, "that in the light of recent developments everything must be done to expedite the uranium program. . . . There is a substantial prospect that the chain reaction will be achieved in the near future, one way or another, and that military applications of transcendental importance may follow. It will not be a calamity if, when we get the answers to the uranium problem, they turn out negative from the military point of view, but if the answers are fantastically positive and we fail to get them first, the results for our country may well be a tragic disaster."[32] Consequently, by December 1941, the OSRD entered into a contract for $300,000 with the University of California for investigations of isotopes and uranium elements. "I am delighted that you are going full-speed on this work, and we all have hopes that your line of approach proves to be very promising," wrote James B. Conant to Lawrence.[33] The great cyclotron at Berkeley now went to war. And almost imperceptibly, rather casually, the Radiation Laboratory acquired a new patron. Who could realize at the time that federal support of science would create new precedents that would extend into the next four decades? For the war veritably transformed the nature of scientific research and its funding.

The efforts of American scientists like Lawrence to secure government support for science were greatly reinforced by a significant group of European refugees who had come to the United States in the wake of Nazi and Fascist persecution. To some extent, the West in 1939 was still less stratified and more hospitable to new ideas and new cultural values than the older East. As the wave of émigré scientists reached the United States after 1933, it brought a bevy of talent to the West. Enrico Fermi, James Franck, Victor Hess, Otto Loewi, Albert Szent-Gyorgi, and Fritz Lipman were among them. This select group also included some of the world's most brilliant younger scientists, such as Wolfgang Pauli, Victor Weisskopf, Emilio Segrè, Leo Szilard, and Hans Bethe.[34] These refugees did much more than to alter the nature—and the level—of scientific inquiry in the West. They also significantly affected the political orientation of American science by seeking out government patronage. Their particular cultural background and their political orientation were to affect the condition of Western science at the outset of the war, just when American scientists were debating the advantages and dangers of federal support of science. Europeans had long been accustomed to government as a patron of science and their attitude differed appreciably from that of their American colleagues. As Henry Smyth wrote in his official report on the atomic bomb in August of 1945: "American-born nuclear physicists were so unaccustomed to the idea of using their science for military purposes that they hardly realized what needed to be done. Consequently, the early efforts for both restricting publication and getting government support were stimulated largely by a small group of foreign-born scientists. . . ."[35] This was evident as early as 1939 in the early stages of planning research on nuclear fission. When President Roosevelt appointed an Advisory Committee on Uranium, he named several Europeans to it in view of their expertise—among them Fermi, Szilard, Teller, and E. P. Wigner, and they strongly urged federal support of a fission research program; the Americans on the committee found the concept alien and preferred to leave the project directly in the hands of the nation's universities.[36]

Apart from providing an impetus for increased government support of science, the émigrés made their most immediate contribution in the field of atomic physics. Of the scores of refugees who contributed to the manufacture of the atomic bomb in wartime, at least five were Nobel Laureates or Laureates-to-be, including the Italian Enrico Fermi, who was associate director of the Los Alamos Laboratory, his collaborator Emilio Segrè, the Swiss Felix Bloch, and the Hungarians Eugene Wigner and Hans Bethe. As Laura Fermi (Enrico Fermi's wife) later recalled, broken English was not at all unusual on the streets of Los Alamos during wartime. The galaxy of talent there was unprecedented, including also the brilliant young Hungarian Edward Teller (later known as Father of the H-Bomb), the encyclopedic Leo Szilard, the erudite Victor Weisskopf, and the imaginative Bruno Rossi. Some of the essential mathematical calculations for the Manhattan Project were provided by the Polish mathematician Stanley Ulam. For special problems at the Los Alamos Laboratory, Director J. Robert Oppenheimer at times called in the Hungarian mathematician John von Neumann, one of the authentic geniuses of the twentieth century, who was also credited with the invention of computers. Of the seven division heads at Los Alamos—in addition to Fermi, the associate director—three were Europeans. Although the Europeans constituted only a minority of the scientists working at Los Alamos, they played a significant role in the inauguration, development, and ultimate completion of the Manhattan Project.[37]

American physicists generally welcomed their European colleagues, particularly in the West. There the reception was unusually warm because they were viewed not necessarily as competitors but as welcome colleagues in their effort to attain international distinction. Enrico Fermi provides a good example. When the news first leaked out early in 1939 that he was resettling in the United States, Provost Monroe E. Deutsch of the University of California asked Ernest O. Lawrence to sound him out about coming to Berkeley for one semester for $3,500 to occupy a Chair of Italian culture. Lawrence quickly wrote Fermi, noting that "the uranium business is certainly exciting." Fermi declined the offer, citing his very recent association with Columbia University which he felt he could not leave so soon after his arrival.[38] Nevertheless, Lawrence secured the services of Fermi's close associate, Emilio Segrè. Segrè first came as a temporary visitor, but Lawrence secured immigrant status for him after Segrè was dismissed from his professorship at the University of Palermo because of Mussolini's anti-Jewish laws. Still, in 1940 Lawrence was not sure whether he would have the funds to keep Segrè in the future. Thus, when an official of a Tulsa, Oklahoma, well drilling company wrote to Lawrence asking him to recommend an émigré who was competent in radioactive research, Lawrence suggested Segrè. Fortunately for the

nuclear research program in World War II—and the ensuing years—
Lawrence did find sufficient funds to keep Segrè as a key member of
the team at the Radiation Laboratory in Berkeley.[39]

The influence of the European émigrés extended beyond physics,
however, to embrace a wide range of scientific activities in the West.
They greatly enriched the field of mathematics in the region, provid-
ing burgeoning western universities with international renown. Jerzy
Neyman and Alexander Tarski at the University of California, Stefan
Bergman and George Polya at Stanford, and Willi Birnbaum at the
University of Washington provided increased distinction for mathematics in the West. Astronomy in the region was enriched as well.
Although the Palomar Observatory was already well known by 1940,
it gained even greater stature when world famous figures like Walter
Baade and Rudolph Minkowsky joined its staff. In Tucson, Bart Bok
did much to develop the Stewart Observatory.[40] At the California
Institute of Technology Max Delbrueck, an erstwhile German physicist turned biologist and geneticist, made that institution the world's
most exciting center for genetics research, and stimulated the new
fields of biophysics, biochemistry, and phage inquiries.[41] Distinguished social scientists such as the psychologist Erik Erikson found
employment at the University of California Medical School, while
Theodore Adorno, a psychologist and sociologist affiliated with
UCLA, coauthored the classic study on *The Authoritarian Personality*
while in Los Angeles during the World War II decade. The refugees
also developed the abstract, highly specialized philosophy of science
as a field in the West. During the World War II years internationally
renowned scholars like Austrian positivist Hans Reichenbach came to
UCLA, while Heinrich Gompertz introduced the subject at the University of Southern California.[42]

If the Europeans did much to enrich science in the West, in theory
as well as in practical applications, the interchange was not one-sided.
American science was on the verge of attaining distinction in 1929
when the Great Depression struck, impeding its progress. The timing
of the European migration was significant, for it came just at a stage
when American scientists were ready for another notable "forward
leap." Many of the Europeans recognized that the United States now
afforded them opportunities which were not available in Europe—
even under the best conditions. They marveled at the funds available
for research, at the scale of projects, at the close cooperative teamwork, and at the extensive laboratories and scientific installations
available for testing theories. This was especially true of the West,
which, younger and more underdeveloped than the East, seemed
particularly hospitable to newcomers and their intellectual baggage.
Thus, the melding of European and American science resulted in a

happy marriage of convenience. And in the West, it provided scientific work with a distinction in less than a decade that would have taken more than a generation in less troubled times.

One of the most significant contributions of the émigrés to science in the West was in the field of psychoanalysis. Already during the 1920s Freudian ideas had enjoyed popularity and notoriety in the United States. By the 1930s American psychiatrists were ready to adopt Freud's theories and were developing closer professional contacts with European and American psychoanalysts.[43] But the war greatly accelerated the integration of European and American psychiatry, and perhaps hastened it by at least one generation. The special strains induced by wartime conditions and the induction of millions of individuals into the armed forces gave a new emphasis to mental health in America as never before. This emphasis was reflected in the appointment of one of the West's most prominent psychiatrists, William C. Menninger, as director of psychiatry in the Office of the Surgeon-General of the United States. In 1941 Menninger supervised 240 psychiatrists in the U.S. Army; by 1945 he had augmented that number to 4,200.[44]

The European émigrés thus came at a crucial time in the development of American psychiatry, for the profession was depleted because many of the best practitioners were serving with the armed services. Moreover, American psychiatrists in wartime were eagerly seeking new ideas and techniques in order to cope with the rapidly extending range of problems with which they were now confronted. One leading psychiatrist of the time, Clarence P. Oberndorf, felt that Americans were long on practice but short on theory, more adept in accumulating clinical experience than in theoretical formulation. This view was challenged by Dr. Douglas W. Orr, an eminent practitioner of the period, who believed that the contribution of the émigrés was not so much in theory as in their dynamic teaching and in their charismatic influence in founding new training facilities.[45] Both of these interpretations, however, emphasized the crucial role of the Europeans in melding their Continental experience with American culture. And much of that melding occurred in the West. Karl Menninger, one of the deans of the profession, summarized the process well when he wrote:

America has been the beneficiary of Europe's tragedies. . . . In a hundred years of development the medical schools and universities had not evolved a single systematic course of training in psychiatry. . . . [It was] not until after the psychoanalytic institutes had shown the way . . . that courses of instruction were developed. It was out of fire and ashes, out of self-destructive rage and sorrow and heartbreak that our

powers of helping our stricken fellow man have thus been extended. . . . Psychoanalysts changed psychiatry from a diagnostic to a
therapeutic science.[46]

Like most westward movements, that of the psychoanalysts also
started in the East. One of the first training centers for psychoanalysis
was established in Chicago in 1932 by Dr. Franz Alexander, a former
student of Sigmund Freud who had founded the Berlin Institute
eleven years earlier. Alexander was a charismatic figure and attracted
a galaxy of talent to the Chicago Institute, among them two talented
physicians, William and Karl Menninger, whose father had founded
the famed Menninger Clinic in Topeka, Kansas, in 1919. The sons
were particularly interested in developing its mental health services.[47]
During the twenties they had traveled to Vienna and Berlin, then the
major centers of psychoanalysis, and acquainted themselves with new
trends and with some of the leading Freudians and practitioners in
the field. After taking further training with Alexander in Berlin, the
Menningers returned to Topeka and there, in 1938, under the supervision of Alexander's Chicago Institute, they founded the first
psychoanalytic training institute west of the Mississippi River—the
Topeka Institute—modeled on those in Vienna and Berlin.[48]

The Topeka Institute was of crucial importance to the development of psychoanalysis in the West in two ways. It played a key
role in facilitating the immigration of European analysts after 1938,
and it gave those already in the country an affiliation. Its founding
coincided with Adolf Hitler's annexation of Austria in 1938, which
led to a mass exodus of Viennese psychoanalysts, many of them Jewish. Freud himself fled to England; scores of others sought asylum in
the United States and elsewhere. One estimate noted that one-half of
Europe's psychoanalysts moved to the United States between 1933
and 1938. The Menningers sponsored dozens of these émigrés, issu-
ing affidavits to allow them entry into the country and offering them
employment either at the clinic or at the institute. So many Europeans
came to Topeka for short or extended stays that the Topeka airfield
became known as the "International Psychoanalytic Airport of the
World."[49]

Many of the prominent analysts who came to join the staff or to
serve as consultants—men and women like Ernst Lewy, Bernard
Kamm, Bernhard Berliner, Fritz Moellenhoff, Ernst Simmel, Otto
Fenichel, and Siegfried Bernfeld—provided an enormous stimulus to
the practice and teaching of psychoanalysis there and, within the
decade, throughout the West. Most émigrés adapted successfully in
relatively short order to life in Topeka, but occasionally difficulties did
crop up. Some, like Ernst Lewy, who was at the Topeka Institute from

1938 to 1944, found the weather oppressive. "We don't seem to be able to improve our adjustment to this climate here," he wrote to his friend Ernst Simmel in California in the summer of 1943. "This is another reason why I should be only too happy to settle down in California sooner or later, rather sooner, if possible."[50] Equally oppressive at times must have been Karl Menninger's concern that the newcomers conform to the customs of their adopted homeland. For example, he attempted (in vain) to get Lewy to abandon his homburg hat on the grounds that it made him look too European,[51] and once "shouted" at Otto Fenichel, who was visiting Topeka, for eating chicken with a knife and fork instead of using his fingers in the American way.[52]

The American Psychiatric Association made special efforts to aid the refugees in adjusting to the United States, and encouraged their move westward. In a special bulletin for immigrants, in 1938, the Association noted that "in the selection of a home in this country, it is important to bear in mind that . . . [in] large communities the field has already become overcrowded. Therefore, the newcomers must be prepared to go to other communities where there is a growing demand for well trained psychoanalysts."[53] And Karl Menninger wrote his friend Ernest Jones that "our larger centers are well supplied with trained analysts and students in training. . . . On the other hand, there are many large cities . . . where there are literally no psychoanalysts. We must hope, therefore, to place our colleagues from Vienna in such cities as these."[54] So from the beachhead at Topeka, the European psychoanalysts began a rapid westward movement.

Psychoanalysis in California had had a slow growth, hampered by the lack of accredited training institutes with which its practitioners could affiliate. By 1930 several lay analysts had settled in Los Angeles, of whom David Brunswick, Margrit Munk, and Marjorie Leonard were most active. They were joined in 1934 by Dr. Ernst Simmel, who had been one of the founders of the Berlin Psychoanalytic Institute. A dynamic organizer, Simmel in the following year founded the first psychoanalytic study group in California. His presence attracted other prominent analysts, including Europeans like Otto Fenichel and Joachim and Irene Haenel as well as Americans such as Charles Tidd and May Romm. When the Topeka Institute, with its large cadre of German and Austrian refugees, was founded in 1938, it authorized some members of the Los Angeles group—notably Simmel, Fenichel, and Tidd—to undertake the training of new analysts in the West under its supervision. (According to prevailing rules of the profession, only an accredited society such as Topeka was authorized to train analysts. The Los Angeles group thus could not function as a self-sufficient facility, but only as an arm of the Topeka Society).[55]

But between 1938 and 1942 the distance between Topeka and Los Angeles created problems. Both the Menningers in Kansas and the Californians were concerned about better communications and favored greater independence for the Pacific Coast group. As Dr. Robert P. Knight, President of the Topeka Society, noted in January 1941: "It becomes more apparent to us here that the best eventual solution will be for you to form a society of your own in California. It is becoming increasingly impractical to direct or supervise psychoanalytic activities in California from this distance." In addition, a major problem became the inclusion of lay analysts—those who were not medical doctors, and who were not recognized under laws of California and other western states. Thus they could function only as psychoanalysts, not as medical practitioners. That issue was particularly pertinent in California because some of the most eminent members of the San Francisco group—such as Siegfried Bernfeld—were not medical doctors.[56] On August 23, 1941, Knight journeyed to Los Angeles and presided over the first meeting of what later became the San Francisco Psychoanalytic Institute. Controversy over whether psychoanalysts should also be medical doctors held up formal establishment of the group for another year. But in 1942 six analysts from San Francisco, two from Los Angeles, one from Seattle, and one from Tucson joined together as the charter sponsors for the new institute. One-half of the founders were Europeans. With a preponderance of San Franciscans, the training school adopted the name of San Francisco Psychoanalytic Institute.

In California three of the émigrés had a particularly important influence in spreading psychoanalytical training although their eminence was closely matched by others. Certainly Ernst Simmel was a major figure. Born in Breslau in 1882, he early became interested in Freud's ideas. A born organizer and administrator, he was in 1920 one of the prime founders of the Berlin Institute. Seven years later he established a therapeutic sanitorium in Berlin-Schloss Tegel, which pioneered new techniques for treatment of the mentally ill. Freud visited it on various occasions and was enthusiastic about its potentials. Another visitor was William Menninger, who was profoundly impressed by what he saw. On his return to the United States he applied Simmel's methods at the Menninger Clinic.[57] Meanwhile, as a Jew and as a socialist, Simmel incurred the wrath of the Nazis in 1933, and fled from Germany. On the recommendation of Franz Alexander in 1934 a group of therapists in Los Angeles invited him to join them there. Soon he organized a formal psychoanalytical study group in Los Angeles and spread psychoanalytical understanding to people in the fields of education, criminology, and social work. A dynamic teacher, he also began publishing numerous papers, on theory, on clinical experience, war neuroses, sanitorium treatment, organic illnesses, and treatment of drug addiction and alcoholism. Much of the success of the Los Angeles group was due to Simmel's great tact and managerial skills. Conscious of the large number of refugees in the western group, he was careful to secure approval from the parent organization—the Topeka Society—for most of his activities. For example, in expressing his desire to appoint a training committee composed of himself, Otto Fenichel, Emanuel Windholz, and William Barrett, he inquired cautiously: "Is there any objection against three psychoanalysts being of European descend [*sic*]?" Whereupon Robert Knight, President of the Topeka Society, noted that "it would be difficult to find in California enough analysts not of European descent to make up a committee of any kind." As a matter of fact, Karl Menninger hoped to lure Simmel to Topeka, but without success. Simmel's aim, above all, was to improve the quality of life. A many-sided man, he died of heart failure in 1947.[58]

Otto Fenichel was another of the major figures among the European psychoanalysts who came west. Trained in Berlin in 1933, he fled to Norway, moved to Prague in 1935, and finally came to Los Angeles in 1938. There he became important in the training of new analysts and became a moving force in the organization of the California institute. Fenichel's influence came not only from his commanding presence as a teacher. In 1934 he had published *The Outline of Clinical Psychoanalysis,* the first textbook in the field, which was widely used in the ensuing decade and influenced an entire generation of analysts.[59]

Among the founding fathers of psychoanalysis in the West Siegfried Bernfeld also ranked high. Considered by Freud as one of his most brilliant students, the Vienna-born Bernfeld was the moving spirit in founding the Institute in San Francisco, and in attracting other brilliant young émigré psychologists like Erik Erikson, then at the University of California in San Francisco. A particularly dynamic teacher, Bernfeld profoundly influenced the young Americans whom he introduced to psychoanalysis training on a high level. Although quite European in his manner and bearing, Bernfeld blended well with his new cultural environment on the Pacific Coast because his major interests centered on the treatment of children and on educational concepts and methods. His influence thus was not narrow or highly specialized but reached out into a variety of fields which benefited from the practical application of Freudian insights and theories.[60]

The extraordinary success of the San Francisco group rapidly led to the founding of other similar institutes in the West. Under William Menninger's prodding the Los Angeles Psychoanalytic Institute was organized in 1946. Within a few years it was larger than its parent in

San Francisco. It also spawned a dissident group which also included eminent émigrés, most notably Dr. Martin Grotjan, who in 1950 organized the competing Psychoanalytic Institute of Southern California.[61]

In 1941 Dr. Douglas W. Orr was completing his psychoanalytic training at the Menninger Clinic when Dr. Leon Saul, a Chicago analyst, urged him to consider Seattle as a good location for a new private practice since that city lacked a certified practitioner. Saul noted that several social agencies there and the University of Washington's Graduate School of Social Work were eagerly seeking the services of a psychoanalyst. Orr moved to Seattle in July 1941 but within a year joined the U.S. Navy and did not return until January 1946. At that time Seattle still lacked training facilities for psychoanalysis, but in August of that year Orr lured Edith Buxbaum to his newly formed Northwest Institute.[62] Buxbaum was a highly reputable training analyst for children at the New York Institute. Born in Vienna in 1902 and educated at the university there, she had also attended some of Freud's famous Wednesday evening meetings, and had received formal training from Anna Freud. "When I visited the Northwest Clinic," she recalled in later years, "they asked me to stay for lunch . . . and incidentally asked me whether I wanted to stay there. . . . I couldn't imagine that such a place, located in such a beautiful country with the great outdoors, would have a need for psychoanalysis . . . I saw Seattle as a frontier town." But after some reflection, and a job offer in social work for her husband, she decided to come. During the next thirty years she became a major figure in the development of psychoanalysis and psychoanalytic training in the Pacific Northwest, and also exerted great influence in child psychology and the development of mental health programs for juveniles.[63] The Northwest Institute received full accreditation from San Francisco in 1950. During the 1950s additional institutes were created throughout the West. Topeka sponsored an institute in Oklahoma City, while Chicago accredited a facility in Denver.[64]

Some of the Europeans tended to be authoritarian. With considerable force they set rigid standards for the training of new analysts and for determining the minimum number of analytic sessions. Their penchant for organization, their capacity to inspire students, and of course their own training directly at the hands of Freud or one of his disciples gave them a measure of authority enjoyed by few others in the field. Thus, they soon exerted a significant influence in American professional organizations. And American-born followers of Freud—who before 1940 often had felt isolated and outnumbered in the field of psychiatry—extended an enthusiastic welcome to the émigrés as new and supportive allies.[65]

By exerting their influence through such professional groups the émigrés contributed to bringing psychoanalytic theories into the mainstream of American medical practices as well as education and social work. When the Austrian analyst Kate Friedlaender—who lived in England—visited the United States in 1947, what impressed her most was postwar America's sudden realization of the importance of psychoanalysis.[66] That was due to the work of William Menninger and his large psychiatric staff in the armed forces whose work touched millions of Americans. But it was certainly also due in part to the persistent work of the émigrés. And as one of them, Rudolf Ekstein, noted, they had far greater influence in the United States than they ever would have had in Europe because of a far more receptive environment.[67] Within a decade after their coming they had begun to affect many aspects of life in the West. Their theories were reflected in the establishment of new counseling services, in greater emphasis on criminal rehabilitation programs, the establishment of new techniques of mental health treatment, and the expansion of drug treatment and alcoholism facilities. In certain fields, such as psychosomatic medicine, they took the lead. Stimulated by Franz Alexander, a pioneer in this area, and promoted by Karl Menninger and Robert P. Knight of Topeka, the practical applications of psychosomatic medicine found much wider acceptance in the West between 1945 and 1955 than in the East, where the Psychoanalytic Institutes in Boston and New York were centers of traditionalism and orthodoxy. In fact, Alexander himself moved west in 1956, joined the staffs of the University of Southern California and Mt. Sinai Hospital, and made Los Angeles a pioneering center of psychosomatic medical studies.[68]

The most visible contribution of the émigrés was in the establishment of the new psychoanalytic training institutes throughout the West in less than a generation.[69] These training centers by the end of World War II provided a firm foundation for a vast network of mental health care facilities that developed in succeeding decades and that added another dimension to the rapidly expanding science establishment in the region which was a direct consequence of wartime research.

The federal government, of course, had played a major role in bringing that science establishment into being, and in 1945 many scientists hoped to continue the close wartime relationships. That was bound to result in the greater politicization of scientists in the United States, and also increased sectional rivalry between East and West over federal largesse. Nor were scientists at the end of World War II united on the specific administrative methods which could be used to extend federal aid. Some, like Frank Jewett, president of the National Academy of Sciences and director of the Bell Telephone Laboratories, viewed the Office of Scientific Research and Development merely as a temporary wartime expedient. Jewett favored only indirect government support of science through tax laws; he believed science should primarily be in the hands of private individuals and corporations. Vannevar Bush, director of the OSRD, also felt that his agency should be abolished at war's end, but that large scale federal aid to university scientists for pure research should be continued in peacetime. Other scientists had become more enamored of the new patron, however, and hoped to institutionalize the wartime partnership.[70]

The issue was crystalized in November 1944 when President Roosevelt expressed his own preferences in a famous letter to Vannevar Bush. "The OSRD represents a unique experiment of teamwork and cooperation in conducting scientific knowledge to the solution of the technical problems paramount in war," the President wrote. "There is no reason why the lessons to be found in the experiment cannot be profitably employed in times of peace."[71]

Bush's reply did not come until after President Roosevelt's death. In a well-known report entitled *Science, the Endless Frontier,* he recommended a plan for government support of science to President Harry Truman. Apparently aware of Roosevelt's oft-stated belief that with the supposed absence of a frontier in twentieth-century America—particularly in the 1930s—the United States had reached the limits of its growth, Bush extended this view further, noting, "It has been basic United States policy that Government should foster the openings of new frontiers. It opened the seas to clipper ships and furnished land for pioneers. Although these frontiers have more or less disappeared, the frontier of science remains. It is in keeping with the American tradition—one which has made the United States great—that new frontiers shall be made accessible for development by all American citizens."[72]

Of the many questions involved in the creation of a federal science agency to succeed the OSRD in peacetime the geographical distribution of federal monies loomed large. That was certainly in the mind of Senator Harley Kilgore (W. Va.) who in 1945 sponsored a bill to create a National Science Foundation with a strong director. As early as 1942 he had begun to sponsor such legislation while stating his belief that eastern universities and scientists had dominated the allocation of federal funds for science during the war.[73] In fact, during the war Otto Stuhlman, a physics professor at the University of North Carolina, had written to Kilgore to complain that fewer than one-half of his colleagues in southern universities were engaged in wartime research—in stark contrast to eastern institutions. By 1945, therefore, Kilgore was convinced that unless some formula for the distribution of federal funds by state was included, the proposed National Science

Foundation would grant the bulk of its monies to scientists in the East—and perhaps a few selected universities on the Pacific Coast.[74]

This fear was echoed by western scientists as well, and reflected in a stimulating article in *Science* in 1948 by Clarence Mills of the Laboratory for Experimental Medicine in Cincinnati. In analyzing the distribution of medical research grants, for example, Mills found that although the Northeast contained only 30 percent of the nation's population, it received approximately 50 to 80 percent of all research funds. Private foundations invariably granted a major portion of their funds to researchers in the Northeast. That was not too surprising since the members of the various selection committees who chose grantees were overwhelmingly from universities in that region. One example was the Committee on Growth of the National Research Council, which before July 1, 1946, had ten of its twelve members holding positions in northeastern universities. After July 1, 1946— when this committee was enlarged—sixteen of nineteen members were affiliated with northeastern universities. As a matter of fact, a small cadre of universities who had members on the committee also garnered the largest share of funds. Representatives of Harvard, Johns Hopkins, Yale, and Columbia awarded their own institutions 29 percent of the total distribution funds available. More than one-half of all research allocations went to universities who had representatives on the selection committee.[75] Clearly, northeastern universities represented a "science establishment" concentrated in the East which was dedicated to preserving its own dominant position.

From this and similar evidence Mills drew some obvious conclusions:

> The time has arrived when the West should take off the stunting dominance of the northeastern seaboard in scientific matters, insisting on autonomy and a just share of public funds for its scientific development. So long as the rich eastern institutions secure the major part of funds disbursed, western institutions will perforce remain relatively pauperized and their most promising young scientists drift eastward. . . .[76]

And to remedy this imbalance, Mills suggested that the greatest good for the greatest number might best be served by distributing federal research funds on a state-population basis. To assure fairness, he recommended the establishment of mechanisms to distribute grants at the state level—ultimately to reach every institution within its borders.

Kilgore's views were opposed by Vannevar Bush and many of his supporters in the East who believed that excellence should be supported wherever it might be. In practice, however, Bush proposed that research facilities that were already strong should be strengthened further—and most of these were located in the East. Such a policy would hardly allow newer institutions and scientists to receive a significant share of federal funds for science. Bush's idea was to have a National Science Foundation with a weak director, but with a strong advisory committee composed of the leading scientists—primarily located in eastern institutions—who would make allocations of federal research funds. This proposal was included in legislation sponsored in 1945 by Warren Magnuson (Wash.) in the Senate.[77]

A concern over eastern domination of the proposed peacetime federal science agency was also strong in the Southwest. Commenting on the various proposals in Congress Chauncey D. Leake, vice-president of the University of Texas, wrote to Senator Kilgore to express his concern that if scientists in the East secured control of a National Science Foundation, they would impose their particular brand of scientific orthodoxy on other parts of the nation. Reflecting the fears of many western scientists, he argued that the "non-establishment" scholars were not well represented on the boards of scientific associations and foundations. The relatively small number of easterners in entrenched positions of power could easily find places on the proposed advisory committee of the National Science Foundation where they could dictate the direction of scientific inquiry in many fields. The proposed advisory board, he wrote, would "omit consideration of an important factor in scientific work. This is assurance of maintaining under any form of Government subsidy for scientific work that freedom for scientists which is requisite for the success of any scientific venture. . . ." Fearful of the possible development of scientific orthodoxy, he recommended that federal control of scientific programs "be placed in professionally chosen groups which would have the widest possible geographic representation, and in which membership would be staggered so that representation would be regularly changed." Going a step further, he urged that no one be selected to serve on a control committee who would at the same time be on the board of a national scientific society or on the board of a national scientific journal.[78]

Leake's recommendations were perhaps too far-reaching, but the western concern did make itself felt in Congress and in ensuing science legislation. When Congress finally enacted the National Science Foundation Act in 1950, it provided for a strong director—chosen by the President—who would work closely with an advisory committee, and with scientific consultants chosen from every part of the nation. Although the eastern institutions still played a major role in determining allocations, nevertheless the function of a strong national director served to check possible inclinations to undue favoritism to any particular section or group of scientists in a given locality or field.[79]

World War II did much to generate the expansion of scientific research and related activities in the West. Indeed, the West made greater strides in developing scientific institutions and in accumulating scientific talent between 1939 and 1945 than at any previous time in its history. The accomplishments included the expansion or creation of new centers of scientific inquiry, such as the Lawrence Radiation Laboratory at Berkeley and the Jet Propulsion Laboratory at Pasadena. Although the majority of federal research contracts were still concentrated in eastern institutions, western universities and research laboratories received a much larger share than before the war. If the University of California and California Institute of Technology were preeminent in western science during the war, state universities in other parts of the West were beginning to receive at least a share of federal science contracts. In addition to expanding scientific research at western universities, the war crisis led to the award of large federal contracts to new research laboratories operated by private corporations such as the Albuquerque and Livermore research centers operated by the Western Electric Company for research in nuclear science. The exigencies of the war also led the federal government to establish a third type of science facility, namely the "science cities." These were complex communities such as Los Alamos and Hanford, which were exclusively created to undertake one or another major federal science project. Since the West contained remote areas and areas with sparse population even at the beginning of the Second World War, it offered special attractions to policymakers such as those on the National Defense Research Council and the OSRD. And the creation of these new facilities hastened the westward trek of scientists that had already begun a decade earlier in peacetime. This migration of scientific talent in itself proved to be a magnet that accelerated the quantity and quality of scientific research west of the Mississippi River. And wartime pressures resulted in large scale federal patronage of science particularly important in a relatively young and still to be developed region like the West.

At the end of World War II the American West was a bustling beehive containing a wide range of important scientific research activities. The range and quality of such research presented a startling contrast to the prewar years. The war had wrought a remarkable transformation of science in the West, with significant implications for the region in succeeding decades.

CHAPTER TEN

Cultural Life in the West: Hollywood in Wartime

The growing eminence of the West in science during World War II was only one reflection of the increased cultural growth of the region in these years. World War II did much to accelerate the development of cultural life in the West. This was particularly true on the Pacific Coast, but its effects were hardly less significant in the western cities of the interior. That history of cultural development still remains to be written. But a selective overview of cultural developments in Hollywood during wartime can provide an awareness of just how profound the widespread influence of wartime activities was in transforming the cultural tone of the region. Western cities which had a somewhat underdeveloped and isolated cultural milieu before the Second World War emerged as increasingly sophisticated cosmopolitan centers. Hollywood may not have been the model for other western cities, but its transformation provides an index to the nature of war-induced cultural changes in the West during wartime.

Among the manifold changes spawned by the global conflict, two were preeminent. As propaganda became a crucial weapon in the ideological struggle with totalitarianism in which the United States was engaged, manipulation of the mass media—and particularly motion pictures—became essential to the war effort. And, *ipso facto,* since the most skilled manipulators of mass or popular culture were already concentrated in Hollywood, that western film center assumed a new role in wartime. Imperceptibly, therefore, the eastern cultural establishment, which long had been wont to sneer at cultural activities in the West, found itself dependent on the center of motion picture activity in the West. Hollywood thus assumed a new national importance. Its prominence had cultural reverberations throughout the West during the war and in the years thereafter.

The war also had another—and unforeseen—impact on Hollywood's cultural life, both then and in the next generation. Southern California became a cultural center for about 10,000 political and religious refugees from Hitler's Europe, who made a profound cultural contribution to the West and the nation. Some worked in the movie industry; others were active in science, literature, the theater, music, art, psychiatry, and other fields. Constituting the cream of European intelligentsia, they brought an intellectual maturity and sophistication to cultural life in the West that it had previously lacked. Rarely had any such small group of western settlers had such far-reaching influence in so many different fields of cultural life as the European refugees who gathered in southern California during wartime.

Like no other event, World War II accentuated the importance of Hollywood as an influence on public opinion in the United States and throughout the world. Between the wars the work of sociologists and psychologists had done much to heighten the public's general awareness of propaganda and its spread by the mass media.[1] Already by 1939 the skillful direction of the Nazi propaganda machine under Joseph Goebbels in Germany had aroused President Franklin D. Roosevelt's advisers who urged him to develop an American propaganda effort which would sustain morale at home while spreading war aims abroad.[2] More than ever, the portrayal of American values and American life styles assumed a major importance. The mass media occupied a central place in this effort. In the battle for men's minds Hollywood now acquired a prominent place. As the Hollywood film producer Walter Wanger said, "The American film is our most important weapon as no country has developed its film industry to compete with ours. The problem of enlightenment of the masses is a major problem and admittedly the film is the greatest visual educational factor accepted by the masses."[3]

The importance of Hollywood as a propaganda tool was recognized by politicians, and particularly by both isolationists and interventionists who were vying for public attention by 1940. Isolationists were eager to extend some control over Hollywood to bend it to their cause while interventionists were just as eager to use American films for their purposes. Their struggle riveted attention on Hollywood and underscored its role as the center of popular culture in America. This courting of Hollywood by the nation's politicians reflected the extraordinary cultural growth of the West. Just two decades earlier an eastern literary critic had written: "There are little gems of Eden along the eastern coast . . . along the western coast [and] . . . for thousands of miles of grey [*sic*] sagebrush and sand, through ghastly white reaches of salt one hears only . . . the barren desert."[4] But by

1940 the eyes of the nation were riveted on America's cultural out-post. How Americans perceived themselves in this war era, and how they visualized their own participation, was to a large extent deter-mined by the impressions they gained from films made in Hollywood.

With the outbreak of war in Europe during 1939 some of the producers in Hollywood began to make films depicting wartime sub-jects. Although most Hollywood pictures between 1939 and 1942 were bland entertainment, a few sought to bring the vividness of the European war to Americans. Pictures such as *Escape* dealt with the story of an American who escaped from Nazi Germany and witnessed German brutality; *Convoy* realistically depicted the submarine war in the North Atlantic endured by British convoys; *Flight Command* fea-tured heroism by the Royal Air Force; *I Married a Nazi* attempted to reveal totalitarian ideology; *The Great Dictator* was Charlie Chaplin's effort to ridicule Adolf Hitler; and *Sergeant York* was the story of an American World War I military hero. These were not expressly propaganda pictures, but they did tend to portray the viciousness of Nazi Germany and the determination and heroism of the British.[5]

Yet even these subdued motion pictures aroused the ire of leading isolationists in the United States, men like U.S. Senators Gerald P. Nye, Burton K. Wheeler, and Charles W. Tobey. Passionately devoted to non-intervention of the United States in the European war, they charged that Hollywood film makers were manipulating public opin-ion so as to brainwash Americans to favor American involvement on the side of the British. In launching an attack on the movie industry Senator Wheeler succeeded in creating a special subcommittee of the Senate Military Affairs Committee in September 1941 to investigate Hollywood. The resolution establishing the committee (largely writ-ten by John T. Flynn, a rabid anti-New Dealer) clearly reflected the prejudices of its sponsors, Senators Gerald P. Nye and Bennett Champ Clark. It noted that "motion pictures and radio are the most potent instruments of communication of ideas," and therefore re-quired investigation since they were being used "to influence public sentiment in the direction of participation by the United States in the present European war."[6]

The subsequent investigation was less of a genuine inquiry than an effort to use the hearings as a platform for isolationist views, to lam-bast interventionists, and to try to extend government control over film making. In many ways, they heralded the hearings held by Senator Joseph P. McCarthy on alleged Communist influences in gov-ernment a decade later. It is doubtful if the investigation had much practical effect except to reflect an increasing recognition by politi-cians of the growing significance of propaganda and image making in American domestic as well as foreign policies. As a contemporary newspaper noted, the inquiry was "a barefaced attempt at censorship and racial persecution."[7]

Senator Nye—one of the best known isolationists of his day—was particularly disturbed by what he considered to be the interventionist tone of Hollywood films. He went so far as to equate "the foreign policy of Hollywood" with the foreign policy of the United States. Bitterly he lashed out at contemporary motion picture trade journals which were openly hostile to this Congressional attempt to muzzle the movie industry or to force it to adopt an isolationist stance.[8] On August 1, 1941, he made a widely publicized radio address in St. Louis under the auspices of the America First Committee, a group dedicated to isolation, in which he accused foreigners and Jews of dominating the movie industry and seeking to bring the nation into war contrary to the national interest, and said that motion picture companies had "become the most gigantic engines of propaganda in existence to arouse the war fever in America and plunge this Nation to her destruction." Although he denied anti-Semitic sentiments, he went out of his way to suggest Jewish domination of Hollywood. "There is Harry and Jack Cohn [Columbia Pictures]," he shouted, "there is Louis B. Mayer [of MGM] . . . the three Warner Brothers, Arthur Loew, Nicholas Katz, and David Bernstein." No non-Jews were mentioned. In addition, he attributed the alleged pro-war sympathies of Hollywood films to foreign refugees whom he charged with dominating American film making.[9]

To a degree, the hostility of isolationists to the movie industry was fueled by their belief that it represented a monopoly controlled by the major studios. Such fears had been reinforced by a recent (1941) study published by the Temporary National Economic Committee, which purported to provide evidence that eight major studios effectively controlled the industry. The Justice Department had begun an antitrust suit against these Big 8 in 1938 and had filed supplemental complaints in 1940.[10] The anti-monopoly sentiment was also fueled by the fear, expressed by Jimmy Fidler, a Hollywood gossip columnist, that the big movie studios were withholding advertising from newspapers like the *Los Angeles Times* to suppress isolationist viewpoints.[11]

Some of Hollywood's leading producers fought back hard to stave off the censorship sought by the isolationists. As a measure of the importance which they attached to this attack on freedom of the screen they hired Wendell Willkie as their legal counsel before the committee. Willkie, the recently defeated 1940 Republican presidential candidate, represented producers like Nicholas Schenck (Loews), Harry Warner (Warner Brothers), and Darryl Zanuck (Twentieth Century-Fox) in rebutting the charges made against them.[12] California's Senator Sheridan Downey also rushed to the defense of one of his state's leading industries. "The world is on fire," he said, "and because a few pale shadows of its conflagration flicker for a moment or two on the screen which is Hollywood, you seek to throw cold water on California. You pursue an illusion. The blaze is in Europe and Asia, not in my state. . . . The potent propaganda is not movies about Hitler; it is Hitler himself."[13] The battle for control of Hollywood was on.

If the isolationists failed to bend the movie industry to their will, the interventionists were more successful. They too hoped to control the mass media, in order to project their liberal New Deal views to the nation and the world in wartime. Movie makers themselves were quite conscious of their increasingly important role. "In the present crisis," noted the famous director Ernst Lubitsch in May of 1942, "the leaders of the motion picture industry have to take into consideration not only what the public wants to see . . . but also what an audience should see."[14] President Roosevelt himself believed that motion pictures were an effective medium for information and entertainment, particularly since about 80 million Americans went to the movies each week, in addition to about 100 million people overseas. To coordinate the various propaganda activities of the federal government the President created the Office of War Information on June 13, 1942, with a special division for motion pictures.[15]

The New Dealers lost little time in seeking to shape the content of Hollywood's film products. Until Pearl Harbor the movie industry had continued to produce bland entertainment films which rarely had a propaganda value—whether they were westerns, romances, musicals, or mysteries. But the men in the Office of War Information, men like Leo Rosten, Archibald MacLeish, or Lowell Mellet, hoped to change all that by persuading the industry to produce films that reflected New Deal liberalism and democratic values. To their chagrin, of 213 war oriented films in production during the summer of 1942, fewer than 50 dealt directly with America's enemies. And fewer still touched on major themes OWI officials considered important—democracy, the home front, the United Nations.[16]

Thus, leading officials in the OWI now stipulated guidelines for film making which Hollywood producers were to follow. Nelson Poynter, an erstwhile journalist now with the OWI, and his staff prepared a manual to guide movie makers in their work. They viewed the war as a people's war for democracy, a war against fascism. This was not a class war, they declared, nor a race war, nor a national conflict. This was a war to create a brave new world. An Allied victory would bring the peoples of the world jobs, better health and housing, and social insurance. It would benefit minorities, and also women, around the world.[17] Here was a New Deal platform extended to reach out to free societies everywhere.

From the issuance of guidelines in the summer of 1942 the OWI moved further toward review of movie scripts to ascertain whether Hollywood movie producers were making "proper" pictures. Before the end of 1942 some studios were submitting scripts to Nelson Poynter, head of the Bureau of Motion Pictures, for his approval. He insisted, for example, that MGM revise its portrayal of President Andrew Johnson in *Tennessee Johnson*, to meet protests by Walter White of the National Association for the Advancement of Colored People; at Poynter's insistence Paramount included explicit speeches about democracy in *So Proudly We Hail*, a story of the siege of Bataan in World War II; and RKO toned down depiction of bloody violence in *Corregidor*. Movie producers were considerably disturbed by this growing censorship.[18] Nevertheless, most films made in Hollywood during 1943 embodied the OWI's suggestions. They included explicit discussion of war themes, avoided blatant stereotypes of the enemy, and provided affirmation of democratic values. After all, noted the *Motion Picture Herald* on August 14, 1943, no one would produce a picture "known in advance to be doomed to domestic exhibition exclusively."[19] By late 1943 the OWI was reading most of the scripts being considered by the major studios and subtly and not so subtly influencing the content of motion pictures produced by Hollywood.

Not only did the OWI manipulate the content of Hollywood films, but it acted as a negative critic. In its weekly analysis of motion pictures for February 26, 1943, for example, Poynter was distressed by *Tarzan Triumphs*, in which Johnny Weissmuller cleared the jungle of Nazi infiltrators while Cheetah the Chimp babbled into a shortwave radio, leading the Germans to believe that they were listening to Adolf Hitler. Such simplistic portrayals bothered Herbert Brucker, a Columbia University journalism professor who headed the OWI's Media Division. He also disliked *Andy Hardy's Double Life* because it dealt with middle class American life at home and made few references to the sacrifices demanded by the war. A western like *Dead Man's Gulch* incurred the wrath of OWI censors who feared that foreigners might consider Americans to be lawless people.[20] In short, the OWI hoped to focus American films on ideological themes, particularly the struggle for democracy and freedom.

The political struggle to control Hollywood's film production reflected its increasingly important role in national affairs. A remote village on the Pacific Coast at the opening of the twentieth century, Hollywood in World War II occupied a central place in America's propaganda arsenal. In a sense this was a reflection of the growing importance of the West in national life. The American West—considered a cultural desert by many easterners before 1940—was irrepressibly forcing itself on the national consciousness as a distinctive cultural region in its own right.

Hollywood also played a significant role in the production of training films for the armed forces. Together with the Chief Signal Officer of the Army's Pictorial Division, the studios made 439 such pictures. During the war the army maintained a branch office in Hollywood to supervise production of these ventures.[21] Many of the army officers involved had graduated from a regular training course which the major Hollywood studios had been offering during the preceding decade. Since there were not enough of these trained individuals in wartime, however, the Army offered commissions to about a hundred Hollywood personalities to make these films. One of the best known was Darryl Zanuck, chairman of the board at Twentieth Century-Fox, who was commissioned as a lieutenant-colonel for the specific purpose of making films to depict Allied combat forces in Alaska and North Africa. He also served as principal advisor on motion pictures to the Chief Signal Officer. Others who received commissions included Frank Capra, Robert Lord, Hal Roach, and Harold Loeb, as well as dozens of directors, camera men, lab cutters, and other specialists.[22]

These appointments aroused controversy and charges of favoritism. The criticisms were so persistent that Senator Harry S. Truman, chairman of the Senate Committee to Investigate the Defense Program, undertook an investigation. Truman charged that the major studios were utilizing wartime conditions to further their control over the industry. Colonel K. B. Lawton—in 1943 Chief of the Army Pictorial Division—admitted that he had approached the industry's Research Council to solicit nominations for specialists to be commissioned. These nominations made their way through the various echelons in the War Department hierarchy and eventually secured approval.[23]

The Truman Committee also criticized the production of training films by the major studios. More than two-thirds of the films were awarded to four major studios, who made them on a non-profit basis. As Colonel Lawton explained, he had had unfortunate experiences with smaller companies and only thereafter turned to the Big Four (MGM, Paramount, Twentieth Century-Fox, RKO). Nevertheless, as a result of the Truman Committee's recommendations the War Department in 1943 reorganized its motion picture contracts policy. Instead of negotiating with the Research Council of the Academy of Motion Picture Arts and Sciences—representing the larger studios—after 1943 it negotiated directly with individual producers, thus providing greater flexibility for the smaller companies.[24]

The war matured Hollywood and led it to produce motion pictures with a greater degree of realism in the postwar decade. This influence stemming from the war was perceived by some of the industry's leaders at the time. Darryl Zanuck said frankly that "we have radiated sweetness and light since the advent of pictures . . . [because]

the profit motive in the final analysis has determined our course. . . . We have carefully refrained for the most part, from even remote contact with the grim and pressing realities before us in the world." But with the challenges brought by the war, he said, "it is up to us to help focus and channelize thoughts . . . [with] substance and reality." And his perception that the impact of the war was to infuse realism into Hollywood movie making was reinforced by Thomas Chapman, Assistant Story Head at Warner Brothers, who said that "we have been thrown . . . into . . . the waters of the real world. Audiences will no longer stomach shoddy unreal stories. . . . They want to see genuine people in honest situations.[25]

That realism was beginning to extend to the portrayal of minorities, particularly blacks, even if the pace was glacial. Dalton Trumbo called attention to the film colony's practices. Trumbo was one of the most prominent screenwriters in wartime Hollywood with credits such as *Thirty Seconds Over Tokyo*. He became a public figure in 1950 when Senator Joseph McCarthy castigated him as a Communist; he was subsequently blacklisted by the industry. In 1943 Trumbo decried Hollywood's stereotyping of black people. "Our current crop of motion pictures [1943] . . . reveals many of the vicious old lies . . ." he said. " 'Two Tickets to London' presents us with a Negro murderer. 'Tales of Manhattan' contains caricatures of the most objectionable sort, which were greeted by Negro picket lines. 'Holiday Inn' was typically insulting mammy and pickaninny bilgewater while 'This Is the Army' Jim-Crowed Negro servicemen into a number with a zoot suit background." But, he continued, "There are . . . hopeful signs to report. 'Bataan' contained an excellent Negro character while in the picture 'In This Our Life' we discovered a Negro law student who represented a complete departure from the stereotype. . . . 'Stage Door Canteen' delivered a blow for democracy in a sequence showing the decoration for bravery of a Negro soldier. But one looks in vain for dramatic material which presents such Negro types as Brigadier General Benjamin O. Davis, Sr., or Captain Hugh Mulzar, skipper of the Liberty Ship 'Booker T. Washington.' Not a single picture . . . deals with Negroes in the war effort." And criticizing the studio policies, he said that "We also shy from Negro writers. . . . Only Langston Hughes and Clarence Muse have been employed as screen writers. Richard Wright . . . has heard no studio clamoring at his door [nor] Saunders Redding, Roi Ottley, Marg Walker, Countee Cullen, Claude McKay. . . ."[26]

This concern with black stereotypes was well articulated by William Grant Still, one of the best-known black composers of the period. Still was employed as a composer by various studios but became increasingly disillusioned by his experience. "When one discusses the Negro 'stereotype' one speaks of something that colored people have

been fighting for many years," he said. "Very often Negroes are engaged to work on music for Negro films and their opinions are then
discarded in favor of what other people think it ought to be. A recent
experience of my own is significant. Employed as a supervisor of
music on an all-Negro film I found that every suggestion I made was
disregarded, everything I did was thrown out with the statement that
it was 'too good'. . . . There is something so fundamentally Negroid
about genuine Negro music . . . that no white man can imitate it."
Pleading for the abandonment of stereotypes he said: "There are
many different kinds of Negro music as there are different types of
colored people. . . . The present war should wrest two major conces-
sions from Hollywood: an open mind with regard to minority groups
and their art forms, and the will to make a positive contribution to
interracial understanding."[27] Still's hopes were to be realized more
fully in succeeding decades.

The war had a profound influence on Hollywood, transforming it
from a somewhat isolated and insulated producer of bland entertainment into the free world's movie capital, charged with a major role in
the Allied war effort. That transformation was already becoming apparent early in the war when a contemporary observer in Hollywood
noted that "Hitler . . . drove hundreds of Continental players, directors, writers, and artisans into exile. Hollywood was their palm
fringed Siberia. Gradually the expatriates were absorbed, and inevitably, their topics of conversation, their convictions. Thus, the film
colony's splendid isolation was, in a sense, Trojan-horsed."[28] The lessening of provincialism in Hollywood was symptomatic of much of
the West during wartime. However, the influence of European refugees who hastened this transformation was not restricted to the motion picture industry but had a similar effect on most other spheres of
western culture.

Indeed, the increasing importance of Hollywood as an emerging
cultural center in the West was one important reason why an increasing flow of European exiles from Hitler's tyranny terminated their
trek in that city. And their coming constituted perhaps the most
significant cultural migration to the West since the region was first
settled. Within a decade after their arrival, they left a profound imprint on cultural life in the West and endowed it with a breadth and
sophistication that it had previously lacked. Between their arrival in
the 1930s and 1969 the refugees garnered twenty-four Nobel Prizes
for the United States! As the cultural historian Peter Gay has noted, in
seeking to place this exodus in historical perspective:

> The exile holds an honored place in the history of Western civiliza-
> tion. Dante and Grotius, Bayle and Rousseau, Heine and Marx did
> their greatest work in enforced residence on alien soil, looking back

with loathing and longing to the country, their own, that had rejected them. The Greek scholars from Byzantium who flooded the Italian city-states early in the fifteenth century and the Huguenot bourgeois who streamed out of France across Western Europe late in the seventeenth century brought with them energy, learning, and scarce, welcome skills; New England was founded by refugees who transformed a savage wilderness into blooming civilization. But these migrations, impressive as they are, cannot compare with the exodus set in motion early in 1933, when the Nazis seized control of Germany; the exiles Hitler made were the greatest collection of transplanted intellect, talent, and scholarship the world has ever seen.[29]

In diverse fields, ranging from literature to art and architecture, from music to psychiatry, to the varied phases of the motion picture industry, to natural science and social science and the humanities, the European émigrés made substantial contributions in the Western communities where they settled. Their story deserves to be told.

Although the majority of the approximately 80,000 refugees who fled from Hitler's Europe to the United States between 1933 and 1941 settled east of the Mississippi River, a contingent of 10,000 to 15,000 traveled westward, establishing an important center in southern California. That region's urban aspect and its pleasant Mediterranean climate were one source of attraction for intellectuals drawn from the capitals of Europe. But of course the job opportunities which Hollywood offered to actors, writers, musicians, artists, and a wide range of other specialties made the southland a magnet as well. Moreover, as a wealthy community with a unique social structure, Hollywood also provided a fertile field for physicians and psychiatrists.[30] While some refugee intellectuals could be found in most western towns and cities, the Los Angeles area came to be their major hub.

In Los Angeles the émigrés conducted an active social life among themselves that centered on European-style salons. One of these crystalized around Thomas Mann, a world-famous novelist and Nobel Prize laureate who opened up his comfortable Pacific Palisades home to the leading literati of the West. Mann, as fellow émigré Ludwig Marcuse commented, played emperor to the émigrés of Southern California. "Everything was expected from him, everything was owed to him, and he was responsible for everything," wrote Marcuse, not entirely without envy.[31] The well-known German novelist, Lion Feuchtwanger, conducted another prominent salon in his pleasant home nearby. Artists and sculptors tended to gather at the apartment of Reinhardt A. Braun, an émigré journalist, who also established a meeting place for displaced European intellectuals. The salons provided havens for the émigrés from which they eventually entered into the mainstream of western American culture.

In Hollywood there were also a number of wealthy individuals who were willing to lend the refugees a helping hand. When Hitler's crushing defeat of France in May of 1940 brought another large wave of displaced persons to the United States, they appealed for help to the film community. The famous German director Ernst Lubitsch had been in Hollywood since 1930 and in 1940 decided to organize motion picture personalities in an aid campaign. Called the European Relief Fund, it was supported by pledges from dozens of Hollywood personalities who agreed to donate 1 percent of their salaries. The fund was to provide temporary maintenance for newly arrived refugees and also to furnish them with sponsors who were necessary to allow them admission on national immigration quotas. In addition, Lubitsch secured the services of Fred Kohner, at the time one of the best-known agents in Hollywood, who had close connections to many of the motion picture industry's leading moguls, to obtain promises of a year of employment for a few well known writers. For example, Kohner approached Jack Warner, Louis Mayer of MGM, and Harry Cohn (Columbia) and secured their sponsorship of Bertolt Brecht, Heinrich Mann, and Alfred Doeblin. After they arrived these highly individualistic writers found that they could not stomach their 9 to 5 schedule in a stable of writers ensconced in small cubicles on movie studio lots. But others adapted—men like Billy Wilder, Walter Reich, Robert Thoeren, Frederick Kohner, and George Froeschel—and within a few years became some of the most prominent film writers in Hollywood. As a group they contributed to raising standards of the American film and attracted a wide array of talent that would not have migrated westward without their presence.[32]

Many of the European writers who came and made Los Angeles a new literary center had well-established reputations. Preeminent among them was Thomas Mann, already famous throughout the world for best-selling novels like *Buddenbrooks* and *The Magic Mountain*. Austere and Germanic in his bearing—a staunch Protestant whose love of freedom led him to oppose Hitler's tyranny—Mann adjusted well to southern California. In fact, his daughter felt that he was inspired by the atmosphere.

> Let me only hint at my belief that the odd elegance of that distant shore, with its almost intangible beauty . . . had a great influence on him and his work. It drove him from his own traditions to stylistic daring and gave him the courage for . . . linguistic experiments.[33]

Mann himself noted with enthusiasm that "I was enchanted by the light, by the special fragrance of the air, by the blue of the sky, the sun, the exhilarating ocean breeze, the spruceness and cleanness of this Southland . . . all these paradisical scenes and colors enraptured me."[34] Reflecting on the condition of writers in exile like himself, he mused: "It is our destiny to carry on this battle against our own land and its cause of whose corruptness we are convinced. What an abnormal, morbid condition . . . for the writer, the bearer of spiritual tradition, when his own country becomes the most hostile, the most sinister foreign land! It is [a] question whether we intend to take up again our former life in our fatherland after its liberation. . . . If I ask myself I must say: No. The idea of returning to Germany . . . is far from me. I am now on the point of becoming an American citizen just as my grandchildren who were born here, and are growing up here, and my attachment to this country has already progressed so far that it would be contrary to my sense of gratitude to part from it again."[35] Accustomed to taking a daily afternoon walk with his poodle, he was an incongruous sight—fastidiously dressed in suit and tie, stepping smartly under the warm blue California sky—where most people were casually dressed in sports clothes and rarely walked when they could ride in cars.[36]

On many an evening a galaxy of literary talent gathered in the hospitable atmosphere of Mann's home. Among those present was Erich Maria Remarque, author of *All Quiet on the Western Front,* perhaps the most famous novel to emerge from the First World War. A great success in Europe as well as the United States, the book was transformed into a memorable motion picture in 1930 featuring Erich von Stroheim who a decade later also resided in Hollywood. The film won many prizes and became one of the all-time classics of the cinema. Another prominent member of the émigré writers' circle was Franz Werfel. Already well known in Europe whence he fled on foot, Werfel wrote the best-selling novel *The Song of Bernadette* in 1942, which Hollywood also turned into a successful movie.[37]

Among the big names of the literati was Lion Feuchtwanger, a novelist and short story writer with a worldwide reputation. His house in Pacific Palisades was another of the gathering places where the refugees could discuss their work, after which, one participant recalled, Frau Marta (Mrs. Feuchtwanger) would serve "Italian salad and homemade Apfel Strudel with whipped cream" to enliven the spirits of her guests, and to recreate a "gemuetlichkeit" which, many of them knew, they had left behind. Feuchtwanger presumed to speak for many of his fellow writers and sought to acquaint Americans with their plight when he noted that:

> The author who had lost the reading public of his own land frequently loses at the same time the core of his economic existence. Very many writers of the highest talent, whose products were in great demand in their own countries, find no markets in foreign lands, either

because their chief merit lies in the stylistic qualities of their language, and these qualities cannot be translated, or because their choice of subjects does not interest the foreign reader. . . . It is surprising how many authors whose accomplishments the entire world has acclaimed in spite of their most earnest efforts now stand helpless and without means. . . . It is no great inconvenience to be forced to live in a hotel room and to be constantly subject to bureaucratic regulations. But not every writer is capable of composing a comprehensive novel in a hotel room; it tears them down double when he does not know whether he will be able to pay his hotel bill tomorrow [or] when his children beg for food.

But Feuchtwanger saw the constructive inducements as well. "For although banishment is destructive," he said, "and makes the victim small and miserable, it also hardens him and adds to his stature. A vast abundance of new materials and new ideas pours in upon him, he is confronted with a variety of impressions he never would have known at home." And he concluded on an upbeat note. "If we make an effort to take a historical view of our life in exile, it becomes evident even now that almost everything that seemed to hamper our work finally contributed to its welfare."[38]

One of the saddest figures was Heinrich Mann, brother of Thomas, who had been as famous as his brother in Europe, but who remained totally unknown in the United States. After a year of unsuccessfully trying out as a script writer in Hollywood, he retreated bitterly into his own world.[39]

In addition to the older writers with established reputations the refugee exodus also brought a younger group who were to gain prominence in the postwar era, many of them adapted to the teamwork required by the major Hollywood studios of their writers. At the same time they also managed to turn out works of their own. Among those who made a successful transition were Leonhard Frank, Joseph Wechsberg, Alfred Polgar, and Raoul Auernheimer. They wrote about their California experience for European audiences and did much to broaden California's image as a cultural center in the intellectual world of Europe.[40] Some also wrote for American readers. Alfred Neuman's *Look Upon This Man* received critical acclaim when it appeared in 1950 as did Victoria Wolf's *Fabulous City* in 1957. Vicki Baum, the well-known author of *Grand Hotel*, became even better known in the United States than in Europe and enjoyed much success with another novel, *Mustard Seed*, in 1953. Her prominence was in part due to a World War II film, *Hotel Berlin*, a Peter Godfrey production, that was directly based on *Grand Hotel*. And that book most probably inspired another best seller, Katherine Anne Porter's *Ship of*

Fools (1964), another offshoot of Vicki Baum's influence, for Katherine Porter had a special sympathy for the émigré writers in southern California.[41]

Not all writers could breach language and cultural barriers, however, and remained obscure. That was true of Alfred Doeblin, author of one of the most successful novels of the Weimar years, *Berlin, Alexanderplatz*. Although he worked as a script writer for MGM for one year, he could never really write in English. He subsisted on charity and a stipend from the European Film Fund. After the war he returned to Europe. His friend, Bruno Frank, also remained unknown outside the émigré circle of southern California.[42] Among the alienated was Bertolt Brecht, who, while living in Hollywood between 1941 and 1947, viewed his experience as justifying his condemnation of capitalism and the United States. Although he was one of the best-paid émigré screen writers of the era, he grew to hate his work. One of his screenplays was Fritz Lang's famous World War II movie, *Hangmen Also Die*, the story of the brutal Nazi Gauleiter of Czechoslovakia who was killed by Czech partisans after mass murders of Czechs by German occupation forces. Brecht deeply resented the changes which the studio made in his work, and later success as a screenwriter hardly mollified him. A performance of his *Galileo* with the help of the famous actor Charles Laughton was not well received. And one of his most famous plays, *The Caucasian Chalk Circle*, which he wrote during these years, did not receive the acclaim with which it was showered in later years.[43]

To say that it was the European émigré writers alone who made Los Angeles a major literary center might be an exaggeration. Already during the 1930s Hollywood had begun to attract a group of distinguished American and English writers: F. Scott Fitzgerald, William Faulkner, Ernest Hemingway, Clifford Odets, Robert Sherwood, and S. J. Perelman, and from England, Aldous Huxley, Christopher Isherwood, Evelyn Waugh, and Somerset Maugham. In a few short years the exiles added an international flavor to Hollywood, making it a literary center with quite a large number of the world's leading writers.[44]

It was rather symbolic, therefore, that in 1943 Los Angeles hosted a national writer's conference. Sponsored by the University of California at Los Angeles and the Hollywood Writers Mobilization, it was chaired by Marc Connelly, a well-known American playwright and film writer. To the conference came not only many leading American writers but also those of Allied nations as well as important figures from the world of motion pictures, radio, and other mass media. Their purpose was to discuss the writer's role in furthering the war effort, and to underscore freedom of expression as a fundamental democratic value. President Roosevelt highlighted the symbolic nature of the gathering when he wrote to Connelly:

> I send these greetings to the Writer's Congress with a deep sense of the significance of a gathering of writers in these times. It is a symbol, it seems to me, of our American faith in the Freedom of Expression—of our reliance upon the talents of our writers to present and clarify the issues of our times. Already, the men and women gathered there have rendered great service in elucidating for the nation the issues of this war.[45]

Over 1,200 people came to attend meetings and seminars and to consider the problems faced by various media—books, radio, motion pictures, music—in articulating wartime problems to the public. During its concluding sessions the Writer's Congress of 1943 adopted a variety of resolutions. These included pledges of international cultural cooperation as well as Pan American cultural unity. The Congress also addressed itself to the problem of securing the more efficient mobilization of writers and scholars. In its final action, the Congress developed an American Writer's Credo designed to provide guidelines for practitioners of the written word. In a manner slightly reminiscent of totalitarian societies like Nazi Germany or the Soviet Union, the Congress unanimously asked American writers to pledge their talents "to the service of the truth . . . [to] dedicate . . . skill and talent to the sacred right of free expression [and to] pledge to know the thought and feeling of the American people in their varied tasks."[46] Irrespective of its impact, the Congress served to focus national and international attention on Los Angeles as a burgeoning center for literary activity, and as a national center for cultural expression through the mass media. As Gustav O. Arlt noted at the time: "The West Los Angeles telephone directory looks like an issue of *Kuerschner's Almanac*. The announcements of a concert series in Los Angeles might have been printed in Paris or Vienna or Milan."[47]

The European émigrés also made significant contributions to the maturation of Los Angeles as an art center in the West, and indeed, the nation. A few of the more famous refugees brought their art collections with them. Erich Maria Remarque brought Cézanne oil and water color paintings, a Delacroix, four Degas pastels, drawings by Toulouse-Lautrec, and works by Picasso, Daumier, and Utrillo. But Remarque was living in a succession of apartments and rented houses during these years and had no room to display his treasures. In 1942, therefore, he decided to lend his collection to the Los Angeles County Art Museum for public display.[48] The movie producer Joseph Von

Sternberg displayed his striking collection of German paintings at the Los Angeles County Museum in 1943.[49] As some of the refugees demonstrated, owning art works was a reflection of sophistication and status, and at the same time constituted a shrewd investment. The Europeans helped to popularize the ownership of distinctive art objects in Hollywood, for as the émigré movie producer and director Ernst Lubitsch once commented: "Owning a Utrillo is like having an indoor Cadillac."[50]

Other émigrés contributed to the expansion of art galleries in Los Angeles and provided an impetus to the city's emergence as a major American art center, second only to New York. Starting in a small way, by the 1950s the galleries of Ralph Altman, Paul Kantor, Frank Klaus Perls, and Felix Landau, to name only a few, became important centers in the emerging art trade of the West. As cultivators of taste, the émigrés brought with them not only a deep appreciation of European classical art, but also a pioneering spirit in regard to modern art which gradually proved infectious for Americans. Karl With, for example, originally an expert in Oriental art, became Director of the Modern Art Institute in Los Angeles after the war. Vincent Price, who established and operated his own art gallery during the war years, later recalled that on a single day his clients included Thomas Mann, Aldous Huxley, Sergei Rachmaninoff, and Franz Werfel (in whose movie version of *The Song of Bernadette* Price had acted).[51]

In various capacities, therefore—as collectors, museum curators, art dealers, and academic teachers—the émigrés made a significant contribution to the maturation of the art scene in the West. They provided an expertise in the realm of classical European art that was largely lacking in the West before 1940 and introduced patrons to the Continental tradition. At the same time they brought sensitivity to the newer and avant-garde trends in European art which were still hardly known in the United States, and particularly in the West. Perhaps the influence of the émigrés would have been less profound in another age. But their coming on the eve of the Second World War coincided with the increasing maturation of the art scene in the West. It was to this movement that the émigrés gave a decided—and far-reaching—impetus. For, as one art critic noted during the period, in evaluating the Santa Fe Fiesta Exhibit in 1941, Western artists were beginning to move beyond the obvious regionalism of the 1920s and 1930s, beyond "piñon studded mesa and mountain, golden aspens, cloud formations on static blue sky." The depth of the land was creeping into their consciousness.[52] To that broadening consciousness the émigrés made a lasting contribution.

In few fields was the contribution of the émigrés more significant than in the world of music in Hollywood. The famous conductor

Bruno Walter felt that the adaptation of émigré musicians was easier in the Los Angeles area than anywhere else in the United States. Hollywood offered more job opportunities than other cities because of the large number of movie studio orchestras. Otto Klemperer and Bruno Walter conducted the Los Angeles Philharmonic in the war years; scores of lesser-known instrumentalists filled the chairs of orchestras in the region. Bronislaw Gimpel, for example, became concertmaster of the Los Angeles Philharmonic, in addition to giving private lessons; Robert Pollack, if not as famous as émigré Jascha Heifetz, became an outstanding violin teacher at the Los Angeles Conservatory of Music. Richard Lert (husband of writer Vicki Baum) did much to raise the professional standards of the Pasadena Civic Orchestra as its conductor. As Walter noted: "Experience has shown me that even the average European [musician] has had little difficulty in building up a new existence in the United States provided he was able from the beginning to see the difference between here and 'over there.'"[53]

A significant number of refugees became prominent film composers. Erich W. Korngold was one of the most talented, garnering two Academy Awards. One of the films for which he wrote a score was *King's Row,* starring a young actor named Ronald Reagan. When Reagan was inaugurated as President in 1981, he chose, as the first piece on the program for the gala Inaugural concert, a suite from Korngold's music for the movie.[54] Friedrich Hollaender, Eugen Zador, and Werner Heyman within a few years made themselves some of the most sought-after composers and arrangers in Hollywood. Others, like Ingolf Dahl, Ernst Toch, Ernest Gold, and Ernst Kanitz, divided their time between writing music for the movies and teaching composition at the University of Southern California. Most of these men at one time or another experienced grave doubts about the time they spent on motion pictures, for they exchanged financial independence for the preoccupation with more serious composition in which they had engaged in Europe. Some felt that their careers had been deflected. And yet one well-known music critic felt that they succeeded in introducing much avant-garde music to a mass audience in America through the medium of the feature film.[55]

Even the major composers of the twentieth century were sometimes drawn to write film music. The eminent French émigré composer Darius Milhaud spent the war years as a professor of music at Mills College in Oakland, California. Although he devoted most of his time to serious composition, he could not resist the lure of Hollywood and went there for a month to compose a score. Los Angeles, he said, "is a city, or rather a vast expanse of country, peopled by a whole *world* of artists, writers and musicians from every country. Some of them have been attracted by the climate [and] by the proximity of the film studios." Milhaud was fascinated by the cultural scene of southern California and made a point of visiting it at least once each year.[56]

One composer who refused to write for the movies was Arnold Schoenberg, one of the giants of modern music. Schoenberg had been invited to join the staff of the Juilliard School in New York City but, suffering from asthma, preferred to live in California. There he became a professor of music at the University of California in Los Angeles. Although several of his students were successful film composers and arrangers (Alfred Newman, Franz Waxman, David Raskin, Eddie Powell), he himself looked upon the medium with disdain. The story was told by Oscar Levant and Mrs. Schoenberg that at one time a representative of the famous producer Irving Thalberg came to Schoenberg to persuade him to write the music for the movie version of Pearl Buck's novel *The Good Earth.* "Think of it!!" said Thalberg's representative to Schoenberg, "A terrific storm is going on; the wheat field is swaying in the wind, and suddenly the earth begins to tremble. In the midst of the earthquake Co-Lan [a character in the film] gives birth to a baby! What an opportunity for music." Whereupon Schoenberg, thoughtful and reflective, replied in his ponderous German accent: "With so much going on, why do you need music?" Instead, Schoenberg devoted himself entirely to teaching and to composing a wide range of works reflecting atonality and counterpoint with which he pioneered new directions for twentieth-century music.[57]

Considering the total number of European immigrants in southern California during the World War II era—no more than 10,000—their contributions to the development of music in the West were astounding. The refugees endowed the musical scene in Los Angeles and other cities in the West with a deeper appreciation of traditional classical musical styles as they had developed in the European continental tradition. At the same time, through composition as well as through performances, they did a great deal to introduce new contemporary music into American repertoire, and so enriched the world of music for millions. And through the medium of motion pictures they did much to raise levels of musical composition for films made in Hollywood. No other group of immigrants to the West had made such substantial contributions to the cultural life of the region as the refugees from Hitler's Europe.

Language and cultural barriers made adjustments for actors and theater folk more difficult than for émigré musicians and artists. By one of the ironies of history, however, the very individuals responsible for the persecution of the émigrés, the Nazis, also created new job opportunities for them in exile. As war clouds gathered in Europe,

Hollywood turned more of its energies to war-inspired films, creating a burgeoning market for actors with German accents who could portray German generals, spies, concentration camp guards, and the like. Most of the émigrés frankly did not relish their roles as Nazis, but it provided them with rare opportunities for employment in their profession. And so Conrad Veidt played the memorable Major Strasser in *Casablanca* (for which the musical score was composed by the émigré Max Steiner); Eric von Stroheim played the ultimate Prussian militarist in *North Star;* Hans von Twardowski brilliantly impersonated the brutal Nazi General Heydrich in *Hangmen Also Die.* Great actors like Peter Lorre and Albert Basserman secured a variety of parts while Alexander Grenach, Fritz Kortner, and Martin Kosleck portrayed the Nazi leaders.[58]

And if Hollywood movie sets during the war became increasingly more realistic and authentic, that was hardly accidental. Behind the scenes at many Hollywood studios were dozens of European refugees. The set designer Hans Peters became one of the most prominent in Hollywood. Many individuals were anonymous, however: a host of former historians, archivists, and painters who found work as costume designers and fabricators and consultants on studio sets. There they applied their Teutonic penchant for accuracy and precision as well as historical knowledge to their newly developed craft.[59]

With somewhat less influence the émigrés also sought to invigorate theatre in Los Angeles. The world-famous Viennese director Max Reinhardt loved southern California and firmly believed that it would be a new Athens. As he wrote to Erika and Klaus Mann (children of Thomas Mann) from Hollywood with some prescience:

> You simply must stay here. It's going to be a new center of culture. America is going to take over the cultural heritage of Europe, and there is no more hospitable landscape . . . than the Californian. Here is a still youthful country. European and American scientists will meet to prepare a home for our old culture and for the new one that is coming into being here.

But Reinhardt was ahead of his time, and the West was not yet ready for a man of his genius. His efforts to attract financial support for legitimate theater in Los Angeles failed, and in 1942 he left dejectedly for New York City. On a more modest scale the young Walter Wicclair, a fledgling theatrical producer from Silesia, organized the *Freie Buehne* in 1940. During the next nine years it produced hundreds of plays in English as well as German at the Coronet Theater in Hollywood where it flourished as one of the finest legitimate playhouses in the region, and expanded the repertoire known to audiences in the United States.[60]

Generalizations about the contributions of the refugee scholars are difficult in view of their diverse fields and temperaments. American scholars tended to be more rigorously empirical than their European colleagues, who sometimes brought new theoretical perspectives to their special fields. Their influence was particularly significant in the West during the 1940s where various disciplines were not as fully developed as they were in older eastern institutions.[61]

As a group, the contributions of European émigrés to the cultural development of the American West were remarkable. In literature, drama, music, art, science, the humanities, medicine, and psychoanalysis, to name only a few major fields, they had a substantial impact. That is not to say that the West was a cultural desert on the eve of World War II. In fact, cultural life in the West had grown during the 1920s, and with encouragement of New Deal programs had continued to flourish during the 1930s. By the time of World War II the region was ready for a "leap forward," for a significant spurt of growth, just as the spread of Nazi totalitarianism in Europe provoked a mass exodus of intellectuals from the continent. The Europeans brought sophistication and an emphasis on theories and abstractions that well supplemented the proverbial American genius for the practical and concrete. Most of the Europeans tried hard to adapt themselves to the tone of American culture at the same time that Americans, under the impact of war, became more hospitable to foreign ideas and insights. The West provided a major arena for the blending of the cultural traditions of Europe and America, for it was more receptive to new influences than the older and more stratified East. If the extraordinary cultural explosion of the West in the 1950s and 1960s is to be understood in historical perspective, then the significant contributions of the émigrés during the World War II era (and beyond) cannot be ignored.

During World War II Hollywood emerged as a major cultural center in the American West, exerting an influence far beyond its immediate environs. Its importance as the nation's motion picture capital was greatly enhanced by World War II in which the movies became an important tool of mass communications and propaganda. This wartime emphasis on Hollywood's role in the national defense effort added a more serious dimension to the movie capital which it had lacked before 1940 and brought the movie colony into the maelstrom of national politics.

But to view Hollywood merely as an entertainment capital is to ignore the cultural life which it spawned, even in an age of popular mass culture. The world of entertainment came to affect writers, musicians, and artists and stimulated the rapid growth of a wide range of cultural endeavors. And these varied activities drew distinguished figures from all over the world which further enhanced the cultural life of the region. The Second World War, by stimulating a mass exodus of many of Europe's leading intellectuals, made a prime contribution to the acceleration of southern California's development as one of the nation's most prominent centers of cultural activities. As no other single event, the coming of the émigrés to Los Angeles during World War II transformed southern California from a provincial and local cultural center to one of national and international dimensions.

Part III
After the Transformation, 1945

CHAPTER ELEVEN

Conclusion:
The West Transformed

The end of hostilities in 1945 left the West somewhat breathless but transformed. The somber, cautious, and rather pessimistic mood of 1941 was but a memory. It had given way to an exhilarating, bubbling, optimistic outlook born of the fast-moving events of the war years. That view was based on the far-reaching changes which the war had wrought in the region. The colonial economy had been liberated; the foundations for another great population boom had been laid; sleepy western towns had been transformed into teeming cities; ethnic diversity had become a new reality in the everyday life of scores of communities in the region; and cultural isolation was largely ended as a diverse array of cultural and scientific institutions and activities was increasingly limiting the once dominant influence of the East.

The war not only changed the physical aspect of the West. It also did much to transform the spirit of the region. By 1945 the self-image of westerners and their perceptions of the West's future was appreciably altered. Some of their dreams were mirrored in the manifold planning activities during and immediately after the war. Such plans were formulated in an urban context, at the state level, and also encompassed the region and its place in the nation and the world. Most of these blueprints for the future were not narrowly conceived but touched on culture, economic development, or politics. And although many of the proposals offered in 1945 remained unfulfilled in succeeding years, they accurately reflected the hopes and aspirations of many westerners at the time and provided a framework for the next generation.[1]

As elsewhere in the nation, the war stimulated a flurry of planning activities in western cities. If at times these efforts seemed disjointed, that was due to the different ideologies within which they were conceived. City officials who believed in comprehensive planning, including social reforms, saw the war years as an unusual opportunity to transform their visions of utopia into reality. Lewis Mumford was representative of the idealists who hoped to utilize central planning under government auspices to build the cities of the future. A contrary point of view was represented by Robert Moses, who conceived of himself as a realist rather than an idealist. His approach was to develop pragmatic responses to specific problems rather than to devise comprehensive schemes. His emphasis was on "practical" public works, transportation, and beautification projects in the cities. The November 1943 issue of *Fortune* contained a feature story on this "battle of the approaches" to city planning.[2] Moses also stressed the importance of private enterprise rather than government in his proposals. By the summer of 1944 Moses was attacking "long-haired planners" with vehemence, charging them with seeking to introduce alien styles into American culture.[3]

In the West both philosophies had their adherents, although by war's end it was clear that most public officials opted for pragmatism. Their visions of the future western city rarely embodied grandiose schemes envisaging utopian communities or extensive social planning. Rather, they focused on practical issues, including full employment, the conversion of industries from war to peace, and improvement of housing and transportation to accommodate the large number of newcomers.

The San Francisco Bay region was typical. There, for example, all attempts by the California State Planning Board between 1940 and 1942 to create a more unified planning region in the area to facilitate wartime production broke down.[4] Until 1942, opposition to the New Deal and fear of further federal centralization dampened most planning efforts. The war stimulated an extraordinary profusion of such plans, encompassing no less than what one observer, Mel Scott, designated as a veritable "renaissance" in American city planning.[5]

The atmosphere of crisis lessened some of the ideological opposition to planning that had existed among many western city officials, often suspicious of federal interference. At the 1943, 1944, and 1945 meetings of the American Municipal Association and the American Society of Planning Officials, for example, scores of westerners— along with those from other regions—now emphasized the need for development of more balanced and integrated communities through planning. Their hope was to turn western boom towns into stable communities, and to diversify their economies.[6]

Hundreds of these western towns and cities thus created postwar development commissions whose task it was to transform western dreams into realities on the local level. In February 1943 for example,

Portland, Oregon created an Area PostWar Development Commission. Its goal was to plan improvements in industrial expansion and transportation, and to provide balance between inner cities and rapidly growing suburban areas. Commission members included prominent local business leaders and representatives from utilities such as the Northwest Electric Company, public officials, representatives of state or federal agencies. In Portland it was this group—on which Edgar Kaiser was active—that invited Robert Moses to Portland to plan a comprehensive program of public improvements eventually totaling $60 million.[7] Late in 1943 San Diego established a similar agency, including city officials, county representatives, and representatives of business and public utilities.[8]

The federal government encouraged such planning efforts, largely through the National Resources Planning Board. Until it was abolished by Congress in 1943, the Board through regional offices lent its technical experts to localities and aided their planning efforts by conducting surveys and inventories of resources. In the Seattle-Tacoma area the NRPB cooperated with the Washington State Planning Commission in giving technical assistance to localities. In Salt Lake City it collected data pertaining to local economic development. But as hostility to centralized planning mounted during the war, Congress in 1943 abolished New Deal agencies, including the NRPB. At the same time the lawmakers established special committees in the House and Senate to consider postwar planning by cities and local governments. Most members opposed federally directed or centralized planning at the local level, and preferred diversified planning by localities, with an emphasis on cooperation with private enterprise.[9]

Yet the experiences of the cities between 1943 and 1945 were of crucial importance to the postwar generation. The long-term impact of postwar planning was in fact more significant than its immediate accomplishments. As a historian of the Sunbelt, Carl Abbott, aptly noted, "The process itself helped to legitimize the idea of urban planning. [It] anticipated the thrust of public policy in sunbelt cities during the next two decades. Agreement on the need to make encouragement of growth an explicit aim of city government [and] on the importance of metropolitan land use and transportation planning . . . constituted a framework for postwar agendas in the majority of sunbelt cities."[10]

The feeling that the West might be on the threshold of a new age was widespread in 1944 and 1945 not only in the cities but at the state level as well. Almost every western state established special committees whose prime task it was to develop plans for postwar growth. Governor Earl Warren of California exemplified the spirit when he declared in 1944 that "we have sniffed our destiny." Speaking to a conference of Pacific Coast sales executives on April 14, 1944, Warren said: "We people out here in the West have our noses high in the air. . . . Anyone who has had the opportunity to travel and consult with Western business, finance, and industrial leaders during the past year has been heartened by the atmosphere of expectancy, faith and determination which is everywhere encountered. Never before have there been quite so many people possessed of faith in our future or quite so intent on giving voice to the conviction that we have our foot in the door of an era of dream realization." And, he continued, "Any summarization of the manner in which California and the West have been able to marshal resources, manpower and initiative in the support of the war effort leads to the perfectly logical conclusion that we possess the essentials for tremendous peace time development."[11]

An intensely practical man, Warren was a prime mover in the establishment of the California State Reconstruction and Reemployment Commission in 1944. It was not intended, he emphasized, as a "superimposed planning agency of government," for that could never "take the place of individual and community effort." In short, he favored a pragmatic planning effort in which private enterprise would play an important role in cooperation with state government. The Commission was to make an inventory of the state's industrial and employment potentials and opportunities and to develop specific plans for their realization. Led by Colonel Alexander Heron, the Commission in 1945 contacted scores of leaders in industry, labor, finance, agriculture, education, government and social welfare. Its function was to mobilize "establishment" as well as "grass roots" individuals in a comprehensive effort to inaugurate a new stage in the state's development.[12]

A similar spirit was the driving force behind Utah's efforts to plan its postwar growth. With a clear realization that the dreams of many westerners for the future of that state's growth would require some planning, Charles W. Eliot, Director of the NRPB, met in August 1942 with Utah's Governor Herbert Maw to lay the groundwork. Maw asked his State Department of Publicity and Development to sponsor a comprehensive program under Ora Bundy whom he appointed as State Director of Postwar Planning. The NRPB provided some staff assistance by lending consultants from its Washington as well as its Region 8 office. As Governor Maw noted, "heartaches, hunger, and misery that followed the first World War could have been avoided, or greatly mitigated, if this Nation had been adequately prepared. . . . Only through careful cooperative community planning can . . . state government . . . lead . . . in preparing a blueprint for the Utah of the Future." The Director and his advisory committee compiled an extensive inventory of the state's present resources and its potentials, comprising more than 300 pages. The first report, which appeared in June of 1943, dealt at length with postwar industrial readjustments, with farming, transportation, power development, the expansion of recreational facilities and tourism, public works program, and improving the machinery for community planning. It constituted a basic framework for postwar planning in succeeding years.[13]

Nevada mounted a particularly aggressive effort to transform its dreams into reality. Governor E. P. Carville was in close touch with Governors Maw of Utah and Sidney Osborn of Arizona, as well as Governor Warren of California. In keeping each other abreast of their postwar planning activities they hoped to have a broader, regional impact. They also shared a similar philosophical outlook. Like Warren, Carville reflected the "Moses approach" whereby private enterprise would bear a major responsibility for statewide development although governmental entities at every level were to provide guidance, direction, and capital. "I know," wrote Carville to fellow Nevadan Charles B. Henderson, who in 1944 was chairman of the board of the Reconstruction Finance Corporation, "it is hard for us in the West to compete with the industrial East but . . . it would be of great help to the West if these plants . . . the Government has constructed . . . could continue under private ownership after the war. We of the West are working quite hard to bring about a better industrial condition here and I hope in some measure the R.F.C. will be able to help us."[14]

Nevada's senior U.S. Senator, Pat McCarran, provided strong leadership to develop a coordinated effort by western states anxious to play a key role in postwar planning. On various occasions he called for meetings of Western senators in his Washington office to plan regional strategy.[15] The *San Francisco News* even felt that his ambitions transcended his native region, and that he was promoting a new economic and political alliance between the West and South since he felt that both sections had been victims of eastern discrimination before the war.[16]

McCarran was also instrumental in organizing western regional conferences dealing with postwar planning. One such meeting convened in Carson City in February 1944. It attracted more than sixty representatives from at least five western states, including California, Nevada, Oregon, Washington, and Utah. Most of the delegates served as members of interstate cooperation commissions in their respective states or on state planning boards. Senator McCarran told the delegates that "the West has been treated as a colonial institution with little more than colonial rights," and urged the West and the South to unite to keep eastern industrialists from throttling the new wartime industries developed in the West. State Attorney General Alan Bible of

Nevada and Robert W. Kenny of California echoed these sentiments. "The East cannot strangle the West's growing might," Kenny shouted. "It has been a tough struggle for the West to achieve what already has been gained. . . . The West should not . . . be at the feudal mercy of the industrial monarchs of the East."

Nevada's Governor Carville, in urging the eleven western states to cooperate, noted that "the very foundation of postwar planning for the western region must be built around the conservation, development, and preservation of all our natural resources [and] the retention and development of already established war plants by private enterprise." The conference adopted several resolutions which constituted a practical program. It urged the transfer of federal war plants to private ownership, a clearly formulated federal policy on reconversion, the addition of western representatives on the War Production Board and other federal agencies, and greater cooperation among western governors to attract private industry and to develop regional markets. In addition, the delegates requested the State Department to thank Mexico in the name of the western states for providing the braceros who had played such a vital role in the western labor force during the war.[17]

In Congress McCarran was a prime mover in the creation of a new committee in the U.S. Senate to deal with industrial centralization.[18] As its chairman, he was in close touch with groups actively engaged in the planning process. One of these was Builders of the West, a regional organization sponsored by private businessmen and government officials who drafted proposals for reconversion. Its executive secretary was Rex L. Nicholson, who had been Regional Director of the Federal Works Agency during the New Deal and now used his contacts to lead this new pressure group. One of its vital concerns was the disposal of federal war plants in the West. McCarran was closely involved with this organization and participated in some of its programs, including radio presentations.[19]

As a major advocate of postwar planning by the states McCarran was active throughout the West. At a meeting of the governors of eleven western states on April 9, 1943, he laid "the blueprint for a new frontier" before them. In his plan for the creation of a new frontier, he argued that it should serve the same purposes as the old frontier, "providing employment and opportunity for all comers, and infusing new blood into the nation's economic and industrial arteries." McCarran urged conservation, power development, road building, new airports, municipal improvements, especially housing, new mineral development and close collaboration of federal agencies in the West with states and localities. Writing to Governor Maw to explain his program, McCarran noted that "much has been said about post-war planning. In fact, too much has been said, and too little done to provide ways and means [for] the development of the west."[20]

Two months later McCarran addressed a joint session of the California legislature to expound on his vision of the future West. He warned against excessive centralization, and letting the federal government take prime responsibility for postwar planning. On the other hand, he vigorously opposed a policy of laissez-faire whereby eastern-dominated industries would have a major voice in the West's postwar development. Instead, he pleaded for regional and state planning in conjunction with federal agencies. Every city and state in the West should develop its own plans, he argued. These should be coordinated as much as possible by state governments. Each should then create its own apparatus to execute its program. Where economic interests overlapped, states should establish regional committees. "Study your problems," he exhorted the legislators, "decide what you want, organize yourself for the task, complete your regional organizations as quickly as possible, and be prepared to make your wishes recognized." This was the alternative to centralization that would preserve democratic processes in the West—and the nation. It was the task of the states to bridge the chasm between people and their government if democracy was to survive.[21]

McCarran spoke not only for his state but clearly had a regional and national perspective. He reflected the intensive ferment in thought and action about the future of the West at the conclusion of the Second World War. And he was not alone. Scores of writers and public figures were actively involved in this effort to create a new self-image for the West to match its spectacular wartime growth. Most realized that the West had reached a critical juncture in its history. The discussions and debates that ensued were voluminous. A very brief account such as this can only hint at the richness and breadth of the ideas and programs that were propounded.

The discussions about the future of the West between 1943 and 1948 ranged over many fields. In cultural life, business, or politics, these years provided a favorable climate for bold speculation about development of the nation's youngest region. Most contemporaries recognized that the war provided a watershed for the West. It created unparalleled opportunities for further growth upon which they had to capitalize if they were to seize the moment.

Although great differences of temperament and style were common among dreamers and planners, certain common elements ran through their analyses. Their mood was one of restrained optimism. Most agreed that the West before the war had been an exploited region. Mobilization removed many shackles of western subservience to the East and opened a new era of unparalleled opportunity. Theirs was not a parochial vision, however. They viewed the postwar expansion of the West in the context of a revitalized national economy whose influence would spread to the entire world, now that in 1945 the United States had emerged as the world's strongest power. In this rise to world eminence the West played a crucial role. It should continue to play a significant part, they felt, particularly as American influence in Latin America and the Far East grew. This was a cosmopolitan vision, in which the future West would be significant both in American domestic and foreign policies.

The recognition that the war had brought the West to a cultural crossroads was clear in the minds of writers between 1943 and 1950 and reflected in their literary outpourings. It was voiced explicitly at regional conferences during these years such as the Writer's Conference sponsored by Reed College in Portland, Oregon, in January 1946. The purpose of that meeting was to assess the cultural progress of the Pacific Northwest and to delimit its regional characteristics which could serve as guidelines for writers of fiction and nonfiction.

In opening the meeting, Peter Odegard, president of Reed College and a distinguished political scientist, placed the West's regional character in historical perspective. He reminded his listeners about the rapid evolution of the Pacific Northwest, from a wilderness to a highly developed region with more than 4 million people. But, asked Odegard, "Where do we go from here? Can the Northwest assume a position of leadership . . . or be contented with the colonial status that has characterized its history and its culture up to now?" And, Odegard continued, "during most of its history the Pacific Northwest has been a colonial outpost of the East. . . . In that respect it was not unique. At one time or another every state has experienced that colonial status." Sectional rivalries were not only economic or physical, he told his hearers, but also psychological. Until psychological attitudes were changed—until westerners shed their feelings of colonial subservience and inferiority—they could not realize the full potential of their region. Within the physical limitations set by nature, Odegard argued, the character of a civilization depended on its cultural resources. The colonial subservience of the Pacific Northwest before World War II, he felt, had roots in the physical features of the economy and the cultural heritage of its inhabitants. The war had liberated them from their economic bonds. It was now up to the writers and the intellectuals to free westerners from the shackles of cultural dependence—from the colonial mentality which still held them in its grip.

Others echoed his sentiments. Among the writers who spoke at the meeting were Carl Van Doren, Luther Evans, Stewart Holbrook, Richard L. Neuberger, Ernest Haycox, Joseph Kinsey Howard, James

Stevens, and Horace R. Cayton. As the older East had been fashioned out of nineteenth-century philosophy, they argued, so the twentieth-century West had an opportunity to construct its own unique cultural world. Would it seize the opportunity?[22]

These themes were taken up by a spate of journalists during and immediately after the war. In one way or another some of these writers hoped to appeal to the millions of newcomers who were expected to seek permanent homes in the West with the war's end. One of the nation's best-known journalists, William Allen White, addressed the issue of the West's future early in the war. "Certainly the constantly moving frontier which was a hundred years going from Pittsburgh to Los Angeles, did make a civilization of its own kind, a golden age here in the American West," wrote White. ". . . The West became what it was because of a vast increment of wealth from the rising price of the virgin land. . . . This tremendous increment transmuted by the democratic process into fluid capital . . . was distributed economically and digested socially, also by the democratic processes, by literate people who were as nearly absolutely free as it was possible in the nineteenth century. . . . It was a new thing in God's world, a strange and beautiful thing, this unfolding of the Golden West." White hoped that this process would continue as westerners took advantage of the technological marvels of their age. "Time and again, in the settlement of the West, has it been made clear that a social order may be erected and maintained under the capitalist profit system. . . . But as our old West worked fairly well despite the rascal . . . in the distribution of the unbelievable billions of dollars of increment from the land, so the new West will work if it is underpinned with the democratic faith. We can, if we will . . . create an equitable order for the distribution of the stupendous increase in human wealth that is rising from the enlargement of mechanical power with the increase of production."[23]

Within a few years White's analysis was followed by a passionate plea from the Plains where John Kinsey Howard wrote of the region in *Montana: High, Wide, and Handsome,* which won the Pulitzer Prize for nonfiction in 1943. "Montana has never had time to develop a Mark Twain or a Bret Harte to chronicle its wealth of frontier history . . . in order that it might become a cultural entity in the national consciousness," Howard noted almost apologetically. He hoped that the West would have a brighter future than Montana had had in the past. His prime reason for writing about eastern exploitation of Montana was to demonstrate that its "unbalance in population will affect all America; and that is the reason for singling out a state whose economy seems most precarious in the hope that discussion of its experience may encourage sympathetic understanding of steps already taken to aid it and help set in motion more such movements for all of the West. Balanced development—that was his hope and his prescription for the future of the West. But, he emphasized, "this isn't solely Montana's problem, nor the west's." Approvingly he cited Frank Lloyd Wright and Baker Brownell who in their *Architecture and Modern Life* (1937) had written that balance of society depended in great measure on regional balance in population. They predicted accurately enough that "with many diversified soils, beautiful climate, with water power and mineral resources, the far west will become no doubt another region of large population" and added, "Any policies that will tend to aid this kind of life and population will contribute to the balance of our society. . . . The social problem in this respect is to prevent the urban east from exploiting other regions as hinterland, draining wealth and youth from the south and west without corresponding return." If regional exploitation were fully recognized as a national problem, and if Americans took steps to curb it to build a more balanced society, then the future of the West would look bright indeed.[24]

A more aggressive stance was taken by A. G. Mezerick, a prolific journalist who specialized in economic affairs. "Why, at this time, a book which stresses the divisions within our country?" asked Mezerick. ". . . The internal stresses which existed before the war are still with us, and more significantly, the war . . . was the instrument with which the corporate clique in the East strengthened its grip on the economic life of the South and West. There can be no internal harmony as long as Eastern corporate power enforces . . . centralized control of major industry, banking and distribution. . . . The South and the West are denied the industries which they could readily support and to which they have every right . . . [they] have been held in the vise of a raw material economy fashioned by that East."

But 1945 was a year of decision. "Western America has a post-war plan. Simply stated, it is to wage war against the financial monopoly now held by the East. The goal is industrial self-determination." His vision of the West's future was grandiose. "The West is playing for a new empire—not only to supply the needs of its own five and one-half million people with manufactured articles, but by utilizing Alaska and its alliance with the undeveloped Canadian Northwest, to become self-sufficient for almost all of its raw materials. Then boldly it expects to ship finished products through the Panama Canal to undersell the East in the South and Southwest, and finally to hit the jackpot—the domination of the world's greatest market, Asia. It will be a breathtaking fight that may change the pattern of our economy."[25]

Mezerick's call was reiterated in more subdued fashion in 1945 by Wendell Berge, Assistant Attorney General in charge of the Anti-

Trust Division of the Department of Justice. "Historians have told us that the vanishing of the geographic frontier constituted a major turning point in our evolution," Berge declared. "All too often in the years before the war it was assumed that the passing of the geographic frontier also meant the disappearance of broad opportunities for economic development." But the war significantly changed that outlook. "Far from being mature or senile our economy had been asleep to its own powers, both in terms of technical progress . . . and of the fields awaiting exploration and enterprise." Berge, too, saw 1945 as a crucial year. At that moment he felt, "the economic future of the West has a critical significance. . . . If the West is denied the chance to develop its resources . . . our economy could not then look forward to expansion but would once more risk contraction and depression. The West is once more the frontier on which the question of America's economic expansion will be decided. All of its trails have not been blazed . . . the full economic greatness of the West is undiscovered. It need not remain so." And in an appeal for sectional harmony he pleaded: "In return for assistance . . . by other sections the development of the West will constitute a magnificent addition to the industrial strength and economic welfare of America."[26]

Many of these arguments were crystallized further and presented to a far-flung national audience by Bernard DeVoto, a distinguished writer who dramatized the problems of his native region in *Harper's Magazine.* As a regular contributor during these years he hammered away consistently at the choices before the West. "New Deal measures, war installations, and war industries have given the West a far greater and more widely distributed prosperity than it has ever had before," he wrote in 1946. "Moreover, during the war a fundamental revolution took place; power and industrial developments in the West have made a structural change in the national economy. . . . if the developments that have occurred are revolutionary those already planned and sure to be carried out are even more revolutionary and some of those which so far are only dreams but may be achieved stagger the mind. Finally, the world movements which are working out a long-term reorientation of human societies whose focus is the Pacific Ocean will be increasingly favorable to the West."

DeVoto felt that this was a moment for which many westerners had waited for decades. "The West sees all this in terms of its historical handicaps; colonial economic status and absentee control. The ancient Western dream of an advanced industrial economy . . . is brighter now than it has ever been before. For the first time there are actual rather than phantasmal reasons for believing that the dream can be realized."[27]

The greatest impediment to the realization of this dream, however, DeVoto saw in a split in the western psyche, in ambiguities surrounding its self-image. "Realization that the dream can be fulfilled has made the West all but drunk," DeVoto noted. "I cannot list here the sectional and interstate associations and committees engaged in implementing the dream, the plans they are working out, the measures they are preparing, or any other specific details. . . . Enough that the West understands the opportunity . . . the possibilities of success and failure . . . and is taking every conceivable measure to . . . insure success. With a conspicuous exception. . . . Whether the great dream will fail or be fulfilled depends on how that split works out. . . . Westerners have always tended to hold themselves cheap and to hold one another cheaper. Western resentment of its Eastern enslavement has always tended to be less a dislike of the enslavement than a belief that it could be made to pay." DeVoto feared that rapacious exploitation of land and natural resources by greedy special interests in the West would seriously undermine the balanced development of the region. In this split of the western psyche DeVoto saw "an almost cosmic irony in that the great dream of the West . . . has been made possible by the developments of our age. While the West moves to build that kind of economy, a part of the West is moving simultaneously to destroy the natural resources forever."[28] Which of the interests in the West would prevail? DeVoto dared not to answer the question but warned his audience about the dichotomy.

The theme that psychological adjustments by westerners were as vital as economic adjustments in postwar America was developed by other writers such as Ladd Haysted. "The West . . . [has] for too long been on the fringes of the fairly tight and integrated balance of the nation. Too many professional Westerners . . . haven't helped the situation. But the war with its annihilation of distance, its cutting across regional and even international lines . . . has shown that we no longer can afford to have any division here at home for any reason. The West cannot longer be divorced from the balance of the nation by any such unwarrantable barrier as calling it a 'society,' a 'state of mind.'" Haysted called for a fuller integration of the West into the nation's life. "Truly, in all the history of this country, where new community after new community has roistered through childhood, come on to maturity, and then been accepted as an equal member . . . there never was a time more propitious for the last child, the youngest member, to be invited to 'belong.' This is the time, with the post-war world at hand, when the twain must meet."[29]

The total impact of the western dreamers of 1945—in the cities, the states, and the region—was to fashion a new self-image for the West. Westerners in 1945 thought of themselves as enterprising innovators, independent pace-setters who had freed themselves from many of the bonds that had tied them to the older East before the war. They were eager to capitalize on their gains and to conquer new challenges before them.

Of course, their vision was not illusory; it was not only a manifestation of their spirit but based on the remarkable material accomplishments of the past four years. The war left an indelible imprint on the economic life of the region. The enormous incursion of new capital by the federal government stimulated an economic boom. In addition to promoting an increase in the production of natural resources, mobilization did much to foster the establishment of new manufacturing facilities in the West. The West acquired new steel and aluminum fabrication plants as well as scores of smaller manufacturing enterprises. More spectacular were the vast new aircraft and shipbuilding operations which were among the largest in the nation. At the same time the rapid growth of scientific research laboratories— particularly on the Pacific Coast—spawned electronics and research industries that contributed to the emergence of a new technologically oriented industrial complex in the West on the eve of the postwar era. That, in turn, served to bolster the expansion of the service industries as the burgeoning population for the first time now provided many western business enterprises with ample markets in the region. The growth of raw materials industries, manufactures, technological development, and service industries provided the West with a diversified economy which lessened its colonial dependence on the East and endowed it with an increased measure of self-sufficiency.

To a considerable extent the influx of more than $40 billion in capital investment between 1941 and 1945, most of it provided by the federal government, was responsible for triggering the economic boom. Such a massive infusion of public funds was not an entirely new departure because since the early nineteenth century the federal government had been directly engaged in promoting western economic growth. In that sense, the West was clearly the offspring of the older East and South. Whether through the construction of canals, roads, and railroads, or through expenditures for military installations, the federal government had taken an active role in providing some of the needed overhead capital for the region's growth. Only the scale and the scope of federal transfer payments during the Second World War made that experience unique.

Western society witnessed another population boom and consequent diversification as a result of the wartime experiences. Population grew by leaps and bounds as more than seven million newcomers streamed into the trans-Mississippi area, many of them war workers with their families. In addition, of the four million men and women in the military services who at one time or another were stationed in the

West, a significant percentage returned in the postwar period to establish permanent residences there.

With the increase of population the ethnic and racial character of the people in the region was also diversified more than in prewar years. To be sure, the West had been home to a wide range of immigrants with varying ethnic and racial backgrounds before 1940. But the population movements spurred by wartime mobilization brought significantly larger numbers of blacks, Mexican-Americans, and Indians to the urban centers, adding to their heterogeneous character. And while the war created these new ethnic and racial enclaves in the western cities, it disrupted older ones such as those peopled by the Japanese, and accelerated their integration into western (and American) society.

Urban growth in the West was enormously stimulated by the war. Placid communities were transformed into boom towns in just a few months. The established cities on the Pacific Coast—Los Angeles, San Francisco, Portland, and Seattle—witnessed significant increases of population, not to speak of smaller cities like San Diego and Tacoma. More than 90 percent of the newcomers to the West Coast settled in urban areas over 10,000. If cities of the interior such as Las Vegas, Phoenix, Tucson, El Paso, Albuquerque, Denver, and Salt Lake City did not have to cope with as great a rush of people as those on the West Coast, yet their growth in wartime was significant. After more than a decade of stagnation during the Great Depression, they were by 1945 oriented toward further expansion. The conditions fostered by the war created a prelude to many of the problems faced by western cities in succeeding decades. Confronted by a sizable increase of population, including rootless and transient elements, the cities experienced increasing social problems. Substandard housing and the growth of new slum areas came to be familiar in most western communities; crime and juvenile delinquency grew sufficiently to arouse increasing public comment; the demands of a growing population for new social services placed serious strains on the financial capabilities of most western city governments at the same time that they strove to provide expanded health care and sewage facilities as well as public schools for the newcomers. The war years were exciting—even exhilarating—for many western cities, but they also ushered in a new age of urban problems.

Some of these problems were directly related to the increased heterogeneity of western urban societies. The ideological overtones set in motion by the war brought American ethnic and racial prejudices into stark relief at the same time that a steady stream of blacks, Mexican-Americans, and Indians poured into the cities—drawn by the lure of new economic opportunities. The newcomers came to face many of the problems that previous generations of migrants had faced before them, but with the added pressures of wartime congestion. They faced discrimination in housing and employment, and the need to adapt to city life in the West. Invariably their migration brought new racial and ethnic strains to western communities and a proliferation of social problems. Still, despite these handicaps, a large number of the new migrants found the betterment of their lives for which they had come. They improved their economic status; they found jobs, improved educational opportunities, and kinship; the very congestion of the neighborhoods in which they congregated stimulated a sense of racial or ethnic pride which sometimes was reflected in political action and increased political influence; and, above all, the war years whetted their desire for more, and heightened their sense of expectations. Somewhat imperceptibly, therefore, the war years became a crucible for civil rights movements in the western cities which came to fruition in later years.

As western cities matured—and came to face some of the same problems as the older urban centers of the East—they also achieved a greater measure of cultural independence. The population increase not only brought new talent to the region, but also provided new audiences for a wide range of cultural activities. Some of these were new cultural attainments in the realm of mass culture, but an increasingly significant portion lay in the realm of serious research and scholarship. Among the many new settlers in the West the contributions of the relatively small number of European émigrés stand out. Representing some of the ablest European intelligentsia, they gave a decided impetus to westerners already seeking emancipation from dependence on the East. In fields such as literature, music, art, the theater, and the cinema, in architecture, science, and a score of other scholarly disciplines, they provided the cultural scene in the West with a maturity and sophistication which by 1945 attracted international attention. Certainly the war did much to foster Hollywood as one of the West's leading cultural centers, for it harbored a galaxy of talent in a variety of fields. And although Hollywood's role as a center of popular culture was widely known, intellectuals and critics have been loath to give it credit for spawning a wide range of "high-brow" or serious cultural activities. The movie colony may not always have been a dependable barometer of good taste or style, but it provided the patronage for a broad spectrum of serious and creative cultural endeavors in the West. Without Hollywood's encouragement of the arts, cultural life in the West would have been more barren. And Hollywood provided a model for the cultural guidance of other cities in the West who before World War II had looked mainly to the East.

The American West emerged from the Second World War as a

transformed region. In 1941 many westerners had feared that the expansion of the region had come to a close. The economy was stagnant, population growth had ceased, and the colonial dependence of the region on the older East pervaded most aspects of life. But by 1945 the war had wrought a startling transformation. Westerners now had visions of unlimited growth and expansion, a newly diversified economy was booming, a vast influx of population was changing the very fabric of western society, and the region had just witnessed a growth in cultural maturity which was totally unprecedented in its history. The West emerged from the war as a path-breaking self-sufficient region with unbounded optimism for its future. World War II had precipitated that transformation, and in retrospect constituted one of the major turning points in the history of the American West.

Appendix

Table 1.

Value Added by Manufactures, by States: 1947 and 1939

(in thousands of dollars)

Division and State	Value added by manufacture 1947	Value added by manufacture 1939
Mountain	839,202	269,381
Montana	92,258	38,828
Idaho	109,694	29,788
Wyoming	34,957	15,336
Colorado	280,774	90,330
New Mexico	55,486	8,640
Arizona	103,958	31,625
Utah	128,298	43,341
Nevada	27,777	11,493
Pacific	5,544,034	1,546,957
Washington	874,036	267,716
Oregon	675,017	156,696
California	3,994,981	1,122,545

Source: Compiled from U.S. Census, *Statistical Abstract,* 1953 (Washington, 1953), p.805.

Table 2.

Major War Supply Contracts and War Facilities, 1940–1945

(in thousands of dollars)

State	Major war supply contracts, June 1940–Sept. 1945		Major war facilities projects, June 1940–June 1945	
	Combat equipment	Other	Industrial	Military
Arizona	94,854	31,115	100,592	134,116
California	14,255,117	2,195,524	1,013,778	1,511,447
Colorado	244,634	116,920	170,350	174,479
Idaho	12,049	6,421	27,049	101,992
Montana	12,966	15,081	12,956	41,106
Nevada	1,521	32,402	151,542	88,050
New Mexico	11,133	9,356	13,325	101,506
North Dakota	1,582	5,938	120	1,572
Oregon	1,629,809	182,825	100,603	163,842
South Dakota	201	4,584	150	65,908
Texas	3,749,561	2,224,979	1,166,836	837,582
Utah	79,136	34,345	284,394	153,097
Washington	3,408,305	379,331	341,058	327,949
Wyoming	12,770	68,419	25,535	23,431

SOURCE: U.S. Census, *County Data Book* (Washington, 1947), p.7.

Table 3.

Expenditures for Plants and Equipment, Western States, 1947 and 1939

(in thousands of dollars)

Division and State	Total expenditures for plant and equipment	Expenditures for new plant and equipment (1947)			Expenditures for used plant and equipment and land	Expenditures for new plant and equipment (1939)		
		Total	New construction	New machinery and equipment		Total	New construction	New machinery and equipment
United States	6,627,029	6,003,873	2,122,143	3,881,730	623,156	1,248,078	391,285	856,793
Mountain	100,745	95,023	33,296	61,727	5,722	15,592	6,469	9,123
Montana	7,788	7,446	1,708	5,738	342	3,046	1,225	1,821
Idaho	12,116	11,447	3,903	7,544	669	1,707	743	964
Wyoming	11,594	10,235	8,756	1,479	1,359	784	308	476
Colorado	33,379	32,189	8,406	23,783	1,190	6,037	2,443	3,594
New Mexico	6,181	5,431	1,810	3,621	750	993	536	457
Arizona	8,761	8,328	3,131	5,197	433	971	264	707
Utah	17,877	16,988	4,171	12,817	889	1,789	859	930
Nevada	3,049	2,959	1,411	1,548	90	265	91	174
Pacific	620,968	553,678	225,377	328,301	67,290	81,348	34,004	47,344
Washington	94,447	81,476	28,707	52,769	12,971	12,862	6,323	6,529
Oregon	72,946	61,669	23,435	38,234	11,277	9,626	3,161	6,465
California	453,575	410,533	173,235	237,298	43,042	58,860	24,510	34,350

SOURCE: U.S. Census, *Statistical Abstract,* 1951 (Washington, 1951), p.770.

Table 4.
Paid Civilian Employment in the Executive Branch of the Federal Government, 1938 and 1945, by State

State or Other Area	December 1938	June 1945
Continental U.S.	831,833	2,915,476
Washington, D.C., metro. area	119,874	257,808
48 states	711,959	2,657,668
Arizona	7,477	17,900
California	48,334	317,236
Colorado	8,692	28,839
Idaho	3,780	9,877
Montana	8,157	9,150
Nevada	1,819	6,753
New Mexico	7,201	16,206
North Dakota	3,820	6,047
Oregon	9,113	18,827
South Dakota	3,886	10,488
Texas	27,777	149,899
Utah	3,886	37,665
Washington	15,520	100,359
Wyoming	3,095	5,067

SOURCE: U.S. Census, *Statistical Abstract,* 1951 (Washington, 1951), p.196.

Table 5.
Personal Income: Select Western States, 1940, 1948
(in millions of dollars)

State	Total Income		Per Capita Income	
	1940	*1948*	*1940*	*1948*
Arizona	251	879	502	1,274
California	5,802	17,633	835	1,752
Colorado	615	1,810	544	1,433
Idaho	235	725	—	1,407
Montana	316	876	566	1,616
Nevada	101	283	890	1,814
New Mexico	198	655	373	1,084
North Dakota	218	813	340	1,401
Oklahoma	851	2,390	366	1,140
Oregon	671	2,278	648	1,621
South Dakota	231	916	360	1,497
Texas	2,762	9,142	430	1,199
Utah	266	810	482	1,241
Washington	1,140	3,608	655	1,600
Wyoming	151	429	606	1,595

SOURCE: *Historical Statistics of the U.S.*, pp. 242–245.

Table 6.

Population Growth of Western States, Estimates, 1940–1945

(in thousands of persons)

Division and State	1940	1941	1942	1943	1944	1945
Mountain	4,172	4,215	4,294	4,443	4,303	4,237
Montana	556	544	522	487	462	463
Idaho	524	515	497	506	539	509
Wyoming	250	259	267	257	251	244
Colorado	1,133	1,138	1,136	1,171	1,148	1,118
New Mexico	534	531	536	541	532	539
Arizona	509	547	611	701	618	602
Utah	554	562	592	635	602	612
Nevada	112	118	133	144	151	148
Pacific	9,824	10,328	11,008	11,799	12,444	13,060
Washington	1,741	1,792	1,909	2,058	2,162	2,274
Oregon	1,100	1,131	1,147	1,233	1,282	1,294
California	6,982	7,405	7,951	8,508	9,001	9,491

SOURCE: U.S. Census, *Statistical Abstract,* 1951 (Washington, 1951), p.28.

Table 7.
Population Growth of Western States, 1920–1950

Division and State	1920	1930	1940	1950	Percent increase 1940 to 1950
United States	105,710,620	122,775,016	131,669,275	150,697,361	14.5
Mountain	3,336,101	2,701,789	4,150,003	5,074,998	22.3
Montana	548,889	537,606	559,456	501,024	5.6
Idaho	431,866	445,032	524,873	588,637	12.1
Wyoming	194,402	225,565	290,742	290,529	15.9
Colorado	939,629	1,035,296	1,123,296	1,325,089	18.0
New Mexico	360,350	423,317	531,818	681,157	28.1
Arizona	334,162	435,573	499,261	749,587	50.1
Nevada	77,407	91,058	110,247	160,083	45.2
Utah	449,396	507,847	550,310	688,862	25.2
Pacific	5,566,871	8,164,423	9,733,262	14,486,527	48.8
Washington	1,356,621	1,563,396	1,726,191	2,378,963	37.0
Oregon	783,389	753,786	1,089,684	1,521,311	39.6
California	3,426,861	5,677,251	6,907,387	10,586,223	53.3

SOURCE: U.S. Census, *Historical Statistics of the U.S.*, p.31.

Table 8.

Population in the West by Sex, Race, Residence, 1940 and 1950

(in thousands)

	1940	*1950*
Total Population	14,379	20,190
Sex		
Male	7,134	9,884
Female	6,750	9,677
Race		
White	13,350	18,574 ·
Black	171	571
Others	363	416
Residence		
Urban	8,409	14,027
Rural	5,969	6,163
Urban White	7,851	12,941
Urban Black and Others	276	707
Rural White	5,498	5,633
Rural Black and Others	257	280

SOURCE: Adapted from U.S. Census, *Historical Statistics,* p.22.

Notes

1. The West on the Eve of War, 1939–1941

1. Walter P. Webb, *Divided We Stand: The Crisis of a Frontierless Democracy* (New York, 1937), pp. 3, 4, 26, 30.

2. On colonialism see Gene M. Gressley, "Colonialism and the American West," *Pacific Northwest Quarterly* 54 (January 1963), pp. 1–8, for a very brief analysis. This is also a theme in A. G. Mezerick, *The Revolt of the South and West* (New York, 1946), pp. 50–76, 112–273; Joseph K. Howard, *Montana: High, Wide, and Handsome* (New Haven, 1943), pp. 83–245; and Bernard DeVoto, "The West Against Itself," *Harper's*, vol. 194 (January 1947), 1–13.

3. Alvin H. Hansen, *Fiscal Policy and Business Cycles* (New York, 1941), pp. 360, 43.

4. Webb, *Divided We Stand*, pp. 157–158, 175. On the myth of the closing of the frontier see also Gerald D. Nash, "The Census of 1890 and the Closing of the Frontier," *Pacific Northwest Quarterly*, vol. 71 (July 1980), pp. 98–100.

5. Wendell Berge, *Economic Freedom for the West* (Lincoln, 1946), p. ix.

6. Ibid., p. 24; Morris E. Garnsey, *America's New Frontier: The Mountain West* (New York, 1950), pp. 168–189; Fritz Machlup, *The Basing Point System* (Philadelphia, 1949), pp. 61–90; Robert A. Lively, *The South in Action* (Durham, 1949), pp. 18–32. Table 1 (Appendix) reveals the position of manufactures in the economy of western states, 1939 and 1947, and reveals the multiplier effects of the war. The most useful, relevant contemporary study analyzing trends in the western economy is K. C. Stokes, *Regional Shifts in Population, Production, and Markets, 1939–1943*, U.S. Department of Commerce, Bureau of Foreign and Domestic Commerce Economic Series #30 (November 1943), pp. 12–17 and Table 1(a), p. 35, showing war output by geographic region.

7. U.S., Temporary National Economic Committee, *Final Report and Recommendations of the Temporary National Economic Committee* in 77th Cong., 1st sess., Senate, Document #35 (Washington, 1943), pp. 53–59, Appendices A, B.

8. Ibid., pp. 55–56, Appendix C; remarks of Chester C. Davis in ibid., p. 57, Appendix E.

9. Leonard J. Arrington, "The New Deal in the West: A Preliminary Statistical Analysis," *Pacific Historical Review*, vol. 38 (August 1969), 311–316.

10. Elwyn P. Robinson, *History of North Dakota* (Lincoln, 1966), p. 400; Herbert S. Schell, *History of South Dakota* (Lincoln, 1975), p. 302; Michael Malone and Richard Roeder, *Montana: A History of Two Centuries* (Seattle, 1976), p. 237.

11. U.S. Census, *Historical Statistics of the U.S., 1780–1970* (2 vols., Washington, 1974), vol. II, 483–485; T.A.B. Larson, *Wyoming's War Years, 1941–1945* (Laramie, 1954), pp. 487–489.

12. On weather conditions see John T. Schlebecker, *Cattle Raising on the Plains, 1900–1961* (Lincoln, 1963), pp. 153–155, 180, 208–209.

13. U.S. Department of Agriculture, Agricultural and Marketing Service, *Livestock and Meat Statistics Bulletin #230* (Washington, 1958), pp. 204, 283; see also Schlebecker, *Cattle Raising*, pp. 152–153.

14. James R. Gray and Chester B. Baker, *Cattle Ranching in the Northern Great Plains*, Montana Agricultural Experiment Station Circular #204 (Bozeman, 1953), p. 7; H. B. Pingrey, *Cattle Ranching in Southeastern New Mexico*, New Mexico Agricultural Experiment Station, *Bulletin #336* (Las Cruces, 1948), p. 18; Day Monroe et al., *Family Income and Expenditures, Pacific Region and Plains and Mountain Region* in U.S. Department of Agriculture, Miscellaneous Publication #336 (Washington, 1939), Part I (Family Income), pp. 91–96; Schlebecker, *Cattle Raising*, p. 166.

15. U.S. Bureau of the Census, *Historical Statistics*, p. 602. See also Russell R. Elliott, *History of Nevada* (Lincoln, 1973), pp. 308–309.

16. 76th Cong., 3d sess., *Cong. Record*, pp. 1465, 1469, 1483, 2783, 5786, 9734–35, Appendix 3806. 76th Cong., 2d sess., Senate, Special Committee to Investigate the National Defense Program, *Hearings* (parts 1 to 43, Washington, 1941–1947), p. 2398, hereafter cited as *Truman Committee Hearings*.

17. American Petroleum Institute, *Petroleum Facts and Figures*, 1959 (New York, 1960), pp. 114, 117, 125–128, 209–211, 379; ibid., 1939 (New York, 1940), pp. 11, 24–26, 40; Harold F. Williamson et al., *The American Petroleum Industry: The Age of Energy, 1899–1959* (Evanston, 1963), pp. 649–651, 718–720; Gerald D. Nash, *U.S. Oil Policy, 1890–1964: Business and Government in Twentieth Century America* (Pittsburgh, 1968), pp. 104–108, 155–158.

18. U.S. Census, *Statistical Abstract, 1941* (Washington, 1942), pp. 4–5, 879–880; Schell, *History of South Dakota*, p. 379; Rufus K. Wyllis, *History of Arizona* (New York, 1945), p. 356. See Table l, Appendix.

19. 77th Cong., 1st sess., Senate, Special Committee to Study and Survey Problems of Small Business Enterprises, *Hearings on Small Business and the War Program* (94 parts, Washington, 1948), hereafter cited as *Small Business Hearings*, Part 1, pp. 126–127.

20. Robinson, *History of North Dakota*, pp. 427–428.

21. Machlup, *The Basing Point System*, pp. 61–90.

22. Lively, *The South in Action*, pp. 20–24; *New York Times*, January 7, 1938.

23. *New York Times*, January 21, 28, 1939; 76th Cong., 1st sess., Senate, Subcommittee of Committee on Interstate Commerce, *Hearings on Freight Rate Discriminations*, February 27–March 8, 1939 (Washington, 1939), p. 546, and 76th Cong., 1st sess., House, Committee on Interstate and Foreign Commerce, *Hearings on Omnibus Transportation Bill* (Washington, 1939), pp. 691–959.

24. For favorable ICC views on the Southern Governors Case see *Railway Age*, 106 (1939), p. 389.

25. For resolutions see *Cong. Record*, 76th Cong., 1st sess., p. 5571; Interstate Commerce Commission, *Class Rate Investigation*, Docket 28300 and 28310; 262 ICC 447; *New York Times*, July 30, 1939.

26. *Cong. Record,* 76th Cong., 1st sess., pp. 3509, 5588, 5984–5985, 6495, 9698–10, 127, 11,766, 12,290; Robert W. Harbeson, "The Transportation Act of 1940," *Journal of Land and Public Utility Economics,* 17 (August 1941), 291–302.

27. U.S., Bureau of the Census, *Statistical Abstract,* 1940, p. 12.

28. Margaret S. Gordon, *Employment Expansion and Population Growth: The California Experience, 1900–1950* (Berkeley, 1954), pp. 4–6; (Davis McEntire) Commonwealth Club of California, *The Population of California* (San Francisco, 1946), pp. 3–12.

29. Table A-2 in Appendix A in Gordon, *Employment Expansion,* p. 162; U.S. Census of Population, 1950, *Special Report,* P-E, #4A, pp. 19–43; Clark Kerr, *Migration to the Seattle Labor Market Area, 1940–1942, University of Washington Publications in the Social Sciences,* vol. 11, No. 3 (Seattle, 1942), p. 160.

30. Marshall Sprague, *Colorado: A Bicentennial History* (New York, 1976), pp. 169–170; Lyle Dorsett, *The Queen City: History of Denver* (Denver, 1977), 237–239; Marshall Sprague, *Newport in the Rockies: The Life and Good Times of Colorado Springs* (Chicago, 1961), pp. 310–311.

31. U.S., Bureau of the Census, *Historical Statistics,* p. 24. See also Elliott, *Nevada,* pp. 312–313, 316–317.

32. U.S., Bureau of the Census, 1950, *Population,* II, Part I, pp. 18, 515.

33. U.S. Bureau of the Census, 1940, *Population,* II, Part 5, p. 51.

34. Lawrence B. De Graaf, "Negro Migration to Los Angeles, 1930–1950" (Ph.D. dissertation, UCLA, 1962), pp. 1–101, provides background information; see also Edward Everett France, "Some Aspects of the Migration of the Negro to the San Francisco Bay Area Since 1940 (Ph.D. dissertation, University of California, 1962), pp. 1–8; on Tucson see Harry T. Getty, *Interethnic Relationships in the Community of Tucson* (Tucson, 1976), pp. 107–108, based on a dissertation completed in 1950; see also Dorsett, *Denver,* pp. 240–241.

35. Nancy L. Gonzales, *The Spanish Americans of New Mexico: A Heritage of Pride* (Albuquerque, 1969), pp. 16–21.

36. Statistics in border states are difficult to evaluate. See U.S. Bureau of the Census, *Historical Statistics,* pp. 107, 117; Paul S. Taylor, *Mexicans in the United States: Migration Statistics, University of California Publications in Economics,* #6 (Berkeley, 1929), p. 240; Heller Committee for Research in Social Economics of the University of California and Constantine Panunzio, *How Mexicans Earn and Live: A Study of the Incomes and Expenditures of One Hundred Mexican Families in San Diego, California, University of California Publications in Economics* #13 (Berkeley, 1933), p. 16; Emory S. Bogardus, "Current Problems of Mexican Immigrants," *Sociology and Social Research,* 25 (November–December 1940), 166–174; John H. Burma, *Spanish Speaking Groups in the United States* (Durham, 1954), p. 91; Faith M. Williams and Alice C. Hanson, *Money Disbursements of Wage Earners and Clerical Workers in Five Cities in the Pacific Region, 1934–1936—Mexican Families in Los Angeles,* U.S. Bureau of Labor Statistics, *Bulletin* #639, part 2 (Washington, 1939), p. 100; see also Robin F. Scott, "The Mexican-American in the Los Angeles Area, 1920–1950" (Ph.D. dissertation, University of Southern California, 1971), pp. 106–192 on Mexican-Americans during the Great Depression.

37. On Chavez see *Biographical Directory of the American Congress, 1774–1971* (Washington, 1971), pp. 729–730. Roy Lujan, a doctoral candidate at the University of New Mexico, is currently writing a political biography of Chavez, whose papers are deposited at the University of New Mexico.

38. Kenneth S. Philp, *John S. Collier's Crusade for Indian Reform, 1928–1954* (Tucson, 1977), and also Donald S. Parman, *The Navajos and the New Deal* (New Haven, 1976).

39. John Modell, *The Economics and Politics of Racial Accommodation: The Japanese of Los Angeles, 1900–1942* (Urbana, 1977), pp. 118–127, 132, 136. Roger Daniels, *The Politics of Prejudice* (Berkeley, 1962).

40. Marvin G. Pursinger, "The Japanese in Oregon in World War II: A Study in Compulsory Relocation" (Ph.D. dissertation, University of Southern California, 1961), and Cheryl Cole, *A History of the Japanese Community in Sacramento, 1885–1972* (San Francisco, 1974); Audrie Girdner and Anne Loftis, *The Great Betrayal: The Evacuation of the Japanese Americans During World War II* (New York, 1969), pp. 33–99.

41. For a short summary see Gerald D. Nash, *The American West in the Twentieth Century* (Albuquerque, 1977), pp. 175–187.

42. Hortense Powdermaker, *Hollywood: The Dream Factory* (Boston, 1950); Leo Rosten, *Hollywood: The Movie Colony, the Movie Makers* (New York, 1941), for a contemporary critic; Robert Sklar, *Movie Made America: A Social History of American Movies* (New York, 1975); see also a more specialized work, Andrew Bergman, *We're in the Money: Depression America and Its Films* (New York, 1971). My conception of "culture" in this study—as part of a broader framework also embracing social structure and the polity—has been influenced by Daniel Bell, *The Coming of Post-Industrial Society* (New York, 1973), p. 12 where he notes that the axial principle of culture "is the desire for the fulfillment and enhancement of the self." See also pp. 13, 37–39, 188–192, 477–480.

2. The New West

1. A brief survey is in Nash, *American West in the Twentieth Century*, pp. 9–10. The term "colonial economy" as used in this study designates an economy based on exploitation of raw materials (such as agriculture, stock raising or mining) sent outside the region for fabrication. "Industrial economy" in this work denotes one deriving significant income from the manufacture of raw materials. In utilizing the concept of "post-industrial economy" I follow the categories outlined by Daniel Bell which include a) an economic sector which is changing from dependence on raw materials and manufacturing to services, b) a shift of occupational distribution to a professional and technical class, or white collar occupations, c) increasing dependence on theoretical knowledge as a source of economic innovation, and d) increased orientation to future planning of technological change. On the colonial economy, see Webb, *Divided We Stand;* on the industrial economy in the West see Leonard J. Arrington, *The Changing Economic Structure of the Mountain West, 1850–1950* (Logan, 1963), pp. 9–21; and Ralph W. Pfouts, ed., *The Techniques of Urban Economic Analysis* (West Trenton, N.J., 1960), particularly the essay by Charles M. Tiebout on Community Income Multipliers, pp. 341–358, and the classic study by Harvey S. Perloff et al., *Regions, Resources, and Economic Growth* (Baltimore, 1960), particularly pp. 93–96 on the multiplier effect in regional growth. A superb distillation is Harvey Perloff, with Vera Dodds, *How a Region Grows* (Washington, 1963), pp. 11–20, 53–62. On the post-industrial economy see Bell, *The Coming of Post-Industrial Society*, pp. 3–14, 17–33. See also Victor R. Fuchs, *The Service Economy* (New York, 1968).

2. The subject matter of this chapter will be treated in greater depth in a

forthcoming book about the economic impact of World War II on the American West.

3. See Table 2 in Appendix for figures on war contracts and federal installations; compilations from annual budgets of the U.S.; for California see Stanley Brubaker, "The Impact of Federal Government Activities on California's Economic Growth, 1930–1956" (Ph.D. dissertation, University of California, 1959). On the remarkable increase of investment wrought by the war see Table 3 in Appendix. Webb, *Divided We Stand*, pp. 157–158; Ransom in *Saturday Review of Literature*, vol. 17 (December 18, 1937), 6–7.

4. The preceding two paragraphs are amplified in Nash, *American West in the Twentieth Century*, pp. 18–41, 155–170, and Edward Ullman, "Amenities as a Factor in Regional Growth," *Geographical Review*, Vol. 44 (January 1954), 119–132.

5. On the nineteenth century see Carter Goodrich, *Government Promotion of American Canals and Railroads* (New York, 1960), Forest G. Hill, *Roads, Rails and Waterways; The Army Engineers and Early Transportation* (Norman, 1957), and W. Turrentine Jackson, *Wagon Roads West: A Study of Federal Road Surveys and Construction in the Trans-Mississippi West, 1846–1869* (Berkeley, 1952). On economic impact of New Deal see Arrington in *Pacific Historical Review*, vol. 38, 311–316. Helpful contemporary publications include studies of the National Resources Planning Board, particularly *Pacific Southwest Region: Industrial Development* (Washington, 1942), pp. 1–2, 4–5, 9–15, 28–52; *Pacific Northwest Region* (Washington, 1942), pp. 3, 10–24, 29–33; *Development of Resources and of Economic Opportunity in the Pacific Northwest* (Washington, 1942), pp. 1–16, 91–170.

6. For a contemporary evaluation of industrial potential see U.S., National Resources Planning Board, *Industrial Location and National Resources* (Washington, 1943), pp. 9–31, 61–63, and passim; on expenditures of the Defense Plant Corporation see Comptroller General of the United States, *Report on Audit of Reconstruction Finance Corporation and Affiliated Corporations as of June 30, 1945: Defense Plant Corporation* in 80th Cong., 1st sess., House, Document $474 (Washington, 1947), p. 4; see also Jesse Jones, *Fifty Billion Dollars: My Thirteen Years with the Reconstruction Finance Corporation, 1932–1945* (New York, 1951); Gerald T. White, *Billions for Defense: Government Financing by the Defense Plant Corporation During World War II* (University, Alabama, 1980).

7. On the Provo plants see Leonard J. Arrington and Anthony T. Cluff, *Federally Financed Industrial Plants Constructed in Utah During World War II* (Logan, 1969), and Leonard J. Arrington and George Jensen, *The Defense Industry of Utah* (Logan, 1965); on Basic Magnesium see 76th Cong., 2d sess., Senate, *Truman Committee Hearings*, pp. 5551–5690 (in Las Vegas, Nevada), Elliott, *History of Nevada*, pp. 310–311; on aluminum see *Truman Committee Hearings*, pp. 713–720, 2111–2884, and "Power to Burn," *Fortune*, vol. 31 (February 1945), 141–146; on Defense Plant Corporation see Jones, *Fifty Billion*, pp. 315–349.

8. *Truman Committee Hearings*, p. 5759 for Henry Kaiser's version. Contemporary literature on Spruce Goose is large. See "Fabulous Team: Kaiser and Hughes," *Time*, vol. 40 (August 31, 1942), 19–20; R. McCormick, "Wing Talk: Important Meeting at Which 200 Ton Cargo Plane Was Conceived," *Collier's*, vol. 110 (October 17, 1942), 8; Raymond Moley, "The Cargo Plane Question," *Newsweek*, vol. 20 (September 28, 1942), 80. "Planes v. Ships: Big

Air Freighters Can Be Built Now Only at the Expense of Other War Equipment," *Business Week* (August 1, 1942), pp. 24ff.

9. *New York Times,* August 24, 25, 29, 1942; September 1, 1942, October 1, 1942, June 9, August 27, 1943, December 16, 24, 1943; "Up in the Air, WPB and the Kaiser-Hughes Plane," *Time,* vol. 42 (November 8, 1943), 83; *New York Times,* November 1, 2, 1947, and March 7, 1980.

10. Valuable is 78th Cong., 2d sess., Senate, Special Committee to Study and Survey Problems of American Small Business Pursuant to Senate Resolution 66, Subcommittee Print #6, "Survey of the Nation's Critical and Strategic Minerals and Metals Program," *Preliminary Report of the SubCommittee on Mining and Minerals Industry* (Washington, 1944), pp. 8–12, 18–42, 52–59. On expansion of the Metals Reserve Corporation see Jesse Jones to Charles B. Henderson, September 26, 1941 in Records of the Metals Reserve Corporation in National Archives, Washington, D.C. My examination of these records convinces me that a detailed history of the Metal Reserves Corporation in the West would be a significant contribution. On problems of western miners see also *Small Business Hearings,* pp. 2337–2402, 3290–3297, and Jones, *Fifty Billion,* pp. 434–450.

11. Clifford Durr, "The Defense Plant Corporation," in Harold Stein (ed.), *Public Administration and Policy Development* (New York, 1952), p. 294–298. Durr was Assistant Counsel of the DPC. Frank A. Howard, *Buna Rubber: The Birth of an Industry* (New York, 1947), pp. 116–120, 133, 274–280; Jones, *Fifty Billion,* pp. 402–433. For a list of all of the synthetic rubber plants sponsored by the RFC including those in the West see Jones, *Fifty Billion,* pp. 610–611. White, *Billions for Defense,* pp. 18, 40, 109.

12. 77th Cong., 1st sess., Senate, Committee on Military Affairs, "Strategic and Critical Materials, Guayule Rubber," *Hearings to Provide for Planting of 45,000 Acres* (December 10, 1941, January 6, 1942) (2 parts, Washington, 1941, 1942), part I, pp. 1–70, part 2, pp. 75–83, and 77th Cong., 2d sess., Senate, *Report* #935 (Washington, 1942), pp. 1–4 ("Report to Accompany S 2152 (Downey Bill) to Provide for Planting of Guayule"); *Truman Committee Hearings* (Salinas), pp. 5537–5545; Truman Committee, 77th Cong., 2d sess., Senate, *Report* #480 (Washington, 1942), pp. 20–21.

13. 77th Cong., 2d sess., House, Committee on Agriculture, *Hearings on HR 6299 to Provide for the Planting of 75,000 Acres of Guayule* (January 7–13, 1942) (Washington, 1942), pp. 2–111; extensive records concerning the guayule experiment can be found in the records of the U.S. Forest Service in the National Archives. Washington, D.C. See also 77th Cong., 2d sess., Senate, Committee on Military Affairs, *Hearing on S. 2775 to Expand the Guayule Program* (September 16, 1942) (Washington, 1942), pp. 1–20, and 77th Cong., 2d sess., Senate, *Report* #1607 (Washington, 1942), pp. 1–2.

14. Arizonans became very excited about the prospects of the guayule program and hoped it might become a major industry. See Carl Hayden to Tom Houck, July 16, 1942, P. V. Carden to Carl Hayden, February 3, 1942; B. H. Ormand to Carl Hayden, May 4, 1942, and Leslie Godding to Carl Hayden, May 9, 1942 in Carl Hayden Papers, Arizona Historical Collections, Arizona State University, Tempe, Arizona, hereafter cited as Hayden Papers. With increasing prices of petroleum, needed to manufacture synthetic rubber, in 1980 the Department of Agriculture began a new program for extensive planting of guayule in the American Southwest. See *New York Times,* November 4, 1980 (Sect. 4, p. 3).

15. Robinson, *History of North Dakota*, p. 427. The North Dakota War Resources Committee and the Greater North Dakota Association directed by Frederick Frederickson were among the most active business groups to solicit war contracts. See also Larson, *Wyoming's War Years*, pp. 244–247, 250–252, 255, and T.A.B. Larson, *History of Wyoming* (Lincoln, 1965), pp. 476, 485, 489–490; Malone and Roeder, *Montana*, pp. 237–238; U.S. Department of Labor, Bureau of Labor Statistics, *Handbook of Labor Statistics* (1947 edition), Bulletin #916 and U.S. Department of Commerce, *Survey of Current Business*, vol. 26 (1946), #8, 19.

16. Franklin D. Roosevelt to Pat McCarran, July 9, 1941; McCarran to Joe Cook, July 11, 1941 in Pat McCarran Papers, Nevada State Archives, Carson City, Nevada, hereafter cited as McCarran Papers. In 1982 this collection was moved to the Nevada State Historical Society in Reno. McCarran spirited the plant away from California interests. See *Las Vegas Age*, August 15, 1941, *Las Vegas Review Journal*, September 23, 1941, November 20, 1941, clippings in McCarran Scrapbooks, McCarran Papers.

17. Elliott, *History of Nevada*, p. 310; Jones, *Fifty Billion*, p. 333.

18. This theme is graphically presented in Arrington, *The Changing Economic Structure of the Mountain West, 1850–1950*.

19. For a general survey see Leonard J. Arrington and George Jensen, *The Defense Industry of Utah* (Logan, 1965), pp. 4–13, 47. For more detailed studies see Leonard J. Arrington and Thomas G. Alexander, "They Kept 'Em Rolling: The Tooele Army Depot, 1942–1962," *Utah Historical Quarterly* (hereafter cited as *UHQ*), vol. 31 (Winter, 1963), 3–14; Leonard J. Arrington and Archer L. Durham, "Anchors Aweigh in Utah: The U.S. Naval Supply Depot at Clearfield, 1942–1962," *UHQ*, vol. 31 (Spring, 1963), 109–118; Leonard J. Arrington and Thomas G. Alexander, "World's Largest Military Reserves: Wendover Air Force Base, 1941–1963," *UHQ*, vol. 31 (Fall, 1963), 324–332; Leonard J. Arrington and Thomas G. Alexander, "Sentinels on the Desert: The Dugway Proving Ground (1942–1963), and Deseret Chemical Depot (1942–1955)," *UHQ*, vol. 32 (Winter, 1964), 32–38; Leonard J. Arrington and Thomas G. Alexander, "Supply Hub of the West: Defense Depot Ogden, 1941–1964," *UHQ*, vol. 32 (Spring, 1964), 99–112; Leonard J. Arrington, Thomas G. Alexander, and Eugene A. Erb, Jr., "Utah's Biggest Business: Ogden Air Materiel Area at Hill Air Force Base, 1938–1965," *UHQ*, vol. 33 (Winter, 1965), 9–16; Thomas G. Alexander, "Ogden's Arsenal of Democracy, 1920–1955," *UHQ*, vol. 33 (Summer, 1965), 240–245; Thomas G. Alexander, "Brief Histories of Three Federal Military Installations in Utah: Kearns Army Air Base," *UHQ*, vol. 34 (Spring, 1966), 123–126. For a descriptive list of military installations in Colorado see Leroy Hafen (ed.), *Colorado and Its People* (3 vols., New York, 1950), vol. 3, 592–598.

20. Most histories of western states include brief mention or lists of these installations in World War II, such as Hafen (ed.), *Colorado and Its People*, vol. 3, 592–598; Elliott, *History of Nevada*, pp. 312–313; Wyllis, *Arizona*, pp. 344–358; Malone and Roeder, *Montana*, p. 238; F. Ross Peterson, *Idaho: A Bicentennial History* (New York, 1976), p. 158; A. M. Gibson, *Oklahoma: A History of Five Centuries* (Norman, 1965), pp. 384–387; Schell, *South Dakota*, pp. 299–302. A graphic illustration of this trend is the increase of federal employees in western states as reflected in Table 4, in Appendix.

21. Marquis and Bessie R. James, *Biography of a Bank* (New York, 1954), pp. 464–471; Federal Reserve Bank of San Francisco, *Bulletin*, June 12, 1945,

p. 4. The multiplier effect of federal expenditures is reflected in the rise of personal income in western states, 1940 and 1948 as reflected in Table 5 in Appendix.

22. See Department of Labor, Bureau of Labor Statistics, *Monthly Labor Review*, vol. 61 (October, 1945), 722–723; Victor R. Fuchs, *Changes in the Location of Manufacturing in the United States Since 1929* (New York, 1962), pp. 2, 26–27, 33, 51–52, 63, 231–236; *Fortune*, vol. 37 (February, 1945), 116–120. Davis McEntire, *The Labor Force in California: A Study of Characteristics and Trends in Labor Force Employment and Occupations in California, 1900–1950* (Berkeley, 1952), pp. 232–240; see also Forest Hill, "The Shaping of California's Industrial Pattern," *Proceedings of the 30th Annual Conference of the Western Economic Association* (1955), pp. 63–68. Essential for tracing the multiplier effect is George Hildebrand and Arthur Mace, Jr., "The Employment Multiplier in an Expanding Industrial Market: Los Angeles County, 1940–47," *Review of Economics and Statistics*, vol. 32 (August 1950), 241–249.

23. Leonard G. Levenson, "Wartime Development of the Aircraft Industry," *Monthly Labor Review*, vol. 59 (November 1944), 909–910; Aircraft Industries Association, *Aircraft Facts and Figures*, 1945, pp. 7–24; William G. Cunningham, *The Aircraft Industry: A Study of Industrial Location* (Berkeley, 1951), pp. 76–81; Arthur P. Allen and Betty V. H. Schneider, *Industrial Relations in the California Aircraft Industry* (Berkeley, 1956), pp. 18–35; a general popular survey is Frank J. Taylor and Lawton Wright, *Democracy's Air Arsenal* (New York, 1947).

24. *Wartime Employment, Production, and Conditions of Work in Shipyards*, Department of Labor, Bureau of Labor Statistics, *Bulletin #824* (Washington, 1945); Frederick C. Lane, *Ships for Victory: A History of Shipbuilding Under the U.S. Maritime Commission in World War II* (Baltimore, 1951), pp. 434–339; Wytze Gorter and George H. Hildebrand, *The Pacific Coast Maritime Shipping Industry, 1930–1948* (2 vols., Berkeley, 1952–54), vol. 1, 7, 16, 37–38, 74–75.

25. "Steel in the West," *Fortune*, vol. 31 (February 1945), 130–134; Ewald T. Grether, *The Steel and Steel Using Industries of California* (Berkeley, 1946).

26. U.S. Census, *Statistical Abstract*, 1951, p. 767; see also a useful pamphlet by Sterling Brubaker, *Significance of Military Installations for California's Economic Growth, 1930–1952* (San Francisco, 1955), published by the Bank of America.

27. On Kaiser see *Current Biography*, 1942 (New York, 1942), pp. 431–435; James, *Biography*, p. 467; *Christian Science Monitor*, September 30, October 6, 19, 20, 29, 1942; *Time*, vol. 37 (March 3, 1941), 67–68; ibid., vol. 40 (September 21, 1942), 171.

28. On Fontana see *New York Times*, August 20, 1942, September 7, 24, 27, 1942, October 18, 21, 22, 23, 25, 28, 1942, November 4, December 31, 1942, January 1, 7, 30, 1943, May 14, 15, 16, 1943; "Steel for West: Companies West of Rockies Propose Big Expansion Program," *Business Week* (June 28, 1941), pp. 18ff.; "Steel Goes West: Kaiser and Columbia Add to Pacific Facilities," *Business Week* (November 21, 1942), p. 52; "Steel Man Kaiser," *Business Week* (March 7, 1942), pp. 33–34; and "Kaiser-Steelmaker," *Newsweek*, vol. 21 (January 11, 1943), p. 50. "Steel—Report on the War Years," *Fortune*, vol. 31 (May 1945), 121–123; Jones, *Fifty Billion*, pp. 332–334.

29. Kaiser employed the well-known Washington lawyer and lobbyist Tom Corcoran to further his ventures into magnesium production. See *Tru-*

man *Committee Hearings,* p. 1571; On aluminum see G. Granville Jensen, *The Aluminum Industry of the Northwest* (Corvallis, 1950), pp. 5–15, Oregon State College Circular #12; Charles M. Wiltse, *Aluminum Policies of the War Production Board and Predecessor Agencies,* May 1940 to November 1945 (Washington, 1946), pp. 173–175; *Small Business Hearings,* pp. 5176–5191; 5258–5260, 5291–5294, 5306–5310, 6028–6032, 6202–6368.

30. Pacific Northwest Regional Planning Commission, *Pacific Northwest Development in Perspective* (Portland, 1943), and Margaret Schleef, "Manufacturing Trends in the Inland Empire" (Pullman, 1947), pp. 3–15, 26–56, 64–66 (Washington State University, Bureau of Economic and Business Research, *Bulletin* #4) provide general accounts; see also Edwin Cohn, Jr., *Industry in the Pacific Northwest and the Location Theory* (New York, 1952), pp. 29–51, and Art Ritchie and William L. Davis (eds.), *The Pacific Northwest Goes to War: State of Washington* (Seattle, 1944), which deals with one state. On Boeing see Harold Mansfield, *Vision: A Saga of the Sky* (New York, 1956), pp. 187–236, and Washington State University, Bureau of Business Research, *The Impact of World War II Subcontracting by the Boeing Airplane Company Upon Pacific Northwest Manufacturing* (Seattle, 1955), pp. 9–20, 22–48, as well as a company publication, Boeing Company, *Pedigree of Champions: Boeing since 1916* (4th ed., Seattle, 1977), passim.

31. Van Buren Stanberg, *Growth and Trends of Manufacturing in the Pacific Northwest, 1939–1947* (Washington, 1950), and Washington State Planning Council, *Employment and Payrolls: Basic Industries of Washington, 1920–1944* (Olympia, 1945).

32. Puget Sound Regional Planning Commission, *The Puget Sound Region: War and Postwar Development* (Washington, 1943). On the extensive efforts to secure steel manufacturing facilities for the Pacific Northwest see *Truman Committee Hearings,* pp. 2084–2102, 5775–5782, 5838–5840, 5908–5832, 5959–5969, 5996–6006; on aluminum see ibid., pp. 2112–2137, 2180, 2222–2254, 2755–2723, and also *Small Business Hearings,* part 42, pp. 5176–5191, 5258–5260, 5291, 5294, 5306–5310; on magnesium see *Truman Committee Hearings,* pp. 5416–5460; on hopes of representatives from the Aluminum Company of America for export of aluminum from the Pacific Northwest to the Orient see *Small Business Hearings,* part 50, pp. 6464–6468.

33. On problems of Denver businessmen in securing war contacts see *Small Business Hearings,* part 21, pp. 2945–2950. Subcontractors in Denver, Fort Collins, and Cheyenne also worked for the Bremerton, Washington shipyards. See ibid., part 30, pp. 4055–4063, and for photographs of the Denver shipyards see ibid., part 30, pp. 4124–4126, 4170–4189. *Rocky Mountain News,* August 19, 23, 1942 and December 1, 1942, and *Denver Post,* August 16, 23, 1942, also with pictures of first launching. Arnold S. Lott, *A Long Line of Ships* (Annapolis, 1954), pp. 212–214. Leroy Hafen (ed.), *Colorado and Its People,* vol. 3, 614–620. During the war the State Historical Society of Colorado sent out a questionnaire to Colorado manufacturing plants inquiring about production. A detailed list of the companies responding, the value of their products, and the number of their employees can be found in Hafen (ed.), *Colorado and Its People,* vol. 3, 620–622; for brief surveys see Carl Ubbelohde, *History of Colorado* (Boulder, 1965), pp. 313–316 and Sprague, *Colorado,* pp. 170–177.

34. Stephen C. Shadegg, "Goodyear Builds Tools of Victory," *Arizona Highways,* vol. 19 (May 1943), 14–19, 42–43, Keith Monroe, "Wings over

Tucson," ibid., vol. 20 (January 1944), 26–29, and "Arizona Lumber Goes to War," ibid., vol. 19 (January 1943), 1–3. Wyllis, *History of Arizona*, pp. 344–358.

35. Arrington, *The Defense Industry of Utah*, pp. 13–43. Arrington and Cluff, *Federally Financed Industrial Plants in Utah*, pp. 33–46.

36. Wartime activities of the U.S. Geological Survey can be followed in the Annual Reports of the Secretary of the Interior. See Secretary of the Interior, *Annual Report*, 1942 (Washington, 1942), pp. 46–49.

37. Ibid., 1943 (Washington, 1943), pp. 34–37; and ibid., 1944 (Washington, 1944), pp. 103–105.

38. Nevertheless, even in states where the war did not immediately stimulate manufacturing, it fostered diversification, or increased production of electric power, according to the authors of state histories. K. Ross Toole, *Montana: An Uncommon Land* (Norman, 1959), p. 254; Robert Karelovitz, *Challenge: The South Dakota Story* (Sioux Falls, 1975), p. 284, Robinson, *History of North Dakota*, p. 424; Malone and Roeder, *Montana*, pp. 237–238; Schell, *History of South Dakota*, pp. 302, 379–382; and South Dakota World War II Historical Commission, *South Dakota in World War II* (Pierre, 1947), passim. Washington State University, *Subcontracting*, pp. 9–10.

39. Harold L. Ickes, "Development of United States Public Land Resources," in Secretary of the Interior, *Annual Report*, 1942 (Washington, 1942), pp. iii–v, 19.

40. 77th Cong., 1st sess., Senate, *Document #35*, "Final Report and Recommendations of the U.S. Temporary National Economic Committee" (Washington, 1941), p. 23. O'Mahoney did not change his views in the course of the war. See "Report of the Hon. Joseph C. O'Mahoney to the Special Committee on Post-War Economic Policy and Planning," in 78th Cong., 1st sess., Senate, *Document #106* (Washington, 1944), pp. 1–3.

41. I have derived biographical data from various sources including the voluminous James E. Murray Papers at the Mansfield Library, University of Montana, Missoula, Montana, hereafter cited as Murray Papers. A competent dissertation is Donald E. Spritzer, "New Dealer from Montana: The Political Career of Senator James E. Murray" (Ph.D. dissertation, University of Montana, 1980). Dr. Spritzer was kind enough to grant me an interview on May 11, 1981. For brief sketches of Murray see *Current Biography*, 1945 (New York, 1945), pp. 414–417; *Biographical Directory of the American Congress, 1774–1971* p. 1457; *New York Times*, October 20, 1943, and *Business Week*, February 10, 1945.

42. 76th Cong., 2d sess., Senate, Resolution #298 (October 8, 1940), printed in *Small Business Hearings*, pp. 1–3.

43. Murray in 77th Cong., 2d sess., Senate, *Report #480* (Washington, 1944), p. 10; Franklin D. Roosevelt to James E. Murray, August 31, 1942, in Murray Papers.

44. Truman in *Truman Committee Hearings*, pp. 881–883; see also pp. 1786–1800, 1856, 1873, 2084–2102.

45. *Small Business Hearings*, pp. 126–140, particularly testimony of J. C. Ingebretsen representing the Los Angeles Chamber of Commerce. Nelson in 77th Cong., 2d sess., House, Committee on Banking and Currency, *Hearings on Conversion of Small Business Enterprises to War Production* (April 27 to May 8, 1942) (Washington, 1942), p. 54. On California pools see ibid., pp. 138–142, hereafter cited as *Banking Hearings*. On pools in Montana see Pat A. Kelley to Senator James E. Murray, January 26, 1943, Murray Papers.

46. Marquis and Bessie James, *Biography of a Bank,* pp. 46off.

47. See also *Federal Register,* Doc. 42–135 (March 26, 1942), and *Banking Hearings,* pp. 19–21, 89–102.

48. Nelson traces his discussions with Murray on this issue in *Banking Hearings,* pp. 53–54; *New York Times,* February 8, 11, 1942, May 6, 15, 25, 1942.

49. 77th Cong., 2d sess., Public Law 603; New York *Times,* June 12, 1942; "History of the Smaller War Plants Corporation," 11 vols., unpublished manuscript in Records of the Smaller War Plants Corporation, National Archives, Washington, D.C., a contemporary administrative history compiled by its staff in 1945, hereafter cited as SWPC History.

50. On Holland see *New York Times,* July 10, 11, 18, September 14, November 7, December 4, 1942. The Lou Holland Papers at the Kansas City Historical Society provide a vivid glimpse of his work with the SWPC. A brief survey of the SWPC can be found in 78th Cong., 1st sess., Senate, *Document #87* (6th Report of SWPC, June 11, 1943) (Washington, 1943), pp. 1–4; a more extensive account is SWPC History, vol. I, 123–143. President Roosevelt wanted to appoint Robert W. Johnson, an old friend (Chairman of Johnson and Johnson, a pharmaceutical manufacturer), but Senators Truman and Murray wanted Holland, although agreeing to Johnson as vice-chairman. See memo of Sidney Weinberg, "Recommendations for Board of Directors of SWPC" (March, 1943), in SWPC Records, Speech File of Maury Maverick.

51. On Johnson see *New York Times,* January 3, 20, 22, 23, 1943, February 8, 12, March 25, 1943; SWPC History, vol. I, 144ff.; 78th Cong., 1st sess., Senate, *Document #98* (Washington, 1943), pp. 1–5 (7th Report of SWPC) details some of the new organizational changes in the West. Before August 1, 1943 the SWPC's only office on the Pacific Coast was in San Francisco. After that date offices were opened in Los Angeles and Seattle while the Denver office was expanded. For specific projects see 78th Cong., 1st sess., Sen. *Document #98,* pp. 13–14, 42–43, and 78th Cong., 1st. sess., Senate, *Document #30* (Washington, 1943), p. 4, for 5th report of chairman of the War Production board on activities of the SWPC and the Smaller War Plants Division of the War Production Board.

52. On Maverick see *Current Biography,* 1944 (New York, 1944), pp. 454–458. Unfortunately, Richard B. Henderson, *Maury Maverick: A Political Biography* (Austin, 1970), completely ignores Maverick's World War II career. Yet the Maury Maverick Papers at the University of Texas are revealing. See Donald Nelson to Maury Maverick, July 11, 1944, Maury Maverick Papers, University of Texas, Austin, Box 2/27, hereafter cited as Maverick Papers. See also SWPC History, vol. 1, 194ff., 46off.; *Business Week,* January 22, 1944, p. 22. Maverick discusses his activities during his first year as chairman of the SWPC in 78th Cong., 2d sess., Senate, *Document #234* (Washington, 1944), pp. 4–7 (9th Report of the SWPC), and also 78th Cong., 2d sess., House, *Hearings Before the Subcommittee of the Committee on Appropriations for 1945* (Washington, 1944), pp. 794–795. There Maverick said: "I once defined a small business as being one which was unable to maintain a representative in Washington."

3. Westward Migrations

1. U.S. Bureau of the Census, *Historical Statistics,* part 1, pp. 24–37. Some contemporary accounts of population changes include Howard Myers, "De-

fense Migration and Labor Supply," *Journal of the American Statistical Association*, vol. 37 (March 1942), 69–76; Elmer C. Bratt and D. S. Wilson, "Regional Distortions Resulting from the War," *Survey of Current Business*, vol. 23 (October 1943), 9–15; Henry S. Shryock, Jr., "Internal Migration and the War," *Journal of the American Statistical Association*, vol. 38 (March 1943), 23–26; Conrad Taeuber, "Wartime Population Changes in the United States," *Milbank Memorial Fund Quarterly*, vol. 24 (July 1946), 238–239; and Henry S. Shryock, Jr., "Wartime Shifts of the Civilian Population," *Milbank Memorial Fund Quarterly*, vol. 25 (July 1947), 269–282. For yearly estimates of population growth in the western states during the war see Table 6 in Appendix; comparative population growth 1920–1950 is detailed in Table 7 in Appendix.

2. For a short survey of these developments see Nash, *American West in Twentieth Century*, pp. 191–211; for a contemporary account by an inveterate traveler see John Gunther, *Inside U.S.A.* (New York, 1946), pp. 1–236; Robert K. Lamb, "Mobilization of Human Resources," *American Journal of Sociology*, vol. 48 (November 1942), 323–330, and Wladimir Woytinsky, "Interstate Migration During the War," *State Government*, vol. 19 (March 1946), 81–84.

3. An extensive literature has arisen on western boom towns. Relevant studies include Lawrence B. Larson, *The Urban West at the End of the Frontier* (Lawrence, 1979), Gunther Barth, *Instant Cities: Urbanization and the Rise of San Francisco and Denver* (New York, 1975), Earl Pomeroy, "The Urban Frontier of the Far West," in John G. Clark (ed.), *The Frontier Challenge: Responses to the TransMississippi West* (Lawrence, 1971), and Carl Abbott, "Boom State and Boom City: Stages in Denver's Growth," *Colorado Magazine*, vol. 50 (Summer 1973), 207–229, and his notable book, *The New Urban America: Growth and Politics in Sunbelt Cities* (Chapel Hill, 1982).

4. U.S. Bureau of the Census, *Current Population Reports* Series P25, #72 (May 1953); Gordon, *Employment Expansion and Population Growth*, pp. 5–7. U.S. Bureau of the Census, *Historical Statistics*, pp. 22–37. Congress made an extensive investigation of these migrations. See 77th Cong., 2d sess., House, Select Committee Investigating National Defense migration pursuant to House Resolution #113 (34 parts, Washington, 1940–1942), *Hearings*, hereafter cited as *Tolan Committee Hearings* [John H. Tolan, chairman].

5. U.S. Bureau of the Census, 1940, *Population*, vol. 2 (Washington, 1942), part 1, p. 516; ibid., *State of Birth of the Native Population*, pp. 15–39; U.S. Bureau of the Census, 1950, *Population*, vol. 2 (Washington, 1952), part 5, p. 57; ibid., Special Report p-E #4A, pp. 19–43; U.S. Bureau of Agricultural Economics, Population Committee for the Central Valley Project Studies, *California Migration*, Statistical Memo #6 by C. N. Reynolds and S. Miles (mimeographed), Berkeley, 1944, pp. 1–8 in University of California Library. Gordon, *Employment Expansion*, pp. 17–24. These changes are placed in context in Henry Shryock, Jr., and Hope T. Eldridge, "Internal Migration in Peace and War," *American Sociological Review*, vol. 12 (February 1947), pp. 27–39.

6. U.S. Bureau of the Census, 1940, *Population*, "Internal Migration in the United States, 1935–1940," pp. 96, 113–114, 118; Kerr, *Migration to the Seattle Labor Market Area, 1940–1942*, p. 160; G. L. Palmer, *Labor Mobility in Six Cities* (New York, 1954), pp. 13–16, 83–91. See also L. V. Fuller, *The Supply of Agricultural Labor as a Factor in the Evolution of Farm Organization in California*, reprinted in 76th Cong., 3d sess., Senate, Committee on Education and Labor, *Hearings*, part 54 (Washington, 1940), pp. 19,777–19,898.

7. Nash, "Census of 1890," in *Pacific Northwest Quarterly*, vol. 71, 98–100; Reynolds and Miles, "Statistical Memo," #6, p. 21.

8. Quote in 78th Cong., 1st sess., Senate, Subcommittee of the Committee on Military Affairs, "Labor Shortages in the Pacific Coast and Rocky Mountain States," *Hearings on Senate Resolution #88 and Senate Resolution #113* (September 9–10, 1943) (Washington, 1943), p. 21, hereafter cited as *Labor Hearings*. See ibid., pp. 35–37, 76, 80, 88 on the high mobility of workers in the Los Angeles and San Francisco areas and also A. J. Reiss, Jr., and E. Katingawa, "Demographic Characteristics and Job Mobility of Migrants in Six Cities," *Social Forces* vol. 32 (October 1953), 70–75; Margaret S. Gordon, "Research Design of the Survey of Patterns and Factors in Mobility of Six Cities," *Journal of the American Statistical Association*, vol. 48 (September 1955), 633.

9. U.S. Bureau of the Census, 1940, *Population*, 1940, vol. 2, part 1, 18, 515; ibid., 1950, *Population*, vol. 2, part 1, 87, part 5, 51, 57; Gordon, *Employment Expansion*, pp. 9–11.

10. U.S. Bureau of the Census, 1940, *Population* (Internal Migration, 1935–1940), pp. 170, 176; Palmer, *Labor Mobility*, pp. 16, 24; Commonwealth Club of California, *The Population of California* (San Francisco, 1946).

11. For a detailed glimpse into the racial mix at one enterprise, the Moore Dry Dock Company in Oakland, California see Katherine Archibald, *Wartime Shipyard* (Berkeley, 1947), pp. 15–109; U.S. Bureau of the Census 1950, *Population*, vol. 2, part 5, 57.

12. 78th Cong., 1st sess., House, Subcommittee of Committee on Naval Affairs, *Hearings on Congested Areas* (8 parts, Washington, D.C., 1944), *Puget Sound, Washington, Area*, p. 1301. The work of the Committee is discussed more fully in Chapters 4 and 5. An interesting discussion of women workers that touches on Seattle is Karen Anderson, *Wartime Women: Sex Roles, Family Relations, and the Status of Women During World War II* (Westport, 1981), pp. 13–15, 36, 45, 52, 128.

13. *Labor Hearings*, p. 4; Roney was Assistant Regional Director for the War Manpower Commission, Region 12, (Pacific Coast).

14. Downey in ibid., p. 5.

15. Ibid., p. 8; see also pp. 18, 21, 59, 70, 96, 116, 118.

16. Douglas in *Truman Committee Hearings*, pp. 1859–1860; Roney in *Labor Hearings*, pp. 15, 18.

17. For Kranz see *Labor Hearings*, p. 61, and for Wilson, ibid., pp. 69–70.

18. Ibid., pp. 7–9. See also pp. 21, 96, 116.

19. Ibid., p. 76; see also pp. 75, 88.

20. Ibid., pp. 31, 70–80, 103–107, 117.

21. *New York Times*, April 9, 1943.

22. *New York Times*, September 4, 1943; *Labor Hearings*, pp. 31, 80–83.

23. For full text of the plan see *Labor Hearings*, pp. 103–107.

24. Ibid., p. 74.

25. Ibid., pp. 75, 85, 95–97, 101–102.

26. Downey in the committee's report as printed in ibid., p. 131.

27. *Truman Committee Hearings*, pp. 2330–2333, 2384–2386.

28. On the West Coast Labor Plan see *New York Times*, September 12, 13, 14, 18, 19, 1943, October 17, 29, 1943, November 2, 7, 17, 1943; "Sternest Manpower Control Yet Clamped on the Pacific Coast," *Newsweek*, vol. 22 (September 13, 1943), 62; "Buffalo Plan and the West Coast Plan," *Time*, vol. 42 (September 27, 1943), 84. "Directives on Effective Use of Manpower Re-

sources," *Monthly Labor Review*, vol. 57 (November, 1943), 932–935; "Byrnes Plan," *New Republic*, vol. 111 (September 25, 1944), 364–366.

29. 77th Cong., 2d sess., Senate, Special Committee to Investigate Farm Labor Conditions in the West, *Hearings on Sen. Resolution 299* (4 parts, Washington, 1943) (November 30–December 3, 1943), part 2, pp. 38, 200–203, hereafter cited as *Farm Labor Hearings*.

30. One concise summary of the Pacific Coast farm labor situation in 1942 is by C. C. Teague (President of the Agricultural Council of California), in ibid., part 2, pp. 493–497; see also Varden Fuller, "A Year on the Farm Labor Front," *Land Policy Review* (Fall 1942), and Lawrence L. Waters, "Transient Mexican Agricultural Labor," *Southwestern Social Science Quarterly*, vol. 22 (June 1941), 49–53, 56–66, and George O. Coalson, "Mexican Contract Labor in American Agriculture," ibid., vol. 33 (December 1952), 228–231.

31. *San Francisco Chronicle*, November 7, 1942; Teague in *Farm Labor Hearings*, part 1, pp. 21–24.

32. *Farm Labor Hearings*, part 2, p. 201.

33. Ibid., part 2, pp. 290–293, 421–424.

34. Ibid., part 1, pp. 40–42; see also letter of George L. Gillette, Director of Farm Machinery and Equipment Division, War Production Board, to Sheridan Downey, December 11, 1942, reprinted in ibid., part 1, pp. 43–44; for details about the impact of WPB Order L-170 on California agriculture see letter of H. B. Walker of the University of California College of Agriculture to Sheridan Downey, January 14, 1943, in ibid., part 1, pp. 46–48.

35. Ibid., part 1, pp. 85–86 and part 2, p. 203.

36. Ibid., part 2, pp. 209–210.

37. *Immigration and Naturalization Reporter*, vol. 5 (July, 1956), 4; Wayne Rasmussen, *A History of the Farm Labor Supply Program, 1943–1947*, U.S. Department of Agriculture, Agricultural Monograph #13 (Washington, 1951), p. 200.

38. On the farm labor shortage see *New York Times*, February 1, 24, March 25, 26, and June 10, 1942; *Farm Labor Hearings*, part 2, pp. 294–296; Richard B. Craig, *The Bracero Program* (Austin, 1971), pp. 38–39, 41–42; Ernesto Galarza, *Merchants of Labor: The Mexican Bracero Story* (Santa Barbara, 1964), p. 46; Carey McWilliams, "They Saved the Crops," *Inter-American* (August 1943), pp. 10–14.

39. *Los Angeles Herald-Express*, June 29, 1942.

40. Setrakian in *Farm Labor Hearings*, part 2, p. 245; letter of Ralph J. Wadsworth to A. Setrakian, June 25, 1942 in ibid., part 2, p. 244. Setrakian expressed similar views at a hearing before the California Senate Interim Planning Committee in Sacramento on June 22, 1943. See *Sacramento Bee*, June 23, 1942.

41. Jensen in *Farm Labor Hearings*, part 2, pp. 292–294; on Olson see *New York Times*, June 16, 1942; Craig, *Bracero Program*, pp. 36–38; for origins see Otey M. Scruggs, "Evolution of the Mexican Farm Labor Agreement of 1942," *Agricultural History*, vol. 34 (July 1960), 140–149; see also Carmela E. Santoro, "United States and Mexican Relations During World War II" (Ph.D. dissertation, Syracuse University, 1967), pp. 125–128. Mexico declared war on the Axis powers on June 1, 1942. Otey M. Scruggs, "The United States, Mexico, and the Wetback, 1942–1947," *Pacific Historical Review*, vol. 32 (May, 1961), 316–329.

42. The subject is discussed in greater detail by Craig, *Bracero Program*,

pp. 38–46; Galarza, *Merchants*, pp. 48, 51–55; Robert C. Jones, *Mexican War Workers in the United States* (Washington, 1945), p. 1. Jones was directly involved with the administration of the program. To understand the context of the 1942 agreement the following dissertations are helpful: Nelson G. Copp, "Wetbacks and Braceros: Mexican Migrant Laborers and American Immigration Policy, 1930–1960" (Ph.D. dissertation, Boston University, 1963), and John C. Elac, "The Employment of Mexican Workers in U.S. Agriculture, 1900–1960" (Ph.D. dissertation, UCLA, 1961), and, for a Mexican view, Gloria R. Vargas y Campos, "El Problema del bracero" (Ph.D. dissertation, Universidad Nacional Autonoma de Mexico, 1964). The text of the Agreement was published as Agreement Between the United States of America and Mexico, August 4, 1942 (Washington, 1942). The best Mexican primary source is Mexico, Secretaria del Trabajo y Prevision Social, Direccion de Prevision Social, *Los Braceros* (Mexico, 1946).

43. Jones, *Mexican War Workers*, pp. 25–27.

44. Galarza, *Merchants*, p. 53; Rasmussen, *Farm Labor Supply Program*, p. 199; A. R. Issler, "Good Neighbors Lend a Hand," *Survey Graphic*, vol. 32 (October 1943), pp. 389–394.

45. Craig, *Bracero Program*, p. 45; Jones, *Mexican War Workers*, pp. 20; Galarza, *Merchants*, p. 54. For a discussion of the bracero impact on the Mexican economy see Howard L. Campbell, "Bracero Migration and the Mexican Economy, 1951–1964" (Ph.D. dissertation, American University, 1972), pp. 38–42. On problems of illegal wetbacks during the war years see 82d Cong., 1st sess., House, Committee on Judiciary, *The Immigration and Naturalization Systems of the United States* (Washington, 1950), pp. 147–150 and also the *Report of the President's Commission on Migratory Labor: Migratory Labor in American Agriculture* (Washington, 1951), pp. 65–76.

46. Galarza, *Merchants*, p. 52; Jones, *Mexican War Workers*, p. 11; *Report of President's Commission on Migratory Labor*, pp. 59–61.

47. Jones, *Mexican War Workers*, p. 14; Rasmussen, *Farm Labor Supply Program*, pp. 207–221. Braceros in the Pacific Northwest were particularly isolated. See Erasmo Gamboa, "Mexican Labor in the Pacific Northwest, 1943–1947," *Pacific Northwest Quarterly*, vol. 73 (October 1982), 175–179.

48. Jones, *Mexican War Workers*, pp. 15–17; Frederick D. Mott, "Health Services for Migrant Farm Families," *American Journal of Public Health*, vol. 35 (April 1945), 308–314, and Henry P. Anderson, *The Bracero Program in California with Particular Reference to Health Status, Attitudes, and Practices* (Berkeley, 1961), passim.

49. On the administrative organization of the *bracero* program in the United States during 1944 see *Mexican War Workers*, pp. 3–5; for Mexico see Robert D. Tomasek, "The Political and Economic Implications of Mexican Labor in the United States under the Non-Quota System, Contract Labor Program, and Wetback Movement" (Ph.D. dissertation, University of Michigan, 1958), pp. 60–63.

50. Jones, *Mexican War Workers*, p. 26; Railroad Retirement Board, "Recruitment of Mexican Workers for Railroad Jobs," *Monthly Review of the Railroad Retirement Board*, vol. 5 (May 1944), 63–68.

51. *Recruiting of Mexican Non-Agricultural Workers; Agreement Between the United States of America*, U.S. Department of State Publication #2108 (Washington, 1944); "Rules of Admission of Mexican Workers as Railroad Track Workers," *Monthly Labor Review*, vol. 57 (August 1943), 240–241; Jones, *Mexican War Workers*, pp. 27–28.

52. Jones, *Mexican War Workers*, p. 29.

53. Ibid., pp. 34–35; for Mexican views of American attitudes see H. C. Woodbridge, "Mexico and United States Racism," *Commonweal*, vol. 42 (June 22, 1945), 234–37.

54. *Business Week*, October 14, 1944.

55. Precise estimates of *bracero* contributions to the Mexican balance of payments during the Second World War vary. Pedro Merla calculated a total of $318 million. See Pedro Merla, "El Bracero Mexicano en la Economica Nacional," *Revista del Trabajo*, vol. 3 (December 1943), 9–10. See also Jones, *Mexican War Workers*, p. 45, and for an extended discussion of the strengths and weaknesses of the program Craig, *Bracero Program*, pp. 12–35; Padilla quoted in Galarza, *Merchants*, p. 48; Camacho quoted in Tomasek, "Mexican Labor," p. 80.

4. Western Cities in Wartime: California

1. Carl Abbott, "The American Sunbelt: Idea and Region," in Gerald D. Nash (ed.), *The Urban West* (Manhattan, Kansas, 1979), pp. 9–10, and Carl Abbott, *The New Urban America*, pp. 98–119. See also Philip J. Funigiello, *The Challenge to Urban Liberalism: Federal-City Relations During World War II* (Knoxville, 1978).

2. U.S. Census, *Statistical Abstract*, 1946 (Washington, 1946), p. 780.

3. Ray West (ed.), *Rocky Mountain Cities* (New York, 1949), p. 8.

4. McWilliams in ibid., 9–12.

5. Earl Pomeroy, *The Territories and the United States* (Philadelphia, 1943), pp. 99–108. West (ed.), *Rocky Mountain Cities*, pp. 14–17, 30.

6. Catherine Bauer, "Cities in Flux," *American Scholar*, vol. 13 (1943–44), 70–71.

7. 78th Cong., 1st sess., House, Subcommittee of Committee on Naval Affairs, *Hearings on Congested Areas* (8 parts, Washington, 1944), hereafter cited as *Congested Area Hearings*. These hearings were scheduled soon after the extensive inquiry of the Tolan Committee on national defense migration. See "Tolan Committee Studies Defense Problems and Migration," *Business Week*, June 21, 1941, pp. 10–11.

8. Bayard O. Wheeler, "The Committee for Congested Production Areas," *Oregon Business Review*, vol. 3 (April 29, 1944), 5–7; see also 78th Cong., 2d sess., House, Subcommittee on Congested Areas, Sub-committee of Committee on Naval Affairs, *Report on the Columbia River Area*, Report #172 (Washington, 1944), and *A Report of the Congested Areas Subcommittee of the Committee on Naval Affairs*, Report #144 (Washington, 1944), p. 1088. Before 1943 other agencies had dealt with problems such as housing in a piecemeal fashion, without much success. See, for example, E. Allen Robinson Memo to J. Bion Philipson, February 27, 1942, concerning housing in Oakland-Berkeley area; J. Bion Philipson to Winters Haydock, January 3, 1943 concerning Los Angeles areas; Winters Haydock memo to Docket, February 18, 1942; J. Bion Philipson to Winters Haydock, January 23, 1943, on Denver, and J. Bion Philipson to Docket, February 13, 1942, on Seattle in Records of the Office of Production Management, Division of Defense Housing Coordination, Box 5, National Archives, Washington, D.C. The Committee also investigated conditions in "undesignated areas" where conditions were not as critical. See Boxes 37 and 38 in Central File, Records of the Committee for Congested Production Areas, National Archives, Washington, D.C., hereafter

cited as CPA Records. On cooperation between the Congressional Committee on Congested areas and the CPA see Harold Smith (Director of the Bureau of the Budget) to Senator Sheridan Downey (Cal.), April 24, 1943, in Central File, CPA Records.

9. Walter W. Cooper in *Congested Area Hearings*, Part 2, San Diego, Calif. Area (Washington, 1943), p. 372, hereafter cited as *Congested Area Hearings: San Diego;* "Boom Town: San Diego," *Life*, vol. 11 (July 28, 1941), 64–69. Walter W. Cooper, "San Diego's War Revenues," *Municipal Finance* (February 1943), pp. 8–12.

10. *Congested Areas Hearings: San Diego*, pp. 374, 390–391.

11. Ibid., 372. See also "Recreation at Emergency Trailer Camps," *Recreation*, vol. 36 (April 1942), 16.

12. *Congested Area Hearings: San Diego*, p. 393. Robert Hays (San Diego Chamber of Commerce) to Charles A. Taylor, September 9, 1943. As W. G. Tuttle (Director of Industrial Relations, Consolidated-Vultee Corporation) noted: "Lack of housing . . . has been a major factor in our inability to recruit persons from out of state." See W. G. Tuttle to Robert Hays, September 10, 1943, CPA Records. Catherine Bauer, "Wartime Housing in Defense Areas," *Architect and Engineer*, vol. 151 (October 1942), 33–35; Abbott, *The New Urban America*, p. 104.

13. Noonan, in *Congested Area Hearings: San Diego*, p. 446.

14. Communication of K. G. Bitter, Secretary of the San Diego County Federated Trades and Labor Council in ibid., pp. 447–448.

15. *Congested Area Hearings: San Diego*, p. 469; see also ibid., pp. 449–453, 463–468.

16. Ibid., p. 524; on problems of shopping for food see ibid., pp. 453–463; on in-plant feeding in Los Angeles see memo of H. C. Legg to Corrington Gill (on Consolidated-Vultee Aircraft), April 27, 1944, in CPA Records. J. Gnarra, "Laundry Solution: Customers Wash Their Own," *Colliers*, vol. 114 (July 8, 1944), 58.

17. *Congested Area Hearings: San Diego*, p. 387.

18. Ibid., p. 393; on sewage problems see Harold Keen, "Sewerage in San Diego for National Defense," *American City*, vol. 58 (September 1943), 56–58, and B. D. Phelps, "San Diego Completes New Sewer Lines," *American City*, vol. 60 (February 1945), 11–12.

19. G. G. Wetherill, "Health Problems in Child Care Centers," *Hygeia*, vol. 21 (September 1943), 634–635; "Changes and Growth Shown in Annual Report," *Educational Victory*, vol. 2 (April 3, 1944), 29–31. Crawford, in *Congested Area Hearings: San Diego*, pp. 538–540; Chief John E. Parrish in ibid., pp. 398–403. R. Barbour, "Secondary School Housing: An Appraisal of a Wartime Expedient," *Elementary School Journal*, vol. 42 (April 1942), 597–602.

20. Levoy in *Congested Area Hearings: San Diego*, p. 423; C. E. Peterson "How San Diego Police Handle Juvenile Delinquency and Other Problems," *Western City* (January 1944), pp. 16–17, and National Probation Association, "The Juvenile Delinquency Problem in San Diego, Report of a Survey by F. H. Hiller" (San Diego, 1943), pp. 1–75.

21. Carter's comments in *Congested Area Hearings: San Diego*, pp. 599–605 and 620–622.

22. Peterson surveys law enforcement problems in ibid., pp. 405–415.

23. On the Navy's role in San Diego see Roger W. Lotchin, "The Metropolitan-Military Complex in Comparative Perspective: San Francisco, Los Angeles, and San Diego in Nash (ed.), *Urban West*, pp. 19–30. Abbott, *New*

Urban American, pp. 100–104. A popular account is by C. Zahn, "What the Blitz-boom did to San Diego," *Travel,* vol. 83 (September 1955, pp. 20–21.

24. Caldwell in *Congested Area Hearings,* Part 8, Los Angeles–Long Beach Area (Washington, 1944, p. 1760, hereafter cited as *Congested Area Hearings: Los Angeles;* see monthly report of H. C. Legg (CPA) to Corrington Gill, March 4, 1944, in Central File, CPA Records.

25. Watson in *Congested Area Hearings: Los Angeles,* p. 1971. A perceptive contemporary traveler's impressions are in A. G. Mezerick, "Journey in America," *New Republic,* vol. 111 (December 19, 1944), 830–831; see also the impressionistic photo essay by R. Butterfield, "Los Angeles," *Life,* vol. 15 (November 22, 1943), 102–104.

26. *Congested Area Hearings: Los Angeles,* pp. 1971, 1806.

27. *Los Angeles Times,* April 27, 1944, reporting on address by Colonel Alexander Heron, Director of the California Reconstruction and Reemployment Division. "Los Angeles' War Pool," *Business Week* (February 7, 1943), p. 68.

28. *Congested Area Hearings: Los Angeles,* pp. 1927–1929, 1942–1945; see also Charles Bayer to Anson Ford, October 30, 1943, Anson Ford Manuscripts, Henry L. Huntington Library, San Marino, California, hereafter cited as Ford Manuscripts. Ford was a longtime member of the Los Angeles Board of Supervisors.

29. On expedients see "For Men Only: Wilmington Hall," *Time,* vol. 40 (Nov. 23, 1942), 27; *Congested Area Hearings: Los Angeles,* pp. 1972, 1974; "Worthy Ideas from Wartime Housing," *Architectural Record,* vol. 94 (November, 1943), 55–60; D. W. Baruch, "Sleep Comes Hard," *Nation,* vol. 160 (January 27, 1945), 95–96.

30. *Congested Area Hearings: Los Angeles,* pp. 1973, 1975; "The Housing Authority of the City of Los Angeles Presents a Solution," *California Arts and Architecture* (May 1943), pp. 48–65.

31. *Congested Area Hearings: Los Angeles,* pp. 1780–1781. A contemporary discussion of rapid transit problems is "Fitzgerald, Go West," *Time,* vol. 44 (December 18, 1944), 82.

32. *Congested Area Hearings: Los Angeles,* p. 1784; the city made considerable strides to improve its streets. See "Los Angeles Plans Unusual Four Level Grade Separation," *American City,* vol. 59 (November 1944), 17ff., and G. T. McCoy, "Three California Cities Complete Street Projects," *American City,* vol. 60 (February 1945), 61; on the broader context see "AIA Activities: Development of a Master Plan for the Los Angeles Metropolitan Area," *Architectural Record,* vol. 91 (March 1942), 10–12.

33. In 1924, 1931, and 1938 the Los Angeles Regional Planning Commission had made studies of the feasibility of using subways or elevated trains, but considered the cost prohibitive. *Congested Area Hearings: Los Angeles,* pp. 1786–1787; for a detailed survey of transportation facilities in wartime Los Angeles see *Statement Prepared for the Los Angeles Product Urgency Committee and the Area Manpower Priorities Committee Outlining the Place of Public Transportation of Passengers in the War Production Effort of the Area,* prepared by the U.S. Office of Defense Transportation, Division of Local Transport, Los Angeles, October 25, 1943, in ibid., pp. 2043–2051 (Appendix).

34. On the streetcar strike see *Los Angeles Times,* September 22, 23, 1943. There is an extensive file on the strike in the Fletcher Bowron Manuscripts, Henry L. Huntington Library, San Marino, California, hereafter cited as

Bowron Manuscripts. Bowron was Mayor of Los Angeles, 1938–45. The streetcar strike and racial tensions are discussed in greater detail in Chapter 6.

35. Fletcher Bowron to Joseph Eastman, May 22, 1944, Bowron Manuscripts, Box 32.

36. Charles L. Senn, "Report on General Smoke and Fume Conditions in Los Angeles County, October 22, 1943, to Los Angeles City Council," in Ford Manuscripts.

37. *Los Angeles Times,* October 29, 1943; "First Annual Report to Los Angeles Board of Supervisors by Los Angeles County Smoke and Fume Commission," in Ford Manuscripts; John A. Ford to Al Waxman (member of the Commission), February 7, 1945, and H. O. Swarthout to Howell H. Barnes (Director, Los Angeles County Mobilization Office), June 18, 1945, in Ford Manuscripts, Box 9. "Fume Nuisance Persists," *Business Week* (November 4, 1944), p. 46.

38. See also Fletcher Bowron to Robert Millikin, October 2, 1945, and John A. Ford to Fletcher Bowron, October 5, 1945, in Ford Manuscripts. For appointment of Director of Air Pollution see *Los Angeles Times,* February 21, 1945 and Harold W. Kennedy (Counsel to County of Los Angeles), "The History, Legal and Administrative Aspects of Air Pollution Control in the County of Los Angeles," pp. 6–8, mimeographed report to Board of Supervisors of Los Angeles County, in Ford Manuscripts (May 9, 1954), Box 9.

39. California Legislature, Assembly, Interim Committee on Juvenile Delinquency, *Preliminary Report* (Sacramento, 1944) touches on the situation; Horrall in *Congested Area Hearings: Los Angeles,* pp. 1770–1771; "Black Legion," *Newsweek,* vol. 20 (August 24, 1942), 34–35; "Police Motors of Los Angeles," *American City,* vol. 57 (January 1942), 13.

40. *Los Angeles Examiner,* October 7, 8, November 5, 1943; *Los Angeles Herald Express,* November 5, 1943; *Los Angeles Daily News,* November 9, 1943; *Congested Area Hearings: Los Angeles,* pp. 1801–1803, 2032, and especially 2036–2042.

41. Fletcher Bowron to Ray L. Chesebro, August 10, 1942, Bowron to City Council, June 6, 1942, Bowron to C. Sheppard; June 2, 1942 in Bowron Manuscripts, Box 29. D. Eddy, "Citizen Army Goes into Action," *American Magazine,* vol. 133 (April, 1942), 106–110.

42. See Caldwell's remarks in *Congested Area Hearings: Los Angeles,* pp. 1760–1762. C. J. Higson, "Los Angeles City Spending Program," *Tax Digest,* vol. 21 (June, 1943), 202–203.

43. Bowron to James M. Landis (Director, Office of Civil Defense), December 28, 1942; Bowron to Secretary of the Navy, October 19, 1942; Bowron to Morgan Adams, September 25, 1942, in Fletcher Bowron Manuscripts, Box 14. In addition, the city had to contend with demands for higher wages from firemen and police. "Cities on the Spot: Police and Fire Fighters in Los Angeles Sue to Recover Depression Pay Cuts," *Business Week* (November 29, 1944), p. 36.

44. *Congested Area Hearings: Los Angeles,* p. 1796. The Council established 64 day nurseries and 69 extended care centers (ages 6 to 16) with funds from the Lanham Act; on one school's program see G. T. Allen, "Cadets Tomorrow: Cadet Nursery School Teachers," *Woman's Home Companion,* vol. 71 (October 1944), 38–39.

45. K. Pearson, "Business in a War Zone," *Nation's Business,* vol. 31 (March 1943), 68–70; Mel Scott, *The San Francisco Bay Region* (Berkeley, 1950), pp.

245–246. Abbott, *The New Urban America*, pp. 109–110; a delightful vignette by Lucius Beebe is "San Francisco: Boom Town de Luxe," *American Mercury*, vol. 56 (January 1941), 66–74.

46. *Congested Area Hearings: San Francisco*, pp. 652, 656, 668; Scott, *San Francisco Bay Area*, p. 247; L. Bradley, "San Francisco: Gibraltar of the West Coast," *National Geographic Magazine*, vol. 82 (March 1943), 279–308.

47. The Minutes of the Area Production Emergency Committee September 24, 1943 to July 6, 1944 provide details. See CPA Records, Central File, Box 111, and also the Daily Diary of CPA activities in the San Francisco Bay Area, October 16, 1943, to August 14, 1944, provides an insight into the administration of the CPA and its policies. See CPA Records, Central File, Box 115. Useful also are the monthly status reports of the San Francisco office of the CPA which provide extensive documentation on local problems. See CPA Records, Box 122, and especially "Composite Report on San Francisco Bay Area," September 10, 1943, 253 pages, prepared by the San Francisco Staff of the CPA and the War Production Board. This is the most comprehensive survey of community problems, including housing, transportation, public utilities, education, health, sanitation, child care and social welfare, in Box 113, CPA Records.

48. Geiger in *Congested Area Hearings: San Francisco*, p. 661.

49. Ibid., pp. 656, 661, 752.

50. Ibid., p. 798.

51. Ibid., 656–658, quotation on p. 659; on expansion of recreational programs see J. Randall, "Golden Gate Is Open Wide," *Recreation*, vol. 35 (January 1942), 6–9.

52. *Congested Area Hearings: San Francisco*, p. 648; J. A. Beeler, "Is the Trolley Coach Stealing the Show?" *American City*, vol. 60 (January 1945), 78–80, and "Pride in Cable Cars," *Business Week* (May 27, 1944), p. 76.

53. James A. Whiteside (Regional Manager, Housing Construction Division, National Housing Administration), memo on manpower situation in San Francisco Bay Area, August 10, 1944, to Charles B. Lawrence, CPA Records.

54. *Congested Area Hearings: San Francisco*, pp. 692–696, 760; a more extended contemporary analysis of Oakland's war problems can be found as follows: problems of new black workers in ibid., pp. 793–1013; crime, ibid., pp. 776–789; public schools, ibid., pp. 789–793; Alameda Air Station, ibid., pp. 770–776; as elsewhere, Oakland had problems in keeping food stores open at night for its 175,000 war workers, and solicited CPA help in dealing with the problem. See R. M. Dorton to Carrington Gill, December 11, 1943 in CPA Records.

55. *Congested Area Hearings: San Francisco*, pp. 901, 927–931, 809. For a more detailed account of Vallejo schools see remarks of Superintendent John Alltucker in ibid., pp. 921–927; housing problems are discussed by Harry Buss, Assistant Labor director of the Vallejo Housing Authority in ibid., pp. 927–931; the transportation situation is well covered by Frank D. Bell, General Manager of the Vallejo Bus Company in ibid., pp. 915–919; conditions in the Mare Island shipyard are discussed in Lott, *Long Line of Ships*, pp. 207–238; on health problems due to inadequate sewers see Rear Admiral W. L. Friedell to Harrison E. Devereaux (Contract Officer, Federal Works Administration), September 23, 1943, CPA Records. For a survey of Vallejo's problems see War Manpower Commission, Manpower Utilization Study IE: JH 217CS, "Adequacy of Community Facilities, Vallejo, California," November 7, 1944 in CPA Records, pp. 1–7. As elsewhere, federal officials believed that

absenteeism could be greatly reduced if only the food stores would remain open at night. In Vallejo, stores were open only one night a week due to opposition of the Butcher's and Retail Clerks Union. See R. M. Dorton (CPA) to J. Wilsie (Executive Director, Vallejo Housing Authority), January 13, 1944, and George P. Tucker to R. M. Dorton, February 28, 1944, and R. M. Dorton to George P. Tucker, March 1, 1944, CPA Records.

56. *Congested Area Hearings: San Francisco,* p. 888. James A. McVittie (City Manager, Richmond, Calif.), *An Avalanche Hits Richmond: A Report* (Richmond, 1944), 141 pp., is the best published contemporary survey; see also "Richmond Took a Beating," *Fortune,* vol. 31 (February 1945), pp. 262–269; and Joseph C. Whitnah, *A History of Richmond, California* (Richmond, 1944).

57. *Congested Area Hearings: San Francisco,* pp. 836–841, 854–855, 859; Scott, *San Francisco Bay Area,* p. 252. James A. McVittie, "A City Earns a Purple Heart," *American City,* vol. 59 (December 1944), 56–58.

58. *Congested Area Hearings: San Francisco,* p. 835. Federal Regional Advisory Council, Region 13, "Composite Report on Richmond Area," June 2, 1942, by Mel Scott and Paul Carrico, pp. 1–28, manuscript in CPA Records.

59. *Congested Area Hearings: San Francisco,* p. 867. With few shopping facilities available, the U.S. Maritime Commission, in addition to building public housing, constructed a public market. C. W. Eliason (Regional Industrial Advisor, U.S. Maritime Commission) to R. M. Dorton, July 12, 1943, CPA Records. On public health and sewage problems see W. T. Harrison (U.S. Public Health Service) to War Production Board, December 2, 1943, CPA Records.

60. *Congested Area Hearings: San Francisco,* pp. 836, 847; see also "Richmond Builds Ships," *Western City* (February 1943), 14–19 on conditions.

61. *Congested Area Hearings: San Francisco,* pp. 852–853. At one point the CPA was so desperate that it considered using Hudson River Line steamers from New York to serve as temporary housing for war workers in the San Francisco Bay region. The United States Maritime Commission felt that the plan was not feasible, however, since it would be difficult to tow the steamers west. See Ed J. Moran (U.S. Maritime Commission) to Charles B. Lawrence, September 5, 1944, CPA Records.

62. 78th Cong., 1st sess., House, Subcommittee of the Committee on Naval Affairs Appointed to Investigate Congestion in Critical War Areas, *Report on the San Francisco Bay Area* (Washington, 1944), p. 810.

63. *Congested Area Hearings: San Francisco,* p. 754; see also pp. 755–757.

64. McVittie in ibid., p. 839; see also McVittie, *An Avalanche Hits Richmond,* pp. 9–94; on the crime situation see also *Congested Area Hearings: San Francisco,* p. 871 and the annual reports of the chief of police, reprinted in ibid., pp. 872–878.

65. McVittie in *Congested Area Hearings: San Francisco,* pp. 838–839; Chief Cooper in ibid., pp. 889, 890; McVittie, *An Avalanche Hits Richmond,* pp. 98–121.

66. *Congested Area Hearings: San Francisco,* pp. 884–888; on relation of lack of recreational areas and juvenile delinquency see lament of Ivan V. Hill, Director of Recreation in Richmond in ibid., pp. 883–885.

67. Ibid., pp. 837, 852–853. The city had an agreement with the Richmond Housing Authority to receive funds in lieu of taxes but under the Lanham Act federal authorities were allowed to deduct the cost of improvements for streets, sewers, and public utilities. Consequently, during 1943 Richmond did not receive a cent of such "in lieu" payments. On prob-

lems of providing banking facilities for Richmond see R. M. Dorton to Corrington Gill, December 1, 1943, and Charles P. Partridge (President, First National Bank of Richmond) to Dorton, November 18, 1943, Dorton to Partridge, December 2, 1943, in CPA Records.

68. *Congested Area Hearings: San Francisco,* p. 870.

69. Ibid., p. 867.

70. 78th Cong., 1st sess., House, Subcommittee of the Committee on Naval Affairs, *Report on the San Francisco Bay Area,* pp. 810–814.

71. Ibid.; Mel Scott, *San Francisco Bay,* pp. 249–248.

72. Quoted in Scott, *San Francisco Bay,* p. 249; County of Marin, Housing Authority, *First Annual Report* (Sausalito, 1943), pp. 1–4; Professor Carroll Pursell of the University of California has written an unpublished history of the wartime housing project in Marin County. See also "Marin City, California," *Architectural Forum* (December 1943), pp. 67–74.

73. It is true, as Carl Abbott has argued, that some of the worst immediate crisis conditions were remedied by 1944 in cities like San Diego and Portland, Oregon. However, many new urban issues were of a long-term nature involving extension of transportation and sewage lines, facilities, and a reorganization of tax levies and revenue arrangements to be worked out with state and federal governments. I agree with Abbott that the World War II experience created a framework and agenda for postwar urban officials. See Abbott, *The New Urban America,* pp. 115, 119. On the shifting relationships between cities and the federal government see Mark Gelfand, *A Nation of Cities: The Federal Government and Urban America, 1933–1965* (New York, 1975).

5. Western Cities in Wartime: The Pacific Northwest, Mountain States, and Southwest

1. A detailed history of Portland during World War II is still needed. A brief survey is in E. Kimbark MacColl, *The Growth of a City: Power and Politics in Portland, Oregon, 1915 to 1950* (Portland, 1979), pp. 228–236, 240–241, 250–252, 575–580, 600–602. A fine collection of documents in the Oregon Historical Society, Portland, Oregon, "Oregon War Industries," Boxes 1 to 9, bears on the wartime activities of Portland business firms who pooled their resources to secure government contracts. See also Anthony Pisano, "Effects of World War II on Portland, Oregon," unpublished manuscript in files of Oregon Historical Society. A useful essay is Carl Abbott, "Portland in the Pacific War: Planning from 1940 to 1945," *Urbanism, Past and Present* (1981), pp. 12–24.

2. On population see U.S. Bureau of the Census, 1940, *County Data Book* (1947), pp. 271-272; see also the contemporary estimates by Acting Mayor Will A. Bowes and George Coplon, Regional Representative of the National Housing Agency, Region IX in *Congested Area Hearings: Columbia River Area* (Washington, 1944), pp. 1615, 1708; for Kaiser's remarks see ibid., p. 1662. A perceptive contemporary traveler's account is Eliot Janeway's "Trouble on the Northwest Frontier: A Correspondent's Travel Report," *Fortune,* vol. 26 (November 1942), 26ff.

3. The correspondence of Robert E. Riley (Mayor of Portland, 1941–48) is revealing. See Robert E. Riley to Julia Spooner, April 8, 1942, in Riley Papers, Oregon Historical Society, Portland; *Congested Area Hearings: Columbia River Area,* pp. 1616, 1639, 1708, 1709–1710. Indeed, groups like the Port-

land Federation of Women's Organizations became greatly concerned over what seemed like the collapse of all zoning regulations. "The Federation especially deplores the fact," wrote Julia Spooner, its Corresponding Secretary, to the Mayor, "that our present critical housing shortage creates a serious problem for the Housing Code Commission in the number of requests for permits for unfit accommodations." Spooner to Riley, April 5, 1942. See also Winters Haydock (National Housing Authority) to Riley, March 30, 1942 in Riley Papers. As the situation worsened, the city hired the famed urban consultant Robert Moses from New York to study transportation problems and the need for public works. See his report to the City Council on November 1, 1943, "Portland Improvement" (November 10, 1943), 85 pp. in Oregon Historical Society. See also *Oregon Journal*, November 2, 1943. See also *Congested Area Hearings: Columbia River Area*, pp. 1616, 1639, 1708, 1709–1710.

4. Bayard O. Wheeler, "The Committee for Congested Production Areas," *Oregon Business Review*, III (April 29, 1944), 3; *Congested Area Hearings: Columbia River Area*, pp. 1639, 1643. See also Federal Reserve Bank of San Francisco, *Monthly Review* (November 1943), p. 54; Board of Governors, *Federal Reserve Bulletin* (January 1944), p. 85 on industrial employment in Portland. In seeking nominees for directors of the Portland Housing Authority Mayor Riley asked Edgar F. Kaiser to suggest the individuals whom he would like to have on the board. Riley to Kaiser, March 30, 1942; see also Walter de Martini to Riley, April 3, 1942, and Donald Nelson to Riley, July 24, 1942, on expansion of public housing, Riley Papers. On Portland housing situation see *Oregon Journal*, June 25, 1944, and Tom Humphrey (Portland representative of the CPA) to Jean Muir *(Oregon Journal)*, June 30, 1944, in CPA Records, Central File, and the CPA "Report on Local Housing Situation," January 5, 1944, in CPA Records.

5. H. D. Freeman, "Story of Vanport City," *American City* (July 1943), 42–43; "Vanport City: Nation's Largest War Housing Project," *Western City* (April 1943), 17; *Congested Area Hearings: Columbia River Area*, pp. 1639–1646.

6. Hamilton in *Congested Area Hearings: Columbia River Area*, pp. 1646–1650; CPA Report on Recreation in Portland for Izak Committee, November 3, 1944. CPA Records, Box 88; Federal Security Agency, "Summary of Community Needs, Portland-Vancouver Area," August 1943, pp. 1–2, Memo in CPA Records, Box 86; in returning a questionnaire concerning needed improvements at Vanport, 279 residents noted their desire for more recreational facilities—and for more racial segregation. See Vanport Questionnaire in CPA Records. Nursery schools in housing projects in the Portland area were so filthy and unattractive that they were filled to less than one-half of capacity. See Tom Humphrey (CPA Representative for Portland), "Information Developed in Conference with Gladys N. Everett" (District Director of Federal Works Agency, Service Projects), October 29, 1943, in CPA Records and Report of Tom Humphrey to Corrington Gill, October 13, 1943, CPA Records.

7. *Congested Area Hearings: Columbia River Area*, p. 1659; pp. 1660–61. Recreational facilities for blacks were virtually nonexistent and their absence presented a problem for city officials. "I have had open Council hearings forced by pressure groups representing both sides of this distressing questions," said Mayor Riley, "I have had many group conferences held in this office between employers, employees, ministers, civil rights advocates, and militant property owners and businessmen." Riley to M. H. Jones, July 1,

1943, Riley Papers. At the same time the CPA was seeking to secure at least one movie theatre for blacks. As Tom Humphrey of the CPA wrote the Mayor, "The problem of Negro migration into this area has been a subject of considerable discussion and concern. . . . In this connection . . . Mr. George Streator (of the War Production Board) [will] visit Portland. Mr. S. is an outstanding and conservative member of the colored race." Tom Humphrey to Mayor Riley, August 9, 1944, CPA Records. Ennis M. Whaley (President, Interracial Council of Vanport City) to Chester A. Moores, June 13, 1943, demanding integration, in Chester A. Moores Papers, Oregon Historical Society, Portland.

8. *Congested Area Hearings: Columbia River Area*, pp. 1615–1617; on Vanport see also David Simpson (President, Portland Chamber of Commerce), to Portland Housing Authority, October 18, 1944, who wanted to turn it into an industrial park. J. T. Marr (Executive Secretary, Oregon State Federation of Labor), to Chester A. Moores (Chairman, Portland Housing Authority) September 20, 1944, Riley Papers. Henry and Edgar F. Kaiser were also unhappy with housing conditions at Vanport. See "Minutes of Recessed Meeting of the Commissioners of the Housing Authority of Portland Held on Thursday, September 9, 1943 at 1:45 PM.," pp. 2–3 in Chester A. Moores Papers, Oregon Historical Society Portland, Oregon. On the problems with electric stoves see also Corrington Gill to Ed. Izac, December 6, 1943, and Tom Humphrey, "Status Report for Portland-Vancouver Area," November 22, 1943, p. 1, CPA Records. See also memo of Robert Lenhart to Gill, December 3, 1943, and Humphrey memo to Gill, November 30, 1943, CPA Records.

9. See description by Edgar F. Kaiser in *Congested Area Hearings: Columbia River Area*, p. 1662, and Paul DeKruif, *Kaiser Wakes the Doctors* (New York, 1943), pp. 114–116, 151–152.

10. Cooper in *Congested Area Hearings: Columbia River Area*, pp. 1624–1626; Bates quoted in ibid., p. 1626. Portland City Auditor, *Annual Report for 6 Months Ended June 30, 1942* (Portland, 1942), passim.

11. E. F. Kaiser in *Congested Area Hearings: Columbia River Area*, p. 1662; see also A. G. Mezerick, "Journey in America," *New Republic*, vol. 111 (December 25, 1944), 864–865.

12. *Congested Area Hearings: Puget Sound, Washington, Area* (Washington, D.C., 1944), pp. 1319, 1322, 1525–1527. On Seattle's turbulent labor problems prior to World War II see Murray Morgan, *Skid Road* (rev. ed. New York, 1960), pp. 220–271.

13. *Congested Area Hearings: Puget Sound, Washington, Area*, pp. 1526–1727; brief discussions are in Roger Sale, *Seattle, Past to Present* (Seattle, 1976), pp. 181–183; Nard Jones, *Seattle* (Garden City, 1972), pp. 261–283, and Gerald B. Nelson, *Seattle, the Life and Times of an American City* (New York, 1977), pp. 149–154. A comprehensive history of wartime Seattle still needs to be written. Also see Tom Collins, *Flying Fortress: The Story of Boeing* (New York, 1943), and James Loutitt, "Industrial Seattle," *Pacific Northwest Industries*, vol. 4 (December 1944), 36–38.

14. On turnover see also the memo of Minor H. Baker (Washington State representative, War Manpower Commission), December 20, 1943, in CPA Records. Shanahan in *Congested Area Hearings: Puget Sound, Washington, Area*, p. 1320.

15. An excellent detailed survey of the Seattle situation is in "Report to Mayor William F. Davin of Seattle by Juvenile Protection Committee of the Council of Social Agencies in Seattle," October 18, 1943 to February 28,

1944," pp. 1–12 in CPA Records. Walter Gordon, "Housing While You Wait: Housing in Washington and Oregon," *Pencil Points* (April, 1943), pp. 48–51; Coplen in *Congested Area Hearings: Puget Sound, Washington, Area,* pp. 1436–1439.

16. *Congested Area Hearings: Puget Sound, Washington, Area,* pp. 1380–1381, 1572–1573.

17. Ibid., pp. 1449–1450; see also ibid., pp. 1353–1357. On efforts of city to prevent commandeering of hotels by armed services see *Business Week* (May 15, 1943), p. 34; Navy projects were more comfortable. "Sand Point Homes," *Architectural Forum,* vol. 91 (April 1942), 54–55.

18. Kimsey, in *Congested Area Hearings: Puget Sound, Washington, Area,* pp. 1329–1336.

19. Mayor Kean's graphic description in ibid., pp. 1367–1379; see also ibid., pp. 1489–1491, and A. G. Mezerick, "Journey into America," *New Republic,* vol. 112 (January 1, 1945), 14–15, on Seattle.

20. *Congested Area Hearings: Puget Sound, Washington, Area,* pp. 1358–1361, 1518–1521, 1596–1597. On the problem of recreational facilities see J. F. Ward to H. C. Legg, February 21, 1944, CPA Records. See also A. A. Sandin, "Orientation of New Pupils," *Elementary School Journal,* vol. 43 (May 1943), 526–529.

21. *Congested Area Hearings: Puget Sound, Washington, Area,* pp. 1338–1339, 1340–1346.

22. Comeaux in ibid., p. 1325; see also ibid., pp. 1326–1329.

23. Unzelman in ibid., pp. 1401, 1407–1408.

24. Dorsett, *Denver* p. 237.

25. Contemporary accounts of population increase include *Denver Bulletin,* November 12, 1942, *Colorado Springs Evening Telegraph,* August 25, 1942, *Denver Post,* June 30, 1942, *Rocky Mountain News,* October 2, 1942; on Mexican-American complaints of discrimination see *Denver Catholic Register,* July 16, 1942, for charges of Juan Noriega, president of Hispanic-American Confederation, and *Colorado Springs Telegraph,* June 15, 1942. See also C. S. Spangler, "History of Region 9, Denver Office," pp. 1–3, and Will N. Leyden, "History of Region 9, Denver Office," pp. 5–7, typescripts in Smaller War Plants Corporation Region 9 Historical Project (1945) in World War II History Collection, Colorado State Historical Society, Denver. See also Dorsett, *Denver,* pp. 237–238.

26. A. G. Mezerick, "Journey in America," *New Republic,* vol. 111 (December 11, 1944), 794–795; on the Denver Arsenal see *Denver Post,* January 7, 1942 and the *Rocky Mountain News,* January 7, August 12, 1942. Lott, *Long Line of Ships,* pp. 210–212, 214; Frederick C. Lane, *Ships for Victory,* pp. 427–430; *Business Week* (December 2, 1944), p. 24.

27. West (ed.), *Rocky Mountain Cities,* p. 286; Leyden, "History," pp. 2–3.

28. Lott, *Long Line of Ships,* pp. 213–214; *Denver Post,* August 9, 1942. On the Denver "Navy Yard" see *Denver Post,* August 16, 23, 1942; *Rocky Mountain News,* August 19, 23, 1942, December 1, 1942, and John W. Hedges, "History of Region 9—Denver Office," pp. 1–6, typescript (1945) in Smaller War Plants Corporation Region 9 Historical Project (1945) in World War II History Collection, Colorado State Historical Society, Denver; "Ships from Denver," *Business Week* (December 13, 1941), p. 22.

29. Dorsett, *Denver,* pp. 239–240; C. Feiss, "How Denver Got Its New Housing Code," *American City,* vol. 59 (November, 1944), 89.

30. Dorsett, *Denver,* pp. 239–240; West, (ed.), *Rocky Mountain Cities,*

p. 313; *Business Week* (July 24, 1943), pp. 30ff. On the impact of military bases see *Denver Post*, November 10, 1942, *Colorado Springs Evening Gazette*, July 11, August 21, 25, 1942; *Colorado Springs Telegraph*, August 4, 25, 1942, September 4, October 6, 1942; publications of individual bases provide information about the impact of service personnel on surrounding communities. See, for example, the *Lowry Field Review Meter*, copies in World War II History Collection, Box 2, Colorado Historical Society, Denver.

31. "School for Bombers," *Arizona Highways* (September–October 1943), pp. 4–13; West (ed.), *Rocky Mountain Cities*, pp. 218–222; Getty, *Interethnic Relationships in the Community of Tucson*, pp. 21, 295; Francis W. Donnell, *History of the Arizona Division of Goodyear Aircraft* (Phoenix, 1947); on efforts to develop a rubber industry near Tucson see Carl Hayden to Tom Houck, July 16, 1942, B. H. Ormand, to Hayden, May 4, 1942, and Hayden to J. C. Elms, July 24, 1942 in Hayden Papers. See also *Arizona Farmer*, July 14, 1945. The rapid growth led to a greater awareness of the need for planning. See A. M. Faure, "Post-War Planning as a Joint City-County Project," *American City*, vol. 59 (October 1944), 89–91.

32. For a concise survey see Elbert B. Edwards, "Clark County: From Wilderness to Metropolitan Area," in *Nevada: The Silver State* (2 vols., Carson City, 1970), vol. II, 677–693; and Elliott, *History of Nevada*, pp. 307–310.

33. Edwards, *Nevada*, vol. II, 683–688; Guy L. Rocha in *Nevada Historical Society Quarterly*, vol. 21 (Fall, 1978), 222–223. Useful is Perry Kaufman, "The Best City of Them All: A City Biography of Las Vegas, 1930–1960" (Ph.D. dissertation, University of California, Santa Barbara, 1974), and Perry Kaufman, "City Boosters, Las Vegas Style," *Journal of the West* vol. 13 (July, 1974), 46–60, and C. Gregory Crampton, *The Complete Las Vegas* (Salt Lake City, 1976); U.S. Bureau of the Census, *County Data Book*, 1940, p. 257.

34. On visiting the Basic Magnesium site McCarran said: "For the first time we have something which is bringing wealth into Nevada instead of taking it out. Every ton of ore which is taken from a mine depletes our wealth. Every ton of concrete poured here adds to our prosperity." *Las Vegas Review Journal*, November 20, 1941. "Minutes of Business and Industry Committee of Clark County Economic Council," July 28, 1943, in Governor E. P. Carville Papers, Nevada State Archives, Carson City, Nevada. U.S. Bureau of the Census, *County Data Book*, 1940, p. 257.

35. One observer estimated that military personnel spent more than $1 million monthly in Las Vegas during wartime. See Kaufman in *Journal of the West*, vol. 13, 49. On McCarran's influence in securing military installations for Nevada see H.H.P. Blandy (Chief, Bureau of Ordnance, U.S. Army) to Pat McCarran, June 14, 1942, and McCarran to E. Snider, July 2, 1942, in McCarran Papers. Edwards, *Nevada*, vol. II, 686–687; Elliott, *Nevada*, p. 313.

36. W. Stout, "Nevada's New Reno," *Saturday Evening Post*, vol. 215 (October 11, 1942), 12–13.

37. R. English, "The Boom Came Back," *Collier's*, vol. 110 (August 22, 1942), 36–37: Edwards, *Nevada*, vol. II, 688; Elliott, *History of Nevada*, p. 314.

38. On Nevada's gambling background see Joseph F. McDonald, "Gambling in Nevada," *Annals of the American Academy of Political and Social Science*, vol. 269 (May 1950), 30–34 and a breezy popular account by Oscar Lewis, *Sagebrush Casinos: The Story of Legal Gambling in Nevada* (New York, 1953), Robert L. Decker, "The Economics of the Legalized Gambling Industry in Nevada" (Ph.D. dissertation, University of Colorado, 1961), and Edward Reid and Ovid Demaris, *The Green Felt Jungle* (New York, 1963). A brief

vivid glimpse is "Las Vegas Gambling," *Life,* vol. 13 (December 21, 1942), 91–94.

39. Dean Jennings, "The Hood Who Invented Las Vegas," *True Magazine,* vol. 48 (August, 1967), 23–25; John Cahlan, "Glamour Was Added," in *Nevada Centennial Magazine* (Las Vegas, 1964), pp. 76–85; see also Fred J. Cook, "Las Vegas: Golden Paradise," *Nation* (October 22, 1960), pp. 297–302; *New York Times,* June 22, 1947.

6. Blacks in the Wartime West

1. Black population growth in the West between 1940 and 1950 can be followed in Table 8; see also U.S. Bureau of the Census, *Census of Population, 1950,* vol. II, *Characteristics of the Population,* part 5, 100–103; De Graaf, "Negro Migration to Los Angeles, 1930–1950," p. 242, and his "Recognition, Racism, and Reflections on the Writing of Western Black History," *Pacific Historical Review* vol. 44, (May 1975), 22–51. *Population—Characteristics,* series Ca–3#s 2, 3, 5, p. 8; *Population—Special Censuses,* Series P-SC, #97, 109, 173, 188. See also U.S. Bureau of the Census, *Historical Statistics,* vol. 1, 22; "Negro Internal Migration, 1940–1943: An Estimate," *Race Relations,* I (September 1943), 10–11.

2. De Graaf, "Negro Migration," pp. 102–121 has a good discussion of the background. See also Ira DeA. Reid, "Special Problems of Negro Migration During the War," *Milbank Memorial Fund Quarterly,* vol. 25 (July 1947), 284–292.

3. Quoted in National Negro Congress, Los Angeles Council, *Jim Crow in National Defense* (Los Angeles, 1940), p. 13.

4. Lester B. Granger, "Negroes and War Production," *Survey Graphic,* vol. 31 (November 1942), 470.

5. 77th Cong., 1st sess., House, *Tolan Committee Hearings* part 16, p. 6536.

6. Ibid., part 16, p. 6530; *California Eagle,* February 3, 1943; Archibald, *Wartime Shipyard,* pp. 58–99.

7. The records of the Fair Employment Practices Committee Region 12 were examined in the Federal Records Center in San Bruno, California in May, 1981. Case files are in RG 28, Administrative Files, hereafter cited as FEPC Records, Region 12. I have examined all of the cases that came before the FEPC, 1941–1945.

8. Charles P. Clark (Associate Counsel of the Committee) Interview with Rayford Logan, Chairman of the Committee for the Participation of Negroes in the National Defense Program, July 11, 1941, in Records of the Special Committee to Investigate National Defense Program, National Archives, Washington, D.C., RG 46, Sen. A-C-30, Box 875, hereafter cited as Truman Committee Records.

9. John P. Davis to Senator Harry Truman, May 27, 1941; see also Charles P. Clark Interview with John Davis (Secretary of the National Negro Congress), on June 19, 1941, Truman Committee Records.

10. Robert C. Weaver to Senator Harry S. Truman, June 23, 1941, Truman Committee Records.

11. *California Eagle,* July 16, 1942.

12. Ibid., August 13, 1942, September 24, 1942.

13. U.S. Bureau of the Census, *County Data Book,* 1940, pp. 64, 76–78, 257; Shryock, Jr., "Wartime Shifts of the Civilian Population," *Milbank Memo-*

rial Fund Quarterly, vol. 25 (July 1947), 269–282, and idem, "Internal Migration and the War," *Journal of the American Statistical Association,* vol. 38 (March 1943), 16–30.

14. 78th Cong., 1st sess., House, *Congested Area Hearings: Los Angeles,* pp. 1763, 1767; Carey McWilliams, "The Los Angeles Archipelago," *Science and Society,* vol. 10 (Winter 1946), 52; U.S. Bureau of the Census, 1950, *Current Population Reports,* Series P-20, #14, p. 2.

15. "Labor in California and the Pacific Northwest," *Monthly Labor Review,* vol. 64 (April 1947), 565; *Congested Area Hearings: Los Angeles,* pp. 1852, 1853, 1859–1860; 77th Cong., 1st sess., House, *Tolan Committee Hearings,* part 34, pp. 13253–13254; Robert C. Weaver, "Negro Employment in the Aircraft Industry," *Quarterly Journal of Economics,* vol. 59 (August 1945), 609–617; De Graaf, "Negro Migration," pp. 187–193.

16. *Los Angeles Times,* August 2, 5, 9, 1944; Fair Employment Practices Committee, "Hearings in re . . . Los Angeles Railway Corp.," pp. 8–127, in FEPC Records, Region 12. See also Charles Wollenberg, *"James v. Marinship:* Trouble on the New Black Frontier," *California History,* vol. 6 (Fall 1981), 262–279; *Business Week,* December 23, 1944, January 13, 1945.

17. 25 Cal. 2d 721; the transcript of the hearing on this case is in the files of the Fair Employment Practices Committee, "California Shipbuilding Company . . . International Brotherhood of Boilermarkers," FEPC Records, Region 12; Harry Kingman to Barney Mayes (Director, Division of Research and Publicity, California State Federation of Labor), January 25, 1944, FEPC Records, Region 12. Kingman hoped the Boilermakers would change their constitution and admit blacks so that the FEPC could dismiss the case.

18. H. C. Legg to Corrington Gill, April 5, 1944, in CPA Records.

19. *Congested Area Hearings: Los Angeles,* pp. 1761, 1764, 1765–1768.

20. *Los Angeles Times,* May 13, and also August 9, 1944.

21. *California Eagle,* April 4, 1946; Arna Bontemps, *Anyplace But Here* (New York, 1966), p. 269; Eugene S. Richardson, "Migration and the Social Education of the Negro," *Journal of Negro Education,* vol. 13 (Winter 1944), 40–46; *Congested Area Hearings: Los Angeles,* pp. 1852–1853; see also Robert E. Colbert, "The Attitude of Older Negro Residents Toward Recent Negro Migrants in the Pacific Northwest," *Journal of Negro Education,* vol. 15 (Fall 1946), 695–703.

22. G. Eleanor Kimble, "Restrictive Covenants," *Common Ground* vol. 6 (Autumn 1945), pp. 45–52; on the San Francisco area see Robert C. Weaver, *The Negro War Worker in San Francisco* (San Francisco, 1944), and Milla Z. Logan, "Racial Discrimination Not Allowed," *Common Ground,* vol. 4 (Summer 1944), 83–86, on successful integration in Marin City. Logan was an employee of the Marin City Housing Authority.

23. Charles B. Spaulding, "Housing Problems of Minority Groups in Los Angeles County," *Annals of the American Academy of Political and Social Science,* vol. 248 (November 1946), 220–225; and Robert C. Weaver, *Negro Ghetto* (New York, 1948).

24. 334 U.S. 72; *California Eagle,* September 5, 1946.

25. *Congested Area Hearings: Los Angeles,* pp. 1761, 1773, 1791. Black population in Los Angeles had been 38, 894 in 1930 and 63,774 in 1940.

26. Caldwell in ibid., p. 1761; see also ibid., pp. 1763–1764, 1858–1859, 1974–1975, and Fletcher Bowron speech, March 25, 1945, on Pacific Parachute Company a successful black-owned enterprise, in Bowron Manuscripts, Box 34.

27. *Congested Area Hearings: Los Angeles,* pp. 1858–1859, 1974–1975, 1977.
28. Ibid., pp. 1765, 1767.
29. Ibid., pp. 1773, 1777, 1946–1947; the CPA was acutely concerned with growing racial tensions in the Los Angeles area. See H. C. Legg to Corrington Gill, April 5, 1944, CPA Records. The CPA divided Los Angeles into "racial tension" areas. The classification included (a) critical tensions (b) serious tensions (c) undercurrents (d) minor incidents. See H. C. Legg memo on Racial Tension areas (1944), CPA Records.
30. Statement of Mayor Fletcher A. Bowron, July 31, 1943, copy in Bowron Papers, pp. 1–4.
31. Memo of D. Dwight Douglas (District Intelligence Officer, 11th Naval District) to Chief of Staff, September 27, 1943, pp. 1–2, in Records of the 11th Naval District, Federal Records Center, Laguna Hills, California, RG 181, File CF-33, declassified, hereafter cited as 11th ND Records. C. H. Fogg, Senior Patrol Officer, noted on October 16, 1943 that attacks by hoodlums on service personnel had been increasing and "that a racial outbreak in Los Angeles may occur at any moment and without fore-warning." Memo on Hoodlum Attacks, C. H. Fogg to Commanding Officer, October 16, 1943, 11th ND Records.
32. Confidential Report of Senior Patrol Officer, Los Angeles, by Theodore J. Heine and Julius Malina, October 13, 1943, pp. 1–2, 11th ND Records.
33. D. Dwight Douglas (District Intelligence Officer), Memo to Commandant, November 1, 1943, pp. 1, 3, 11th ND Records.
34. D. Dwight Douglas Memo to Commandant, October 19, 1943, "Negro Situation in 11th Naval District," p. 3, in 11th ND Records.
35. *California Eagle,* October 21, 1943.
36. Ibid., November 4, 1943; D. Dwight Douglas Memo, November 16, 1943, 11th ND Records.
37. *Congested Area Hearings: San Francisco,* p. 661.
38. Ibid., p. 752.
39. Ibid., p. 798.
40. Ibid., pp. 857–860, 862–863; quotation from Hall on p. 856. Joseph James, "Race Relations on the Pacific Coast, San Francisco," *Journal of Educational Sociology,* vol. 19 (November 1945), pp. 166–168. James was president of the San Francisco branch of the NAACP.
41. CPA Final Report—San Francisco Bay area (1944), p. 19, manuscript in CPA Records, notes that "the housing agencies were very definitely influenced by . . . local resistance which delayed programming . . . but progress is now visible." See also Charles S. Johnson, *The Negro Worker in San Francisco* (San Francisco, 1944), pp. 1–8, and *Congested Area Hearings: San Francisco,* pp. 900–902.
42. *San Francisco Call-Bulletin,* July 18, 19, 1944, and *San Francisco Chronicle,* July 18, 19, 1944; Theodore Rosequist Memo to James A. Whiteside, August 2, 1944 and attachment, "Notes Taken at July 31 meeting of the Port Chicago Citizens Disaster Committee," and W. S. Van Winkle to Hiram Johnson, August 21, 1944, in CPA Records. See Florence Murray, *The Negro Handbook, 1946–47* (New York, 1947), pp. 347–349, for a brief summary.
43. Earl Warren to James A. Whiteside, August 28, 1944, W. S. Van Winkle (Chairman of Port Chicago Citizens Disaster Committee) to Sheridan Downey, August 29, 1944 in CPA Records; Lott, *Long Line of Ships,* pp. 255–257; Buford Rowland and William B. Boyd, *U.S. Navy Bureau of Ordnance in*

World War II (Washington, 1952), p. 211. A detailed account is in "U.S. Naval Administration in World War II," unpublished narrative histories in Naval History Division, Office of the Chief of Naval Operations (8 vols.), Bureau of Ordnance; *California Eagle,* September 21, 1944. The best summary account of this affair is Charles Wollenberg, "Black vs. Navy Blue: The Mare Island Mutiny Court Martial," *California History,* vol. 59 (January 1980), 62–74, which also provides extensive bibliographical references.

44. Calshipbuilding Company, *Calship* (San Pedro, Calif., 1947) estimated that the Kaiser yards on the Pacific Coast employed about 15 percent blacks and 5 percent Mexican-Americans. See Oregon Shipbuilding Company Records, Oregon Historical Society, Portland; *Congested Area Hearings: Columbia River Area,* p. 1637.

45. On discrimination see *Congested Area Hearings: Columbia River Area,* p. 1615; R. K. Miller to Ed Izak, October 29, 1943 in ibid., p. 1740; Jenkins's remarks in ibid., pp. 1638–1639. The CPA was also concerned with providing more recreational facilities for the Portland area, particularly in securing a movie house for blacks, who were being excluded from existing theatres. See CPA, Portland Office, Status Report, December 4, 1943, pp. 3–5, CPA Records. For complaints about discrimination see *The People's Observer,* July 16, 1943 (a black newspaper), and *Oregon Journal,* April 4, May 12, May 30, 1944, clippings in Oregon Historical Society. Some church leaders questioned the rise of black crime, *Portland Oregonian,* October 2, 1942. On efforts to open war industry jobs to blacks see *Portland Oregonian,* February 26, March 13, March 14, March 21, April 1, 1942. On contemporary concerns about a growing black population see *Portland Oregonian,* September 23, October 4, 8, November 8, 13, 17, 1942, and July 30, 1943 on job discrimination.

46. On the opening of a Race Relations Clinic see *Oregon Journal,* September 20, 1945 and *Portland Oregonian,* September 21, 1945; on pressures exerted by newly organized Urban League chapter see *Portland Oregonian,* October 24, November 25, December 14, 1945; "Negroes in Oregon," *Phylon,* vol. 30 (Fall 1969), 282–286.

47. U.S. Bureau of the Census, 1940, *Population,* p. 400; ibid., 1950, *Population,* part 47, p. 61. An excellent account of racial tensions in Seattle is in Howard A. Droker, "Seattle Race Relations During the Second World War," *Pacific Northwest Quarterly,* vol. 67 (October 1976), 163–174.

48. Taffinder in *Congested Area Hearings: Puget Sound, Washington Area,* p. 1285; Sprague in ibid., p. 1541; *Northwest Enterprise,* June 21, 1944.

49. Kean in *Congested Area Hearings: Puget Sound, Washington Area,* p. 1374, 1368; Robert W. O'Brien and Lee M. Brooks, "Race Relations in the Pacific Northwest," *Phylon,* vol. 7 (First Quarter 1946), 26–27.

50. Lillard in *Congested Area Hearings: Puget Sound, Washington Area,* p. 1524.

51. Ibid., p. 1524.

52. Jack B. Burke (FEPC Examiner) to Harry Kingman, January 26, 1944, FEPC Records, Region 12.

53. Edgar F. Kaiser to Harry Kingman, December 1, 1943, FEPC Records, Region 12.

54. Ibid.; Harry L. Kingman to Edgar F. Kaiser, January 13, 1943; Harry Kingman to Milo Dempster, August 25, 1944; FEPC Records, Region 12; Dempster was with the Federal Public Housing Authority at Marinship in Sausalito, California, which had one of the best housing integration records in the nation.

55. Memo from Fay W. Hunter (War Manpower Commission) to Lee Still (Oregon Manpower Director), September 5, 1944, including detailed table, "Employment in the Portland Metropolitan Area," September 1, 1944, FEPC Records, Region 12.

56. See also Frank Coleman to George H. Johnson, "Analysis and Recommendations—Petition for Rehearing by Kaiser Co., Oregon Shipbuilding Corp. and California Shipbuilding Corp.," February 4, 1944, pp. 1–14 concerning FEPC rulings in this case, in FEPC Records, Region 12; Edward Rutledge (FEPC Examiner) to Claude Barnett (Staff Director, Associated Negro Press), November 9, 1944; George Johnson (Vice-Chairman, FEPC) to James Clow (Chairman, Portland chapter of NAACP), December 28, 1943. An extensive file on the discriminatory practices of the Boilermaker's Union in the Portland, Oregon area is in FEPC Records, Region 12.

57. James Clow to Harry Kingman, December 21, 1943; Edward Rutledge to Clow, November 9, 1944, FEPC Records, Region 12.

58. Memorandum of Edward Rutledge to Harry Kingman, November 6, 1944, pp. 3–4, FEPC Records, Region 12.

59. Memo of Clarence R. Johnson (FEPC) to Robert C. Weaver (War Production Board), January 17, 1942 concerning "Employment of Negroes and Other Minorities at Boeing"; for statement of one black worker who was refused a union card see "Statement of Eugene Hawkins in Securing Employment at Boeing Aircraft Co.," January 14, 1942. For the union's defense of discrimination see G. R. Cotton (President, Aeronautical Mechanics, Lodge 751, Seattle Industrial District) to FEPC, January 16, 1942 in FEPC Records, Region 12.

60. Dorsett, *Queen City,* pp. 239–240; West (ed.), *Rocky Mountain Cities,* p. 315.

61. West (ed.), *Rocky Mountain Cities,* p. 315; on social problems of black servicemen in Colorado Springs (Camp Kit Carson) see "Letters and Histories Sent to Colorado Defense Council–Colorado Springs, October 25, 1944," p. 3 in War Records Survey #657, World War II History Collection, Colorado State Historical Society. During World War II 188 local Colorado Defense Councils were established.

62. Dorsett, *Queen City,* pp. 240–242; West (ed.), *Rocky Mountain Cities,* p. 315.

62. Quoted in Getty, *Tucson,* pp. 16, 76.

63. Caldwell, quoted in West (ed.), *Rocky Mountain Cities,* p. 224; Getty, *Tucson,* pp. 107–108, 167.

64. Robert E. Brown (FEPC Examiner) to Will Maslow (Director of Field Operations, FEPC), February 5, 1944, FEPC Records, Region 12. The FEPC files contain an extensive collection on discrimination against blacks at the Basic Magnesium Plant. See Box 827, FEPC Records, Region 12.

65. For a specific complaint of alleged beatings see affidavit of Clinton Shaw, September 27, 1943, FEPC Records, Region 12, and in same location the affidavit of Estoly Ward, September [8], 1943. Ward was a CIO organizer at Basic Magnesium where his union was also involved in a jurisdictional dispute with AF of L unions.

66. Florence Mayberry to Harry Kingman, November 18, 1944, FEPC Records, Region 12; some mines in Nevada refused to employ blacks although they hired Mexicans and Indians. See FEPC, Final Disposition Report, Mt. City Copper Co. in Rio Tinto, Nevada, June 14, 1944; on the other hand, the International Smelting and Refining Company employed blacks at

its Victoria Mine near Wendover, Nevada and at its Bailey Triumph Mine in Idaho. See F. A. Wardlaw, Jr., to Harry Kingman, June 20, 1944, in FEPC Records, Region 12.

67. Box 831 in FEPC Records, Region 12 contains an extensive file concerning discriminatory practices at Hawthorne; see also FEPC complaints 12–GR 477 (Johnson), 12 GR–448 (Nimitz and Bragg), and 12–GR 446 (Kelly), FEPC Records, Region 12.

68. Rear Admiral C. H. Wright (Commandant, 12th Naval District) to Commanding Officer, Hawthorne Naval Ammunition Depot, October 2, 1944, "Alleged Discriminatory Practices Against Negroes at the Naval Ammunition Depot, Hawthorne, Nevada," pp. 1–3, 5–6 in FEPC Records, Region 12.

7. Spanish-Speaking Americans in Wartime

1. U.S. Bureau of the Census, 1940, *Population* (Washington, 1943), pp. 42, 73. A competent study is Robin F. Scott, "The Mexican-American in the Los Angeles Area, 1920–1950: From Acquiescence to Activity" (Ph.D. dissertation, University of Southern California, 1971).

2. Nancy L. Gonzales, *The Spanish-Americans of New Mexico* (Albuquerque, 1969), pp. 16–21. Charles P. and Nellie H. Loomis, "Skilled Spanish-American War Industry Workers from New Mexico," *Applied Anthropology,* vol. 2 (October–December 1942), 33–36, and Charles P. Loomis, "Wartime Migration from the Spanish-American Villages of New Mexico," *Rural Sociology,* vol. 7 (December, 1942) 384–395. Memo from Dora T. Hettower to Victor Borella (Director, Division of Inter-American Activities in the United States), June 5, 1943, in Records of the Office of Inter-American Affairs, RG 229, Central Files, in National Archives, Suitland, Maryland, hereafter cited as CIAA Records.

3. U.S. Bureau of the Census, 1940, *Population*, p. 632. Ruth D. Tuck, *Not with the Fist: Mexican Americans in a Southwest City* (New York, 1946), p. 174, and Ruth Tuck, "Behind the Zoot Suit Riots," *Survey Graphic,* vol. 32 (August 1943), 313–316; Celia S. Heller, *Mexican-American Youth: Forgotten Youth at the Crossroads* (New York, 1968), p. 80. *Time,* vol. 6 (September 13, 1943), 25; see also Edward McDonagh, "Status Levels of Mexicans," *Sociology and Social Research,* vol. 33 (July–August 1949), 452–453.

4. Tuck, "Behind the Zoot Suit Riots," pp. 315. Beatrice Griffith, *American Me* (Boston, 1948), p. 267; Tuck, *Not with the Fist,* p. 140; National Catholic Welfare Conference, *The Spanish Speaking of the Southwest and West,* 2d report, San Antonio (1944), p. 17; see also Elis M. Tipton, "What We Want Is Action," *Common Ground,* vol. 7 (Autumn 1946), 76–80.

5. Barron B. Beshoar, "Report from the Mountain States," *Common Ground,* vol. 4 (Spring 1943), 23–30. Beshoar was regional chief of information for the War Manpower Commission, encompassing Colorado, Utah, Idaho, Montana, and Wyoming.

6. Dorsett, *Queen City,* pp. 240–242; West (ed.), *Rocky Mountain Cities,* p. 315.

7. U.S. Bureau of the Census, *County Data Book,* 1940, p. 64; June Caldwell in West (ed.), *Rocky Mountain Cities,* pp. 222–224; Getty, *Tucson,* pp. 40–41, 45. Businesses owned by Mexican-Americans included Jerome's Department Store, Martin's Drug Stores, and Ronstadt's Hardware Store.

8. On military contributions see Raul Morin, *Among the Valiant: Mexican-Americans in WW II and Korea* (Los Angeles, 1963), p. 22.

9. Quote from Heller, *Mexican-American Youth,* pp. 58–62; Norman D. Humphrey, "The Stereotype and the Social Types of Mexican-American Youths," *Journal of Social Psychology,* vol. 22 (1945), 69–78; Carey McWilliams, "Los Angeles Pachuco Gangs," *New Republic,* vol. 18 (January 18, 1943), 76; incisive is Emory S. Bogardus, "Gangs of Mexican-American Youth," *Sociology and Social Research,* vol. 28 (September–October 1945), 65; Griffith, *American Me,* p. 45; Heller, *Mexican-American Youth,* p. 58. Octavio Paz, *The Labyrinth of Solitude: Life and Thought in Mexico,* translated by Lysander Kemp (New York, 1961), p. 14. See also Burma, *Spanish-Speaking Groups,* p. 11; Morin, *Among the Valiant,* p. 20.

10. A standard account is George C. Barker, *Pachuco* (Tucson, 1950), by a contemporary anthropologist. Beatrice Griffith, "The Pachuco Patois," *Common Ground,* vol. 7 (Summer, 1947), pp. 77–84; Barker, *Pachuco,* p. 21; see also George C. Barker, "The Social Functions of Language," *ETC,* vol. II (Summer 1945), 228–234.

11. Karl Holton, Los Angeles County Probation Department, in Papers of Sleepy Lagoon Defense Committee, 1942–1945, Special Collections Library, University of California, Los Angeles, Box. 5.

12. *Los Angeles Times,* August 10, 1942.

13. See also Lloyd E. Fisher, *The Problem of Violence: Observations on Race Conflict in Los Angeles* (Los Angeles, 1946), p. 14; Carey McWilliams, "The Zoot Suit Riots," *New Republic,* vol. 108 (June 21, 1943), p. 819; *Los Angeles Times,* August 19, 1942, and October 27, 1942.

14. The facts of the case can be gleaned from *Los Angeles Times,* August 2, 3, 1942; *Los Angeles Daily News,* August 3, 1942; *People v. Zamora,* 66 Cal. Appell. 2d (1944), 174–177, 200–201; Carey McWilliams, *North from Mexico* (New York, 1944), pp. 228–233, 237; McWilliams was as biased in favor of *pachucos,* in whose defense he was involved, as the Hearst Press was biased against them. Eleanor Roosevelt was very much interested in the Sleepy Lagoon Case. See Walter H. C. Laves to Mrs. F. D. Roosevelt, November 30, 1942 in CIAA Records. Laves was Director of the Division of Inter-American Activities in the CIAA. *Los Angeles Times,* June 17, 1943; see also Laves to Robert Redfield, November 3, 1942 CIAA Records.

15. *Los Angeles Times,* October 27, 1942, January 11, 12, 13, 1943; *People v. Zamora,* 66 Cal. Appel. 2d (1944), 173.

16. California, Senate, Joint Committee on Un-American Activities in California, *Report of Joint Fact Finding Committee on Un-American Activities in California to the California Legislature* (Sacramento, 1943), pp. 160, 216; McWilliams, *North from Mexico,* pp. 229–243.

17. I am indebted to Alice Greenfield McCormick, the secretary of the Sleepy Lagoon Defense Committee, for granting me permission to read through the Committee's files, hereafter cited as Sleepy Lagoon Papers, housed at UCLA. Orson Welles to San Quentin Parole Board, March 1, 1944, Sleepy Lagoon Papers. See also *People v. Zamora,* 66 Cal. Appel. 2d (1944), and *Los Angeles Times,* October 5, 1944.

18. Interview with Guy Endore (1964), pp. 173, 181–185, in Oral History Collection, UCLA. Carey McWilliams, quoted in *Los Angeles Times,* May 9, 1978.

19. *Final Report of the Los Angeles County Grand Jury for the Year 1942,* p. 45.

20. *Los Angeles Times,* October 27, 1942; *Los Angeles Herald and Express,* October 27, 1942; *Los Angeles Daily News,* November 1, 1942; John Ford, *Thirty Explosive Years in Los Angeles County* (San Marino, 1961), p. 136. Ford was a

long-time county supervisor; Tuck in *Survey Graphic*, vol. 32 (1943), 313; Scott, "Mexican-American," pp. 234–235.

21. Griffith, *American Me*, p. 45; Bogardus in *Sociology and Social Research*, vol. 28, p. 56; see also in this connection Ralph H. Turner and Samuel J. Surace, "Zoot Suiters and Mexicans: Symbols in Crowd Behavior," *American Journal of Sociology*, vol. 62 (July 1956), 14–20. Mauricio Mazon, "Social Upheaval in World War II: 'Zoot Suiters' and Servicemen in Los Angeles, 1943" (Ph.D. dissertation, University of California, Los Angeles, 1976), provides an interesting psychological, but one-dimensional, perspective on the zoot suit riots.

22. *Thirty Explosive Years*, p. 135; McDonagh in *Sociology and Social Research* (1944), p. 451; Turner and Surace in *American Journal of Sociology*, vol. 62 (1956), 17. Griffith, *American Me*, pp. 17–19; *Westwood Hills Press*, May 14, 1943; *Los Angeles Times*, May 12, 1943; *Santa Monica Outlook*, May 10, 1943; on dismissal of charges against the accused see *Westwood Hills Press*, May 21, 1943. My generalization is based on an analysis of cases by Martin Dickinson (Commanding Officer, U.S. Naval Training School, Naval Reserve Armory, Los Angeles), "Report on Local Disturbances by the Civilian and Service Personnel," for Commandant, 11th Naval District, June 10, 1943, 16 pp. in 11th ND Records, File p8–5.

23. Dickinson, "Report on Local Disturbances," p. 1.

24. Ibid., p. 14.

25. Ibid., p. 1 on Short, p. 2 on Henderson, p. 16 on Coleman.

26. Ibid., p. 4.

27. McWilliams, "Zoot-Suit Riots," *New Republic* (June 21, 1943), p. 818.

28. *California Eagle*, January 1, 1943, for Dixon's statement; *Hollywood Citizen-News*, June 4, 1943, section 2.

29. Quotations, in order, can be found in *Los Angeles Herald-Express*, June 5, 1943, and *Los Angeles Daily News*, June 7, 1943.

30. Griffith, *American Me*, p. 22; the events are described from different perspectives in *Los Angeles Times*, June 4, 5, 1943; *Newsweek*, June 21, 1943; McWilliams, "The Zoot Suit Riots," *New Republic*, vol. 108 (June 21, 1943), p. 818; McWilliams, *North from Mexico*, pp. 244–258; for later views see the novel by David Chavez, *Zoot Suit* (New York, 1980), and Richard A. Garcia in *Los Angeles Times*, August 27, 1978 on the play by Luis Valdez which romanticized zoot suiters.

31. *Los Angeles Times*, June 8, 1943.

32. Telegram, Rear Admiral D. W. Bagley, 11th Naval District, to All Units, June 10, 1943 in ND Records.

33. Rear Admiral D. W. Bagley to Senor Alfredo Calles, June 10, 1943; telegram, Calles to Bagley, June 9, 1943, in ND Records. *Los Angeles Times* and *Los Angeles Daily News* for June 6, 7, 8, 9, 10, and 11, 1943, provide coverage of the riots.

34. Major General Maxwell Murray to Commanders, All Units, Southern California Sector, June 11, 1943, in ND Records.

35. S. F. Heim (Commandant, Naval Operating Base, Terminal Island) to D. W. Bagley, August 2, 1943; Memo, "Organization for Detachments Called Out for Riot Duty," July 30, 1943, in ND Records.

36. C. H. Fogg (Senior Patrol Officer) to D. W. Bagley, July 29, 1943, p. 1, ND Records.

37. Ibid., pp. 2–3.

38. Fletcher A. Bowron to Elmer Davis, June 28, 1943, Bowron Manuscripts.

39. Telephone conversation between Admiral D. W. Bagley and Captain B. F. Heim at 1035, June 11, 1943, in ND Records.

40. John M. Clark to Reginald Garcia (Chairman, Committee for the Defense of Mexican-American Youth), November 24, 1942, Sleepy Lagoon Papers.

41. Los Angeles County Grand Jury, "Report of the Special Committee on Racial Problems," in *Final Report of the 1943 Los Angeles County Grand Jury*, p. 27.

42. *Los Angeles Daily News*, June 10, 1943; *Los Angeles Times*, June 16, 17, 18, 1943; *Time*, June 21, 1943, pp. 18–19; Griffith, *American Me*, p. 28.

43. Ford, *Thirty Exciting Years*, pp. 135–136; Scott, "Mexican-American," pp. 249–252.

44. Ruth Ginsburg, "A New Program in Spanish for Los Angeles," *California Journal of Secondary Education*, vol. 18 (October 1943), 347–348.

45. McWilliams was active in this group. See McWilliams, in *North from Mexico*, pp. 238–251, 255–257. Los Angeles County Probation Department, *42d Annual Report*, p. E; Scott, "Mexican-American," pp. 242–253.

46. Joseph P. Hill, "The Church and the Zoot Suiter," National Catholic Welfare Conference, *Conference Report: Catholic Council for the Spanish Speaking* (1946), p. 16.

47. Barker, *Pachuco*, p. 23; Getty, *Tucson*, pp. 65–66; 206–207.

48. See his speech as reported in *Albuquerque Journal*, June 15, 1942; see also *Colorado Springs Telegraph*, June 15, 1942.

49. Memo of Ignacio L. Lopez to Harry L. Kingman, March 1, 1945 in FEPC Records, Region 12; see also National Catholic Welfare Conference, *Spanish Speaking of the Southwest*, p. 1. On social theory concerning the functioning of closely knit Mexican American communities see Griffith, *American Me*, pp. 233–243; Tuck, *Not with the Fist*, pp. 145–172; Burma, *Spanish-Speaking Groups*, pp. 72–99; Lee Grebler, Joan W. Moore and Ralph Guzman, *The Mexican-American People* (New York, 1970), pp. 517–572. Particularly relevant is Ralph C. Guzman, "The Political Socialization of the Mexican-American People" (Ph.D. dissertation, UCLA, 1970), pp. 56–89, 196–277 on the role of charismatic leaders. Since Spanish-speaking Americans in California were more likely to be immigrants or first-generation Mexican-Americans, this may explain why they were more reluctant to use the FEPC than Spanish-speaking Americans in the Southwest, whose families had been settled in the region for hundreds of years and who were more familiar with American governmental institutions.

50. These cases are filed alphabetically in Records of the Fair Employment Practices Committee, Regions 10, 11, 13 in National Archives, Washington, D.C. See also letter of Senator Edwin C. Johnson (Col.) to Lawrence M. Cramer (Executive Secretary, FEPC), March 14, 1944, on the Utah case, in FEPC Records, Region 10.

51. E. G. Trimble, "Discrimination in the Southwest," Report to Lawrence W. Cramer, October 23, 1943, pp. 1–6, FEPC Records, Region 10; see also FEPC Records, Region 10–11, in National Archives, Washington, D.C.

52. Victor Borella to John Lockwood, December 9, 1943; Nelson Rockefeller to Carl Hayden, March 9, 1943, in CIAA Records.

53. Joseph E. Weckler to William Sheperd (President, U.S. Junior Chamber of Commerce), June 1, 1943, CIAA Records. See also James M. Landis (Director, Office of Civilian Defense), Memo on Volunteer Opportunities in Civil Defense for Minorities, Operations Letter #99, December 18, 1942,

pp. 1–2, CIAA Records. Memo, Joseph E. Weckler to Walter T. Prendergast, January 23, 1943, CIAA Records.

54. Donald W. Rowland, *History of the Office of the Coordinator of Inter-American Affairs* (Washington, 1947), pp. 105–114.

55. "Confidential Report of the Conference on the Spanish-Speaking Minority Program in the Southwest," held by the Division of Inter-American Activities in the United States, Coordinator of Inter-American Affairs (CIAA), Washington, D.C., July 12–14, 1943, mimeographed, pp. 5–6, 20–23, CIAA Records.

56. "Committee Reports of the Conference on Educational Problems in the Southwest—With Special Reference to the Educational Problems of the Spanish Speaking Communities" (n.p., n.d.), p. 1, mimeographed copy in University of New Mexico Library.

57. Ibid., pp. 2–3, 13; quotations on pp. 4, 13, respectively.

58. Coordinator of Inter-American Affairs, Conference on the Problems of Education Among Spanish-Speaking Populations of Our Southwest, "Recent Educational and Community Experiments and Projects in New Mexico Affecting the Spanish-Speaking Population" (n.p., n.d.), p. 12, mimeographed copy in University of New Mexico Library.

59. Ibid., pp. 7–9.

60. Joseph E. Weckler (Assistant to the Director, Division of Inter-American Activities in the United States), memo, May 1, 1943, CIAA Records.

61. On Barelas see "Proposed Project Authorization, Barelas Community Center (Ident. #A1A6–4265), pp. 1–2 in CIAA Records, Central File. An extensive file on CIAA aid to the Albuquerque, N.M. public schools is in Box 29. On Texas projects see "Confidential Report . . . Washington Conference," pp. 17–20, and Jane W. Pijoan to Harold W. Janis, November 5, 1943 in CIAA Records.

62. Getty, *Tucson,* pp. 45–47, 50–51, 116–118, 158–164.

8. Western Indians and Japanese-Americans

1. John Adair, "The Navajo and Pueblo Veteran, A Force for Culture Change," *The American Indian,* vol. 4, #1 (1947), 5–11; Adair's views were based on his doctoral dissertation: "A Study of Culture Resistance: The Veterans of World War II at Zuni Pueblo" (Ph.D. dissertation, University of New Mexico, 1948). See also John Adair and Evan Z. Vogt, "Navajo and Zuni Veterans: A Study of Contrasting Modes of Culture Change," *American Anthropologist,* vol. 51 (Oct.–Dec. 1949), 547–561; Evan Z. Vogt, "Between Two Worlds: Case Study of a Navajo Veteran," *The American Indian,* vol. 5, #1 (1949), 13–21; and Evan Z. Vogt, *Navajo Veterans: A Study of Changing Values,* in *Papers of the Peabody Museum of Archeology and Ethnology,* vol. 41, #1 (Cambridge, 1951).

2. John Collier in *Indians at Work* (December 1941), p. 3. See also Tom Holm, "Fighting a White Man's War: The Extent and Legacy of American Indian Participation in World War II," *Journal of Ethnic Studies,* vol. 9 (Summer, 1981), 69–81. Collier wanted Indian conscripts to be registered by race. See John Collier to Brigadier-General Lewis Hershey, June 12, 1941, Records of the Office of Indian Affairs, RG 75, National Archives, Washington, D.C., hereafter cited as OIA Records.

3. William Hagan, *American Indians* (Chicago, 1961), pp. 158–159 is very

superficial; for examples of Indian responses see *Indians at Work* (April 1941), p. 18; ibid. (February 1942), pp. 8–9; ibid. (March 1942), pp. 11–14; ibid. (April 1942), pp. 6–8, 17–20; Charles H. Lange, *Cochiti* (Austin, 1960), p. 188. Lange, a distinguished anthropologist, was a Cochiti himself. Contemporary articles include Elizabeth S. Sergeant, "The Indian Goes to War," *New Republic,* vol. 107 (November 30, 1942), 708; Stanley Vestal, "The Plains Indian and the War," *Saturday Review of Literature,* vol. 25 (May 16, 1942), 9; John Collier, "The Indian in a Wartime Nation," *Annals of the American Academy of Political and Social Science,* vol. 223 (September 1942), 29–35; See also Robert Ritzenthaler, "The Impact of War on an Indian Community," *American Anthropologist,* vol. 45 (April–June 1943), 325–326.

4. Statistics on Indian involvement from report of John Collier in U.S. Department of the Interior, *Annual Report,* 1945 (Washington, 1945), pp. 233, 249–250. See also *Indians at Work* (January–February 1945), pp. 6–9 for a detailed analysis; for a general discussion see Harold Fey and D'Arcy McNickle, *Indians and Other Americans* (New York, 1959), pp. 149–150.

5. LaFarge in *Indians at Work* (January 1942), p. 11. On Indian participation elsewhere see Monthly Service Reports, World War II, Cheyenne and Arapaho Agency, OIA Records.

6. *Santa Fe New Mexican,* December 13, 1941.

7. Margretta Dietrich, "Braves on the Warpath," *New Mexico Magazine* vol. 21 (June 1943), pp. 14–15.

8. On Indian participation in war bond purchases see *Indians at Work* (February 1942), pp. 11–12; report of Indian Commissioner Collier in U.S. Department of the Interior, *Annual Report,* 1943, pp. 273–274; ibid., 1944, pp. 235–239; ibid., 1945, p. 250; on Jemez Pueblo dancers see *Albuquerque Journal,* May 3, 1942.

9. On statistics see U.S. Office of Indian Affairs, *Indians in the War* (Washington, 1945), pp. 1–11, 14–15; for a detailed list of dead and wounded by state, see ibid., pp. 16–24, 30–41. *New York Times,* February 14, 1943 for General MacArthur's praise of Indian soldiers, and January 19, 1944, and January 23, 1945.

10. On Tinker see *Indians at Work* (January 1942), p. 13, and ibid. (May–June 1942), p. 13; *New York Times,* June 13, 14, 1942. See also October 25, November 11, 1942. Samuel Eliot Morison, *Coral Sea, Midway, and Submarine Action, May, 1942–August, 1942* in *History of United States Naval Operations in World War II* (Boston, 1950), p. 151.

11. The records pertaining to the organization of a separate Indian unit are in the National Archives in Washington, D.C., Records of the Adjutant General.

12. Doris Paul, *The Navajo Code Talkers* (New York, 1970), pp. 7–11.

13. Text of Johnston's memorandum, "Plan for Recruiting Indian Signal Corps Personnel," in Paul, *The Navajo Code Talkers,* pp. 153–156; Vogel's Memo to Vandergrift, March 6, 1942 in ibid., pp. 156–157. Original copies can be examined at the Navajo Tribal Museum in Window Rock, Arizona.

14. In order to expedite his induction, Johnston waived a commission and agreed to serve as a noncommissioned officer. See his letter to General Vandergrift requesting enlistment, September 14, 1942, printed in Paul, *The Navajo Code Talkers,* pp. 157–159.

15. Quoted in Paul, *The Navajo Code Talkers,* pp. 53–54; Richard Tregaskis, *Guadalcanal Diary* (New York, 1942), p. 32; a more detailed account of the activities of the code talkers is in Paul, *The Navajo Code Talkers,* pp. 66–101.

They were particularly important in the capture of Iwo Jima.

16. Margretta Dietrich (comp.), *Hello and Many Lucks* (Santa Fe, N.M., 1945), pp. 8–9. This is a remarkable collection of letters written by Indian service men and women. Mrs. Dietrich, widow of a U.S. Senator, was president of the Santa Fe Indian Club and carried on an extensive correspondence which was published in a limited edition of 300 copies each. See also Margretta Dietrich (comp.), *Doing Fine and Thanks a Million* (Santa Fe, N.M., 1943).

17. Dietrich (comp.), *Doing Fine*, p. 54; ibid., p. 65; Dietrich (comp.), *Hello and Many Lucks*, p. 41.

18. Dietrich (comp.), *Hello and Many Lucks*, p. 54.

19. *Santa Fe New Mexican*, August 8, 1942.

20. Dietrich (comp.), *Hello and Many Lucks*, p. 11; Nakai quoted in Paul, *Navajo Code Talkers*, p. 108.

21. Dietrich (comp.), *Doing Fine*, p. 19; ibid., pp. 31–32; ibid., p. 35.

22. Ibid., p. 43; ibid., p. 46.

23. Ibid., pp. 47–48; ibid., p. 59.

24. Quoted in Paul, *Navajo Code Talkers*, p. 85.

25. Quoted in ibid., p. 87; for other cases of mistaken identity see ibid., pp. 87–91. Understandably, the code talkers reflected strong anti-Japanese sentiments. When one of them, Scotty Begay, heard about a Japanese-American teacher in a Navajo school in Arizona, he wrote an angry letter to W. W. Midgley, chairman of the Selective Service Board in Flagstaff, Arizona. "What is this I hear about Jap school teachers in Navajo schools?" he noted. "Has Collier gone crazy all the way? We are using the Navajo language here to keep the Japs from knowing what we are doing. Will these teachers back there learn our language?" Secretary Ickes strongly opposed discrimination against Japanese in Indian schools, however. See Scotty Begay to W. W. Midgley (May 30, 1944) who sent a copy to Secretary of War Henry L. Stimson. Harold L. Ickes to Henry L. Stimson, July 5, 1944, and John S. Collier to Margretta Dietrich (chairman, New Mexico Association for Indian Affairs), November 1, 1943, OIA Records.

26. Fay and McNickle, *Indians*, p. 179; Ruth Underhill, *Red Man's America* (Chicago, 1953), p. 239; Lange, *Cochiti*, p. 188; Adair and Vogt, *American Anthropologist*, vol. 51. 558–561.

27. *Indians at Work* (January–February 1945), p. 6.

28. Ibid. (Winter, 1942), vol. 10, 2–6, 18–19; *Albuquerque Journal*, May 18, 1943. The Office of Indian Affairs also sent a Los Angeles clothing manufacturer who was looking for a new factory site to the Pima Reservation. See Willard Beatty (OIA, Director of Education) to A. E. Robinson (Superintendent of Pima Agency), November 9, 1944 and George C. Wells (Superintendent of Indian Education at Phoenix) to Beatty, November 20, 1944, RG 29, OIA Records. On contemporary accounts of Pimas in wartime see 78th Cong., 2d sess., House, Subcommittee of the Committee on Indian Affairs, *Hearings on Indian Affairs, H. Resolution 166* (5 parts, Washington, 1944), part 3, pp. 928–936, hereafter cited as *Hearings on Indian Affairs*.

29. Archibald, *Wartime Shipyard*, p. 105.

30. Quote from Carlson in Frederick Sleight, "Indians Work for the Navy," *Indians in the War*, p. 42; a more detailed discussion of the Clearfield Depot is in Leonard Arrington and Archer L. Durham, "Anchors Aweigh in Utah," *Utah Historical Quarterly* vol. 31 (1963), 109–118; see also *Salt Lake City Tribune Magazine*, January 9, 1944.

31. L. E. Correll to Commissioner, July 16, 1941; C. W. Spaulding to Commissioner, July 18, 1941; see also Lem Towers (Superintendent, Pawnee, Okla. Agency) to Commissioner, July 15, 1941, and George Trombold to John Woolery (Senior Employment agent at Chilocco), June 24, 1941, OIA Records.

32. For general works see Joseph H. Cash, *The Sioux People* (Rapid City, 1979), pp. 79–80; Stanley Vestal, "The Plains Indian and the War," *Saturday Review of Literature*, vol. 25 (May 16, 1942), 9; Michael Lawson, *Dammed Indians* (Norman, 1982), p. 37; Tom Holm, "Fighting a White Man's War," *Journal of Ethnic Studies*, vol. 9 (January 1981), 69–81.

33. John Useem, Gordon Macgregor, and Ruth Hill Useem, "Wartime Employment and Adjustments of the Rosebud Sioux," *Applied Anthropology* vol. 2 (January 1943), 1–2.

34. Ibid., pp. 3–5; Cash, *Sioux People*, p. 78.

35. 78th Cong., 2d sess., *Hearings on Indian Affairs*, 1944, part 3, pp. 175–179 for the text of the resolution.

36. Eleanor Williams, "Rosebud's Tribal Land Enterprise," *Indians at Work* (March–April 1944), pp. 14–17.

37. 78th Cong., 2d sess., *Hearings on Indian Affairs*, 1944, part 3, p. 185.

38. James N. Howard, "The Dakota Indian Victory Dance, World War II," *North Dakota History*, vol. 18 (January 1951), 33–35; Williams in *Indians at Work* (March–April 1944), p. 14.

39. Useem et al., in *Applied Anthropology*, vol 2, 3–4.

40. Ibid., pp. 5–9; for contemporary testimony amplifying these conditions among Rosebud Sioux see 78th Cong., 2d sess., *Hearings on Indian Affairs*, 1944, part 3, pp. 174, 180–182, 188.

41. Katie Jordan and Tonita Mirabal, "War's Impact on New Mexico Indians," *El Palacio*, vol. 51 (June 1944), 110, 13.

42. Tonita Mirabal in ibid., p. 112.

43. Bernice Brode, "Maid Service," Los Alamos Scientific Laboratory *Community News*, June 30, 1960, p. 8. On the impact of the cash economy on Navajos, see also 78 Cong., 2d sess., *Hearings on Indian Affairs*, 1944, part 3, pp. 864–886.

44. Bernice Brode, "Los Alamos and the Indians," Los Alamos Scientific Laboratory *Community News*, August 25, 1960, p. 5.

45. *Navajos and World War II* (Tsaile, Arizona, 1977), p. 48, a series of taped oral interviews, transcribed.

46. Tonita Mirabal in *El Palacio*, vol. 51, 113.

47. *Indians at Work* (April 1942), p. 7.

48. Ibid. (July 1942), p. 18. See also Howard, "The Dakota Indian Victory Dance, World War II," *North Dakota History*, vol. 18 (January 1951), 36.

49. Ruth Kirk, "Dances for War and Peace," *New Mexico Magazine*, vol. 21 (July 1943), pp. 9–10. See also Adair, "Veterans of World War II at Zuni Pueblo," passim; Dietrich in *New Mexico Magazine*, vol. 21 (June 1943), p. 29.

50. Ruth Kirk, "War Rituals at Zuni," *New Mexico Magazine*, vol. 23 (August 1945), pp. 14–15; *Navajos and World War II*, pp. 59, 82; Dietrich (comp.), *Doing Fine*, p. 74.

51. Katie Jordan in *El Palacio*, vol. 51, 110.

52. Dietrich (comp.), *Doing Fine*, p. 18; ibid., p. 29; Dietrich (comp.), *Hello and Many Lucks*, p. 5; Navajo quoted in Paul, *Navajo Code Talkers*, p. 108.

53. Dietrich, *New Mexico Magazine* (June 1943), p. 15.

54. Tonita Mirabal in *El Palacio*, vol. 51, 112; Walter C. Eels, "Educational

Opportunities for the Indian," *The American Indian,* vol. 2 (Fall, 1945), 17–21.

55. Joe S. Sando, *The Pueblo Indians* (San Francisco, 1976), p. 113. Sando was himself a World War II veteran.

56. Katie Jordan in *El Palacio,* vol. 51, 110.

57. Dietrich in *New Mexico Magazine* (June 1943), p. 30.

58. Dietrich (comp.), *Hello and Many Lucks,* pp. 38–39.

59. Lois E. Harlin, "The National Congress of American Indians," *Indians at Work* (November–December 1944), pp. 20–21.

60. Ibid., p. 22. See also 78th Cong., 2d sess., House, *Hearings on Indian Affairs,* 1944, (3 parts, Washington, 1945), part 3, pp. 1000–1004 for President (Judge) Johnson's views, and p. 1064.

61. On the significance of the war veterans see Eric T. Hagberg and Robert Bunker, "Pueblo Sovereignty, Post-war," *New Mexico Quarterly Review,* vol. 18 (Summer 1948), 223–224; see also Theodore H. Haas, "The Legal Aspects of Indian Affairs from 1887 to 1957," *Annals of the American Academy of Political and Social Science,* vol. 311 (May 1957), pp. 16–22.

62. The literature on this subject is voluminous. For an overview see Thomas Le Duc, "The Work of the Indian Claims Commission Under the Act of 1946," *Pacific Historical Review,* vol. 26 (February 1957), 1–16, and Randolph C. Downes, "The Indian Claims Bill," *The American Indian,* vol. 3 (Spring, 1946), 1–8. For text of Republican platform of 1944 advocating creation of the Indian Claims Commission see *New York Times,* June 28, 1944.

63. On conflicts see David H. French, *Factionalism at Isleta Pueblo* (Seattle, 1948) and Bernard J. Siegel and Alan R. Beals, "Pervasive Factionalism," *American Anthropologist,* vol. 62 (April 1960), 397–398, 403–406.

64. On Cochiti see Lange, *Cochiti,* pp. 71, 174, 395–396, and Stuart Levine and Nancy Lurie, *The American Indian Today* (Deland, 1965), p. 61; on Pueblos see J. R. Fox, "Veterans and Factions in Pueblo Society," *Man,* vol. 61 (October 1962), 174–176; on Zuni see Adair, "The Veterans of World War II at Zuni Pueblo," pp. 4–5, 31–45, 161–167, and Adair and Vogt, "Navajo and Zuni Veterans," in *American Anthropologist,* vol. 51, 547–561, and Vogt, *The Navajo War Veteran,* passim.

65. References to Hayes are extensive. See Fay and McNickle, *American Indians,* pp. 44–46; Virgil J. Vogel, *This Country Was Ours* (New York, 1974), pp. 329–334; Ralph and Natasha Friar, *The Only Good Indian: The Hollywood Gospel* (New York, 1972), pp. 216–218; Wilcomb Washburn, *Red Man's Land—White Man's Law* (New York, 1971), p. 80. A 1955 movie, *The Outsider,* dealt with the life of Hayes.

66. "Address by Dillon S. Meyer before . . . the National Council of Churches of Christ," Buck Hill Falls, Pennsylvania, December 12, 1951, quoted in Fay and McNickle, *American Indians,* pp. 150–151.

67. Commissioner of Indian Affairs, *Annual Report,* 1946 (Washington, 1947), p. 456.

68. Quoted in Paul, *Navajo Code Talkers,* p. 111.

69. 79th Cong., 2d sess., Senate, Committee on Indian Affairs, *Testimony on Senate Joint Resolution 79* (Washington, 1946), 3 ff.; *New York Times,* December 3, 5, 10, 12, 16, 24, 1947.

70. The literature on internment of Japanese-Americans is large. See Gardner and Loftis, *The Great Betrayal;* Morton Grodzins, *Americans Betrayed* (Chicago, 1949); Dorothy S. Thomas and Richard S. Nishimoto, *The Spoilage* (Berkeley, 1946); Roger Daniels, *Concentration Camps, U.S.A.* (New York, 1974). Each of these works has an extensive bibliography.

71. Report of Munson in Franklin D. Roosevelt Memo, November 8, 1941, Franklin D. Roosevelt Papers, quoted in Roger Daniels, *The Decision to Evacuate the Japanese* (New York, 1972), pp. 28, 33–35.

72. Grodzins, *Americans Betrayed*, pp. 97–99, 106–108, 144–145, 155–156, 285–287, 405–407; Stetson Conn et al., *United States Army in World War II: The Western Hemisphere Guarding the United States and Its Outposts* (Washington, 1964), pp. 116–118.

73. 77th Cong., 2d sess., *House Report #2124* (Washington, 1942), pp. 314–315; for detailed accounts see Grodzins, *Americans Betrayed*, pp. 185–210; Daniels, *Decision*, pp. 70–73; Conn, *U.S. Army*, pp. 207–210; Jacobus Ten Broek, E. N. Barnhart, and F. W. Matson, *Prejudice, War and the Constitution* (Berkeley, 1958).

74. Quoted in Grodzins, *Americans Betrayed*, p. 94. See also Girdner and Loftus, *The Great Betrayal*, pp. 339–340 on attitudes of western state governors.

75. *New York Times*, March 19, 1942; the ten detention centers were Manzanar and Tule Lake in California, Minidoka in Idaho, Heart Mountain in Wyoming, Topaz in Utah, Granada in Colorado, Poston, Gila River, and Jerome in Arizona, and Rohwer in Arkansas.

76. John Modell, "The Japanese of Los Angeles: A Study in Growth and Accommodation, 1900–1946" (Ph.D. dissertation, Columbia University, 1969), pp. 379–386. This study has the most detailed examination of the Japanese-Americans in the Los Angeles area; see also *Los Angeles News*, January 28, 1942; *Congressional Record*, 77th Cong., 2d sess., (1942), A 457–459; 78th Cong., 1st sess., Senate, Committee on Military Affairs, Subcommittee on Japanese War Relocation Centers, *Report* (Washington, 1942), pp. 92–98. Girdner and Loftis, *The Great Betrayal*, pp. 327–354; Daniels, *Decision*, provide details. Modell, "Japanese of Los Angeles," pp. 339–410 provides an excellent account of the Japanese evacuation there.

77. Modell, *The Japanese of Los Angeles*, pp. 280–283, pays some attention to the evacuation in San Francisco. For Sacramento see Cole, *A History of the Japanese Community in Sacramento: 1883–1972*, pp. 43–62.

78. *Portland Oregonian*, January 24, 1942; for a detailed study of Japanese evacuation see Pursinger, "Oregon's Japanese in World War II," pp. 68–319.

79. *Portland Oregonian*, January 13, 30, 1942; *Oregon Voter*, February 7, 1942.

80. *San Francisco Chronicle*, February 21, 1942; see also 77th Cong., 2d sess., *Tolan Committee Hearings*, part 30, pp. 11, 397–411, 404.

81. Sale, *Seattle*, pp. 175–176; Jones, *Seattle*, p. 281.

82. Jones, *Seattle*, p. 284.

83. Sale, *Seattle*, p. 177; for an account by one of those evacuated see Nelson, *Seattle*, pp. 149–154. For the general context see Girdner and Loftis, *The Great Betrayal*, pp. 23–24, 76–77, 86–87, 114–115; Seattle *Post-Intelligencer*, February 28, March 1, 3, 1942; John L. DeWitt, *Final Report, Japanese Evacuation from the Pacific Coast* (Washington, 1943), pp. 105–108; 77th Cong., 2d sess., House, *Report of the Select Committee Investigating National Defense Migration* (Washington, 1942), pp. 15–29, Appendix A.

84. Jones, *Seattle*, p. 286.

85. *Boise Capital News*, May 22, 1942.

86. *New York Times*, April 12, 1942; *Portland Oregonian*, April 29, 1942.

87. *Los Angeles Times*, November 23, December 12, 1944.

88. U.S. War Relocation Authority, *A Story of Human Conservation* (Wash-

ington, 1946); Harold Fistere, *Final Report of the Northwest Area (WRA) Office* (Washington, 1946), pp. 69–70; Modell, "Japanese in Los Angeles," pp. 392–410, and Pursinger, "Oregon's Japanese," pp. 32–425, have extensive coverage.

89. Larry Tajiri, "Farewell to Little Tokyo," *Common Ground*, vol. 3 (Spring, 1943), 90, 91, 92.

90. Transcript of oral interview with Chikaji Teramoto (a Nisei in Sacramento) by Cheryl Cole, in Cole, *A History of the Japanese Community in Sacramento: 1883–1972*, p. 120.

9. Science in the Wartime West

1. The two standard works on the OSRD are James Phinney Baxter III, *Scientists Against Time* (Boston, 1946), and Irvin Stewart, *Organizing Scientific Research for War* (Boston, 1948); Records of the OSRD are in the National Archives; on Los Alamos, see the official history by Richard G. Hewlett and Oscar Anderson, Jr., *The New World* (University, Pa., 1962), pp. 229–252, 309–318, 374–376; more extensive is "Manhattan District History," in Records of Nuclear Regulatory Agency, Washington, D.C. On Hanford, see ibid., pp. 188–190, 212–226, 304–310; computation of the value from government contracts in the West made from data in Baxter, *Scientists Against Time*, p. 460. See also Daniel J. Kevles, *The Physicists* (New York, 1978), pp. 302–323.

2. A. Hunter Depree, *Science in the Federal Government—A History of Policies and Activities to 1940* (Cambridge, 1957), pp. 302–325; Millikan was an enthusiastic supporter of the Allied cause; on the other hand, Frank B. Jewett, a distinguished scientist, felt the war diverted the energies of scientists away from serious, productive research. See ibid., pp. 309, 324.

3. Ibid., pp. 344–371.

4. General works that include a discussion of scientists in the West include Laura Fermi, *Illustrious Immigrants: The Intellectual Migration from Europe, 1930–1941* (Chicago, 1971), Donald Fleming and Bernard Bailyn (eds.), *The Intellectual Migration* (Cambridge, 1969), and Jarrell C. Jackman and Carla M. Borden (eds.), *The Muses Flee Hitler: Cultural Transfer and Adaptation* (Washington, 1983), pp. 169–234.

5. Baxter, *Scientists Against Time*, pp. 203–204, 210, 261; on Pauling see ibid., pp. 20, 265. Clayton Koppes prepared a detailed history of the Jet Propulsion Laboratory; see *JPL* (New Haven, 1982).

6. Baxter, *Scientists Against Time*, pp. 174, 179–181.

7. Ibid., p. 391.

8. Bernard Jaffe, *Men of Science in America* (New York, 1944), p. 476. Brief summaries of the Radiation Laboratory's work can be found in Baxter, *Scientists Against Time*, pp. 429–431. I have relied largely on the following: Ernest O. Lawrence, "History of the University of California Radiation Laboratory" [1945], and "Research and Development at the University of California Radiation Laboratory" [an unpublished historical account written by its staff in wartime], and Marcus Lathrop, "Report on Ernest O. Lawrence Correspondence Files, 1939–1941," [1945] in Ernest O. Lawrence Papers, Bancroft Library, University of California, Berkeley. Lathrop, a physicist on the staff of the Radiation Laboratory, was a close associate of Lawrence. On formulation of his report see Marcus Lathrop to Ernest O. Lawrence, November 17, 1945 in Lawrence Papers.

9. Baxter, *Scientists Against Time*, pp. 21–22, 159, 445.

10. Ibid., p. 238. On Hanford see the manuscript volumes in the office of the Nuclear Regulatory Agency in Hanford, Washington, entitled "Construction, Hanford Engineer Works," and "Design and Procurement History of Hanford Engineer Works and Clinton Semi-Works."

11. Robert E. McKee, *The Zia Corporation in Los Alamos* (El Paso, 1950); Marjorie Chambers, "Technically Sweet Los Alamos: The Development of a Federally Sponsored Scientific Community" (Ph.D. dissertation, University of New Mexico, 1974).

12. On Los Alamos, in addition to Hewlett and Anderson, *The New World,* pp. 229–236, see James W. Kunetka, *City of Fire: Los Alamos and Birth of the Atomic Age* (Englewood Cliffs, 1978); Roland E. Pettit, *Los Alamos Before the Dawn* (Los Alamos, 1972); and Fermor Church, *When Los Alamos Was a Ranch School* (Los Alamos, 1974); Peggy Bond Church, *The House at Potowi Bridge* (Albuquerque, 1960); on Lovelace Clinic see *Lovelace Foundation for Medical Education and Research* (Albuquerque, n.p., n.d.), pp. 4–5, 13; Frank D. Reeve, *History of New Mexico* (3 vols., New York, 1961), vol. 3, 6–7; *Albuquerque Journal,* December 5, 1965.

13. Jaffe, *Men of Science in America,* p. 476.

14. Bush's views are in Carnegie Institution of Washington, *Yearbook* #38 (Washington, 1939), pp. 5–7 and ibid, #39 (Washington, 1940), pp. 4–5, and ibid., #40 (Washington, 1941), pp. 3–5.

15. George H. Hildebrand to Vannevar Bush, July 25, 1940, OSRD Records, Office File of Vannevar Bush, National Archives, Washington, D.C. This letter has also been reprinted in James L. Penick et al. (eds.), *The Politics of American Science, 1939 to the Present* (revised ed., Cambridge, 1972), pp. 53–55.

16. Los Alamos Scientific Laboratory, "Manhattan District History," *Report LAMS 2532* (Los Alamos, 1961); Leslie R. Groves, *Now It Can Be Told* (New York, 1962); Kevles, *The Physicists,* pp. 329–332; Hewlett and Anderson, *The New World,* pp. 229–230; "Manhattan District History" Book VIII; Los Alamos Project (Y), vol. I, General, 2.1–2.7, mss. in library, Los Alamos Scientific Laboratory.

17. Ernest O. Lawrence to Warren Weaver, February 24, 1940; Lathrop Report, pp. 1–3, Lawrence Papers. See also Daniel S. Greenberg, *The Politics of Pure Science* (New York, 1967), p. 65.

18. Ernest O. Lawrence, "History," pp. 1–2, Lawrence Papers.

19. "Research and Development at the Radiation Laboratory," Book I, pp. 6–28, Lawrence Papers; Hewlett and Anderson, *The New World,* pp. 33–34, 50, 53–60, 141–147, 155–159; Donald Cooksey, a staff member, provided a fine photograph of Lawrence and the staff in 1938, reproduced in ibid., opposite p. 32.

20. Ernest O. Lawrence to Warren Weaver, October 14, 1939, Lathrop Report, p. 10, Lawrence Papers. See also Raymond B. Fosdick, *The Story of the Rockefeller Foundation* (New York, 1952), pp. 171–175, and Warren Weaver, *Scene of Change* (New York, 1970), p. 76.

21. Ernest O. Lawrence to Vannevar Bush, June 8, 1939, Lawrence Papers. See also Lawrence to Bush, April 4, 1940, Lawrence to Bush, May 22, 1940 and Bush to Lawrence, August 30, 1940, in Lawrence Papers, on the close working relationship of the two men.

22. Ernest O. Lawrence to Warren Weaver, April 7, 1938; Lawrence to Weaver, April 23, 1939; Lathrop Report, pp. 5, 8, Lawrence Papers.

23. Ernest O. Lawrence to Warren Weaver, September 10, 1939, Lathrop

Report, pp. 9–10, Lawrence Papers.

24. Ernest O. Lawrence to Warren Weaver, October 14, 1939, Lathrop Report, p. 10, Lawrence Papers.

25. Ernest O. Lawrence to Warren Weaver, November 22, 1939, Lathrop Report, p. 12, Lawrence Papers.

26. Lathrop Report, p. 18, Lawrence Papers.

27. R. H. Fowler to Ernest O. Lawrence, January 28, 1941; John D. Cockroft to Lawrence, December 28, 1940, Lathrop Report, pp. 25–26, Lawrence Papers.

28. Ernest O. Lawrence, "History of Radiation Laboratory," Addendum, p. 1 [p. 7], Lawrence Papers.

29. Quotations from ibid., pp. 1–2 [pp. 7–8]. See also James B. Conant, *My Several Lives: Memoirs* (New York, 1970), 272–274; Arthur Compton, *Atomic Quest* (New York, 1956), pp. 98–100, 138–142. On typical aspects see Stephan Groneff, *Manhattan Project* (Boston, 1967).

30. Vannevar Bush to Frank B. Jewett, April 19, 1941, Lathrop Report, p. 28, Lawrence Papers.

31. Ernest O. Lawrence to Lyman J. Briggs, July 10, 1941, Lathrop Report, p. 33; "Research and Development at the Radiation Laboratory," Lawrence Papers, p. 6.

32. Ernest O. Lawrence to Arthur H. Compton, October 22, 1941, Lathrop Report, pp. 35–36, Lawrence Papers.

33. James B. Conant to Ernest O. Lawrence, December 20, 1941, Lathrop Report, pp. 38–40; "Research and Development at the Radiation Laboratory," Lawrence Papers, pp. 7–9.

34. A brief general survey is in Fermi, *Illustrious Immigrants*, 180ff. and Jackman and Borden (eds.), *Muses Flee Hitler*, 169–188; Emilio Segrè, *Enrico Fermi, Physicist* (Chicago, 1970); H. G. Rorschach, Jr., "The Contributions of Felix Bloch and Will V. Houston to the Electron Theory of Metals," *American Journal of Physics*, vol. 38 (July 1970), 897–904. Grace Spruch, "Victor Weisskopf: International Scientist," *New Scientist*, vol. 46 (May 21, 1970), 387–388.

35. Henry D. Smyth, *Atomic Energy for Military Purposes* (Princeton, 1945), p. 245.

36. Fermi, *Illustrious Immigrants*, pp. 184–185.

37. Hewlett and Anderson, *The New World*. A good description of life among émigré scientists in wartime Los Alamos is in Laura Fermi, *Atoms in the Family: My Life with Enrico Fermi* (Chicago, 1954), pp. 200–249. Alice K. Smith, "Los Alamos: Focus of an Age," *Bulletin of Atomic Scientists*, vol. 26 (June, 1970), 15–20.

38. Monroe E. Deutsch to Ernest O. Lawrence, February 6, 1939; Lawrence to Enrico Fermi, February 7, 1939; Fermi to Lawrence, February 17, 1939, Lawrence Papers.

39. S. A. Scherbatsky to Ernest O. Lawrence, February 27, 1940; Lawrence to Scherbatsky, March 7, 1940; Lawrence to Lt. Colonel E. G. Hollingsworth, November 9, 1940, Lawrence Papers.

40. Fermi, *Illustrious Immigrants*, pp. 296–297.

41. James D. Watson, *The Double Helix* (New York, 1968), pp. 217–223; James D. Watson, "Growing Up in the Phage Group," in John Cairns, Gunther S. Stent, and James D. Watson (eds.), *Phages and the Origins of Molecular Biology* (Cold Spring Harbor, 1966), pp. 239–245.

42. Fermi, *Illustrious Immigrants*, pp. 359–360.

43. Franz Alexander, *The Western Mind in Transition* (New York, 1960), and

Karl Menninger, *A Psychiatrist's World* (New York, 1959) trace the movement in broad strokes.

44. A detailed narrative of the development of psychiatry in the armed forces is U.S., Department of the Army, Office of the Surgeon-General, *Neuropsychiatry in World War II* (2 vols., Washington, 1966–1973), vol. 1, 5–23, 53–66, 67–91. See also John A. P. Millet, "Psychoanalysis in the United States," in *Psychoanalytic Pioneers*, edited by Franz Alexander, Samuel Eisenstein, and Martin Grotjan (New York, 1966), p. 563.

45. Clarence P. Oberndorf, *A History of Psychoanalysis in America* (New York, 1953), pp. 207–208, 247–248; the contrary view was expressed by Orr, a prominent contemporary, in a personal communication to Gerald D. Nash, March 4, 1981.

46. Menninger, *A Psychiatrist's World*, p. 853.

47. Ibid., p. 853; Fermi, *Illustrious Immigrants*, pp. 150–151, 159; Millet, "Psychoanalysis," p. 581.

48. Ann Applebaum et al., "Activity Therapy in Psychiatric Treatment," *Bulletin of the Menninger Clinic*, vol. 39 (1975), 50; John A. P. Millet, "Changing Faces of Psychoanalytic Training," in L. Salzman and J. H. Masserman (eds.), *Modern Concepts of Psychoanalysis* (New York, 1962), pp. 127–130; Millet, "Psychoanalysis," pp. 557–558.

49. Fermi, *Illustrious Immigrants*, p. 150.

50. Ernst Lewy to Ernst Simmel, August 6, 1943, in Ernst Simmel Papers, Los Angeles Psychoanalytic Institute, Los Angeles, California.

51. Douglas W. Orr, "Some Psychoanalytic Reminiscences," unpublished manuscript in possession of Dr. Orr, p. 29; a copy of these reminiscences is on file in the office of the Executive Secretary of the American Psychiatric Association, New York, N.Y. I have used a copy sent to me by Dr. Orr.

52. Hannah Fenichel, Oral History Interview by Dr. Will Horowitz, February 16, 1963, p. 5, transcript on file in Library of Los Angeles Psychoanalytic Institute.

53. American Psychiatric Association, *Bulletin of Information to be Supplied Only to Psychoanalysts Who Desire to Emigrate to the U.S.A.* (1938), mimeographed, copy in Library of Los Angeles Psychoanalytic Institute, pp. 1, 2.

54. Karl Menninger to Ernest Jones, April 26, 1938 in Papers of the Los Angeles Psychoanalytic Institute, hereafter cited as LAP Papers.

55. A brief general survey is in Albert Kandelin, "California's First Psychoanalytical Society," *Bulletin of the Menninger Clinic*, vol. 12 (1965), 351–358; the files of the Los Angeles Psychoanalytic Institute contain a substantial correspondence on the evolution of the Institute. See, for example, Karl Menninger to Ernst Simmel, July 24, 1942; Simmel to Menninger, July 21, 1942, Menninger to Simmel, June 5, 1942, Simmel to Menninger, June 1, 1942, LAP Papers.

56. Knight, quoted in Kandelin, *Bulletin of the Menninger Clinic*, p. 353; Ralph Greenson, Oral History Interview by Dr. Robert J. Stoller, December 12, 1962, pp. 2–5, transcript in Library of Los Angeles Psychoanalytic Institute. Greenson was the first graduate of the Institute. See also Frances Deri, Oral History Interview by Dr. Albert Kandelin, February 3, 1963, pp. 1–5, transcript in Library of Los Angeles Psychoanalytic Institute. Ernst Lewy to Ernst Simmel, July 1, 1942, and Ernst Simmel to Margrit Munk, July 18, 1942, Simmel Papers. On Bernfeld's sensitivity to his lay status see Siegfried Bernfeld to Margrit Munk, October 11, 1943, Simmel Papers. The Bernfeld Papers are in the Library of Congress.

57. On Simmel see the sketch in Alexander et al., *Psychoanalytical Pioneers* by John S. Peck, pp. 374–379; Orr, "Some Psychoanalytical Reminiscences," pp. 37–40; I have also consulted the Ernst Simmel Papers in the Special Collections Library of the University of California at Los Angeles.

58. Ernst Simmel to Robert Knight, April 4, 1942; Knight to Simmel, April 13, 1942, Simmel Papers; on Menninger's concern about Lewy see Karl Menninger to Simmel, October 13, 1943, Simmel Papers. My generalizations are also based on recollections of students and colleagues such as Ralph Greenson, Oral History Interview, pp. 5–8; David Brunswick, Oral History Interview by Dr. Will Horowitz, February 20, 1963, pp. 2–6; and Dr. Charles Tidd, Oral History Interview by Dr. Robert Stoller, March 4, 1963, pp. 2–3, manuscript transcripts in files of Los Angeles Psychoanalytic Institute.

59. On Fenichel see sketch by Ralph R. Greenson in Alexander et al., *Psychoanalytic Pioneers,* pp. 439–449; Hannah Fenichel Interview, pp. 1–5, 7–10; Emanuel Windholz, "Psychoanalysis Comes to the West Coast," pp. 3–8, unpublished paper presented May 1, 1975 at the annual meeting of the American Psychiatric Association in Los Angeles, copy in files of American Psychiatric Association, New York City. Windholz was an eminent Czech member of the group.

60. On Bernfeld see sketch by Rudolf Ekstein in Alexander et al., *Psychoanalytic Pioneers,* pp. 415–429.

61. Millet, "Psychoanalysis," p. 583; Siegmund Gabe, "Highlights in the Development of the Southern California Psychoanalytic Society and Institute," pp. 1–5, unpublished paper presented at the May 1, 1975 annual meeting of the American Psychiatric Association, copy in files of American Psychiatric Association, New York City.

62. On Seattle see A. C. Stewart and H. A. Dickel, "Psychoanalytic Development in Three States," *Northwest Medicine,* vol. 41 (August, 1942), 284–288 for background; see also Douglas W. Orr, "Psychoanalytic Beginnings in Seattle and San Diego," pp. 1–4, unpublished paper presented at annual meeting of American Psychiatric Association, Los Angeles, May 1, 1975, copy in American Psychiatric Association office, New York.

63. Quotation from Edith Buxbaum, "Seattle Psychoanalytic History Series: Part II" in Seattle Psychoanalytic Society, *Bulletin,* vol. 3, 3; see also Emmet Watson, "Fascinating Buxbaum: Analyst . . . and Much More," *Seattle Post-Intelligencer,* October 7, 1975.

64. A convenient list is in Oberndorf, *History,* p. 264.

65. Karl Menninger, "The Contributions of Psychoanalysis to American Psychiatry," in *A Psychiatrist's World,* pp. 834–843; Franz Alexander and Sheldon T. Selesnick, *The History of Psychiatry* (New York, 1965), pp. 410–412; on the impact of psychoanalysis on social psychiatry, child psychology, and psychosomatic medicine see ibid., pp. 269–401; M. Levin, "The Impact of Psychoanalysis on Training in Psychiatry," in *Twenty Years of Psychoanalysis,* edited by F. Alexander and H. Ross (New York, 1953). See also D. Blain, "The Organization of Psychoanalysis in the United States," in *Handbook of Psychoanalysis,* edited by S. Arieti (2 vols., New York, 1959), vol. 2.

66. Kate Friedlaender, in Alexander et al., *Psychoanalytical Pioneers,* pp. 517–518.

67. Quoted in Fermi, *Illustrious Immigrants,* p. 172. Said Ekstein, "We could not have done as well had we remained in Europe. It is amazing how much we European analysts have accomplished here."

68. Alexander, in *Psychoanalytical Pioneers,* pp. 580–585.

69. Bertram Lewis and Helen Ross, *Psychoanalytic Education in the United States* (New York, 1960), pp. 3–4, 10, 19, 20–26. This book summarizes a survey and report on institutes in the United States.

70. 79th Cong., 1st sess., Senate, Subcommittee on War Mobilization, *Report on the Government's Wartime Research and Development, 1940–44*, Part II (Washington, 1945), pp. 20–22; 80th Cong., 1st sess., House, Committee on Interstate and Foreign Commerce, *Hearings on National Science Foundation* [March, 1947] (Washington, 1947), pp. 73–76. Bush to Harley Kilgore, December 7, 1942, in 78th Cong., 1st sess., Senate, Subcommittee on Military Affairs, *Hearings on Scientific and Technological Mobilization* [June 17, 1943] (Washington, 1943), III, pp. 259–263.

71. FDR to Vannevar Bush, November 17, 1944, Roosevelt Papers. This letter is also reprinted in Bush, *Science, the Endless Frontier*, p. iii.

72. Vannevar Bush, *Science, the Endless Frontier*, p. 11; see also Bush, quoted in *Physics Today* (August, 1961), p. 33. Vannevar Bush, *Pieces of the Action* (New York, 1970), p. 3, discusses disappearance of the frontier; see also Bush's testimony in 79th Cong., 1st sess., House, Committee on Military Affairs, *Hearings on Research and Development* (Washington, 1945), pp. 3–5.

73. 77th Cong., 2d sess., Senate Bill #2721; see also 78th Cong., 1st sess., Senate, *Hearings on Scientific and Technological Mobilization*, vol. I, 1–3; 78th Cong., 1st sess., *Report on the Government's Wartime Research and Development*, II, pp. 26–29. The sectional aspect also is noted in memorandum of J. Donald Kingsley to John R. Steelman, December 31, 1946 in Harry S. Truman Papers, Harry S. Truman Library, printed in Penick (ed.), *Politics of American Science*, p. 121.

74. Otto Stuhlman to Senator H. M. Kilgore, April 30, 1943 in 78th Cong., 1st sess., Senate, *Hearings on Scientific and Technological Mobilization*, III, p. 237.

75. Clarence Mills, "Distribution of American Research Funds," *Science*, vol. 107 (February 6, 1948), 127–128.

76. Ibid., p. 130; see also Greenberg, *The Politics of Pure Science*, pp. 212–215.

77. Bush, *Science, the Endless Frontier*, pp. 32–40; 79th Cong., 1st sess., Senate, Subcommittee of the Committee on Military Affairs, *Hearings on Science Legislation* (Washington, 1946), pp. 103–105, 225–227, 98off.

78. Leake in 79th Cong., 1st sess., *Hearings on Science Legislation*, pp. 967–968.

79. The National Science Foundation Act is in 81st Cong., 2d sess., Public Law 507 (ch. 71). In this connection, even Vannevar Bush feared that applied research would drive out basic research, and postulated "Bush's Law." See James L. McCamy, *Science and Public Administration* (University, Ala., 1960), pp. 64–65; Bush, *Science, the Endless Frontier*, p. 83.

10. Cultural Life in the West

1. Stuart Chase, *The Tyranny of Words* (New York, 1938). Paul Lazarsfeld, a Viennese refugee, was doing important work on propaganda at Columbia University by 1940. See Paul Lazarsfeld, *Radio and the Printed Page* (New York, 1940), *The People's Choice* (New York, 1944), and *The People Look at Radio* (Chapel Hill, 1946).

2. Richard Steele, "Preparing the Public for War: Efforts to Establish a National Propaganda Agency, 1940–1941," *American Historical Review*, vol. 75

(October 1970), 1640–1653; Clayton R. Koppes and Gregory D. Black, "What to Show the World: The Office of War Information and Hollywood, 1942–1945," *Journal of American History*, vol. 64 (June 1977), 87–105; James McGregor Burns, *Roosevelt: Soldier of Freedom* (New York, 1972), pp. 381–389.

3. Walter Wanger to Gardner Cowles, Jr., July 30, 1942, Office of War Information Records, Director's Records, RG 208, National Archives, Washington, D.C. quoted in Gregory D. Black and Clayton R. Koppes, "OWI Goes to the Movies: The Bureau of Intelligence Criticism of Hollywood, 1942–43," *Prologue*, vol. 6 (Spring 1974), 49; Walter Wanger, "OWI and Motion Pictures," *Public Opinion Quarterly*, vol. 7 (Spring 1943), 100–110.

4. Stuart P. Sherman, quoted in Nash, *The American West in the Twentieth Century*, pp. 122–123.

5. 76th Cong., 2d sess., Senate, Subcommittee of Committee on Military Affairs, *Hearings on Motion Picture Industry* (Washington, 1942), pp. 57, 60, 113–115, hereafter cited as *Wheeler Hearings;* see also Charles Higham and Joel Greenberg, *Hollywood in the Forties* (New York, 1968), pp. 86–92; Lewis Jacobs, "World War II and the American Film," *Cinema Journal*, vol. 7 (Winter 1967–68), 1–21. An interesting analysis by an OWI employee is Dorothy B. Jones, "The Hollywood War Film: 1942–44," *Hollywood Quarterly*, vol. 1 (1946–47), 1–11; see also Peter Sonderbergh, "On War and the Movies," *Centennial Review* vol. 11 (Summer 1967), pp. 504–518.

6. *Wheeler Hearings*, p. 1; on origins of inquiry see ibid., pp. 66–68; 77th Cong., 1st sess., Senate Resolution 152, *Congressional Record*, p. 6565 (1941).

7. *Chicago Sentinel*, August 14, 1941; see also Wayne S. Cole, *Senator Gerald P. Nye and American Foreign Policy* (Minneapolis, 1962), pp. 176–201.

8. Nye in *Wheeler Hearings*, pp. 7, 12–15.

9. *New York Times*, August 2, 1941; *Wheeler Hearings*, pp. 9, 11, 47, 54, 75; *Vital Speeches of the Day*, vol. 7 (September 15, 1941), 720–723.

10. Temporary National Economic Committee, *Monograph* #43 (Washington, 1940); *Wheeler Hearings*, pp. 25–47, 91–108; *U.S. v. Paramount Pictures et al.* in U.S. District Court for the Southern District of New York. The Department of Justice had filed an anti-trust suit against the Big 8 in July 1938 and augmented it with a supplemental complaint on November 14, 1940.

11. On this dispute see *Wheeler Hearings*, pp. 138–196.

12. Ibid., pp. 213–290, 322–335, 338–391, 410–427; Jack Warner, *My First One Hundred Years* (New York, 1965), pp. 212–214.

13. Downey in *Wheeler Hearings*, p. 209.

14. *National Board of Review Magazine*, vol. 17 (May 1942), 20; see also Peter Sonderbergh, "Hollywood and World War II," *University of Dayton Review*, vol. 5 (Winter 1968–69), 13–21, and a popular contemporary perspective in Louella Parsons, "Hollywood Meets the War Challenge," *Photoplay Movie Mirror*, vol. 20 (March 1942), 100.

15. Steele, "Preparing the Public for War," 164; Sidney Weinberg, "What to Tell America: The Writers Quarrel in OWI," *Journal of American History*, vol. 55 (June 1968), 73–89.

16. Black and Koppes, "OWI Goes to the Movies," p. 49; Sonderbergh, "Hollywood and World War II," pp. 17–18; Movies at War, Reports of War Activities, Motion Picture Industry, 1942–1945, vol. I, #1, 1–5.

17. Koppes and Black, "What to Show the World," pp. 91–92.

18. Ibid., pp. 98–104; *Variety*, December 23, 1943; Frank S. Nugent, "Hollywood Faces Reality," *New York Times Magazine*, March 8, 1942, p. 17. Ken D. Jones and Arthur F. McClure, *Hollywood at War: The American Motion Picture*

and World War II (New York, 1973), pp. 15–16.

19. Quoted in Koppes and Black, "What to Show the World," p. 101.

20. Black and Koppes, "OWI Goes to the Movies," pp. 50–57.

21. *Truman Committee Hearings*, pp. 6868–6878.

22. Ibid., pp. 1903–1904; for a complete list of officers see Exhibit 704, on pp. 7137–3739; 55 of these individuals were from 9 major studios. See ibid., exhibit 690, pp. 6879, 7099.

23. *Truman Committee Hearings*, pp. 6880–6886, 6888–6898, 7100–7114.

24. Ibid., pp. 6904–6905.

25. Darryl Zanuck, "The Responsibilities of the Industry," in *Proceedings of the Writers' Congress, Los Angeles* (Berkeley, 1944), pp. 31, 33, 42.

26. Dalton Trumbo, "Minorities and the Screen," in ibid., pp. 488, 499, 500.

27. Still in ibid., pp. 277, 278, 279.

28. Nugent, "Hollywood Faces Reality," p. 16.

29. Peter Gay, "Weimar Culture: The Outsider as Insider," in Fleming and Bailyn (eds.), *The Intellectual Migration*, pp. 11–12; see also Fermi, *Illustrious Immigrants*, p. 12.

30. Some aspects of the refugee migration are touched on in Jarrell C. Jackman, "Exiles in Paradise: A Cultural History of German Emigres in Southern California, 1933–1950" (Ph.D. dissertation, University of California, Santa Barbara, 1977), and summarized in Jarrell C. Jackman, "Exiles in Paradise: German Emigres in Southern California, 1933–1950," *Southern California Quarterly*, vol. 61 (Summer, 1979), 183–203; among the many reminiscences consult Salka Viertel, *The Kindness of Strangers* (New York, 1969) and Erich Maria Remarque, *Shadows in Paradise*, translated by Ralph Manheim (New York, 1972); Gerald D. Nash, oral interview with Marta Feuchtwanger in Pacific Palisades, June 14, 1981.

31. Ludwig Marcuse, *Mein Zwanzigstes Jahrhundert: Auf dem Weg zu Einer Autobiographie* (Munich, 1960), p. 288; Gerald D. Nash, oral interview with Marta Feuchtwanger, Pacific Palisades, California, June 14, 1981; Jackman, "Exiles," in *Southern California Quarterly*, vol. 61, 196–199; Marta Mierendorff, *Exiltag an der Pazifischen Westkueste* (Los Angeles, 1973), p. 4.

32. Frederick Kohner, *Der Zauberer von Sunset Boulevard* (Munich, 1974), pp. 189–190; Joseph Wechsberg, *The First Time Around: Some Irreverent Recollections* (Boston, 1970), pp. 217–218; Viertel, *Kindness of Strangers*, pp. 241, 248, 250–251, 258–259. Remarque, *Shadows in Paradise*, p. 229; Jackman, "Exiles in Paradise," pp. 88–92, 107–108, 186; John Spalek and Joseph Strelka (eds.), *Deutsche Exilliteratur seit 1933*, vol. I, *Kalifornien* (Bern, 1976), 715–832 has broad coverage.

33. Monica Mann, *Past and Present* (New York, 1960), p. 132.

34. Thomas Mann, *The Story of a Novel: The Genesis of Dr. Faustus*, translated by Richard and Clara Winston (New York, 1981), pp. 64, 186; see also Thomas Mann, *Letters of Thomas Mann*, translated by Richard and Clara Winston (New York, 1971), pp. 362, 366.

35. Thomas Mann, "The Exiled Writer's Relation to His Homeland," in *Writers' Conference, Los Angeles*, pp. 339–340, 343.

36. *Aufbau*, August 7, 1942, p. 15.

37. Luizi Korngold, *Erich Korngold: Ein Lebensbild* (Vienna, 1967), p. 68; Leonhard Frank, *Heart on the Left*, translated by Cyrus Brooks (London, 1954), p. 164; Marcuse, *Mein Zwanzigstes Jahrhundert*, p. 266; on Werfel see Lore B. Foltin (ed.), *Franz Werfel* (Pittsburgh, 1961), and Werner Braselman,

Franz Werfel (Wuppertal, 1960), Remarque, *Shadows in Paradise*, pp. 228–231.

38. On Feuchtwanger see Lion Feuchtwanger, *Stories from Near and Far* (New York, 1945), passim, and "The Working Problems of the Writer in Exile," in *Writers' Conference, Los Angeles*, pp. 345, 346, 348.

39. Heinrich Mann, *Briefe an Karl Lemke und Klaus Pinkus* (Berlin, n.d.), p. 193; Bertolt Brecht somewhat unfairly criticized Thomas Mann—whose conservative politicial views he resented, anyhow—for not doing enough for his older brother. See Bertolt Brecht, *Arbeitsjournal*, vol. II (Frankfurt am Main, 1973), 643.

40. See Leonhard Frank, *The Baroness* (London, 1950), and *Heart on the Left* (London, 1954); Raoul Auernheimer, *Das Wirtshaus Zur Verlorenen Zeit: Erlebnisse und Bekenntnisse* (Vienna, 1948); Joseph Wechsberg, *The First Time Around* (New York, 1964); Alfred Polgar, *Anderseits: Erzaehlungen und Erwaegungen: Standtpunkte* (Amsterdam, 1948), passim.

41. Higham and Greenberg, *Hollywood in the Forties*, p. 91; Vicki Baum, *It Was All Quite Different: The Memoirs of Vicki Baum* (New York, 1964), p. 218; for Katherine Anne Porter see her remarks at University of California at Los Angeles during the 1943 Writers' Congress, in *Writers' Congress, Los Angeles* (1943), p. 329; a concise contemporary assessment of the impact of foreign writers is by Gustav O. Arlt, "The Cultural Contributions of Exiled Intellectuals to America and the World," in *Writers' Congress Proceedings*, 1943, p. 356.

42. Alfred Doeblin, *Briefe* (Freiburg, 1970), p. 273; Marcuse, *Mein Zwanzigstes Jahrhundert*, p. 276; Jackman, "Exiles," *Southern California Quarterly*, p. 194; Harold von Hofe, "German Literature in Exile: Alfred Doeblin," *German Quarterly*, vol. 17 (January, 1948), 28.

43. An excellent account is James K. Lyon, "Bertolt Brecht's Hollywood Years: The Dramatist as Film Writer," *Oxford German Studies*, vol. 6 (1971–72), 145–174; see also Bertolt Brecht, *Arbeitsjournal*, vol. II, 643.

44. A detailed cultural history of Los Angeles has not yet been written. Some perceptive comments can be found in Christopher Rand, *Los Angeles* (New York, 1970), originally written as profiles for the *New Yorker* Magazine.

45. Franklin D. Roosevelt to Marc Connelly, September 8, 1943, *Writers' Congress, Los Angeles*, p. 5; *Los Angeles Times*, October 2, 3, 4, 1943; *New York Times*, October 10, 1943.

46. *Writers' Congress, Los Angeles*, pp. 611–613; text of resolutions can be found on pp. 606–610.

47. Arlt, "The Cultural Contributions of Exiled Intellectuals to America and the World," in *Writers' Congress, Los Angeles*, p. 353. Arlt was a well-known professor of German at the University of California and a staunch advocate of the émigré intellectuals.

48. *Los Angeles Times*, January 14, 1942; *Los Angeles County Museum Newsletter*, November 23, 1942; *Time*, November 8, 1943.

49. *Los Angeles Times*, May 23, 1943.

50. *Beverly Hills Press*, April 22, 1954. See also Carla Higgins, "Art Collecting in the Los Angeles Area, 1910–1960" (Ph.D. dissertation, UCLA, 1963), pp. 238–239.

51. I've checked biographical data in *Who's Who in American Art*, 1980 (New York, 1980), pp. 424, 578 and *Who's Who in Los Angeles County, 1950–51*, ed. by Alice Catt Armstrong (Los Angeles, 1950), pp. 161, 270. Vincent Price, *I Like What I Know* (New York, 1959), pp. 177–180, 181–186; Viertel, *Kindness of Strangers*, p. 217.

52. Dorothy B. Hughes in *Art Digest*, vol. 10 (October 1, 1941), 10.

53. Bruno Walter, *Themes and Variation* (London, 1947), p. 375; Otto Klemperer, *Meine Erinnerungen* (Berlin, 1963), passim.

54. Luizi Korngold, *Erich Korngold: Ein Lebensbild*, p. 80; *New York Times*, January 19, 1981; *Baker's Biographical Dictionary of Musicians*, 6th ed., revised by Nicolas Slonimsky (New York, 1978), pp. 914–915, and Stanley Sadie (ed.), *The New Grove Dictionary of Music and Musicians* (20 vols., New York, 1980), vol. 10, pp. 210–211.

55. See comments of Fred W. Sternfeld, "Music and the Feature Films," *Musical Quarterly*, vol. 33 (October 1947), 517, 519–532; Howard Swan, in *Music in the Southwest: A History* (San Marino, 1952), pp. 274–275 also noted that the émigrés were responsible for more performances of contemporary music in Los Angeles than anywhere else in the United States outside New York City. *Baker's Biographical Dictionary of Musicians* has excellent articles about these men and their careers.

56. Darius Milhaud, *Notes Without Music* (New York, 1953), pp. 289–290.

57. The literature on Schoenberg is extensive. The story about Thalberg is recounted in Walter H. Rubsamen, "Schoenberg in America," *The Musical Quarterly*, vol. 37 (October, 1951), 485–486; an intimate memoir by one of his students is Dika Newlin, *Schoenberg Remembered: Diaries and Recollections, 1938–1976* (New York, 1980), pp. 13–81, 89–234, 329–338; on the premiere of one of his last works, "A Survivor at Auschwitz," I have consulted Schoenberg's letters in the Kurt Frederick Manuscripts, Fine Arts Library, University of New Mexico, Albuquerque, N.M. In 1974 the University of Southern California announced plans for establishment of a Schoenberg Institute at the university. See *Los Angeles Times*, January 20 and February 6, 1974.

58. Higham and Greenberg, *Hollywood in the Forties*, pp. 87–92; Fritz Kortner, *Aller Tage Abend* (Munich, 1959), p. 550; Kohner, *Der Zauberer*, p. 208.

59. Higham and Greenberg, *Hollywood in the Forties*, p. 92; Guenther Anders, *Die Schrift an der Wand: Tagebuecher 1951 bis 1955* (Munich, 1967), pp. 1–5. Author Anders worked as a costume cleaner in Hollywood, 1941–1943, then left in disgust for New York, and returned to Germany after the war. See also Jackman, "Exiles in Paradise," pp. 133–135, 183–187.

60. Reinhardt quoted in Erika and Klaus Mann, *Escape to Life* (Boston, 1939), p. 265. See also Gottfried Reinhardt, *Der Liebhaber: Erinnerungen seines Sohnes Gottfried Reinhardt an Max Reinhardt* (Munich, 1973), pp. 269–270; Jackman, "Exiles in Paradise," pp. 172–180.

61. A brief list of émigré scholars is found in Bailyn and Fleming (eds.), *The Intellectual Migration*, pp. 675–718; on Max Delbrueck see Cairns, Stent, and Watson (eds.), *Phages and the Origins of Molecular Biology*, and Watson, *The Double Helix*, and for mathematics James R. Newman (ed.), *The World of Mathematics* (New York, 1956); and Laura Fermi, *Illustrious Immigrants*, pp. 175–214.

11. Conclusion

1. Abbott, *The New Urban America*, pp. 98–119; Funigiello, *The Challenge to Urban Liberalism*, pp. 187–245.

2. "City-Planning: Battle of the Approaches," *Fortune*, vol. 28 (November 1943), 164–168, 222–223.

3. "Mr. Moses Dissects the 'Long-Haired Planners,'" *New York Times Magazine*, vol. 6 (June 1944), 16–17; Moses in 78th Cong., 2d sess., House, Special Committee on Post-War Economic Policy and Planning Pursuant to House Resolution 408 and House Resolution 60, *Hearings* (6 parts, Washington, 1944), part 6, pp. 1780–1784.

4. Scott, *San Francisco Bay Area,* pp. 246–248; Abbott, *New Urban America,* pp. 102, 110; see also Philip M. Hauser, "Wartime Population Changes and Post-War Prospects," *Journal of Marketing,* vol. 8 (January 1944), 238–248; Hugh Pomeroy, "Impact of the War on Communities," *Proceedings of the National Conference on Planning,* 1942 (Chicago, 1942), pp. 27–38.

5. Mel Scott, *American City Planning,* pp. 400–407; Abbott, *The New Urban America,* p. 111; L. P. Cookingham, "The Effect of War upon Cities," *Planning* 1943 (Chicago, 1943), pp. 15–26.

6. An excellent detailed analysis of city planning in Los Angeles is by Martin Schiesl, "City Planning and the Federal Government in World War II: The Los Angeles Experience," *California History,* vol. 58 (April 1979), 127–143; Abbott, *The New Urban America,* pp. 110–114; Carl Feiss, "How Cities Are Preparing for the Post-War Era," *Planning,* 1944 (Chicago, 1944), pp. 46–50.

7. Moses, *Portland Improvement,* pp. 114–116; Arthur McVoy, "How Cities Are Preparing for the Post-War Period: Portland," *Planning, 1944* (Chicago: American Society of Planning Officials, 1944), pp. 78–80. An excellent detailed discussion is in Abbott, "Portland in the Pacific War: Planning from 1940 to 1945," *Urbanism, Past and Present* (1981), pp. 12–24.

8. "California County Plans for Peace Era," *American City,* vol. 58 (August 1943), 77; "Blueprint for San Diego," *Business Week* (March 31, 1945), pp. 36–37; "San Diego Faces Postwar Transition with Confidence," *American City,* vol. 60 (July 1945), 95.

9. The work of the NRPB with cities is discussed in Marion Clawson, *New Deal Planning: The National Resources Planning Board* (Baltimore, 1981), pp. 34–35, 166, 180–181, and in Abbott, *New Urban America,* pp. 111–112; Funigiello, *Challenge to Urban Liberalism,* pp. 163–186; Gelfand, *A Nation of Cities,* pp. 102–104. Congressional efforts to promote city planning are briefly covered in Funigiello, *Challenge to Urban Liberalism,* pp. 217–245; for discussion of national planning legislation see 78th Cong., 2d sess., House, Special Committee on Postwar Economic Policy and Planning Pursuant to House Resolutions 408 and 60, *Hearings* and 79th Cong., 1st sess., Senate, Special Committee on Post-war Economic Policy and Planning Pursuant to Senate Resolution 102, *Hearings* (6 parts, Washington, 1944–45); see also 78th Cong., 2d sess., House, Committee on Public Buildings and Grounds, *Hearings* (Washington, 1944).

10. Abbott, *New Urban America,* pp. 118–119.

11. *Vital Speeches,* vol. 10 (May 1, 1944), 432.

12. For activities of this agency consult California, State Reconstruction and Reemployment Commission, *Annual Reports,* 1946 (San Francisco, 1946); *Hearings on Post-War Problems in San Francisco Bay,* August 23–24, 1944 (San Francisco, 1944); *California Planning* (Sacramento, 1946); *California State Reconstruction and Reemployment Commission—Objectives—Organization—Program* (Sacramento, 1944); *The Timing of Public Works in California* (Sacramento, 1945).

13. Ora Bundy (comp.), *After Victory: Plans for Utah and the Wasatch Front* (Salt Lake City, 1943), pp. iv–v; for list of consultants see p. ii; Herbert Maw to the People of Utah, June 9, 1943, insert in the report. I consulted the copy in the Western History Research Center, University of Wyoming; *Salt Lake City Tribune,* June 10, 1943.

14. Quote from Orville P. Carville to Charles B. Henderson, March 9, 1944; on relation with other states see Carville to F. O. Case (General Manager, Basic Magnesium Corp.), March 10, 1944; Sidney Osborn (Governor of

Arizona) to Carville, March 21, 1944, Carville to Osborn, March 29, 1944; Charles B. Henderson to Carville, March 20, 1944, in Carville Papers.

15. See, for example, correspondence relating to meeting of western senators on regional development of natural resources on October 4, 1943. Burton K. Wheeler (Mont.) to McCarran, September 29, 1943, Ed V. Robertson (Wyo.) to McCarran, September 30, 1943, Dennis Chavez (N.M.) to McCarran, September 30, 1943, Clyde Reed (Kansas) to McCarran, September 30, 1943, Arthur Capper (Kansas) to McCarran, September 30, 1943, in McCarran Papers.

16. *San Francisco News,* February 14, 1944 in McCarran Scrapbooks, McCarran Papers.

17. *Reno Evening Gazette,* February 8, 11, 12, 13, 1944; *Nevada (Reno) State Journal,* February 2, 8, 9, 11, 12, 13, 1944; *Las Vegas Evening Review Journal,* February 8, 10, 1944; *San Francisco Chronicle,* February 12, 13, 1944; *Salt Lake City Tribune,* February 12, 1944.

18. 78th Cong., 2d sess., Senate, Committee on Centralization of Heavy Industry in the U.S., *Hearings Pursuant to Senate Resolution 190* (5 parts, Washington, 1944–45); see also *Cong. Record,* 78th Cong., 1st sess. (October 5, 1943), pp. 8065–8067; and Maury Maverick to Pat McCarran, July 14, 1944, McCarran Papers.

19. See Rex L. Nicholson to Pat McCarran, July 10, 1944, McCarran to Rex Nicholson, July 15, 1944; transcript of radio broadcast, April 27, 1944 over CBS on the Builders of the West, in McCarran Papers.

20. McCarran press release, April 9, 1943; McCarran to Herbert B. Maw, April 2, 1943, McCarran Papers.

21. McCarran's speech, "The West: Key to Full Employment and Our Post-War Prosperity," is in *Cong. Record,* 78th Cong., 2d sess. (June 21, 1944), vol. 90, part 10, pp. A 3205–3213. See also *Sacramento Union,* June 10, 1944.

22. V.L.O. Chittick (ed.), *Northwest Harvest: A Regional Stocktaking* (New York, 1948), pp. ix–x; quotations on 9, 10, 12–13; see also V. Oakes, "West Coast Dreams," *Asia,* vol. 45 (August 1945), 373–375.

23. William A. White, *The Changing West* (New York, 1939), quotations on pp. v, vi, 136, 137; on this theme note also "Industrial Revolution," *Newsweek,* vol. 28 (September 23, 1946), 70–72.

24. Howard, *Montana, High, Wide, and Handsome,* quotations on pp. 6, 7 (Wright and Brownell), p. 321; in a similar vein see Morris E. Garnsey, "Future of the Mountain States," *Harper's,* vol. 191 (October 1945), 329–336.

25. Mezerick, *Revolt of the South and West,* quotations on pp. ix, xiv, 290; see also A. G. Mezerick, "West Coast Versus East," *Atlantic Monthly,* vol. 173 (May 1944), 48–52. In a similar vein see "Postwar Hopes and Fears on the West Coast," *Business Week* (November 20, 1943), p. 20.

26. Wendell Berge, *Economic Freedom for the West* (Lincoln, 1946), pp. x, 148, 149.

27. Bernard DeVoto, "The Anxious West," *Harper's,* vol. 193 (December 1946), 489, 490.

28. DeVoto, "The West Against Itself," *Harper's,* vol. 194 (January 1947), 13.

29. Ladd Haysted, *If the Prospect Pleases: The West the Guidebooks Never Mention* (Norman, 1946), pp. 205, 208.

Bibliography

Manuscripts

Bowron, Fletcher. Papers. Henry L. Huntington Library, San Marino, California.

Carville, E. P. Papers. Nevada State Archives, Carson City, Nevada.

Ford, Anson L. Papers. Henry L. Huntington Library, San Marino, California.

Frederick, Kurt. Papers. Fine Arts Library, University of New Mexico, Albuquerque, N.M.

Hayden, Carl. Papers. Arizona State University, Phoenix, Arizona.

Lawrence, Ernest O. Papers. Bancroft Library, University of California, Berkeley.

Los Angeles Psychoanalytic Institute. Papers. Los Angeles Psychoanalytic Institute, Los Angeles, California.

McCarran, Pat. Papers. Nevada State Historical Society, Reno, Nevada.

Maverick, Maury. Papers. University of Texas, Austin, Texas.

Moores, Chester A. Papers. Oregon Historical Society, Portland, Oregon.

Murray, James E. Papers. University of Montana, Missoula, Montana.

Riley, Robert E. Papers. Oregon Historical Society, Portland, Oregon.

Simmel, Ernst. Papers. Los Angeles Psychoanalytic Institute, Los Angeles, California.

———. Papers. UCLA, Los Angeles, California.

Sleepy Lagoon Defense Committee. Papers. Special Collections, UCLA, Los Angeles, California.

Truman, Harry S. Papers. Harry S. Truman Library, Independence, Missouri.

World War II History Collection, Colorado Historical Society, Denver, Colorado.

Archives

U.S. Committee for Congested Production Areas. Records. National Archives, Washington, D.C.

U.S. Coordinator of Inter-American Affairs. Records. National Archives, Suitland, Maryland.

U.S. Eleventh Naval District. Records. Federal Records Center, Laguna Hills, California.
U.S. Fair Employment Practices Commission, Records. National Archives, Washington, D.C.
U.S. Fair Employment Practices Commission, Region 12, Records. Federal Records Center, San Bruno, California.
U.S. Metals Reserve Corporation, Records. National Archives, Washington, D.C.
U.S. Office of Indian Affairs, Records. National Archives, Washington, D.C.
U.S. Office of Production Management, Records. National Archives, Washington, D.C.
U.S. Senate. Special Committee to Investigate National Defense Program, 1941–1947, Records. National Archives, Washington, D.C.
U.S. Smaller War Plants Corporation, Records. National Archives, Washington, D.C.

Government Documents

Biographical Directory of the American Congress, 1774–1971. Washington, 1971.
California, Senate, Joint Committee on Un-American Activities in California. *Report of Joint Fact Finding Committee on Un-American Activities in California to the California Legislature.* Sacramento, 1943.
California, State Reconstruction and Reemployment Commission, *Annual Reports,* 1946. San Francisco, 1946.
———. *California State Reconstruction and Reemployment Commission—Objectives—Organization—Program.* Sacramento, 1944.
———. *The Timing of Public Works in California.* Sacramento, 1945.
Report of the President's Commission on Migratory Labor: Migratory Labor in American Agriculture. Washington, 1951.
U.S. Bureau of the Census. *County Data Book,* 1947. Washington, 1947.
———. *Historical Statistics of the United States.* 2 vols. Washington, 1976.
———. *Statistical Abstract,* 1938–1946. Washington, 1946.
U.S. Department of Agriculture, Agricultural and Marketing Service. *Livestock and Meat Statistics.* Bulletin #230. Washington, 1958.
———. *Miscellaneous Publication #336.* "Family Income and Expenditures, Pacific Region, and Plains and Mountain Region," by Day Monroe et al. Washington, 1939.
U.S. Department of the Army, Office of the Surgeon-General. *Neuro-Psychiatry in World War II.* 2 vols. Washington, 1966–1973.
U.S. Department of the Interior. *Annual Reports,* 1939–1946. Washington, 1946.
U.S. National Resources Planning Board. *Development of Resources and of Economic Opportunity in the Pacific Northwest.* Washington, 1942.
———. *Industrial Location and Natural Resources.* Washington, 1943.
———. *Pacific Northwest Region.* Washington, 1942.
———. *Pacific Southwest Region: Industrial Development.* Washington, 1942.
U.S. Temporary National Economic Committee. *Final Report and Recommendations of the Temporary National Economic Committee.* Washington, 1943.

Congressional Hearings

U.S. Congress. House. 76th Cong., 1st sess., Committee on Interstate and Foreign Commerce. *Hearings on Omnibus Transportation Bill.* Washington, 1939.

U.S. Congress. Senate. 76th Cong., 1st sess., Subcommittee of Committee on Interstate Commerce. *Hearings on Freight Rate Discriminations.* Washington, 1939.

U.S. Congress. Senate. 76th Cong., 2d sess., Special Committee to Investigate the National Defense Program. *Hearings* (Parts 1–43). Washington, 1941–1947.

U.S. Congress, Senate. 76th Cong., 2d sess., Subcommittee of Committee on Military Affairs. *Hearings on Motion Picture Industry.* Washington, 1942.

U.S. Congress. Senate. 77th Cong., 1st sess., Committee on Military Affairs. *Hearings to Provide for Planting of 45,000 Acres of Guayule Rubber* (2 parts). Washington, 1942.

U.S. Congress. Senate. 77th Cong., 1st sess., Special Committee to Study and Survey Problems of Small Business Enterprises. *Hearings on Small Business and the War Program* (94 Parts). Washington, 1948.

U.S. Congress. House. 77th Cong., 2d sess., Committee on Agriculture. *Hearings on HR 6299 to Provide for the Planting of 75,000 Acres of Guayule.* Washington, 1942.

U.S. Congress. House. 77th Cong., 2d sess., Committee on Banking and Currency. *Hearings on Conversion of Small Business Enterprises to War Production.* Washington, 1942.

U.S. Congress. Senate. 77th Cong., 2d sess., Committee on Military Affairs. *Hearing on S.2775 to Expand the Guayule Program.* Washington, 1942.

U.S. Congress. House. 77th Cong., 2d sess., Select Committee Investigating National Defense Migration Pursuant to House Resolution #113. *Hearings* (34 parts). Washington, 1940–1942.

U.S. Congress. Senate. 77th Cong., 2d sess., Special Committee to Investigate Farm Labor Conditions in the West. *Hearings on Sen. Resolution 299* (4 parts). Washington, 1943.

U.S. Congress. Senate. 78th Cong., 1st sess., Subcommittee of the Committee on Military Affairs, *Hearings on Labor Shortages in the Pacific Coast and Rocky Mountain States.* Washington, 1943.

U.S. Congress. Senate. 78th Cong., 1st sess., Subcommittee on Military Affairs. *Hearings on Scientific and Technological Mobilization.* Washington, 1943.

U.S. Congress, House, 78th Congress, 1st sess., Subcommittee of Committee on Naval Affairs. *Hearings on Congested Areas* (8 parts). Washington, 1944.

U.S. Congress. Senate. 78th Cong., 2d sess., Committee on Centralization of Heavy Industry in the U.S. *Hearings Pursuant to Senate Resolution 190* (5 parts). Washington, 1944–1945.

U.S. Congress. House. 78th Cong., 2d sess., Special Committee on Post-War Economic Policy and Planning Pursuant to House Resolution 408 and House Resolution 60. *Hearings* (6 parts). Washington, 1944.

U.S. Congress. House. 78th Cong., 2d sess., Subcommittee of the Committee on Indian Affairs. *Hearings on Indian Affairs—H. Resolution 166* (5 parts). Washington, 1944.

U.S. Congress. House. 79th Cong., 1st sess., Committee on Military Affairs. *Hearings on Research and Development,* Washington, 1945.

U.S. Congress. Senate. 79th Cong., 1st sess., Special Committee on Post-War Economic Policy and Planning Pursuant to Senate Resolution 102. *Hearings* (6 parts). Washington, 1944–1945.

U.S. Congress. Senate. 79th Cong., 1st sess., Subcommittee of the Committee on Military Affairs. *Hearings on Science Legislation.* Washington, 1946.

U.S. Congress. House. 80th Cong., 1st sess., Committee on Interstate and

Foreign Commerce. *Hearings on National Science Foundation.* Washington, 1947.

Newspapers

Albuquerque Journal, 1939–1945.
California Eagle, 1939–1945.
Christian Science Monitor, 1939–1946.
Colorado Springs Telegraph, 1939–1945.
Denver Bulletin, 1939–1946.
Denver Post, 1939–1945.
Las Vegas Review Journal, 1939–1945.
Los Angeles Daily News, 1939–1946.
Los Angeles Examiner, 1939–1946.
Los Angeles Herald-Express, 1939–1946.
Los Angeles Times, 1939–1945.
Nevada (Reno) State Journal, 1939–1945.
New York Times, 1939–1946.
Oregon Journal, 1939–1946.
The People's Observer (Portland, Oregon), 1939–1945.
Portland Oregonian, 1939–1945.
Reno Evening Gazette, 1939–1945.
Rocky Mountain News, 1939–1946.
Sacramento Bee, 1939–1946.
Salt Lake City Tribune, 1939–1946.
San Francisco Call Bulletin, 1939–1945.
San Francisco Chronicle, 1939–1945.
Santa Fe New Mexican, 1939–1945.
Westwood Hills Press, 1939–1945.

Periodicals

Arizona Farmer, 1939–1945.
Business Week, 1939–1945.
Collier's, 1938–1946.
Fortune, 1939–1946.
Indians at Work, 1940–1946.
Los Angeles County Museum Newsletter, 1941–1945.
New Republic, 1939–1946.
Newsweek, 1939–1946.
Railway Age, 1937–1945.
Time, 1938–1946.
U.S. Department of Labor. Bureau of Labor Statistics, *Monthly Labor Review,* 1939–1946.

Books

Abbott, Carl. *The New Urban America: Growth and Politics in Sunbelt Cities.* Chapel Hill, 1982.
Alexander, Franz. *The Western Mind in Transition.* New York, 1960.
Alexander, Franz, Samuel Eisenstein, and Martin Grotjan (eds.). *Psychoanalytic Pioneers.* New York, 1966.

Alexander, Franz, and H. Ross (eds.). *Twenty Years of Psychoanalysis.* New York, 1953.

Alexander, Franz, and Sheldon T. Selesnick. *The History of Psychiatry.* New York, 1965.

Allen, Arthur P., and Betty V. H. Schneider. *Industrial Relations in the California Aircraft Industry.* Berkeley, 1956.

Anders, Guenther. *Die Schrift an der Wand: Tage-Buecher 1937 bis 1955.* Munich, 1967.

Anderson, Henry P. *The Bracero Program in California with Particular Reference to Health Status, Attitudes, and Practices.* Berkeley, 1961.

Anderson, Karen. *Wartime Women: Sex Roles, Family Relations and the Status of Women during World War II.* Westport, 1981.

Archibald, Katherine. *Wartime Shipyard.* Berkeley, 1947.

Arieti, S. (ed.). *Handbook of Psychoanalysis.* 2 vols. New York, 1959.

Arrington, Leonard J. *The Changing Economic Structure of the Mountain West, 1850–1950.* Logan, 1963.

Arrington, Leonard J. and Anthony Cluff. *Federally Financed Industrial Plants Constructed in Utah during World War II.* Logan, 1969.

Arrington, Leonard J., and George Jensen. *The Defense Industry of Utah.* Logan, 1965.

Auernheimer, Raoul. *Das Wirtshaus zur Verlorenen Zeit: Erlebnisse und Bekenntnisse.* Vienna, 1948.

Barker, George C. *Pachuco.* Tucson, 1950.

Barth, Gunther. *Instant Cities: Urbanization and the Rise of San Francisco and Denver.* New York, 1975.

Baum, Vicki. *It Was All Quite Different: The Memoirs of Vicki Baum.* New York, 1964.

Baxter, James Phinney III. *Scientists Against Time.* Boston, 1946.

Bell, Daniel. *The Coming of Post-Industrial Society.* New York, 1973.

Berge, Wendell. *Economic Freedom for the West.* Lincoln: 1946.

Bergman, Andrew. *We're in the Money: Depression America and Its Films.* New York, 1971.

Boeing Company. *Pedigree of Champions: Boeing since 1916.* 4th ed. Seattle, 1977.

Bontemps, Arna. *Anyplace but Here.* New York, 1966.

Braselman, Werner. *Franz Werfel.* Wuppertal, 1960.

Brecht, Bertolt. *Arbeits Journal.* vol II. Frankfurt am Main, 1973.

Bundy, Ora (comp.). *After Victory: Plans for Utah and the Wasatch Front.* Salt Lake City, 1943.

Burma, John H. *Spanish Speaking Groups in the United States.* Durham, 1954.

Burns, James M. *Roosevelt: Soldier of Freedom.* New York, 1972.

Bush, Vannevar. *Pieces of the Action.* New York, 1970.

———. *Science, the Endless Frontier.* New York, 1947.

Buxbaum, Edith. "Seattle Psychoanalytic History Series: Part II" *Bulletin,* vol. 3 (n.d.), pp. 1–3.

Cash, Joseph H. *The Sioux People.* Rapid City, 1979.

Ceplair, Larry, and Steven Englund. *The Inquisition in Hollywood.* Garden City, 1980.

Chittick, V.L.O. (ed.). *Northwest Harvest: A Regional Stocktaking.* New York, 1948.

Church, Fermor. *When Los Alamos Was a Ranch School.* Los Alamos, 1974.

Church, Peggy Bond. *The House at Potowi Bridge.* Albuquerque, 1960.

Clawson, Marion. *New Deal Planning: The National Resources Planning Board.* Baltimore, 1981.

Cohn, Edwin, Jr. *Industry in the Pacific Northwest and the Location Theory.* New York, 1952.

Cole, Charyl L. *A History of the Japanese Community in Sacramento, 1883–1972: Organizations, Businesses, and General Response to Majority Domination and Stereotypes.* San Francisco, 1974.

Cole, Wayne S. *Senator Gerald P. Nye and American Foreign Policy.* Minneapolis, 1962.

Collins, Tom. *Flying Fortress: The Story of Boeing.* New York, 1943.

Commonwealth Club of California. *The Population of California.* San Francisco, 1946.

Compton, Arthur. *Atomic Quest.* New York, 1972.

Conant, James B. *My Several Lives: Memoirs.* New York, 1970.

Conn, Stetson, et al. *United States Army in World War II: The Western Hemisphere Guarding the United States and Its Outposts.* Washington, 1964.

Craig, Richard B. *The Bracero Program.* Austin, 1971.

Cunningham, William G. *The Aircraft Industry: A Study of Industrial Location.* Berkeley, 1951.

Daniels, Roger. *Concentration Camps U.S.A.* New York, 1974.

———. *The Decision to Evacuate the Japanese.* New York, 1972.

———. *The Politics of Prejudice.* Berkeley, 1962.

De Kruif, Paul. *Kaiser Wakes the Doctors.* New York, 1943.

Dietrich, Margretta (comp.). *Doing Fine and Thanks a Million.* Santa Fe, 1943.

———. *Hello and Many Lucks.* Santa Fe, 1945.

Doeblin, Alfred. *Briefe.* Freiburg, 1970.

Donnell, Francis W. *History of the Arizona Division of Goodyear Aircraft.* Phoenix, 1947.

Dorsett, Lyle W. *The Queen City: History of Denver.* Denver, 1977.

Dupree, A. Hunter. *Science in the Federal Government: A History of Policies and Activities to 1940.* Cambridge, 1957.

Elliott, Russell R. *History of Nevada.* Lincoln, 1973.

Fermi, Laura. *Atoms in the Family: My Life with Enrico Fermi.* Chicago, 1954.

———. *Illustrious Immigrants: The Intellectual Migration from Europe 1930–1941.* Chicago, 1971.

Feuchtwanger, Lion. *Stories from Near and Far.* New York, 1945.

Fey, Harold, and D'Arcy McNickle. *Indians and Other Americans.* New York, 1959.

Fisher, Lloyd E. *The Problem of Violence: Observations on Race Conflict in Los Angeles.* Los Angeles, 1946.

Fleming, Donald, and Bernard Bailyn (eds.). *The Intellectual Migration.* Cambridge, 1969.

Foltin, Lore B. (ed.). *Franz Werfel.* Pittsburgh, 1961.

Ford, John. *Thirty Explosive Years in Los Angeles County.* San Marino, 1961.

Fosdick, Raymond B. *Story of the Rockefeller Foundation.* New York, 1970.

Frank, Leonhard. *Heart on the Left.* Translated by Cyrus Brooks. London, 1954.

French, David J. *Factionalism at Isleta Pueblo.* Seattle, 1948.

Friar, Ralph, and Natasha Friar. *The Only Good Indian: The Hollywood Gospel.* New York, 1972.

Fuchs, Victor R. *Changes in the Location of Manufacturing in the United States Since 1929.* New York, 1962.

————. *The Service Economy.* New York, 1968.

Funigiello, Philip J. *The Challenge to Urban Liberalism: Federal-City Relations During World War II.* Knoxville, 1978.

Galarza, Ernesto. *Merchants of Labor: The Mexican Bracero Story.* Santa Barbara, 1964.

Garnsey, Morris E. *America's New Frontier: The Mountain West.* New York, 1950.

Gelfand, Mark. *A Nation of Cities: The Federal Government and Urban America, 1933–1965.* New York, 1975.

Getty, Harris T. *Inter-Ethnic Relationships in the Community of Tucson.* Tucson, 1976.

Gibson, A. M. *Oklahoma: A History of Five Centuries.* Norman, 1965.

Girdner, Audrie, and Anne Loftis. *The Great Betrayal: The Evacuation of the Japanese Americans During World War II.* New York, 1969.

Gonzales, Nancy L. *The Spanish-Americans of New Mexico: A Heritage of Pride.* Albuquerque, 1969.

Goodrich, Carter. *Government Promotion of American Canals and Railroads.* New York, 1960.

Gordon, Margaret S. *Employment Expansion and Population Growth: The California Experience, 1900–1950.* Berkeley, 1954.

Gorter, Wytze, and George H. Hildebrand. *The Pacific Coast Maritime Shipping Industry, 1930–1948.* 2 vols. Berkeley, 1952–54.

Gray, James R., and Chester B. Baker. *Cattle Ranching in the Northern Great Plains.* Montana Agricultural Experiment Station Circular #204. Bozeman, 1953.

Grebler, Lee, Joan W. Moore, and Ralph Guzman. *The Mexican-American People.* New York, 1970.

Greenberg, Daniel S. *The Politics of Pure Science.* New York, 1967.

Grether, Ewald T. *The Steel and Steel Using Industries of California.* Berkeley, 1946.

Griffith, Beatrice. *American Me.* Boston, 1948.

Groneff, Stephan. *Manhattan Project.* Boston, 1967.

Groves, Leslie R. *Now It Can Be Told.* New York, 1962.

Grodzins, Morton. *Americans Betrayed.* Chicago, 1949.

Gunther, John. *Inside U.S.A.* New York, 1946.

Hafen, LeRoy (ed.). *Colorado and Its People.* 3 vols. New York, 1950.

Hansen, Alvin H. *Fiscal Policy and Business Cycles.* New York, 1941.

Haysted, Ladd. *If the Prospect Pleases: The West the Guidebooks Never Mention.* Norman, 1946.

Heller, Celia S. *Mexican-American Youth: Forgotten Youth at the Crossroads.* New York, 1968.

Heller Committee for Research in Social Economics of the University of California and Constantine Panunzio. *How Mexicans Earn and Live. A Study of Income and Expenditures of One Hundred Mexican Families in San Diego, California.* Berkeley, 1933.

Henderson, Richard B. *Maury Maverick: A Political Biography.* Austin, 1970.

Hewlett, Richard G., and Oscar Anderson, Jr. *The New World.* University, Penna., 1962.

Higham, Charles, and Joel Greenberg. *Hollywood in the Forties.* New York, 1968.

Hill, Forest G. *Roads, Rails and Waterways: The Army Engineers and Early Transportation.* Norman, 1957.

Howard, Frank A. *Buna Rubber: The Birth of an Industry.* New York, 1947.

Howard, Joseph K. *Montana: High, Wide, and Handsome.* New Haven, 1943.

Jackman, Jarrell C. and Carla M. Borden (eds.), *The Muses Flee Hitler: Cultural Transfer and Adaptation, 1930–1945.* Washington, 1983.

Jackson, W. Turrentine. *Wagon Roads West: A Study of Federal Road Surveys and Construction in the Trans-Mississippi West, 1846–1869.* Berkeley, 1952.

Jaffe, Bernard. *Men of Science in America.* New York, 1944.

James, Marquis, and Bessie James. *Biography of a Bank.* New York, 1956.

Jensen, G. Granville. *The Aluminum Industry of the Northwest.* Corvallis, 1950.

Johnson, Charles S. *The Negro Worker in San Francisco.* San Francisco, 1944.

Jones, Jesse. *Fifty Billion Dollars: My Thirteen Years with the Reconstruction Finance Corporation, 1932–1945.* New York, 1951.

Jones, Ken D., and Arthur F. McClure. *Hollywood at War: The American Motion Picture and World War II.* New York, 1973.

Jones, Nard. *Seattle.* Garden City, 1972.

Jones, Robert C. *Mexican War Workers in the United States.* Washington, 1945.

Karelovitz, Robert. *Challenge: The South Dakota Story.* Sioux Falls, 1975.

Kerr, Clark. *Migration to the Seattle Labor Market Area, 1940–1942. University of Washington Publications in the Social Sciences,* vol. 11, #3. Seattle, 1942.

Kevles, Daniel J. *The Physicists.* New York, 1978.

Kohner, Frederick. *Der Zauberer von Sunset Boulevard.* Munich, 1974.

Korngold, Luizi. *Erich Korngold: Ein Lebensbild.* Vienna, 1967.

Kortner, Fritz. *Aller Tage Abend.* Munich, 1959.

Kunetka, James W. *City of Fire: Los Alamos and Birth of the Atomic Age.* Englewood Cliffs, 1978.

Lane, Frederick C. *Ships for Victory: A History of Shipbuilding Under the U.S. Maritime Commission in World War II.* Baltimore, 1951.

Lange, Charles H. *Cochiti.* Austin, 1960.

Larson, Lawrence B. *The Urban West at the End of the Frontier.* Lawrence, 1979.

Lazarsfeld, Paul. *The People's Choice.* New York, 1944.

———. *Radio and the Printed Page.* New York, 1940.

Levine, Stuart, and Nancy Lurie. *The American Indian Today.* Deland, Florida, 1965.

Lewin, Bertram, and Helen Ross. *Psychoanalytic Education in the United States.* New York, 1960.

Lott, Arnold S. *A Long Line of Ships.* Annapolis, 1954.

Maccoll, E. Kimbark. *The Growth of a City: Power and Politics in Portland, Oregon, 1915 to 1950.* Portland, 1979.

Machlup, Fritz. *The Basing Point System.* Philadelphia, 1949.

Malone, Michael, and Richard Roeder. *Montana: A History of Two Centuries.* Seattle, 1976.

Mann, Erika, and Klaus Mann. *Escape to Life.* Boston, 1939.

Mann, Heinrich. *Briefe an Karl Lemke und Klaus Pinkus.* Berlin, n.d.

Mann, Monica. *Past and Present.* New York, 1960.

Mann, Thomas. *The Story of a Novel: The Genesis of Dr. Faustus.* Translated by Richard and Clara Winston. New York, 1981.

———. *Letters of Thomas Mann.* Translated by Richard and Clara Winston. New York, 1971.

Mansfield, Harold. *Vision: A Saga of the Sky.* New York, 1956.

Marcuse, Ludwig. *Mein Zwanzigstes Jahrhundert: Auf Dem Weg zu Einer Autobiographie.* Munich, 1960.

McCamy, James L. *Science and Public Administration.* University, Alabama, 1960.

McEntire, Davis. *The Labor Force in California: A Study of Characteristics and*

Trends in Labor Force Employment and Occupations in California, 1900–1950. Berkeley, 1952.

McKee, Robert E. *The Zia Corporation in Los Alamos.* El Paso, 1950.

McVittie, James A. *An Avalanche Hits Richmond: A Report.* Richmond, 1944.

McWilliams, Carey. *North from Mexico.* New York, 1944.

Menninger, Karl. *A Psychiatrist's World.* New York, 1959.

Mezerick, A. G. *The Revolt of the South and West.* New York, 1946.

Mierendorff, Marta. *Exiltag an der Pazifischen Westkueste.* Los Angeles, 1973.

Milhaud, Darius. *Notes without Music.* New York, 1953.

Modell, John. *The Economics and Politics of Racial Accommodation: The Japanese of Los Angeles, 1900–1942.* Urbana, 1977.

Morgan, Murray. *Skid Road.* Rev. ed. New York, 1960.

Morin, Raoul. *Among the Valiant: Mexican-Americans in WW II and Korea.* Los Angeles, 1963.

Morison, Samuel Eliot. *Coral Sea, Midway and Submarine Action, May, 1942–August, 1942.* Boston, 1950.

Murray, Florence. *The Negro Handbook, 1946–1947.* New York, 1947.

Nash, Gerald D. *The American West in the Twentieth Century.* Albuquerque, 1977.

———. *U.S. Oil Policy, 1890–1964: Business and Government in Twentieth Century America.* Pittsburgh, 1968.

———. (ed.). *The Urban West.* Manhattan, Kansas, 1979.

National Catholic Welfare Conference, *The Spanish Speaking of the Southwest and West.* San Antonio, 1944.

Navajos and World War II. Tsaile, Arizona, 1977.

Nelson, Gerald B. *Seattle, The Life and Times of an American City.* New York, 1977.

Newlin, Dika, *Schoenberg Remembered: Diaries and Recollections, 1938–1976.* New York, 1980.

Newman, James R. (ed.). *The World of Mathematics.* New York, 1956.

Oberndorf, Clarence P. *A History of Psychoanalysis in America.* New York, 1953.

Pacific Northwest Regional Planning Commission. *Pacific Northwest Development in Perspective.* Portland, 1943.

Palmer, G. L. *Labor Mobility in Six Cities.* New York, 1954.

Parman, Donald S. *The Navajos and the New Deal.* New Haven, 1976.

Paul, Doris. *The Navajo Code Talkers.* New York, 1970.

Paz, Octavio. *The Labyrinth of Solitude: Life and Thought in Mexico.* Translated by Lysander Kemp. New York, 1961.

Penick, James L., et al. (eds.). *The Politics of American Science, 1939 to the Present.* Rev. ed. Cambridge, 1972.

Perloff, Harvey S., with Vera Dodds. *How a Region Grows.* Washington, 1963.

Perloff, Harvey S., et al. *Regions, Resources, and Economic Growth.* Baltimore, 1960.

Peterson, F. Ross. *Idaho: A Bicentennial History.* New York, 1976.

Pettitt, Roland E. *Los Alamos Before The Dawn.* Los Alamos, 1972.

Pfouts, Ralph W. (ed.). *The Techniques of Urban Economic Analysis.* West Trenton, N.J., 1960.

Philp, Kenneth S. *John S. Collier's Crusade for Indian Reform, 1928–1954.* Tucson, 1977.

Pingree, H. B. *Cattle Ranching in Southeastern New Mexico.* New Mexico Agricultural Experiment Station. Bulletin #336. Las Cruces, 1948.

Polgar, Alfred. *Anderseits: Erzaehlungen und Erwaegungen: Standpunkte.* Amsterdam, 1948.

Pomeroy, Earl. *The Territories and the United States.* Philadelphia, 1943.

Powdermaker, Hortense. *Hollywood: The Dream Factory.* Boston, 1950.

Price, Vincent. *I Like What I Know.* New York, 1959.

Proceedings of the Writers' Congress, Los Angeles. Berkeley, 1944.

Puget Sound Regional Planning Commission. *The Puget Sound Region: War and Postwar Development.* Washington, 1943.

Rand, Christopher. *Los Angeles.* New York, 1970.

Rasmussen, Wayne P. *A History of the Farm Labor Supply Program, 1943–1947.* Washington, 1951.

Reeve, Frank D. *History of New Mexico.* 3 vols. New York, 1961.

Reinhardt, Gottfried. *Der Liebhaber: Erinnerungen Seines Sohnes Gottfried Reinhardt an Max Reinhardt.* Munich, 1973.

Remarque, Erich Maria. *Shadows in Paradise.* Translated by Ralph Manheim. New York, 1972.

Ritchie, Art, and William L. Davis (eds.). *The Pacific Northwest Goes to War: State of Washington.* Seattle, 1944.

Robinson, Elwyn B. *History of North Dakota.* Lincoln, 1966.

Rosten, Leo. *Hollywood: The Movie Colony, the Movie Makers.* New York, 1941.

Rowland, Buford, and William B. Boyd. *U.S. Navy Bureau of Ordnance in World War II.* Washington, 1952.

Rowland, Donald W. *History of the Office of the Coordinator of Inter-American Affairs.* Washington, 1947.

Sale, Roger. *Seattle, Past to Present.* Seattle, 1976.

Salzman, L., and J. H. Masserman (eds.). *Modern Concepts of Psychoanalysis.* New York, 1962.

Sando, Joe. *The Pueblo Indians.* San Francisco, 1976.

Schell, Herbert S. *History of South Dakota.* Lincoln, 1975.

Schlebecker, John T. *Cattle Raising on the Plains, 1900–1961.* Lincoln, 1963.

Scott, Mel. *The San Francisco Bay Region.* Berkeley, 1950.

Segrè, Emilio. *Enrico Fermi, Physicist.* Chicago, 1970.

Sklar, Robert. *Movie Made America: A Social History of American Movies.* New York, 1975.

Smyth, Henry D. *Atomic Energy for Military Purposes.* Princeton, 1945.

South Dakota World War II Historical Commission. *South Dakota in World War II.* Pierre, 1947.

Spalek, John, and Joseph Strelka (eds.). *Deutsche Exilliteratur seit 1933.* vol. I. *Kalifornien.* Bern, 1976.

Sprague, Marshall. *Colorado: A Bicentennial History.* New York, 1976.

Stanberg, Van Buren. *Growth and Trends of Manufacturing in the Pacific Northwest, 1939–1947.* Washington, 1950.

Stein, Harold (ed.). *Public Administration and Policy Development.* New York, 1952.

Stewart, Irvin. *Organizing Scientific Research for War.* Boston, 1948.

Stokes, K. C. *Regional Shifts in Population, Production, and Markets, 1939–1943.* Washington, 1943.

Swan, Howard. *Music in the Southwest: A History.* San Marino, 1952.

Taylor, Frank J., and Lawton Wright. *Democracy's Air Arsenal.* New York, 1947.

Taylor, Paul S. *Mexicans in the United States: Migration Statistics.* Berkeley, 1929.

Ten Broek, Jacobus, E. N. Barnhart, and F. W. Matson. *Prejudice, War, and the Constitution.* Berkeley, 1958.

Thomas, Dorothy S., and Richard S. Nishimoto. *The Spoilage*. Berkeley, 1946.
Toole, K. Ross. *Montana: An Uncommon Land*. Norman, 1959.
Tregaskis, Richard. *Guadalcanal Diary*. New York, 1942.
Tuck, Ruth D. *Not with the Fist: Mexican Americans in a Southwest City*. New York, 1946.
Ubbelohde, Carl. *History of Colorado*. Boulder, 1965.
Underhill, Ruth. *Red Man's America*. Chicago, 1953.
Viertel, Salka. *The Kindness of Strangers*. New York, 1969.
Vogel, Virgil J. *This Country Was Ours*. New York, 1974.
Vogt, Evan Z. *Navajo Veterans: A Study of Changing Values. Papers of the Peabody Museum of Archeology and Ethnology*. vol. 41, #1. Cambridge, 1951.
Walter, Bruno. *Themes and Variation*. London, 1947.
Warner, Jack. *My First Hundred Years*. New York, 1965.
Washburn, Wilcomb. *Red Man's Land—White Man's Law*. New York, 1971.
Washington State Planning Council. *Employment and Payrolls: Basic Industries of Washington, 1920–1944*. Olympia, 1945.
Washington State University. Bureau of Business Research. *The Impact of World War II Subcontracting by the Boeing Airplane Company upon Pacific Northwest Manufacturing*. Seattle, 1955.
Watson, James D. *The Double Helix*. New York, 1968.
Weaver, Robert C. *Negro Ghetto*. New York, 1948.
———. *The Negro War Worker in San Francisco*. San Francisco, 1944.
Weaver, Warren. *Scene of Change*. New York, 1970.
Webb, Walter P. *Divided We Stand: The Crisis of a Frontierless Democracy*. New York, 1937.
Wechsberg, Joseph. *The First Time Around: Some Irreverent Recollections*. Boston, 1970.
West, Ray (ed.). *Rocky Mountain Cities*. New York, 1949.
White, Gerald T. *Billions for Defense: Government Financing by the Defense Plant Corporation during World War II*. University, Alabama, 1982.
White, William A. *The Changing West*. New York, 1939.
Williams, Faith M., and Alice C. Hanson. *Money Disbursements of Wage Earners and Clerical Workers in Five Cities in the Pacific Region, 1934–1936, Mexican Families in Los Angeles*. Washington, 1939.
Williamson, Harold F., et al. *The American Petroleum Industry: The Age of Energy, 1899–1959*. Evanston, 1963.
Wiltse, Charles M. *Aluminum Policies of the War Production Board and Predecessor Agencies*. Washington, 1946.
Wyllis, Rufus K. *History of Arizona*. New York, 1945.

Articles

Abbott, Carl. "The American Sunbelt: Idea and Region." In Gerald D. Nash (ed.), *The Urban West*. Manhattan, Kansas, 1979, pp. 9–16.
———. "Boom State and Boom City: Stages in Denver's Growth," *Colorado Magazine*, vol. 50 (1973), 207–230.
———. "Portland in the Pacific War: Planning from 1940 to 1945," *Urbanism, Past and Present* (1981), pp. 12–24.
Adair, John. "The Navajo and Pueblo Veterans: A Force for Culture Change," *The American Indian*, vol. 4 #1 (1947), 5–11.
Adair, John, and Evan Z. Vogt. "Navajo and Zuni Veterans: A Study of Contrasting Modes of Culture Change," *American Anthropologist*, vol. 51 (October–December 1949), 547–561.

Alexander, Thomas G. "Brief Histories of Three Federal Military Installations in Utah: Kearns Army Air Base." *Utah Historical Quarterly*, vol. 34 (Spring 1966), 123–126.

————. "Ogden's Arsenal of Democracy, 1920–1955." *Utah Historical Quarterly*, vol. 33 (Summer 1965), 240–245.

Applebaum, Ann. "Activity Therapy in Psychiatric Treatment," *Bulletin of the Menninger Clinic*, vol. 39 (1975), 50–57.

"Arizona Lumber Goes to War." *Arizona Highways*, vol. 19 (January 1943), 1–3.

Arrington, Leonard J. "The New Deal in the West: A Preliminary Statistical Analysis." *Pacific Historical Review*, vol. 38 (August 1969), 311–316.

Arrington, Leonard J., and Thomas G. Alexander. "Sentinels on the Desert: The Dugway Proving Ground (1942–1963) and Deseret Chemical Depot (1942–1955). *Utah Historical Quarterly*, vol. 32 (Winter 1964), 32–38.

————. "Supply Hub of the West: Defense Depot Ogden, 1941–1964." *Utah Historical Quarterly*, vol. 32 (Spring 1964), 99–112.

————. "They Kept 'Em Rolling: The Tooele Army Depot, 1942–1962." *Utah Historical Quarterly*, vol. 31 (Winter 1963), 3–14.

————. "World's Largest Military Reserves: Wendover Air Force Base, 1941–1963." *Utah Historical Quarterly*, vol. 31 (Fall 1963), 324–332.

Arrington, Leonard J., Thomas G. Alexander, and R. Erb, Jr. "Utah's Biggest Business: Ogden Air Materiel Area at Hill Air Force Base, 1938–1965." *Utah Historical Quarterly*, vol. 33 (Winter 1965), 9–16.

Arrington, Leonard J., and Archer L. Durham. "Anchors Away in Utah: The U.S. Naval Supply Depot at Clearfield, 1942–1962." *Utah Historical Quarterly*, vol. 31 (Spring 1963), 109–118.

Barbour, R. "Secondary School Housing: An Appraisal of a Wartime Expedient." *Elementary School Journal*, vol. 42 (April 1942), 597–602.

Barker, George C. "The Social Functions of Language." *ETC*, vol. 2 (Summer 1945), 228–234.

Bauer, Catherine. "Cities in Flux." *American Scholar*, vol. 13 (1943–44), 70–77.

————. "Wartime Housing in Defense Areas." *Architect and Engineer*, vol. 151 (October 1942), 33–35.

Beshoar, Barron B. "Report from the Mountain States." *Common Ground*, vol. 4 (Spring 1943), 23–30.

Black, Gregory D., and Clayton R. Koppes. "OWI Goes to the Movies: The Bureau of Intelligence Criticism of Hollywood, 1942–43." *Prologue*, vol. 6 (Spring 1974), 49–55.

Bogardus, Emory S. "Current Problems of Mexican Immigrants." *Sociology and Social Research*, vol. 25 (November–December, 1940), 166–174.

————. "Gangs of Mexican-American Youth." *Sociology and Social Research*, vol. 28 (September–October 1945), 65–68.

Bratt, Elmer C., and D. S. Wilson. "Regional Distortions Resulting from the War." *Survey of Current Business*, vol. 23 (October 1943), 9–15.

Brode, Bernice. "Los Alamos and the Indians." *Los Alamos Scientific Laboratory Community News*, August 25, 1960, p. 5.

————. "Maid Service." *Los Alamos Scientific Laboratory Community News*, June 30, 1960, p. 8.

"City Planning: Battle of the Approaches." *Fortune*, vol. 28 (November 1943), 164–168, 222–223.

Coalson, George. "Mexican Contract Labor in American Agriculture." *Southwestern Social Science Quarterly*, vol. 33 (December 1952), 228–237.

Colbert, Robert E. "The Attitude of Older Negro Residents Toward Recent

Negro Migrants in the Pacific Northwest." *Journal of Negro Education*, vol. 15 (Fall 1946), 695–703.

Collier, John. "The Indian in a Wartime Nation." *Annals of the American Academy of Political and Social Science*, vol. 223 (September 1942), 29–38.

Cookingham, L. P. "The Effect of the War upon Cities." *Planning*, 1943 (Chicago, 1943), pp. 15–26.

Cooper, Walter W. "San Diego's War Revenues." *Municipal Finance* (February 1943), pp. 8–12.

De Graaf, Lawrence B. "Recognition, Racism, and Reflections on the Writing of Western Black History." *Pacific Historical Review*, vol. 44 (May 1975), 22–51.

DeVoto, Bernard. "The Anxious West." *Harper's*, vol. 193 (December 1946), 489–495.

———. "The West Against Itself." *Harper's*, vol. 194 (January 1947), 1–13.

Dietrich, Margretta. "Braves on the Warpath." *New Mexico Magazine*, vol. 21 (June 1943), pp. 14–15.

Downes, Randolph C. "The Indian Claims Bill." *The American Indian*, vol. 3 (Spring 1946), 1–8.

Droker, Howard A. "Seattle Race Relations During the Second World War." *Pacific Northwest Quarterly*, vol. 67 (October 1976), 163–174.

Edwards, Elbert B. "Clark County: From Wilderness to Metropolitan Area." In *Nevada: The Silver State*. 2 vols. Carson City, 1970. II, 677–693.

Eels, Walter C. "Educational Opportunities for the Indian." *The American Indian*, vol. 2 (Fall 1945), 17–21.

Faure, A. M. "Post-War Planning as a Joint City-County Project." *American City*, vol. 59 (October 1944), 89–91.

Feiss, Carl. "How Cities Are Preparing for the Post-War Era." *Planning*, 1944 (Chicago, 1944), pp. 46–50.

———. "How Denver Got Its New Housing Code." *American City*, vol. 59 (November 1944), 89–90.

Fox, J. R. "Veterans and Factions in Pueblo Society." *Man*, vol. 61 (October 1962), 174–176.

Freeman, H. D. "Story of Vanport City." *American City* (July 1943), pp. 42–43.

Gamboa, Erasmo. "Mexican Labor in the Pacific Northwest." *Pacific Northwest Quarterly*, vol. 73 (October 1982), 173–179.

Garnsey, Morris E. "Future of the Mountain States." *Harper's*, vol. 191 (October 1945), 324–336.

Ginsburg, Ruth. "A New Program in Spanish for Los Angeles." *California Journal of Secondary Education*, vol. 18 (October 1943), 347–348.

Gordon, Margaret S. "Research Design of the Survey of Patterns and Factors in Mobility of Cities." *Journal of the American Statistical Association*, vol. 48 (September 1955), 633–641.

Gordon, Walter. "Housing While You Wait: Housing in Washington and Oregon." *Pencil Points* (April 1943), pp. 48–51.

Granger, Lester B. "Negroes and War Production." *Survey Graphic*, vol. 31 (November 1942), 470–478.

Gressley, Gene M. "Colonialism and the American West." *Pacific Northwest Quarterly*, vol. 54 (January 1963), 1–8.

Griffith, Beatrice. "The Pachuco Patois." *Common Ground*, vol. 8 (Summer 1947), 127–141.

Haas, Theodore H. "The Legal Aspects of Indian Affairs from 1887 to 1957." *Annals of the American Academy of Political and Social Science*, vol. 311 (May 1957), 16–22.

Hagberg, Eric T., and Robert Bunker. "Pueblo Sovereignty, Post-War." *New Mexico Quarterly Review*, vol. 28 (Spring 1946), 223–224.

Harlin, Lois E. "The National Congress of American Indians." *Indians at Work* (November–December 1944), pp. 20–21.

Hauser, Philip M. "Wartime Population Changes and Post-War Prospects." *Journal of Marketing*, vol. 8 (January 1944), 238–248.

Hildebrand, George, and Arthur Mace, Jr. "The Employment Multiplier in an Expanding Industrial Market: Los Angeles County, 1940–47." *Review of Economics and Statistics*, vol. 32 (August 1950), 241–249.

Hill, Forest. "The Shaping of California's Industrial Pattern." *Proceedings of the 30th Annual Conference of the Western Economic Association* (1955), pp. 63–68.

Holm, Tom. "Fighting a White Man's War: The Extent and Legacy of American Indian Participation in World War II." *Journal of Ethnic Studies*, vol. 9 (Summer 1981), 69–81.

Howard, James N. "The Dakota Indian Victory Dance, World War II." *North Dakota History*, vol. 18 (January 1951), 33–38.

Humphrey, Norman D. "The Stereotype and the Social Types of Mexican-American Youths." *Journal of Social Psychology*, vol. 22 (1945), 69–77.

Issler, A. R. "Good Neighbors Lend a Hand." *Survey Graphic*, vol. 32 (October 1943), 389–394.

Jackman, Jarrell C. "Exiles in Paradise: A Cultural History of German Emigres in Southern California, 1933–1950." *Southern California Quarterly*, vol. 61 (Summer 1979), 183–203.

Jacobs, Lewis. "World War II and the American Film." *Cinema Journal*, vol. 7 (Winter, 1967–68), 1–21.

James, Joseph. "Race Relations on the Pacific Coast, San Francisco." *Journal of Educational Sociology*, vol. 12 (November 1945), 166–172.

Janeway, Eliot. "Trouble on the Northwest Frontier: A Correspondent's Travel Report." *Fortune*, vol. 26 (November 1942), 26–32.

Jennings, Dean. "The Hood Who Invented Las Vegas." *True Magazine*, vol. 48 (August 1967), 23–25.

Jones, Dorothy B. "The Hollywood War Film, 1942–44." *Hollywood Quarterly*, vol. 1 (1946–47), 1–11.

Jordan, Katie, and Tonita Mirabal. "War's Impact on New Mexico Indians." *El Palacio*, vol. 51 (June 1944), 110–115.

Kandelin, Albert. "California's First Psychoanalytical Society." *Bulletin of the Menninger Clinic*, vol. 12 (1965), 357–362.

Kaufman, Perry. "City Boosters, Las Vegas Style." *Journal of the West*, vol. 13 (July 1974), 46–60.

Keen, Harold. "Sewerage in San Diego for National Defense." *American City*, vol. 58 (September 1943), 56–58.

Kimble, G. Eleanor. "Restrictive Covenants." *Common Ground*, vol. 5 (Autumn 1945), 45–52.

Kirk, Ruth. "Dances for War and Peace." *New Mexico Magazine*, vol. 21 (July 1943), 9–10.

———. "War Rituals at Zuni." *New Mexico Magazine*, vol. 23 (August 1945), pp. 14–15.

Koppes, Clayton R., and Gregory D. Black. "What to Show the World: The Office of War Information and Hollywood, 1942–1945." *Journal of American History*, vol. 64 (June 1977), 87–105.

Lamb, Robert K. "Mobilization of Human Resources." *American Journal of Sociology*, vol. 48 (November 1942), 323–330.

LeDuc, Thomas. "The Work of the Indian Claims Commission under the Act of 1946." *Pacific Historical Review*, vol. 27 (February 1957), 1–16.

Logan, Millaz. "Racial Discrimination not Allowed." *Common Ground*, vol. 4 (Summer 1944), 83–86.

Loomis, Charles P. "Wartime Migration from the Spanish-American Villages of New Mexico." *Rural Sociology*, vol. 7 (December 1942), 384–395.

Loomis, Charles P., and Nellie H. Loomis. "Skilled Spanish-American War Industry Workers from New Mexico." *Applied Anthropology*, vol. 2 (October–December 1942), 33–36.

Lotchin, Roger W. "The Metropolitan-Military Complex in Comparative Perspective: San Francisco, Los Angeles, and San Diego." In Gerald D. Nash (ed.), *The Urban West*. Manhattan, Kansas, 1979, pp. 19–30.

Lyon, James K. "Bertolt Brecht's Hollywood Years: The Dramatist as Film Writer." *Oxford German Studies*, vol. 6 (1971–72), 145–174.

McDonald, Joseph F. "Gambling in Nevada." *Annals of the American Academy of Political and Social Science*, vol. 269 (May 1950), 30–34.

McDonagh, Edward. "Status Levels of Mexicans." *Sociology and Social Research*, vol. 33 (July–August 1949), 452–459.

McVittie, James A. "A City Earns a Purple Heart." *American City*, vol. 59 (December 1944), 56–58.

McVoy, Arthur. "How Cities Are Preparing for the Post-War Period: Portland." *Planning* (Chicago, 1944), pp. 78–80.

McWilliams, Carey. "Los Angeles Archipelago." *Science and Society*, vol. 10 (Winter 1946), 52–55.

———. "Los Angeles Pachuco Gangs." *New Republic*, vol. 108 (January 18, 1943), 76–77.

———. "They Saved the Crops." *Inter-American* (August 1943), pp. 10–14.

———. "The Zoot Suit Riots." *New Republic* vol. 108 (June 21, 1943), pp. 819–820.

Merla, Pedro. "El bracero Mexicano en la economica nacional." *Revista del Trabajo*, vol. 3 (December 1943), 9–10.

Mezerick, A. G. "Journey in America." *New Republic*, vol. 111 (December 19, 1944), 830–831.

———. "Journey in America." *New Republic*, vol. 111 (December 25, 1944), 864ff.

———. "West Coast Versus East." *Atlantic Monthly*, vol. 173 (May 1944), 48–52.

Mills, Clarence. "Distribution of American Research Funds." *Science*, vol. 107 (February 6, 1948), 127–128.

Monroe, Keith. "Wings Over Tucson." *Arizona Highways*, vol. 20 (January 1944), 26–29.

Mott, Frederick D. "Health Services for Migrant Farm Families." *American Journal of Public Health*, vol. 35 (April 1945), 308–314.

Myers, Howard. "Defense Migration and Labor Supply." *Journal of the American Statistical Association*, vol. 37 (March 1942), 69–76.

Nash, Gerald D. "The Census of 1890 and the Closing of the Frontier." *Pacific Northwest Quarterly*, vol. 71 (July 1980), 98–100.

"Negro Internal Migration: An Estimate." *Race Relations*. vol. I (September 1943), 10–11.

Oakes, V. "West Coast Dreams." *Asia*. vol. 45 (August 1945), 373–375.

O'Brien, Robert W., and Lee M. Brooks. "Race Relations in the Pacific Northwest." *Phylon*, vol. 7 (1946), 26–32.

Peterson, C. E. "How San Diego Police Handle Juvenile Delinquency and Other Problems." *Western City* (January, 1944), pp. 16–17.

Phelps, B. D. "San Diego Completes New Sewer Lines." *American City*, vol. 60 (February 1945), 11–12.

Pomeroy, Earl. "The Urban Frontier of the Far West." In John G. Clark (ed.), *The Frontier Challenge: Responses to the Trans-Mississippi West.* Lawrence, 1971.

Pomeroy, Hugh. "Impact of the War on Communities." *Proceedings of the National Conference on Planning,* 1942 (Chicago, 1942), 27–38.

Reid, Ira DeA. "Special Problems of Negro Migration During the War." *Milbank Memorial Fund Quarterly,* vol. 25 (July 1947), 284–292.

Reiss, A. J., Jr., and E. Katingawa. "Demographic Characteristics and Job Mobility of Migrants in Six Cities." *Social Forces,* vol. 32 (1953), 70–75.

Richardson, Eugene S. "Migration and the Social Education of the Negro." *Journal of Negro Education,* vol. 13 (Winter 1944), 40–46.

Ritzenthaler, Robert. "The Impact of the War on an Indian Community." *American Anthropologist,* vol. 45 (April–June 1943), 325–335.

Rorschach, H. G., Jr. "The Contributions of Felix Bloch and Will V. Houston to the Electron Theory of Metals." *American Journal of Physics,* vol. 38 (1970), 897–904.

Rubsamen, Walter H. "Schoenberg in America." *The Musical Quarterly,* vol. 37 (October 1951), 485–492.

Schiesl, Martin. "City Planning and the Federal Government in World War II: The Los Angeles Experience." *California History,* vol. 58 (April 1979), 127–143.

Schleef, Margaret. "Manufacturing Trends in the Inland Empire." Washington State University, Bureau of Economic and Business Research. *Bulletin* #4 (1947), pp. 3–66.

Scruggs, Otey M. "Evolution of the Mexican Farm Labor Agreement of 1942." *Agricultural History,* vol. 34 (July 1960), 140–149.

——. "The United States, Mexico, and the Wetback, 1942–1947." *Pacific Historical Review,* vol. 32 (May 1961), 316–329.

Sergeant, Elizabeth S. "The Indian Goes to War." *New Republic,* vol. 107 (November 30, 1942), 708.

Shadegg, Stephen C. "Goodyear Builds Tools of Victory." *Arizona Highways,* vol. 19 (May 1943), 14–19, 42–43.

Shryock, Henry S., Jr. "Internal Migration and the War." *Journal of the American Statistical Association,* vol. 38 (March 1943), 23–30.

——. "Wartime Shifts of the Civilian Population." *Milbank Memorial Fund Quarterly,* vol. 25 (July 1947), 269–282.

Shryock, Henry S., Jr., and Hope T. Eldredge. "Internal Migration in Peace and War." *American Sociological Review,* vol. 12 (February 1947), 27–39.

Siegel, Bernard J., and Alan R. Beals. "Pervasive Factionalism." *American Anthropologist,* vol. 62 (April 1960), 398–407.

Smith, Alice K. "Los Alamos: Focus of an Age." *Bulletin of Atomic Scientists,* vol. 26 (June 1970), 15–20.

Sonderbergh, Peter. "Hollywood and World War II." *University of Dayton Review,* vol. 5 (Winter 1968–69), 16–21.

——. "On War and the Movies." *Centennial Review* vol. 11 (Summer 1967), pp. 504–518.

Spaulding, Charles B. "Housing Problems of Minority Groups in Los Angeles County." *Annals of the American Academy of Political and Social Science,* vol. 248 (November 1946), 220–225.

Spruch, Grace, "Victor Weisskopf: International Scientist." *New Scientist*, vol. 46 (May 21, 1970), 387–388.

Steele, Richard. "Preparing the Public for War: Efforts to Establish a National Propaganda Agency, 1940–1941." *American Historical Review*, vol. 75 (October 1970), 1640–1653.

Sternfeld, Fred W. "Music and the Feature Films." *Musical Quarterly*, vol. 33 (October 1947), 519–532.

Stewart, A. C., and H. A. Dickel, "Psychoanalytic Development in Three States." *Northwest Medicine*, vol. 41 (August 1942), 284–288.

Stout, W. "Nevada's New Reno." *Saturday Evening Post*, vol. 215 (October 11, 1942), 12–13.

Taeuber, Conrad. "Wartime Population Changes in the United States." *Milbank Memorial Fund Quarterly*, vol. 24 (July 1946), 238–239.

Tajiri, Larry. "Farewell to Little Tokyo." *Common Ground*, vol. 3 (Spring 1943), 90–93.

Tipton, Elis M. "What We Want Is Action." *Common Ground*, vol. 7 (Autumn 1946), 76–80.

Tuck, Ruth D. "Behind The Zoot Suit Riots." *Survey Graphic*, vol. 32 (August 1943), 313–320.

Turner, Ralph H., and Samuel J. Surace. "Zoot Suiters and Mexicans: Symbols in Crowd Behavior." *American Journal of Sociology*, vol. 62 (July 1956), 14–20.

Ullman, Edward. "Amenities as a Factor in Regional Growth." *Geographical Review*, vol. 44 (January 1954), 119–132.

U.S. Railroad Retirement Board. "Recruitment of Mexican Workers for Railroad Jobs." *Monthly Review of the Railroad Retirement Board*, vol. 5 (May 1944), 63–68.

Useem, John, Gordon MacGregor, and Ruth Hill Useem. "Wartime Employment and Adjustments of the Rosebud Sioux." *Applied Anthropologist*, vol. 2 (January 1943), 1–2.

Vestal, Stanley. "The Plains Indian and the War." *Saturday Review of Literature*, vol. 25 (May 16, 1942), 9.

Vogt, Evan Z. "Between Two Worlds: Case Study of a Navajo Veteran." *The American Indian*, vol. 5 #1 (1949), 13–21.

Von Hofe, Harold. "German Literature in Exile: Alfred Doeblin." *German Quarterly*, vol. 17 (January 1948), 28–35.

Wanger, Walter. "OWI and Motion Pictures." *Public Opinion Quarterly*, vol. 7 (Spring 1943), 100–110.

Waters, Lawrence L. "Transient Mexican Agricultural Labor." *Southwestern Social Science Quarterly*, vol. 22 (June 1941), 49–66.

Watson, James D. "Growing Up in the Phage Group." In John Cairns, Gunther S. Stent, and James D. Watson (eds.), *Phages and the Origins of Molecular Biology*. Cold Spring Harbor, 1966, pp. 239–245.

Weaver, Robert C. "Negro Employment in the Aircraft Industry." *Quarterly Journal of Economics*, vol. 59 (August 1945), 187–193.

Weinberg, Sidney. "What to Tell America, the Writers Quarrel in OWI." *Journal of American History*, vol. 55 (June 1968), 73–89.

Wetherill, G. G. "Health Problems in Child Care Centers." *Hygeia*, vol. 21 (September 1943), 634–635.

Wheeler, Bayard O. "The Committee for Congested Production Areas." *Oregon Business Review*, vol. 3 (April 29, 1944), 5–11.

Wollenberg, Charles. "Black vs. Navy Blue: The Mare Island Mutiny Court

Martial." *California History,* vol. 59 (January 1980), 62–74.

———. *"James v. Marinship:* Trouble on the New Black Frontier." *California History,* vol. 60 (Fall 1981), 262–279.

Woodbridge, W. C. "Mexico and United States Racism." *Commonweal,* vol. 42 (June 22, 1945), 234–237.

Woytinsky, Wladimir. "Interstate Migration During the War." *State Government,* vol. 19 (March 1946), 81–84.

Dissertations

Adair, John. "A Study of Culture Resistance: The Veterans of World War II at Zuni Pueblo." Ph.D. dissertation, Anthropology, University of New Mexico, 1948.

Brubaker, Stanley. "The Impact of Federal Government Activities on California's Economic Growth, 1930–1956." Ph.D. dissertation, History, University of California, 1959.

Campbell, Howard Z. "Bracero Migration and the Mexican Economy, 1951–1964." Ph.D. dissertation, Latin American Studies, American University, 1972.

Campos, Gloria R. Vargas. "El Problema del Bracero." Ph.D. dissertation, Universidad Nacional Autonoma de Mexico, 1964.

Chambers, Marjorie. "Technically Sweet Los Alamos: The Development of a Federally Sponsored Scientific Community." Ph.D. dissertation, History, University of New Mexico, 1974.

Copp, Nelson G. "Wetbacks and Braceros: Mexican Migrant Laborers and American Immigration Policy, 1930–1960." Ph.D. dissertation, History, Boston University, 1963.

Decker, Robert. "The Economics of the Legalized Gambling Industry in Nevada." Ph.D. dissertation, Economics, University of Colorado, 1961.

De Graaf, Lawrence B. "Negro Migration to Los Angeles, 1930–1950." Ph.D. dissertation, History, UCLA, 1962.

Elac, John C. "The Employment of Mexican Workers in U.S. Agriculture, 1900–1960." Ph.D. dissertation, International Relations, UCLA, 1961.

France, Edward Everett. "Some Aspects of the Migration of the Negro to the San Francisco Bay Area since 1940." Ph.D. dissertation, University of California, 1962.

Guzman, Ralph C. "The Political Socialization of the Mexican-American People." Ph.D. dissertation, Political Science, UCLA, 1970.

Higgins, Carla. "Art Collecting in the Los Angeles Area, 1910–1960." Ph.D. dissertation, Fine Art, UCLA, 1963.

Kaufman, Perry. "The Best City of Them All: A City Biography of Las Vegas, 1930–1960." Ph.D. dissertation, History, University of California, Santa Barbara, 1974.

Modell, John. "The Japanese of Los Angeles: A Study in Growth and Accommodation, 1900–1946." Ph.D. dissertation, Political Science, Columbia University, 1960.

Pursinger, Marvin G. "The Japanese in Oregon in World War II: A Study in Compulsory Relocation." Ph.D. dissertation, History, University of Southern California, 1961.

Santoro, Carmela. "United States and Mexican Relations During World War II." Ph.D. dissertation, History, Syracuse University, 1967.

Scott, Robin F. "The Mexican-American in the Los Angeles Area, 1920–1950:

From Acquiescence to Activity." Ph.D. dissertation, History, University of Southern California, 1971.

Spritzer, Donald E. "New Dealer from Montana: The Political Career of Senator James E. Murray." Ph.D. dissertation, History, University of Montana, 1980.

Tomasek, Robert D. "The Political and Economic Implications of Mexican Labor in the United States Under the Non-Quota System, Contract Labor Program, and Wetback Movement." Ph.D. dissertation, History, University of Michigan, 1958.

Index